CROSSING
CULTURES

READINGS
FOR
COMPOSITION

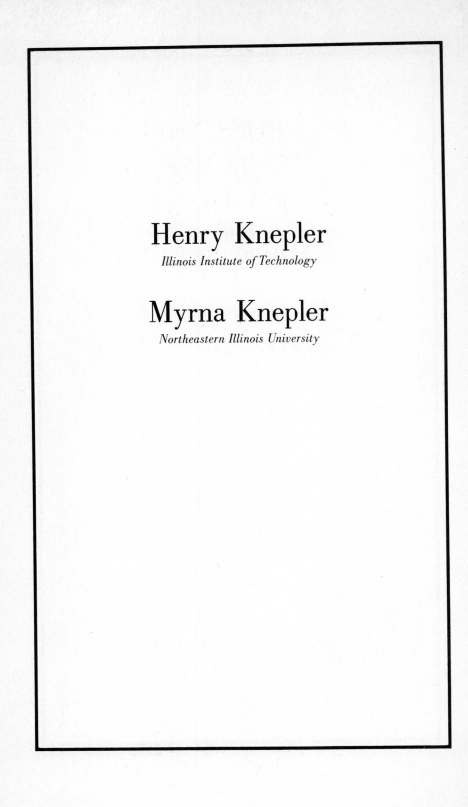

Henry Knepler
Illinois Institute of Technology

Myrna Knepler
Northeastern Illinois University

CROSSING CULTURES

READINGS FOR COMPOSITION

MACMILLAN PUBLISHING CO., INC.

NEW YORK

Copyright © 1983, Macmillan Publishing Co., Inc.

Printed in the United States of America

Macmillan Publishing Co., Inc.
866 Third Avenue, New York, New York 10022

Collier Macmillan Canada, Inc.

Library of Congress Cataloging in Publication Data
Main entry under title:

Crossing cultures.
    1. College readers.   2. English language—
Rhetoric.   3. Cross-cultural studies—Addresses,
essays, lectures.   I. Knepler, Henry W.
II. Knepler, Myrna.
PE1417.C75 1983   808'.0427   82-14944
ISBN 0-02-365200-4

Printing: 1 2 3 4 5 6 7 8   Year: 3 4 5 6 7 8 9 0

ISBN   0-02-365200-4

ACKNOWLEDGMENTS

Arno Press. WALTER WHITE. "I Learn What I Am," from *A Man Called White*. Copyright ©
1948 by Walter White. Permission to reprint material from *A Man Called White* granted
by Arno Press.

Jonathan Cape Limited. DESMOND MORRIS, PETER COLLETT, PETER MARSH, and MARIE O'SHAUGH-
NESSY, "The Hand Purse," from *Gestures*. Copyright © 1980 by Desmond Morris, Peter
Collett, Peter Marsh, and Marie O'Shaughnessy. Permission to reprint material from *Ges-
tures* granted by Jonathan Cape Limited.

Change Magazine. HENRY KNEPLER, "Beyond American Expressland," in *Change*, February–
March 1980. Copyright © 1980 by *Change* Magazine. Reprinted by permission of
Change Magazine.

The Dial Press. JAMES BALDWIN, "Stranger in the Village," from *Notes of a Native Son*. Copy-
right © 1963 by James Baldwin. Reprinted by permission of The Dial Press. JACK
AGUEROS, "Halfway to Dick and Jane," in Thomas Wheeler, *The Immigrant Experience*.
Copyright © 1971 by Jack Agueros. Reprinted by permission of The Dial Press.

Doubleday & Company, Inc. EDWARD T. HALL. "Private Space," from *The Hidden Dimension*.
Copyright © 1966 by Edward T. Hall. Reprinted by permission of Doubleday & Company, Inc.

Dow Jones & Company, Inc. ELIZABETH HANSON WARREN, "Blessings of Emptiness," in *The
National Observer*, November 8, 1975. Reprinted by permission of *The National
Observer*, © 1975, Dow Jones & Company, Inc. All Rights Reserved.

Elsevier-Dutton Publishing Co., Inc. CAROLINA MARIA DE JESUS, *Child of the Dark*, translated by
David S. Clair. Copyright © 1962 by E. P. Dutton & Co., Inc., and Souvenir Press Ltd.
Reprinted by permission of the publisher, E. P. Dutton, Inc. JOAN MORRISON and CHAR-
LOTTE FOX ZABUSKY, "Vo Thi Tam," from *American Mosaic: An Oral History of Immi-
gration*. Copyright © 1980 by Joan Morrison and Charlotte Zabusky. Reprinted by per-
mission of the publisher, E. P. Dutton, Inc.

Esquire Magazine. ADAM SMITH, "The Japanese Model," in *Esquire*, October 1980. Copyright
© 1980 by Esquire Publishing, Inc. Reprinted with permission from *Esquire* (October
1980).

Harcourt Brace Jovanovich, Inc. IRVING HOWE, "Ellis Island," from *World of Our Fathers*.
Copyright © 1976 by Irving Howe. Permission granted by Harcourt Brace Jovanovich,
Inc. ALFRED KAZIN, "The Kitchen," from *A Walker in the City*. Copyright © 1951 by

v

Alfred Kazin. Permission granted by Harcourt Brace Jovanovich, Inc. GEORGE ORWELL, "Shooting an Elephant," from *Shooting an Elephant and Other Essays*. Copyright © 1950 by George Orwell. Permission granted by Harcourt Brace Jovanovich, Inc. JAMES THURBER, "Ivorytown, Rinsoville, Anacinburg and Crisco Corners," from *The Beast in Me and Other Animals*. Copyright © 1948 by James Thurber; renewed 1975 by Helen W. Thurber. Reprinted by permission of Helen Thurber. LEONORE TIEFER, "The Kiss," in *Human Nature*, July 1978. Copyright © 1978 by Human Nature, Inc. Reprinted by permission of the publisher.

Harold Matson Company, Inc. PETER FREUCHEN, "The Eskimo House," from *Book of the Eskimos*. Copyright © 1961 by Peter Freuchen. Reprinted by permission of Harold Matson Company, Inc.

Harper & Row, Publishers, Inc., and Lippincott & Crowell Publishers. GWENDOLYN BROOKS, "We Real Cool. The Pool Players. Seven at the Golden Shovel," from *The World of Gwendolyn Brooks*. Copyright © 1959 by Gwendolyn Brooks. Reprinted by permission of Harper & Row, Publishers, Inc. COUNTEE CULLEN, "Incident," from *On These I Stand*. Copyright © 1925 by Harper & Row, Publishers, Inc.; renewed 1953 by Ida M. Cullen. Reprinted by permission of Harper & Row, Publishers, Inc. HARRY GOLDEN, "For Two Cents Plain," from *Only in America*. Copyright © 1958 by Harry Golden. Reprinted by permission of Harper & Row, Publishers, Inc. NORMAN PODHORETZ, "The Brutal Bargain," from *Making It*. Copyright © 1967 by Norman Podhoretz. Reprinted by permission of the author and Georges Borchardt, Inc.

Houghton Mifflin Company. MARY ANTIN, "The Promised Land," from *The Promised Land*. Copyright © 1912 by Houghton Mifflin Company; renewed 1940 by Mary Antin. Reprinted by permission of Houghton Mifflin Company. WILLA CATHER, "Ántonia," from *My Ántonia*. Copyright © 1918, 1926, 1946 by Willa Sibert Cather; renewed 1954 by Edith Lewis; renewed 1977 by Walter Havighurst. Reprinted by permission of Houghton Mifflin Company. JEAN WAKATSUKI HOUSTON and JAMES D. HOUSTON, "Arrival at Manzanar," from *Farewell to Manzanar*. Copyright © 1973 by James Houston. Reprinted by permission of Houghton Mifflin Company.

Macmillan Publishing Co., Inc. VINE DELORIA, JR., *Custer Died for Your Sins*. Copyright © 1969 by Vine Deloria, Jr. Reprinted with permission of Macmillan Publishing Co., Inc. MICHAEL HARRINGTON, "The Invisible Poor," from *The Other America*. Copyright © 1962 by Michael Harrington. Reprinted with permission of Macmillan Publishing Co. MICHAEL NOVAK, "In Ethnic America," from *The Rise of the Unmeltable Ethnics*. Copyright © 1971, 1972 by Michael Novak. Reprinted with permission of Macmillan Publishing Co., Inc. WILLIAM BUTLER YEATS, "The Second Coming," from *Collected Poems*. Copyright © 1924 by Macmillan Publishing Co., Inc.; renewed 1952 by Bertha Georgie Yeats. Reprinted with permission of Macmillan Publishing Co., Inc.

Edward B. Marks Music Corporation. JAMES WELDON JOHNSON, "Lift Ev'ry Voice and Sing," song in Maya Angelou, *I Know Why the Caged Birds Sing*. Used by Permission.

McGraw-Hill Book Company. CLYDE KLUCKHOHN, "Customs," from *Mirror for Man*. Reprinted by permission of McGraw-Hill Book Company.

David McKay. HARRY MARK PETRAKIS, "Barba Nikos," from *Stelmark: A Family Recollection*. Copyright © 1972 by Harry Mark Petrakis. Used by permission of Toni Strassman, Agent.

William Morrow & Company, Inc. NIKKI GIOVANNI, "They Clapped," from *My House*. Copyright © 1972 by Nikki Giovanni. By permission of William Morrow & Company.

MS Magazine. ROBIN LAKOFF, "You Are What You Say," in *MS*, July 1974. Copyright © 1974 by *MS* Magazine. By permission of the publisher.

Natural History Magazine. LAURA BOHANNAN, "Shakespeare in the Bush," in *Natural History*, August–September 1966. Copyright © 1966 by Laura Bohannan. With permission from *Natural History*, Vol. 75, no. 7, 1966. CONRAD P. KOTTACK, "Rituals at McDonald's," in *Natural History*, January 1978. Copyright © 1978 by The American Museum of Natural History. With permission from *Natural History*, Vol. 87, no. 1, 1978.

The New Republic, Inc. EVE MERRIAM, "A Wasp Hymn," in *The New Republic*, July 12, 1969. Copyright © 1969 by The New Republic, Inc. Reprinted by permission of *The New Republic*.

Newsweek, Inc. ROBERT CLAIBORNE, "A Wasp Stings Back," in *Newsweek*, September 30, 1974. Copyright © 1974 by Newsweek, Inc. All Rights Reserved. Reprinted by permission. "Soapland Today," from "Television's Hottest Show," in *Newsweek*, September 28, 1981. Copyright © 1981 by Newsweek, Inc. All Rights Reserved. Reprinted by permission.

The New York Review of Books. IVAN ILLICH, "Effects of Development," from "Problems of Development," in *The New York Review of Books*, November 6, 1969. Copyright © 1969 by Nyrev, Inc. Reprinted with permission from *The New York Review of Books*.

W. W. Norton Company, Inc. LILLIAN SMITH, "When I Was a Child," from *Killers of the Dream*. Copyright © 1949, 1961 by Lillian Smith. Selection is reprinted with the permission of W. W. Norton & Company, Inc.

The Putnam Publishing Group. ASHLEY MONTAGU, "American Men Don't Cry," from *The American Way of Life*. Copyright © 1952, 1962, 1967 by Ashley Montagu. Reprinted by permission of G. P. Putnam's Sons.

Ramparts Magazine. FRANK CHIN, "Confessions of a Number One Son," in *Ramparts*, Copyright 1973 by Noah's Ark, Inc. Reprinted by permission.

Random House, Inc., Alfred A. Knopf, Inc., Pantheon Books. MAYA ANGELOU. "Graduation," from *I Know Why the Caged Bird Sings*. Copyright © 1969 by Maya Angelou. Reprinted by permission of Random House, Inc. MARSTON BATES, "On Being Human," from *Gluttons and Libertines*. Copyright © 1967 by Marston Bates. Reprinted by permission of Random House, Inc. PETER FARB, "How to Talk About the World," from *Word Play: What Happens When People Talk*. Copyright © 1973 by Peter Farb. Reprinted by permission of Alfred A. Knopf, Inc. MAXINE KINGSTON, "Girlhood Among Ghosts," from *The Woman Warrior*. Copyright © 1975, 1976 by Maxine Hong Kingston. Reprinted by permission of Alfred A. Knopf, Inc. ANDREA LEE, *Russian Journal*. Copyright © 1979, 1980, 1981 by Andrea Lee. Reprinted by permission of Random House, Inc. JONATHAN SCHELL, "The War Comes to Ben Suc," from *The Village of Ben Suc*. Originally appeared in the *New Yorker* in slightly different form. Copyright © 1967 by Jonathan Schell. Reprinted by permission of Alfred A. Knopf, Inc. RICHARD SENNETT AND JONATHAN COBB, "Third Generation," from *The Hidden Injuries of Class*. Copyright © 1972 by Richard Sennett and Jonathan Cobb. Reprinted by permission of Alfred A. Knopf, Inc. Originally appeared in the *New Yorker* in slightly different form. PIRI THOMAS, "Alien Turf," from *Down These Mean Streets*. Copyright © 1967. Reprinted by permission of Alfred A. Knopf, Inc. ALVIN TOFFLER, *Future Shock*. Copyright © 1970 by Alvin Toffler. Reprinted by permission of Random House, Inc. MALCOLM X with ALEX HALEY, "Hair," from *The Autobiography of Malcolm X*. Copyright © 1964 by Alex Haley and Malcolm X. Copyright © 1965 by Alex Haley and Betty Shabazz. Reprinted by permission of Random House, Inc.

Simon & Schuster. JOAN DIDION, "Norte americana," from *A Book of Common Prayer*. Copyright © 1977 by Joan Didion. Reprinted by permission of SIMON & SCHUSTER, a Division of Gulf & Western Corporation. JANE HOWARD, *Families*. Copyright © 1978 by Jane Howard. Reprinted by permission of SIMON & SCHUSTER, a Division of Gulf & Western Corporation. JOHN NEIHARDT, "War Games," from *Black Elk Speaks*. Copyright © 1932, 1959, etc., by John G. Neihardt. Published by Simon & Schuster Pocket Books and by the University of Nebraska Press. Reprinted by permission of Hilda Neihardt Petri.

Souvenir Press of London. CAROLINA MARIA DE JESUS, *Beyond All Pity*. Reprinted with permission of Souvenir Press of London.

Stein and Day, Publishers. DESMOND MORRIS, PETER COLLETT, PETER MARSH, and MARIE O'SHAUNESSY, "The Hand Purse," from *Gestures*. Copyright © 1980 by Desmond Morris, Peter Collett, Peter Marsh, and Marie O'Shaunessy. Reprinted with permission of Stein and Day Publishers.

University of Arizona Press. HELEN SEKAQUAPTEWA, "Marriage," from *Me and Mine: The Life Story of Helen Sekaquaptewa as Told to Louise Udall*. Copyright © 1969 by the University of Arizona Press. Reprinted with permission of the publisher.

University of New Mexico Press. N. SCOTT MOMADAY, "The Way to Rainy Mountain," from *The Way to Rainy Mountain*, Copyright © 1969 by the University of New Mexico Press. First published in *The Reporter*, January 26, 1967. Reprinted by permission from the University of New Mexico Press.

University of Notre Dame Press. ERNESTO GALARZA, "The Barrio," from *Barrio Boy*. Copyright © 1971 by Ernesto Galarza. Permission granted by the University of Notre Dame Press.

University of Pennsylvania Press. WILLIAM LABOV, "The Logic of Non-standard English," from *Language in the Inner City* © 1972 by William Labov. Reprinted by permission of William Labov.

Verbatim Magazine. MYRNA KNEPLER, "Sold at Fine Stores, Naturellement," in *Verbatim*, February 1978. Copyright © 1978 by *Verbatim*, Vol. 4, no. 4. Permission granted by the publisher.

A. P. Watt Ltd. WILLIAM BUTLER YEATS, "The Second Coming," in *Collected Poems*. Copyright © 1924 by Macmillan Publishing Co., Inc.; renewed 1952 by Bertha Georgie Yeats. Reprinted by permission of Michael and Anne Yeats and Macmillan London Limited.

Western Review Magazine. ARTHUR L. CAMPA, "Anglo vs. Chicano: Why?" in *Western Review*, 1972. Copyright © 1972. Reprinted by permission of Mrs. Arthur L. Campa.

*For
Elizabeth,
Elinor and
Anne*

PREFACE

Crossing Cultures is a collection of varied readings on a common theme: the diverse ways in which men and women live in different societies and social circumstances. The selections discuss the origins of that diversity as well as its consequences, and in particular provide examples of encounters between people of differing life ways.

American awareness of cultural differences has risen considerably in the last few decades. The Black liberation movement of the 1960's, the rise of ethnic consciousness in the 1970's and, most recently, the arrival of Vietnamese and Cuban refugees, among many others, has affected our consciousness, conscience, and attitude. At the same time, Americans have also become increasingly concerned with the need to interact with the rest of the world— with the recognition, in fact, that such interaction can no longer be avoided. Hundreds of thousands of Americans are abroad, not as tourists merely but working as professionals. Three hundred thousand foreign students attend American colleges and universities, a number that may double by the 1990's. What happens in Afghanistan affects American participation in the Olympic Games; what happens in the Persian Gulf affects our position in line at the gas pump.

Crossing Cultures is an attempt to introduce some of these contemporary concerns in the context of the composition course, not as a strange marriage of convenience, but because we have found in working with our students that crosscultural subjects and composing can work in tandem surprisingly well. It seems to us that there are three reasons for this.

Class discussion of crosscultural subjects has a powerful impact on students, because it challenges accepted beliefs by asking them to consider the lives, ideas, and aspirations of people often very different from themselves, and also because it may appeal to particular ethnic backgrounds and pride. When challenged "where they live," people are much more likely to want to express themselves forcefully, and to marshal arguments with care.

Secondly, because of the nature of the subject, *Crossing Cultures* is particularly strong in first person narratives, the kind of writing that students, especially some of those who think they have "nothing to say," will be able to carry through successfully. Such students will begin their college writing tasks with what they know best—their own experiences. From this kind of narrative students move to selections in which narration becomes a vehicle for expository and persuasive ends. In addition, the book contains examples of more objective forms of writing with various patterns of organization.

Finally, crosscultural readings are, we have found, effective in making students aware of the fact that, whatever writing they will do, will be for an audience, often an audience whose background differs widely from their own. The confrontation with different lives, experiences and points of view helps to make them conscious of the possible gaps between the writer's intentions and a reader's response to them.

Most of the sixty-four selections in *Crossing Cultures* are essays, some of the length of student essays, others much longer. A few pieces of fiction and poetry whose subjects seemed particularly apt are also included. All the selections fit the crosscultural theme, but they were chosen because we found them exciting, interesting or provocative, because they stuck in our minds long after reading them. A few of the essays of considerable power were written by untrained writers, and styles range from the very straightforward or simple to the highly complex, allusive. Well-known authors are included, as well as some often-used selections, together with some surprises.

We believe that the thematic organization of this book offers advantages to the student whose growth in writing ability is likely to arise from a growth of understanding of his own ideas and those of others. We have, however, also provided a table which places selections in one or more rhetorical categories. In some cases that was rather easy to do; in others, of course, categories are less meaningful, and we have placed such selections in two of the groups.

Each of the ten parts of *Crossing Cultures* is provided with an introduction that states the theme of that section and briefly introduces each selection. A headnote precedes each piece; it gives biographical information and refers the reader to other works of interest by the author. All prose selections are followed by "Words to Know," a rather comprehensive list of words and phrases, including proper nouns (persons, places) that the students may need to look up. This is followed by two sets of questions: "Some of the Issues" focuses on content, beginning with questions testing the students' understanding of what they have read. "The Way We Are Told" is designed to make students realize that a writer constantly has to make choices: it leads them to examine an author's strategies to reach his or her audience, by organizing materials effectively, by choosing words and phrases appropriately, and by making transitions. Lastly we suggest one or more topics for writing assignments, connected either to the theme of the selection or its method of organization.

We are grateful to several colleagues for their advice, in particular to Susan Feinberg, Robert F. Irving, and Leon Stover, all at the Illinois Institute of Technology; to C. Jeriel Howard and Rory Stephens at Northeastern Illinois University; and to Takeko Stover, Roosevelt University. At Macmillan Patricia Cabeza, Susan Didriksen, William F. Oldsey, and William D. Winschief were of great help. John Boles, Rutgers University, John Harwood, The Pennsylvania State University, Anita Hochser, University of Michigan—Flint, Frank Hubbard, University of Wisconsin—Milwaukee, Carolyn Johnson, Montgomery Community College, George Miller, University of Delaware, and James T. Nardin, Louisiana State University advised us in the selection and preparation of the text. Etta Carter and Carol Wiggins assisted us generously in preparing the manuscript.

CONTENTS

ONE · Growing Up Different 1

Maya Angelou
GRADUATION 4

"Days before, we had made a sign for the store, and as we turned out the lights Momma hung the cardboard over the doorknob. It read clearly: CLOSED. GRADUATION."

Lillian Smith
WHEN I WAS A CHILD 15

"Though you ate with your nurse when you were little, it was bad to eat with any colored person after that. It was bad just as other things were bad that your mother had told you."

Maxine Hong Kingston
GIRLHOOD AMONG GHOSTS 23

"When I went to kindergarten and had to speak English for the first time, I became silent."

Jack Agueros
HALFWAY TO DICK AND JANE: A PUERTO RICAN PILGRIMAGE 29

"When you got to the top of the hill, something strange happened: America began, because from the hill south was where the 'Americans' lived. Dick and Jane were not dead; they were alive and well in a better neighborhood."

Black Elk, as told to John G. Neihardt
WAR GAMES   42

"When the ponies came together on the run, they would rear and flounder and scream in a big dust, and the riders would seize each other wrestling until one side had lost all its men."

Countee Cullen
INCIDENT   45

"Now I was eight and very small."

TWO · Heritage   47

N. Scott Momaday
THE WAY TO RAINY MOUNTAIN   49

"At the end of a long and legendary way was my grandmother's grave. Here and there on the dark stones were ancestral names. Looking back once, I saw the mountain and came away."

Harry Golden
FOR TWO CENTS PLAIN   56

"My uncle Berger once operated one of those sweet potato pushcarts with the stove on the bottom, and years later he always said that he began life in America as an engineer."

Harry Mark Petrakis
BARBA NIKOS   62

"One of our untamed games was to seek out the owner of a pushcart or a store, unmistakably an immigrant, and bedevil him with a chorus of insults and jeers. To prove allegiance to the gang it was necessary to reserve our fiercest malevolence for a storekeeper or peddler belonging to our own ethnic background."

Arthur L. Campa
ANGLO VS. CHICANO: WHY?   68

"A century of association has inevitably acculturated both Hispanos and Anglo-Americans to some extent, but there still persist a number of culture traits that neither group has relinquished."

THREE · Families 75

Jane Howard
FAMILIES 77

"Good families are much to all their members, but everything to none."

Alfred Kazin
THE KITCHEN 83

"All my memories of that kitchen are dominated by the nearness of my mother sitting all day long at her sewing machine, by the clacking of the treadle against the linoleum floor, by the patient twist of her right shoulder as she automatically pushed at the wheel with one hand."

Willa Cather
ÁNTONIA 87

"My grandmother always spoke in a very loud tone to foreigners, as if they were deaf. She made Mrs. Shimerda understand the friendly intention of our visit, and the Bohemian woman handled the loaves of bread and even smelled them."

Helen Sekaquaptewa
MARRIAGE 93

"The groom may follow the bride to her home as soon as he likes. Some go right away, some wait a long time before claiming their brides."

Carolina Maria De Jesus
DIARY 101

"I went to the junk dealer to sell the paper. 55 cruzeiros. I hurried back, bought milk and bread. I made a chocolate drink for the children, made the beds, put beans on the stove, and swept the shack."

FOUR · Encounters 105

Walter White
I LEARN WHAT I AM 108

"In the flickering light the mob swayed, paused, and began to flow toward us. In that instant there opened up within me a great awareness; I knew then who I was. I was a Negro."

Piri Thomas
ALIEN TURF   114

"This crap kept up for a month. They tried to shake me up. Every time they threw something at me, it was just to see me jump."

Jeanne Wakatsuki Houston and James D. Houston
ARRIVAL AT MANZANAR   127

"Mama took out another dinner plate and hurled it at the floor, then another and another, never moving, never opening her mouth, just quivering and glaring at the retreating dealer, with tears streaming down her cheeks."

Vine Deloria Jr.
CUSTER DIED FOR YOUR SINS   134

"The American public feels most comfortable with the mythical Indians of stereotypeland who were always THERE. These Indians are fierce; they wear feathers and grunt."

Frank Chin
CONFESSIONS OF A NUMBER ONE SON   138

"Or sometimes I'd die shouting something paradoxical. 'The river does not contend against the willow, yet the doorknob still turns,' I'd say, and crash, I was dead."

Michael Novak
IN ETHNIC AMERICA   148

"We did not feel this country belonged to us. We felt fierce pride in it, more loyalty than anyone could know. But we felt blocked at every turn."

Robert Claiborne
A WASP STINGS BACK   156

"As a Wasp, the mildest thing I can say about the stereotype emerging from the current wave of anti-Wasp chic is that I don't recognize myself."

Rarihokwats (Jerry Gambill)
ON THE ART OF STEALING HUMAN RIGHTS   160

"Tell the Indian he has a voice and go through the motions of listening. Then interpret what you have heard to suit your own needs."

Jonathan Swift
A MODEST PROPOSAL   164

" . . . a fair, cheap and easy method of making these children sound and useful members of the Commonwealth."

Eve Merriam
A WASP HYMN   173

"All men are brothers: White Anglo-Saxon Protestants and others."

FIVE · Identities   175

Mary Antin
THE PROMISED LAND   178

"A fairy godmother took us children to a wonderful country called 'uptown' where, in a dazzlingly beautiful palace called a 'department store' we exchanged our hateful homemade European costumes for real American machine-made garments."

Norman Podhoretz
THE BRUTAL BARGAIN   183

"One of the longest journeys in the world is the journey from Brooklyn to Manhattan."

Richard Sennett and Jonathan Cobb
THIRD GENERATION   193

"This man is someone who feels he has done a good job establishing a stable family and margin of security in contrast to the life of poverty and turmoil he knew as a child during the Depression. Why then is he so defensive?"

Ernesto Galarza
THE BARRIO   199

"Don Salvador had told us, saluting and marching as he talked to our class, that the Cinco de Mayo was the most glorious date in human history. The Americans had not even heard about it."

Malcolm X
HAIR   203

"I took the little list of ingredients . . . to a grocery store, where I got a can of Red Devil lye, two eggs, and two medium-sized white potatoes."

Gwendolyn Brooks
WE REAL COOL   206

"The pool players. Seven at the Golden Shovel."

SIX · Defining America   207

Michel Guillaume St. Jean de Crèvecoeur
WHAT IS AN AMERICAN?   209

"Here individuals of all nations are melted into a new race of men, whose labours and posterity will one day cause great changes in the world."

Henry James
THE AMERICAN   214

"Frigid yet friendly, frank yet cautious, shrewd yet credulous, positive yet sceptical, confident yet shy . . ."

Joan Didion
NORTEAMERICANA   218

"She understood that something was always going on in the world but believed that it would turn out all right."

Michael Harrington

THE INVISIBLE POOR   221

"The very development of the American city has removed poverty from the living, emotional experience of millions of middle-class Americans."

James Thurber

IVORYTOWN, RINSOVILLE, ANACINBURG, AND CRISCO CORNERS   226

"A soap opera is an endless sequence of narratives whose only cohesive element is the eternal presence of its bedevilled and beleaguered characters."

Newsweek

SOAPLAND TODAY   237

"To the extent that some viewers look to soaps to tell them what real life is like, today's younger generation may enter adulthood with some very odd notions about what to expect."

Conrad Phillip Kottak

RITUALS AT MC DONALD'S   241

"While McDonald's is definitely a mundane, secular institution—just a place to eat—it also assumes some of the attitudes of a sacred place."

SEVEN • New Worlds   251

Jacob A. Riis

IN THE GATEWAY OF NATIONS   253

"How it all came back to me; that Sunday in early June when I stood, a lonely immigrant lad, at the steamer's rail and looked out upon the New World of my dreams."

Irving Howe

ELLIS ISLAND   263

"Especially bewildering is the idea that that if you say you have a job waiting for you in the United States, you are liable to deportation . . ."

Vo Thi Tam

FROM VIETNAM, 1979   268

"After seven days we ran out of water, so all we had to drink was the sea water, plus lemon juice."

Andrea Lee

RUSSIAN JOURNAL   273

"At seven o'clock the head of the university began to speak. At the first few phrases, I felt stealing irresistibly over me the memory of my own freshman year: the universal confusion; the unexpected liberty; awe; the endlessly proffered, absurd advice, which we ritually ignored."

Elizabeth Hanson

BLESSINGS OF EMPTINESS   280

"Mrs. Hirata was not attracted to American life because we have cars and big television sets and lots of appliances. She likes the United States because of the emptiness."

Laura Bohannan

SHAKESPEARE IN THE BUSH   284

"They threatened to tell me no more stories until I told them one of mine . . . Realizing that here was my chance to prove Hamlet universally intelligible, I agreed."

Jonathan Schell

THE VILLAGE OF BEN SUC   296

"You know that's the first time I've ever seen a dead guy, and I don't feel bad. I just don't. That's all."

James Baldwin

STRANGER IN THE VILLAGE   303

"All of the physical characteristics of the Negro which had caused me, in America, a very different and almost forgotten pain were nothing less than miraculous—or infernal—in the eyes of the village people."

George Orwell
SHOOTING AN ELEPHANT   315

"In Moulmein, in Lower Burma, I was hated by large numbers of people—the only time that I have been important enough for this to happen to me."

Nikki Giovanni
THEY CLAPPED   322

" . . . they finally realized they are strangers all over."

EIGHT · Change   325

Alvin Toffler
FUTURE SHOCK   327

"Future shock is the dizzying disorientation brought on by the premature arrival of the future. It may well be the most important disease of tomorrow."

Adam Smith
THE JAPANESE MODEL   335

"What are the Japanese doing right? And how have they done it on a crowded group of islands, without enough coal and oil, without significant natural resources, without adequate farmland?"

Henry Knepler
BEYOND AMERICAN EXPRESSLAND   340

"We see—or saw—ourselves as straightforward, with a tinge of innocence, only a little cleaner in mind and body than the natives upon whom we visit the rational accomplishments of our culture."

Ivan Illich
EFFECTS OF DEVELOPMENT   351

"Once the Third World has become a mass market for the goods, products, and processes which are designed by the rich for themselves, the discrepancy between demand for these Western artifacts and the supply will increase indefinitely."

William Butler Yeats
THE SECOND COMING   358

"Things fall apart; the centre cannot hold."

NINE • Defining Cultures   359

Marston Bates
ON BEING HUMAN   361

"The outstanding peculiarity of man is the great control of custom, of culture, over behavior."

Clyde Kluckhohn
CUSTOMS   371

"A humble cooking pot is as much a cultural product as is a Beethoven sonata."

Peter Freuchen
THE ESKIMO HOUSE   376

"You enter the winter house through an entrance tunnel, usually about fifteen feet long so as to provide both ventilation and protection against the outside cold."

Ashley Montagu
AMERICAN MEN DON'T CRY   382

"American men don't cry, because it is considered unmasculine to do so. Only sissies cry. Crying is a 'weakness' characteristic of the female, and no American male wants to be identified with anything in the least weak or feminine."

Leonore Tiefer
THE KISS   385

"When the Thonga first saw Europeans kissing they laughed remarking, 'Look at them. They eat each other's saliva and dirt.'"

TEN · Communicating   389

Peter Farb
HOW TO TALK ABOUT THE WORLD   391

"Anyone who visits an exotic culture quickly learns that people are linguistically deaf to categories he considers obvious."

William Labov
THE LOGIC OF NONSTANDARD ENGLISH   396

"Our work in the speech community makes it painfully obvious that in many ways working-class speakers are more effective narrators, reasoners and debaters than many middle-class speakers who temporize, qualify, and lose their argument in a mass of irrelevant detail."

Robin Lakoff
YOU ARE WHAT YOU SAY   405

"If we refuse to talk 'like a lady,' we are ridiculed and criticized as being unfeminine."

Myrna Knepler
SOLD AT FINE STORES EVERYWHERE, NATURELLEMENT   412

"Madison Avenue, when constructing ads for high-priced non-necessary items, may use French phrases to suggest to readers that they are identified as super-sophisticated, subtly sexy, and privy to the secrets of old world charm and tradition."

Edward T. Hall
PRIVATE SPACE   418

"Germans sense their own space as an extension of their ego. One sees a clue to this feeling in the term 'Lebensraum,' which is impossible to translate because it summarizes so much."

Desmond Morris
THE HAND PURSE   424

"Many gestures have more than one meaning, as you travel from place to place, but it is unusual to find one with such a variety of meanings, even over a wide range of territory."

ALTERNATE TABLE OF CONTENTS

Description *(Selections which contain substantial descriptive passages)*

—Jack Agueros, HALFWAY TO DICK AND JANE: A PUERTO RICAN PILGRIMAGE   29

—N. Scott Momaday, THE WAY TO RAINY MOUNTAIN   49

—Harry Golden, FOR TWO CENTS PLAIN   56

—Alfred Kazin, THE KITCHEN   83

—George Orwell, SHOOTING AN ELEPHANT   315

—Peter Freuchen, THE ESKIMO HOUSE   376

Narration *(Personal)*

—Maya Angelou, GRADUATION   4

—Lillian Smith, WHEN I WAS A CHILD   15

—Maxine Hong Kingston, GIRLHOOD AMONG GHOSTS   23

—Jack Agueros, HALFWAY TO DICK AND JANE: A PUERTO RICAN PILGRIMAGE   29

—Black Elk, as told to John G. Neihardt, WAR GAMES   42

—Harry Golden, FOR TWO CENTS PLAIN   56

—Helen Sekaquaptewa, MARRIAGE   93

—Walter White, I LEARN WHAT I AM   108

—Piri Thomas, ALIEN TURF   114

xxvii

—Jeanne Wakatsuki Houston and James D. Houston, ARRIVAL AT
    MANZANAR   127

—Mary Antin, THE PROMISED LAND   178

—Norman Podhoretz, THE BRUTAL BARGAIN   183

—Ernesto Galarza, THE BARRIO   199

—Malcolm X, HAIR   203

—Vo Thi Tam, FROM VIETNAM, 1979   268

—Laura Bohannan, SHAKESPEARE IN THE BUSH   284

—George Orwell, SHOOTING AN ELEPHANT   315

—Marston Bates, ON BEING HUMAN   361

Narration *(Observation and Reporting)*

—Richard Sennett and Jonathan Cobb, THIRD GENERATION   193

—*Newsweek*, SOAPLAND TODAY   237

—Jacob A. Riis, IN THE GATEWAY OF NATIONS   253

—Irving Howe, ELLIS ISLAND   263

—Andrea Lee, RUSSIAN JOURNAL   273

—Jonathan Schell, THE VILLAGE OF BEN SUC   296

Analysis

—Alvin Toffler, FUTURE SHOCK   327

—Henry Knepler, BEYOND AMERICAN EXPRESSLAND   340

—Robin Lakoff, YOU ARE WHAT YOU SAY   405

Classification and Division

—Rarihokwats (Jerry Gambill), ON THE ART OF STEALING HUMAN
    RIGHTS   160

—Leonor Tiefer, THE KISS   385

—Peter Farb, HOW TO TALK ABOUT THE WORLD   391

—Desmond Morris, THE HAND PURSE   424

Comparison and Contrast

—Arthur L. Campa, ANGLO VS. CHICANO: WHY? 68

—Ernesto Galarza, THE BARRIO 199

—Michel Guillaume St. Jean de Crèvecoeur, WHAT IS AN
    AMERICAN? 209

—Elizabeth Hanson, BLESSINGS OF EMPTINESS 280

—Laura Bohannan, SHAKESPEARE IN THE BUSH 284

—Adam Smith, THE JAPANESE MODEL 335

—William Labov, THE LOGIC OF NON-STANDARD ENGLISH 396

—Myrna Knepler, SOLD AT FINE STORES EVERYWHERE,
    NATURELLEMENT 412

—Edward T. Hall, PRIVATE SPACE 418

Definition

—Jane Howard, FAMILIES 77

—Michel Guillaume St. Jean de Crèvecoeur, WHAT IS AN
    AMERICAN? 209

—Conrad Phillip Kottak, RITUAL AT MC DONALD'S 241

—Marston Bates, ON BEING HUMAN 361

—Clyde Kluckhohn, CUSTOMS 371

Argument and Persuasion

—Maya Angelou, GRADUATION 4

—Lillian Smith, WHEN I WAS A CHILD 15

—Vine Deloria Jr., CUSTER DIED FOR YOUR SINS 134

—Frank Chin, CONFESSIONS OF A NUMBER ONE SON 138

—Michael Novak, IN ETHNIC AMERICA 148

—Robert Claiborne, A WASP STINGS BACK 156

—Rarihokwats (Jerry Gambill), ON THE ART OF STEALING HUMAN
    RIGHTS 160

—Michael Harrington, THE INVISIBLE POOR 221

—Jonathan Swift, A MODEST PROPOSAL   164

—Norman Podhoretz, THE BRUTAL BARGAIN   183

—Malcolm X, HAIR   203

—James Baldwin, STRANGER IN THE VILLAGE   303

—Ivan Illich, EFFECTS OF DEVELOPMENT   351

—William Labov, THE LOGIC OF NONSTANDARD ENGLISH   396

Irony, Humor and Satire

—Vine Deloria Jr., CUSTER DIED FOR YOUR SINS   134

—Frank Chin, CONFESSIONS OF A NUMBER ONE SON   138

—Rarihokwats (Jerry Gambill), ON THE ART OF STEALING HUMAN
  RIGHTS   160

—Jonathan Swift, A MODEST PROPOSAL   164

—Eve Merriam, A WASP HYMN   173

—Joan Didion, NORTEAMERICANA   218

—James Thurber, IVORYTOWN, RINSOVILLE, ANACINBURG, AND
  CRISCO CORNERS   226

Journals

—Carolina Maria De Jesus, DIARY   101

—Andrea Lee, RUSSIAN JOURNAL   273

Fiction

—Harry Mark Petrakis, BARBA NIKOS   62

—Willa Cather, ÁNTONIA   87

—Henry James, THE AMERICAN   214

—Joan Didion, NORTEAMERICANA   218

Poetry

—Countee Cullen, INCIDENT 45

—Eve Merriam, A WASP HYMN 173

—Gwendolyn Brooks, WE REAL COOL 206

—Nikki Giovanni, THEY CLAPPED 322

—William Butler Yeats, THE SECOND COMING 358

ONE

Growing Up Different

Generations of American children learned to read with Dick and Jane. When they entered the first grade in public school, they met Dick, Jane, and their dog Spot—white, bright, blonde suburban children with a pipe-smoking, genial father and a kindly mother whose only job was to keep an immaculate house and look after them.

The American dream which they represented was in reality something distant and unattainable to many, if not most, of the children who encountered it. But it was so well established that it persisted; a very long time passed before voices were raised insistently to point out its unreality. This homogenized, one-culture dream world of Dick and Jane contrasts to the encounters with reality that are described in the selections that follow, but somehow Dick and Jane hover over them. Each of these selections recalls key childhood experiences that caused the writer to discover the fact of cultural difference and its consequences.

In the opening selection, the Black poet and actress Maya Angelou recalls her graduation from the eighth grade in Stamps, a tiny rural community in Arkansas. She looks back at that event, which starts out as "a dream of a day," as her first jolting awareness that she, like others of her race, is assigned the scraps from the table—put in her place, casually and unthinkingly, by the white commencement speaker.

In contrast to Angelou, Lillian Smith, the author of the second selection, grew up in a Dick-and-Jane environment, turn-of-the-century version: the privileged child of upper middle-class white parents in Florida, raised in an atmosphere of religion and strict morality. She describes that setting with great care because it is important not only for the story she tells but to explain the bitterness she feels. Her description focuses on a single event, the meaning of which she could not fully grasp as a child. Only as an adult, many years later, did she see how that short experience had exploded the myths of her childhood.

In the third selection, Maxine Hong Kingston describes her childhood in the Chinese community in Stockton, California. It is a world in which the Chinese traditions, learned through her mother's stories, have a greater reality than the family's daily life in California. Their word for the non-Chinese is "ghosts." When school introduces her into the company of black and white "ghosts," she turns completely silent.

Jack Agueros, whose parents migrated from Puerto Rico to New York shortly before he was born, grew up during the Depression of the 1930s. In "Halfway to Dick and Jane: A Puerto Rican Pilgrimage," he describes his emergence from the shelter of family and early childhood into a world that resisted accepting him and that he found hard to accept. He finds himself between two cultures and expresses the tensions of that position.

Children all over America used to play cowboys and Indians; some still do. Indians did not play the same game. Black Elk's childhood games were very rough, foreshadowing the rough adult existence to come.

A poem by Countee Cullen concludes this part of the anthology. It sums up, in a few lines, a first contact with pain inflicted by prejudice.

GRADUATION

Maya Angelou

Maya Angelou, born Marguerite Johnson, spent her childhood in Stamps, Arkansas, the small town in which her story is set. The author of several books of prose and poetry, she has also acted on stage and screen, hosted a television show, and appeared in the popular television series "Roots." She has taught and served as writer-in-residence at several universities and worked as the northern coordinator of the Southern Christian Leadership Conference at the invitation of Dr. Martin Luther King, Jr.

This selection is taken from *I Know Why The Caged Bird Sings* (1970), the first volume in an autobiographical series that includes *Gather Together in My Name* (1975), *Singin' and Swingin' and Merry Like Christmas* (1976), and *The Heart of a Woman* (1981).

The children in Stamps trembled visibly with anticipation. Some adults were excited too, but to be certain the whole young population had come down with graduation epidemic. Large classes were graduating from both the grammar school and the high school. Even those who were years removed from their own day of glorious release were anxious to help with preparations as a kind of dry run. The junior students who were moving into the vacating classes' chairs were tradition-bound to show their talents for leadership and management. They strutted through the school and around the campus exerting pressure on the lower grades. Their authority was so new that occasionally if they pressed a little too hard it had to be overlooked. After all, next term was coming, and it never hurt a sixth grader to have a play sister in the eighth grade, or a tenth-year student to be able to call a twelfth grader Bubba. So all was endured in a spirit of shared understanding. But the graduating classes themselves were the nobility. Like travelers with exotic destinations on their minds, the graduates were remarkably forgetful. They came to school without their books, or tablets or even pencils. Volunteers fell over themselves to secure replacements for the missing equipment. When accepted, the willing workers might or might not be thanked, and it was of no importance to the pregraduation rites. Even teachers were respectful of the now quiet and aging seniors, and tended to speak to them, if not as equals, as beings only slightly lower than themselves. After tests were returned and grades given, the student body, which acted like an extended family, knew who did well, who excelled, and what piteous ones had failed.

Unlike the white high school, Lafayette County Training School distinguished itself by having neither lawn, nor hedges, nor tennis court, nor climbing ivy. Its two buildings (main classrooms, the grade school and home

economics) were set on a dirt hill with no fence to limit either its boundaries
or those of bordering farms. There was a large expanse to the left of the
school which was used alternately as a baseball diamond or a basketball
court. Rusty hoops on the swaying poles represented the permanent recrea-
tional equipment, although bats and balls could be borrowed from the P.E.
teacher if the borrower was qualified and if the diamond wasn't occupied.

Over this rocky area relieved by a few shady tall persimmon trees the   3
graduating class walked. The girls often held hands and no longer bothered
to speak to the lower students. There was a sadness about them, as if this old
world was not their home and they were bound for higher ground. The boys,
on the other hand, had become more friendly, more outgoing. A decided
change from the closed attitude they projected while studying for finals.
Now they seemed not ready to give up the old school, the familiar paths and
classrooms. Only a small percentage would be continuing on to college—one
of the South's A & M (agricultural and mechanical) schools, which trained
Negro youths to be carpenters, farmers, handymen, masons, maids, cooks
and baby nurses. Their future rode heavily on their shoulders, and blinded
them to the collective joy that had pervaded the lives of the boys and girls
in the grammar school graduating class.

Parents who could afford it had ordered new shoes and ready-made   4
clothes for themselves from Sears and Roebuck or Montgomery Ward. They
also engaged the best seamstresses to make the floating graduating dresses
and to cut down secondhand pants which would be pressed to a military
slickness for the important event.

Oh, it was important, all right. Whitefolks would attend the ceremony,   5
and two or three would speak of God and home, and the Southern way of
life, and Mrs. Parsons, the principal's wife, would play the graduation march
while the lower-grade graduates paraded down the aisles and took their seats
below the platform. The high school seniors would wait in empty classrooms
to make their dramatic entrance.

In the Store I was the person of the moment. The birthday girl. The   6
center. Bailey had graduated the year before, although to do so he had had
to forfeit all pleasures to make up for his time lost in Baton Rouge.

My class was wearing butter-yellow piqué dresses, and Momma   7
launched out on mine. She smocked the yoke into tiny crisscrossing puckers,
then shirred the rest of the bodice. Her dark fingers ducked in and out of
the lemony cloth as she embroidered raised daisies around the hem. Before
she considered herself finished she had added a crocheted cuff on the puff
sleeves, and a pointy crocheted collar.

I was going to be lovely. A walking model of all the various styles of   8
fine hand sewing and it didn't worry me that I was only twelve years old

and merely graduating from the eighth grade. Besides, many teachers in Arkansas Negro schools had only that diploma and were licensed to impart wisdom.

The days had become longer and more noticeable. The faded beige of former times had been replaced with strong and sure colors. I began to see my classmates' clothes, their skin tones, and the dust that waved off pussy willows. Clouds that lazed across the sky were objects of great concern to me. Their shiftier shapes might have held a message that in my new happiness and with a little bit of time I'd soon decipher. During that period I looked at the arch of heaven so religiously my neck kept a steady ache. I had taken to smiling more often, and my jaws hurt from the unaccustomed activity. Between the two physical sore spots, I suppose I could have been uncomfortable, but that was not the case. As a member of the winning team (the graduating class of 1940) I had outdistanced unpleasant sensations by miles. I was headed for the freedom of open fields.

Youth and social approval allied themselves with me and we trammeled memories of slights and insults. The wind of our swift passage remodeled my features. Lost tears were pounded to mud and then to dust. Years of withdrawal were brushed aside and left behind, as hanging ropes of parasitic moss.

My work alone had awarded me a top place and I was going to be one of the first called in the graduating ceremonies. On the classroom blackboard, as well as on the bulletin board in the auditorium, there were blue stars and white stars and red stars. No absences, no tardinesses, and my academic work was among the best of the year. I could say the preamble to the Constitution even faster than Bailey. We timed ourselves often: "WethepeopleoftheUnitedStatesinordertoformamoreperfectunion . . ." I had memorized the Presidents of the United States from Washington to Roosevelt in chronological as well as alphabetical order.

My hair pleased me too. Gradually the black mass had lengthened and thickened, so that it kept at last to its braided pattern, and I didn't have to yank my scalp off when I tried to comb it.

Louise and I had rehearsed the exercises until we tired out ourselves. Henry Reed was class valedictorian. He was a small, very black boy with hooded eyes, a long, broad nose and an oddly shaped head. I had admired him for years because each term he and I vied for the best grades in our class. Most often he bested me, but instead of being disappointed I was pleased that we shared top places between us. Like many Southern Black children, he lived with his grandmother, who was as strict as Momma and as kind as she knew how to be. He was courteous, respectful and soft-spoken to elders, but on the playground he chose to play the roughest games. I admired him. Anyone, I reckoned, sufficiently afraid or sufficiently dull could be polite. But to be able to operate at a top level with both adults and children was admirable.

His valedictory speech was entitled "To Be or Not to Be." The rigid   14
tenth-grade teacher had helped him write it. He'd been working on the dramatic stresses for months.

The weeks until graduation were filled with heady activities. A group   15
of small children were to be presented in a play about buttercups and daisies and bunny rabbits. They could be heard throughout the building practicing their hops and their little songs that sounded like silver bells. The older girls (nongraduates, of course) were assigned the task of making refreshments for the night's festivities. A tangy scent of ginger, cinnamon, nutmeg and chocolate wafted around the home economics building as the budding cooks made samples for themselves and their teachers.

In every corner of the workshop, axes and saws split fresh timber as the   16
woodshop boys made sets and stage scenery. Only the graduates were left out of the general bustle. We were free to sit in the library at the back of the building or look in quite detachedly, naturally, on the measures being taken for our event.

Even the minister preached on graduation the Sunday before. His sub-   17
ject was, "Let your light so shine that men will see your good works and praise your Father, Who is in Heaven." Although the sermon was purported to be addressed to us, he used the occasion to speak to backsliders, gamblers and general ne'er-do-wells. But since he had called our names at the beginning of the service we were mollified.

Among Negroes the tradition was to give presents to children going only   18
from one grade to another. How much more important this was when the person was graduating at the top of the class. Uncle Willie and Momma had sent away for a Mickey Mouse watch like Bailey's. Louise gave me four embroidered handkerchiefs. (I gave her three crocheted doilies.) Mrs. Sneed, the minister's wife, made me an underskirt to wear for graduation, and nearly every customer gave me a nickel or maybe even a dime with the instruction "Keep on moving to higher ground," or some such encouragement.

Amazingly the great day finally dawned and I was out of bed before I   19
knew it. I threw open the back door to see it more clearly, but Momma said, "Sister, come away from that door and put your robe on."

I hoped the memory of that morning would never leave me. Sunlight   20
was itself still young, and the day had none of the insistence maturity would bring it in a few hours. In my robe and barefoot in the backyard, under cover of going to see about my new beans, I gave myself up to the gentle warmth and thanked God that no matter what evil I had done in my life He had

allowed me to live to see this day. Somewhere in my fatalism I had expected
to die, accidentally, and never have the chance to walk up the stairs in the
auditorium and gracefully receive my hard-earned diploma. Out of God's
merciful bosom I had won reprieve.

Bailey came out in his robe and gave me a box wrapped in Christmas 21
paper. He said he had saved his money for months to pay for it. It felt like
a box of chocolates, but I knew Bailey wouldn't save money to buy candy
when we had all we could want under our noses.

He was as proud of the gift as I. It was a soft-leather-bound copy of a 22
collection of poems by Edgar Allan Poe, or, as Bailey and I called him,
"Eap." I turned to "Annabel Lee" and we walked up and down the garden
rows, the cool dirt between our toes, reciting the beautifully sad lines.

Momma made a Sunday breakfast although it was only Friday. After 23
we finished the blessing, I opened my eyes to find the watch on my plate. It
was a dream of a day. Everything went smoothly and to my credit. I didn't
have to be reminded or scolded for anything. Near evening I was too jittery
to attend to chores, so Bailey volunteered to do all before his bath.

Days before, we had made a sign for the Store, and as we turned out 24
the lights Momma hung the cardboard over the doorknob. It read clearly:
CLOSED. GRADUATION.

My dress fitted perfectly and everyone said that I looked like a sunbeam 25
in it. On the hill, going toward the school, Bailey walked behind with Uncle
Willie, who muttered, "Go on, Ju." He wanted him to walk ahead with us
because it embarrassed him to have to walk so slowly. Bailey said he'd let
the ladies walk together, and the men would bring up the rear. We all
laughed, nicely.

Little children dashed by out of the dark like fireflies. Their crepe-paper 26
dresses and butterfly wings were not made for running and we heard more
than one rip, dryly, and the regretful "uh uh" that followed.

The school blazed without gaiety. The windows seemed cold and 27
unfriendly from the lower hill. A sense of ill-fated timing crept over me, and
if Momma hadn't reached for my hand I would have drifted back to Bailey
and Uncle Willie, and possibly beyond. She made a few slow jokes about my
feet getting cold, and tugged me along to the now-strange building.

Around the front steps, assurance came back. There were my fellow 28
"greats," the graduating class. Hair brushed back, legs oiled, new dresses and
pressed pleats, fresh pocket handkerchiefs and little handbags, all homesewn.
Oh, we were up to snuff, all right. I joined my comrades and didn't even see
my family go in to find seats in the crowded auditorium.

The school band struck up a march and all classes filed in as had been 29
rehearsed. We stood in front of our seats, as assigned, and on a signal from

the choir director, we sat. No sooner had this been accomplished than the band started to play the national anthem. We rose again and sang the song, after which we recited the pledge of allegiance. We remained standing for a brief minute before the choir director and the principal signaled to us, rather desperately I thought, to take our seats. The command was so unusual that our carefully rehearsed and smooth-running machine was thrown off. For a full minute we fumbled for our chairs and bumped into each other awkwardly. Habits change or solidify under pressure, so in our state of nervous tension we had been ready to follow our usual assembly pattern: the American national anthem, then the pledge of allegiance, then the song every Black person I knew called the Negro National Anthem. All done in the same key, with the same passion and most often standing on the same foot.

Finding my seat at last, I was overcome with a presentiment of worse things to come. Something unrehearsed, unplanned, was going to happen, and we were going to be made to look bad. I distinctly remember being explicit in the choice of pronoun. It was "we," the graduating class, the unit, that concerned me then.

The principal welcomed "parents and friends" and asked the Baptist minister to lead us in prayer. His invocation was brief and punchy, and for a second I thought we were getting back on the high road to right action. When the principal came back to the dais, however, his voice had changed. Sounds always affected me profoundly and the principal's voice was one of my favorites. During assembly it melted and lowed weakly into the audience. It had not been in my plan to listen to him, but my curiosity was piqued and I straightened up to give him my attention.

He was talking about Booker T. Washington, our "late great leader," who said we can be as close as the fingers on the hand, etc. . . . Then he said a few vague things about friendship and the friendship of kindly people to those less fortunate than themselves. With that his voice nearly faded, thin, away. Like a river diminishing to a stream and then to a trickle. But he cleared his throat and said, "Our speaker tonight, who is also our friend, came from Texarkana to deliver the commencement address, but due to the irregularity of the train schedule, he's going to, as they say, 'speak and run.'" He said that we understood and wanted the man to know that we were most grateful for the time he was able to give us and then something about how we were willing always to adjust to another's program, and without more ado—"I give you Mr. Edward Donleavy."

Not one but two white men came through the door offstage. The shorter one walked to the speaker's platform, and the tall one moved over to the center seat and sat down. But that was our principal's seat, and already occu-

30

31

32

33

pied. The dislodged gentleman bounced around for a long breath or two before the Baptist minister gave him his chair, then with more dignity than the situation deserved, the minister walked off the stage.

Donleavy looked at the audience once (on reflection, I'm sure that he 34 wanted only to reassure himself that we were really there), adjusted his glasses and began to read from a sheaf of papers.

He was glad "to be here and to see the work going on just as it was in 35 the other schools."

At the first "Amen" from the audience I willed the offender to imme- 36 diate death by choking on the word. But Amens and Yes, sir's began to fall around the room like rain through a ragged umbrella.

He told us of the wonderful changes we children in Stamps had in store. 37 The Central School (naturally, the white school was Central) had already been granted improvements that would be in use in the fall. A well-known artist was coming from Little Rock to teach art to them. They were going to have the newest microscopes and chemistry equipment for their laboratory. Mr. Donleavy didn't leave us long in the dark over who made these improvements available to Central High. Nor were we to be ignored in the general betterment scheme he had in mind.

He said that he had pointed out to people at a very high level that one 38 of the first-line football tacklers at Arkansas Agricultural and Mechanical College had graduated from good old Lafayette County Training School. Here fewer Amen's were heard. Those few that did break through lay dully in the air with the heaviness of habit.

He went on to praise us. He went on to say how he had bragged that 39 "one of the best basketball players at Fisk sank his first ball right here at Lafayette County Training School."

The white kids were going to have a chance to become Galileos and 40 Madame Curies and Edisons and Gauguins, and our boys (the girls weren't even in on it) would try to be Jesse Owenses and Joe Louises.

Owens and the Brown Bomber were great heroes in our world, but what 41 school official in the white-goddom of Little Rock had the right to decide that those two men must be our only heroes? Who decided that for Henry Reed to become a scientist he had to work like George Washington Carver, as a bootblack, to buy a lousy microscope? Bailey was obviously always going to be too small to be an athlete, so which concrete angel glued to what county seat had decided that if my brother wanted to become a lawyer he had to first pay penance for his skin by picking cotton and hoeing corn and studying correspondence books at night for twenty years?

The man's dead words fell like bricks around the auditorium and too 42 many settled in my belly. Constrained by hard-learned manners I couldn't look behind me, but to my left and right the proud graduating class of 1940 had dropped their heads. Every girl in my row had found something new to do with her handkerchief. Some folded the tiny squares into love knots, some into triangles, but most were wadding them, then pressing them flat on their yellow laps.

On the dais, the ancient tragedy was being replayed. Professor Parsons sat, a sculptor's reject, rigid. His large, heavy body seemed devoid of will or willingness, and his eyes said he was no longer with us. The other teachers examined the flag (which was draped stage right) or their notes, or the windows which opened on our now-famous playing diamond.

Graduation, the hush-hush magic time of frills and gifts and congratulations and diplomas, was finished for me before my name was called. The accomplishment was nothing. The meticulous maps, drawn in three colors of ink, learning and spelling decasyllabic words, memorizing the whole of *The Rape of Lucrece*—it was for nothing. Donleavy had exposed us.

We were maids and farmers, handymen and washerwomen, and anything higher that we aspired to was farcical and presumptuous.

Then I wished that Gabriel Prosser and Nat Turner had killed all whitefolks in their beds and that Abraham Lincoln had been assassinated before the signing of the Emancipation Proclamation, and that Harriet Tubman had been killed by that blow on her head and Christopher Columbus had drowned in the *Santa María*.

It was awful to be Negro and have no control over my life. It was brutal to be young and already trained to sit quietly and listen to charges brought against my color with no chance of defense. We should all be dead. I thought I should like to see us all dead, one on top of the other. A pyramid of flesh with the whitefolks on the bottom, as the broad base, then the Indians with their silly tomahawks and teepees and wigwams and treaties, the Negroes with their mops and recipes and cotton sacks and spirituals sticking out of their mouths. The Dutch children should all stumble in their wooden shoes and break their necks. The French should choke to death on the Louisiana Purchase (1803) while silkworms ate all the Chinese with their stupid pigtails. As a species, we were an abomination. All of us.

Donleavy was running for election, and assured our parents that if he won we could count on having the only colored paved playing field in that part of Arkansas. Also—he never looked up to acknowledge the grunts of acceptance—also, we were bound to get some new equipment for the home economics building and the workshop.

He finished, and since there was no need to give any more than the most perfunctory thank-you's, he nodded to the men on the stage, and the tall white man who was never introduced joined him at the door. They left with the attitude that now they were off to something really important. (The graduation ceremonies at Lafayette County Training School had been a mere preliminary.)

The ugliness they left was palpable. An uninvited guest who wouldn't [50] leave. The choir was summoned and sang a modern arrangement of "Onward, Christian Soldiers," with new words pertaining to graduates seeking their place in the world. But it didn't work. Elouise, the daughter of the Baptist minister, recited "Invictus," and I could have cried at the impertinence of "I am the master of my fate, I am the captain of my soul."

My name had lost its ring of familiarity and I had to be nudged to go [51] and receive my diploma. All my preparations had fled. I neither marched up to the stage like a conquering Amazon, nor did I look in the audience for Bailey's nod of approval. Marguerite Johnson, I heard the name again, my honors were read, there were noises in the audience of appreciation, and I took my place on the stage as rehearsed.

I thought about colors I hated: ecru, puce, lavender, beige and black. [52]

There was shuffling and rustling around me, then Henry Reed was giv- [53] ing his valedictory address, "To Be or Not to Be." Hadn't he heard the whitefolks? We couldn't *be*, so the question was a waste of time. Henry's voice came out clear and strong. I feared to look at him. Hadn't he got the message? There was no "nobler in the mind" for Negroes because the world didn't think we had minds, and they let us know it. "Outrageous fortune"? Now, that was a joke. When the ceremony was over I had to tell Henry Reed some things. That is, if I still cared. Not "rub," Henry, "erase." "Ah, there's the erase." Us.

Henry had been a good student in elocution. His voice rose on tides of [54] promise and fell on waves of warnings. The English teacher had helped him to create a sermon winging through Hamlet's soliloquy. To be a man, a doer, a builder, a leader, or to be a tool, an unfunny joke, a crusher of funky toadstools. I marveled that Henry could go through with the speech as if we had a choice.

I had been listening and silently rebutting each sentence with my eyes [55] closed; then there was a hush, which in an audience warns that something unplanned is happening. I looked up and saw Henry Reed, the conservative, the proper, the A student, turn his back to the audience and turn to us (the proud graduating class of 1940) and sing, nearly speaking,

> "*Lift ev'ry voice and sing*
> *Till earth and heaven ring*
> *Ring with the harmonies of Liberty . . .*"

It was the poem written by James Weldon Johnson. It was the music composed by J. Rosamond Johnson. It was the Negro national anthem. Out of habit we were singing it.

Our mothers and fathers stood in the dark hall and joined the hymn of encouragement. A kindergarten teacher led the small children onto the stage and the buttercups and daisies and bunny rabbits marked time and tried to follow:

> *"Stony the road we trod*
> *Bitter the chastening rod*
> *Felt in the days when hope, unborn, had died.*
> *Yet with a steady beat*
> *Have not our weary feet*
> *Come to the place for which our fathers sighed?"*

Every child I knew had learned that song with his ABC's and along with "Jesus Loves Me This I Know." But I personally had never heard it before. Never heard the words, despite the thousands of times I had sung them. Never thought they had anything to do with me.

On the other hand, the words of Patrick Henry had made such an impression on me that I had been able to stretch myself tall and trembling and say, "I know not what course others may take, but as for me, give me liberty or give me death."

And now I heard, really for the first time:

> *"We have come over a way that with tears*
> *has been watered,*
> *We have come, treading our path through*
> *the blood of the slaughtered."*

While echoes of the song shivered in the air, Henry Reed bowed his head, said "Thank you," and returned to his place in the line. The tears that slipped down many faces were not wiped away in shame.

We were on top again. As always, again. We survived. The depths had been icy and dark, but now a bright sun spoke to our souls. I was no longer simply a member of the proud graduating class of 1940; I was a proud member of the wonderful, beautiful Negro race.

QUESTIONS

Words to Know

strutted (paragraph 1), exotic (1), rites (1), extended family (1), pervaded (3), forfeit (6), piqué (7), smocked (7), decipher (9), parasitic (10), heady (15), fatalism (20), piqued (31), Booker T. Washington (32), Galileo (40), Madame Curie (40), Edison (40), Gauguin (40), Jesse Owens (40), Joe Louis (40), Brown Bomber (41), George Washington Carver (41), *The Rape of Lucrece* (44), Gabriel Prosser (46), Nat Turner (46), Harriet Tubman (46), abomination (47), perfunctory (49), palpable (50), "Invictus" (50), ecru (52), puce (52), elocution (54), soliloquy (54), rebutting (55).

Some of the Issues

1. How does Angelou establish the importance of the graduation? How does she build it stage by stage?
2. Why does Angelou distinguish between the high school graduates. (paragraph 3, end) and the eighth-graders like herself? How do their attitudes differ? Why is she happier?
3. At what point in the narrative do we first get the idea that things may be going wrong with the "dream of a day"? What are later indications that something is wrong?
4. In paragraph 29, the children are confronted with a change in the usual order of things. Why does Angelou make this seem important? Why does the principal "rather desperately" signal for the children to sit down?
5. How do the first words Mr. Donleavy says indicate what his attitude is?

The Way We Are Told

6. Paragraph 1 talks about the graduates and their schoolmates. Paragraphs 2 and 3 describe the school. Why does Angelou write in that order? What distinguishes paragraph 1 from 2 and 3 in addition to the content?
7. Why does Angelou introduce Henry Reed so early (paragraphs 12 and 13?
8. Explain the irony Angelou sees in Henry Reed's "To be or not to be" speech.

Some Subjects for Essays

9. Have you ever experienced an event—a dance, a party, a trip—that you
    looked forward to and that turned out to be a disaster? Or have you ever
    dreaded an event, such as an interview or a blind date, that turned out
    better than you had expected? Tell it, trying to make the reader feel the
    anticipation and the change through the specific, descriptive details you
    cite, rather than by telling him directly. (You will find that the indirect
    way—making the reader feel or see the event—is more effective than
    simply saying, "I was bored" or "I found out it was a great evening after
    all.")
10. Describe a ceremony you have witnessed or participated in. Do it in two
    separate essays. In the first, describe the event simply in a neutral way.
    In the second, tell it from the point of view of a witness or participant.

WHEN I WAS A CHILD

Lillian Smith

Lillian Smith was born in 1897, in Jasper, Florida, "a small Deep South town whose population was about equally Negro and white." Her novel *Strange Fruit* (1944) was, in its day, a daring treatment of race relations, dealing with the love of a black woman and a white man. It sold three million copies and was translated into 15 languages. The autobiographical *Killers of the Dream* (1949), from which the following selection is taken, explores the psychology of prejudice. Lillian Smith died in 1966.

I was born and reared in a small Deep South town whose population was about equally Negro and white. There were nine of us who grew up freely in a rambling house of many rooms, surrounded by big lawn, back yard, gardens, fields, and barn. It was the kind of home that gathers memories like dust, a place filled with laughter and play and pain and hurt and ghosts and games. We were given such advantages of schooling, music, and art as were available in the South, and our world was not limited to the South, for travel to far places seemed a natural thing to us, and usually one of the family was in a remote part of the earth.

We knew we were a respected and important family of this small town but beyond this we gave little thought to status. Our father made money in lumber and naval stores for the excitement of making and losing it—not for what money can buy nor the security which it sometimes gives. I do not remember at any time wanting "to be rich" nor do I remember that thrift and saving were ideals which our parents considered important enough to urge upon us. In the family there was acceptance of risk, a mild delight in burning bridges, an expectant "what next?" We were not irresponsible; living according to the pleasure principle was by no means our way of life. On the contrary we were trained to think that each of us should do something of geniune usefulness, and the family thought it right to make sacrifices, if necessary, to give each child preparation for such work. We were also trained to think learning important, and books; but "bad" books our mother burned. We valued music and art and craftsmanship but it was people and their welfare and religion that were the foci around which our lives seemed naturally to move. Above all else, the important thing was what we "planned to do." That each of us must do something was as inevitable as breathing for we owed a "debt to society which must be paid." This was a family commandment.

15

While many neighbors spent their energies in counting limbs on the   3
family tree and grafting some on now and then to give symmetry to it, or in
licking scars to cure their vague malaise, or in fighting each battle and turn
of battle of that Civil War which has haunted the southern conscience so
long, my father was pushing his nine children straight into the future. "You
have your heritage," he used to say, "some of it good, some not so good; and
as far as I know you had the usual number of grandmothers and grandfath-
ers. Yes, there were slaves, too many of them in the family, but that was your
grandfather's mistake, not yours. The past has been lived. It is gone. The
future is yours. What are you going to do with it?" He asked this question
often and sometimes one knew it was but an echo of a question he had spent
his life trying to answer for himself. For the future held my father's dreams;
always there, not in the past, did he expect to find what he had spent his life
searching for.

We lived the same segregated life as did other southerners but our par-   4
ents talked in excessively Christian and democratic terms. We were told ten
thousand times that status and money are unimportant (though we were well
supplied with both); we were told that "all men are brothers," that we are a
part of a democracy and must act like democrats. We were told that the
teachings of Jesus are important and could be practiced if we tried. We were
told that to be "radical" is bad, silly too; and that one must always conform
to the "best behavior" of one's community and make it better if one can. We
were taught that we were superior to hate and resentment, and that no member of the Smith family could stoop so low as to have an enemy. No matter
what injury was done us, we must not injure ourselves further by retaliating.
That was a family commandment.

We had family prayers once each day. All of us as children read the   5
Bible in its entirety each year. We memorized hundreds of Bible verses and
repeated them at breakfast, and said "sentence prayers" around the family
table. God was not someone we met on Sunday but a permanent member of
our household. It never occurred to me until I was fourteen or fifteen years
old that He did not chalk up the daily score on eternity's tablets.

Despite the strain of living so intimately with God, the nine of us were   6
strong, healthy, energetic youngsters who filled days with play and sports and
music and books and managed to live most of the time on the careless level
at which young lives should be lived. We had our times of anxiety of course,
for there were hard lessons to be learned about the soul and "bad things" to
be learned about sex. Sometimes I have wondered how we learned them with
a mother so shy with words.

She was a wistful creature who loved beautiful things like lace and sun-   7
sets and flowers in a vague inarticulate way, and took good care of her chil-

dren. We always knew this was not her world but one she accepted under duress. Her private world we rarely entered, though the shadow of it lay heavily on our hearts.

Our father owned large business interests, employed hundreds of colored and white laborers, paid them the prevailing low wages, worked them the prevailing long hours, built for them mill towns (Negro and white), built for each group a church, saw to it that religion was supplied free, saw to it that a commissary supplied commodities at a high price, and in general managed his affairs much as ten thousand other southern businessmen managed theirs.   8

Even now, I can hear him chuckling as he told my mother how he won his fight for Prohibition. The high point of the campaign was election afternoon, when he lined up the mill force of several hundred (white and black), passed out a shining silver dollar to each one, marched them in and voted liquor out of our county. It was a great day. He had won the Big Game, a game he was always playing against all kinds of evil. It did not occur to him to scrutinize the methods he used. Evil was a word written in capitals; the devil was smart; if you wanted to win you outsmarted him. It was as simple as that.   9

He was a hardheaded, warmhearted, high-spirited man born during the Civil War, earning his living at twelve, struggling through decades of Reconstruction and post-Reconstruction, through populist movement, through the panic of 1893, the panic of 1907, on into the twentieth century accepting his region as he found it, accepting its morals and its mores as he accepted its climate, with only scorn for those who held grudges against the North or pitied themselves or the South; scheming, dreaming, expanding his business, making and losing money, making friends whom he did not lose, with never a doubt that God was by his side whispering hunches as to how to pull off successful deals. When he lost, it was his own fault. When he won, God had helped him.   10

Once while we were kneeling at family prayers the fire siren at the mill sounded the alarm that the mill was on fire. My father did not falter. The alarm sounded again and again—which signified the fire was big. With dignity he continued his talk with God while his children sweated and wriggled and hearts beat out of their chests in excitement. He was talking to God— how could he hurry out to save his mills! When he finished his prayer, he quietly stood up, laid the Bible carefully on the table. Then, and only then, did he show an interest in what was happening in Mill Town. . . . When the telegram was placed in his hands telling of the death of his beloved favorite son, he gathered his children together, knelt down, and in a steady voice which contained no hint of his shattered heart, loyally repeated, "God is our   11 refuge and strength, a very present help in trouble. Therefore will we not fear, though the earth be removed, and though the mountains be carried into the midst of the sea." On his deathbed, he whispered to his old Business Partner in Heaven: "I have fought a good fight . . . I have kept the faith."

Against this backdrop the drama of the South was played out one day in my life: 12

A little white girl was found in the colored section of our town, living with a Negro family in a broken-down shack. This family had moved in a few weeks before and little was known of them. One of the ladies in my mother's club, while driving over to her washerwoman's, saw the child swinging on a gate. The shack, as she said, was hardly more than a pigsty and this white child was living with dirty and sick-looking colored folks. "They must have kidnapped her," she told her friends. Genuinely shocked, the clubwomen busied themselves in an attempt to do something, for the child was very white indeed. The strange Negroes were subjected to a grueling questioning and finally grew evasive and refused to talk at all. This only increased the suspicion of the white group. The next day the clubwomen, escorted by the town marshal, took the child from her adopted family despite their tears.   13

She was brought to our home. I do not know why my mother consented to this plan. Perhaps because she loved children and always showed concern for them. It was easy for one more to fit into our ample household and Janie was soon at home there. She roomed with me, sat next to me at the table; I found Bible verses for her to say at breakfast; she wore my clothes, played with my dolls and followed me around from morning to night. She was dazed by her new comforts and by the interesting activities of this big lively family; and I was as happily dazed, for her adoration was a new thing to me; and as time passed a quick, childish, and deeply felt bond grew up between us.   14

But a day came when a telephone message was received from a colored orphanage. There was a meeting at our home. Many whispers. All afternoon the ladies went in and out of our house talking to Mother in tones too low for children to hear. As they passed us at play, they looked at Janie and quickly looked away again, though a few stopped and stared at her as if they could not tear their eyes from her face. When my father came home Mother closed her door against our young ears and talked a long time with him. I heard him laugh, heard Mother say, "But Papa, this is no laughing matter!" And then they were back in the living room with us and my mother was pale and my father was saying, "Well, work it out, Mame, as best you can. After all, now that you know, it is pretty simple."   15

In a little while my mother called my sister and me into her bedroom   16
and told us that in the morning Janie would return to Colored Town. She
said Janie was to have the dresses the ladies had given her and a few of my
own, and the toys we had shared with her. She asked me if I would like to
give Janie one of my dolls. She seemed hurried, though Janie was not to leave
until next day. She said, "Why not select it now?" And in dreamlike stiffness
I brought in my dolls and chose one for Janie. And then I found it possible
to say, "Why is she leaving? She likes us, she hardly knows them. She told
me she had been with them only a month."

"Because," Mother said gently, "Janie is a little colored girl."   17
"But she's white!"   18
"We were mistaken. She is colored."   19
"But she looks—"   20
"She is colored. Please don't argue!"   21
"What does it mean?" I whispered.   22
"It means," Mother said slowly, "that she has to live in Colored Town   23
with colored people."
"But why? She lived here three weeks and she doesn't belong to them,   24
she told me so."
"She is a little colored girl."   25
"But you said yourself she has nice manners. You said that," I persisted. 26
"Yes, she is a nice child. But a colored child cannot live in our home."   27
"Why?"   28
"You know, dear! You have always known that white and colored peo-   29
ple do not live together."
"Can she come to play?"   30
"No."   31
"I don't understand."   32
"I don't either," my young sister quavered.   33
"You're too young to understand. And don't ask me again, ever again,   34
about this!"

Mother's voice was sharp but her face was sad and there was no cer-   35
tainty left there. She hurried out and busied herself in the kitchen and I
wandered through that room where I had been born, touching the old familiar things in it, looking at them, trying to find the answer to a question that
moaned like a hurt thing. . . .

And then I went out to Janie, who was waiting, knowing things were   36
happening that concerned her but waiting until they were spoken aloud.

I do not know quite how the words were said but I told her she was to   37
return in the morning to the little place where she had lived because she was
colored and colored children could not live with white children.

"Are you white?" she said.   38

"I'm white," I replied, "and my sister is white. And you're colored. And   39
white and colored can't live together because my mother says so."

"Why?" Janie whispered.   40

"Because they can't," I said. But I knew, though I said it firmly, that   41
something was wrong. I knew my father and mother whom I passionately
admired had betrayed something which they held dear. And they could not
help doing it. And I was shamed by their failure and frightened, for I felt
they were no longer as powerful as I had thought. There was something Out
There that was stronger than they and I could not bear to believe it. I could
not confess that my father, who always solved the family dilemmas easily
and with laughter, could not solve this. I knew that my mother who was so
good to children did not believe in her heart that she was being good to this
child. There was not a word in my mind that said it but my body knew and
my glands, and I was filled with anxiety.

But I felt compelled to believe they were right. It was the only way my   42
world could be held together. And, slowly, it began to seep through me: *I
was white. She was colored. We must not be together. It was bad to be
together. Though you ate with your nurse when you were little, it was bad
to eat with any colored person after that. It was bad just as other things
were bad that your mother had told you. It was bad that she was to sleep
in the room with me that night. It was bad. . . .*

I was overcome with guilt. For three weeks I had done things that white   43
children were not supposed to do. And now I knew these things had been
wrong.

I went to the piano and began to play, as I had always done when I was   44
in trouble. I tried to play my next lesson and as I stumbled through it, the
little girl came over and sat on the bench with me. Feeling lost in the deep
currents sweeping through our house that night, she crept closer and put her
arms around me and I shrank away as if my body had been uncovered. I
had not said a word, I did not say one, but she knew, and tears slowly rolled
down her little white face. . . .

And then I forgot it. For more than thirty years the experience was   45
wiped out of my memory. But that night, and the weeks it was tied to,
worked its way like a splinter, bit by bit, down to the hurt places in my
memory and festered there. And as I grew older, as more experiences collected around that faithless time, as memories of earlier, more profound
hurts crept closer, drawn to that night as if to a magnet, I began to know
that people who talked of love and children did not mean it. That is a hard
thing for a child to learn. I still admired my parents, there was so much that
was strong and vital and sane and good about them and I never forgot this;

I stubbornly believed in their sincerity, as I do to this day, and I loved them. Yet in my heart they were under suspicion. Something was wrong.

QUESTIONS

Words to Know

rambling (paragraph 1), expectant (2), foci (2), grafting (3), symmetry (3), malaise (3), retaliating (4), wistful (7), duress (7), prevailing (8), scrutinize (9), Reconstruction (10), populist (10), grueling (13), evasive (13), dazed (14), dilemmas (41).

Some of the Issues

1. Paragraphs 2 and 3 describe the lives and attitudes of Smith's family, contrasting them to other families in their environment. What was her and her family's attitude toward their neighbors? Cite some words and phrases that make the comparison explicit.
2. Paragraphs 4, 5, and 6 describe the religious life of the family. What is the significance of their religious beliefs in relation to the rest of the story Smith tells?
3. How do the three anecdotes in paragraphs 9 and 11 add to our understanding of the values of Smith's father?
4. The values of Smith's parents are in some sense in conflict with their actions. Could Smith's parents be called hypocrites? What evidence can you cite that Smith would object to such a label?

The Way We Are Told

5. Smith spends more time setting the background than telling the story of Janie. What effect does that lengthy introduction have on the narrative?
6. Cite elements in paragraph 4 that will be important to the way Smith sees the story of Janie.
7. How does paragraph 15 prepare the reader for what is to follow? How does Smith create suspense?

8. Compare the final few paragraphs, which return the narrative to Smith and her family, to the opening section (before the discovery of Janie). How do these last paragraphs differ in tone and attitude from the earlier ones?

Some Subjects for Essays

9. One factor in the story changes everything: Janie is Black. Do you know, or have you experienced, a case when finding out something new about a person fundamentally changed your or someone else's attitude toward that person? After describing the circumstances, examine any justification for the change.
10. Are there parts of your family's or community's value system that you have come to question? If so, examine the changes and your reason for change. If not, explain how the values you grew up with have served you.
11. We generally believe that our actions should be in accord with our value systems; otherwise, we are guilty of hypocrisy. In an essay, try to argue the opposite: try to show, by means of logic annd examples, that it is not always possible to live up to this ideal.

GIRLHOOD AMONG GHOSTS

Maxine Hong Kingston

Maxine Hong Kingston's parents came to America from China in the 1930s. She was born in Stockton, California, graduated from the University of California at Berkeley and lives with her husband and child in Honolulu.

This selection is taken from her autobiography, *The Woman Warrior: Memories of a Girlhood Among Ghosts* (1976). The ghosts Kingston refers to are of several kinds: the spirits and demons which Chinese peasants believed in, the ghosts of the dead, and, more significantly, the whole of non-Chinese America, peopled with strange creatures who are not quite human but who are very powerful, and whose behavior is often inexplicable. These ghosts help Kingston explain the conflicts and difficulties of her bi-cultural childhood.

Kingston's most recent book is *China Men*.

Long ago in China, knot-makers tied string into buttons and frogs, and rope into bell pulls. There was one knot so complicated that it blinded the knot-maker. Finally an emperor outlawed this cruel knot, and the nobles could not order it anymore. If I had lived in China, I would have been an outlaw knot-maker. 1

Maybe that's why my mother cut my tongue. She pushed my tongue up and sliced the frenum. Or maybe she snipped it with a pair of nail scissors. I don't remember her doing it, only her telling me about it, but all during childhood I felt sorry for the baby whose mother waited with scissors or knife in hand for it to cry—and then, when its mouth was wide open like a baby bird's, cut. The Chinese say "a ready tongue is an evil." 2

I used to curl up my tongue in front of the mirror and tauten my frenum into a white line, itself as thin as a razor blade. I saw no scars in my mouth. I thought perhaps I had had two frena, and she had cut one. I made other children open their mouths so I could compare theirs to mine. I saw perfect pink membranes stretching into precise edges that looked easy enough to cut. Sometimes I felt very proud that my mother committed such a powerful act upon me. At other times I was terrified—the first thing my mother did when she saw me was to cut my tongue. 3

"Why did you do that to me, Mother?" 4

"I told you." 5

23

"Tell me again."   6

"I cut it so that you would not be tongue-tied. Your tongue would be   7
able to move in any language. You'll be able to speak languages that are
completely different from one another. You'll be able to pronounce anything.
Your frenum looked too tight to do those things, so I cut it."

"But isn't 'a ready tongue an evil'?"   8

"Things are different in this ghost country."   9

"Did it hurt me? Did I cry and bleed?"   10

"I don't remember. Probably."   11

She didn't cut the other children's. When I asked cousins and other   12
Chinese children whether their mothers had cut their tongues loose, they
said, "What?"

"Why didn't you cut my brothers' and sisters' tongues?"   13

"They didn't need it."   14

"Why not? Were theirs longer than mine?"   15

"Why don't you quit blabbering and get to work?"   16

If my mother was not lying she should have cut more, scraped away   17
the rest of the frenum skin, because I have a terrible time talking. Or she
should not have cut at all, tampering with my speech. When I went to kindergarten and had to speak English for the first time, I became silent. A
dumbness—a shame—still cracks my voice in two, even when I want to say
"hello" casually, or ask an easy question in front of the check-out counter,
or ask directions of a bus driver. I stand frozen, or I hold up the line with
the complete, grammatical sentence that comes squeaking out at impossible
length. "What did you say?" says the cab driver, or "Speak up," so I have to
perform again, only weaker the second time. A telephone call makes my
throat bleed and takes up that day's courage. It spoils my day with self-
disgust when I hear my broken broken voice come skittering out into the
open. It makes people wince to hear it. I'm getting better, though. Recently
I asked the postman for special-issue stamps; I've waited since childhood for
postmen to give me some of their own accord. I am making progress, a little
every day.

My silence was thickest—total—during the three years that I covered   18
my school paintings with black paint. I painted layers of black over houses
and flowers and suns, and when I drew on the blackboard, I put a layer of
chalk on top. I was making a stage curtain, and it was the moment before
the curtain parted or rose. The teachers called my parents to school, and I
saw they had been saving my pictures, curling and cracking, all alike and
black. The teachers pointed to the pictures and looked serious, talked seriously too, but my parents did not understand English. ("The parents and
teachers of criminals were executed," said my father.) My parents took the

pictures home. I spread them out (so black and full of possibilities) and pretended the curtains were swinging open, flying up, one after another, sunlight underneath, mighty operas.

During the first silent year I spoke to no one at school, did not ask before 19
going to the lavatory, and flunked kindergarten. My sister also said nothing for three years, silent in the playground and silent at lunch. There were other quiet Chinese girls not of our family, but most of them got over it sooner than we did. I enjoyed the silence. At first it did not occur to me I was supposed to talk or to pass kindergarten. I talked at home and to one or two of the Chinese kids in class. I made motions and even made some jokes. I drank out of a toy saucer when the water spilled out of the cup, and everybody laughed, pointing at me, so I did it some more. I didn't know that Americans don't drink out of saucers.

I liked the Negro students (Black Ghosts) best because they laughed the 20
loudest and talked to me as if I were a daring talker too. One of the Negro girls had her mother coil braids over her ears Shanghai-style like mine; we were Shanghai twins except that she was covered with black like my paintings. Two Negro kids enrolled in Chinese school, and the teachers gave them Chinese names. Some Negro kids walked me to school and home, protecting me from the Japanese kids, who hit me and chased me and stuck gum in my ears. The Japanese kids were noisy and tough. They appeared one day in kindergarten, released from concentration camp, which was a tic-tac-toe mark, like barbed wire, on the map.

It was when I found out I had to talk that school became a misery, that 21
the silence became a misery. I did not speak and felt bad each time that I did not speak. I read aloud in first grade, though, and heard the barest whisper with little squeaks come out of my throat. "Louder," said the teacher, who scared the voice away again. The other Chinese girls did not talk either, so I knew the silence had to do with being a Chinese girl.

Reading out loud was easier than speaking because we did not have to 22
make up what to say, but I stopped often, and the teacher would think I'd gone quiet again. I could not understand "I." The Chinese "I" has seven strokes, intricacies. How could the American "I," assuredly wearing a hat like the Chinese, have only three strokes, the middle so straight? Was it out of politeness that this writer left off strokes the way a Chinese has to write her own name small and crooked? No, it was not politeness; "I" is a capital and "you" is lower-case. I stared at that middle line and waited so long for its black center to resolve into tight strokes and dots that I forgot to pronounce it. The other troublesome word was "here," no strong consonant to hang on to, and so flat, when "here" is two mountainous ideographs. The teacher, who had already told me every day how to read "I" and "here,"

put me in the low corner under the stairs again, where the noisy boys usually sat.

When my second grade class did a play, the whole class went to the auditorium except the Chinese girls. The teacher, lovely and Hawaiian, should have understood about us, but instead left us behind in the classroom. Our voices were too soft or nonexistent, and our parents never signed the permission slips anyway. They never signed anything unnecessary. We opened the door a crack and peeked out, but closed it again quickly. One of us (not me) won every spelling bee, though. 23

I remember telling the Hawaiian teacher, "We Chinese can't sing 'land where our fathers died.'" She argued with me about politics, while I meant because of curses. But how can I have that memory when I couldn't talk? My mother says that we, like the ghosts, have no memories. 24

After American school, we picked up our cigar boxes, in which we had arranged books, brushes, and an inkbox neatly, and went to Chinese school, from 5:00 to 7:30 P.M. There we chanted together, voices rising and falling, loud and soft, some boys shouting, everybody reading together, reciting together and not alone with one voice. When we had a memorization test, the teacher let each of us come to his desk and say the lesson to him privately, while the rest of the class practiced copying or tracing. Most of the teachers were men. The boys who were so well behaved in the American school played tricks on them and talked back to them. The girls were not mute. They screamed and yelled during recess, when there were no rules; they had fistfights. Nobody was afraid of children hurting themselves or of children hurting school property. The glass doors to the red and green balconies with the gold joy symbols were left wide open so that we could run out and climb the fire escapes. We played capture-the-flag in the auditorium, where Sun Yat-sen and Chiang Kai-shek's pictures hung at the back of the stage, the Chinese flag on their left and the American flag on their right. We climbed the teak ceremonial chairs and made flying leaps off the stage. One flag headquarters was behind the glass door and the other on stage right. Our feet drummed on the hollow stage. During recess the teachers locked themselves up in their office with the shelves of books, copybooks, inks from China. They drank tea and warmed their hands at a stove. There was no play supervision. At recess we had the school to ourselves, and also we could roam as far as we could go—downtown, Chinatown stores, home—as long as we returned before the bell rang. 25

At exactly 7:30 the teacher again picked up the brass bell that sat on his desk and swung it over our heads, while we charged down the stairs, our cheering magnified in the stairwell. Nobody had to line up. 26

Not all of the children who were silent at American school found voice 27 at Chinese school. One new teacher said each of us had to get up and recite in front of the class, who was to listen. My sister and I had memorized the lesson perfectly. We said it to each other at home, one chanting, one listening. The teacher called on my sister to recite first. It was the first time a teacher had called on the second-born to go first. My sister was scared. She glanced at me and looked away; I looked down at my desk. I hoped that she could do it because if she could, then I would have to. She opened her mouth and a voice came out that wasn't a whisper, but it wasn't a proper voice either. I hoped that she would not cry, fear breaking up her voice like twigs underfoot. She sounded as if she were trying to sing though weeping and strangling. She did not pause or stop to end the embarrassment. She kept going until she said the last word, and then she sat down. When it was my turn, the same voice came out, a crippled animal running on broken legs. You could hear splinters in my voice, bones rubbing jagged against one another. I was loud, though. I was glad I didn't whisper. There was one little girl who whispered.

QUESTIONS

Words to Know

frenum (paragraph 2), tauten (3), tampering (17), skittering (17), wince (17), intricacies (22), ideographs (22), mute (25), Sun Yat-sen (25), Chiang Kai-shek (25).

Some of the Issues

1. After reading the selection explain why Kingston says in the first paragraph, "In China, I would have been an outlaw knot-maker." Why does she call herself an outlaw? And, considering the legend she tells, why would she have been a knot-maker?
2. "Maybe that's why my mother cut my tongue." That startling sentence introduces a remembered conversation with her mother. Is it possible that the tongue-cutting never took place? What evidence do you find either way?

3. Kingston is silent in some situations but not in others. When is she the one and when the other?
4. How did the American and the Chinese schools differ in the way they were run? In the way they affected the children?

The Way We Are Told

5. Kingston uses several symbols: the knot, the tongue, the Chinese letter *I*. Explain their meaning and use.
6. What is the effect of the first sentence of paragraph 2?
7. Kingston departs from strict chronological order in telling her story. What is the effect?

Some Subjects for Essays

8. Kingston suggests that in Chinese-American culture girls are brought up very differently from boys. In your own experience of the culture in which you were raised does gender make an important difference in upbringing? Give examples in your answer.
9. Kingston describes times when she was embarrassed or "tongue-tied." Describe a time when you were afraid to speak. Include descriptions of your feelings before, during, and after the incident.

HALFWAY TO DICK AND JANE: A PUERTO RICAN PILGRIMAGE

Jack Agueros

Jack Agueros was born in New York City of parents who had recently
migrated from Puerto Rico. He grew up in Spanish Harlem, attended
Brooklyn College, and has served in the New York City administration.
This selection was his first published work.

I was born in Harlem in 1934. We lived on 111th Street off Fifth Avenue. It 1
was a block of mainly three-story buildings—with brick fronts, or brownstone, or limestone imitations of brownstone. Our apartment was a three-
room first-floor walk-up. It faced north and had three windows on the street,
none in back. There was a master bedroom, a living room, a kitchen-dining
room, a foyer with a short hall, and a bathroom. In the kitchen there was an
air shaft to evacuate cooking odors and grease—we converted it to a chim-
ney for Santa Claus.

The kitchen was dominated by a large Victorian china closet, and the 2
built-in wall shelves were lined with oilcloth, trimmed with ruffle, both decorated by brilliant and miniature fruits. Prominent on a wall of the kitchen
was a large reproduction of a still life, a harvest table full of produce, framed
and under glass. From it, I learned to identify apples, pumpkins, bananas,
pears, grapes, and melons, and "peaches without worms." A joke between
my mother and me. (A peach we had bought in the city market, under the
New Haven's elevated tracks, bore, like the trains above, passengers.)

On one shelf of the kitchen, over the stove, there was a lineup of 3
ceramic canisters that carried words like "nutmeg," "ginger," and "basil." I
did not know what those words meant and I don't know if my mother did
either. "Spices," she would say, and that was that. They were of a yellow
color that was not unlike the yellow of the stove. The kitchen was itself
painted yellow, I think, very pale. But I am sure of one thing, it was not
"Mickey Moused." "Mickey Mousing" was a technique used by house paint-
ers to decorate the areas of the walls that were contained by wood molding.
Outside the molding they might paint a solid green. Inside the wood mold,
the same solid green. Then with a twisted-up rag dipped in a lighter green
they would trace random patterns.

29

We never used wallpaper or rugs. Our floors were covered with lino- 4
leum in every room. My father painted the apartment every year before
Christmas, and in addition, he did all the maintenance, doing his own plas-
tering and plumbing. No sooner would we move into an apartment than my
father would repair holes or cracks, and if there were bulges in the plaster,
he would break them open and redo the area—sometimes a whole wall. He
would immediately modify the bathrooms to add a shower with separate
valves, and usually as a routine matter, he cleaned out all the elbow traps,
and changed all the washers on faucets. This was true of the other families
in the buildings where I lived. Not a December came without a painting of
the apartment.

We had Louis XIV furniture in the living room, reflected in the curved 5
glass door and curved glass sides of the china closet. On the walls of the living
room hung two prints that I loved. I would spend hours playing games with
my mother based on the pictures, making up stories, etc. One day at Brooklyn College, a slide projector slammed, and I awoke after having dozed off
during a dull lecture to see Van Gogh's "The Gleaners" on the screen. I
almost cried. Another time I came across the other print in a book. A scene
of Venice by Canaletto.

The important pieces of the living room, for me, were a Detrola radio 6
with magic-eye tuning and the nightingale, Keero. The nightingale and the
radio went back before my recollection. The bird could not stop singing, and
people listened on the sidewalk below and came upstairs offering to buy
Keero.

The Detrola, shaped like a Gothic arch with inlaid woodwork, was a 7
great source of entertainment for the family. I memorized all the hit songs
sung by Libertad Lamarque and Carlos Gardel. Sundays I listened to the
Canary Hour presented by Hartz Mountain Seed Company. Puppy, a white
Spitz, was my constant companion. Puppy slept at the foot of my bed from
the first day he came to our house till the day he died, when I was eleven or
twelve and he was seven or eight.

I am an only child. My parents and I always talked about my becoming 8
a doctor. The law and politics were not highly regarded in my house. Lawyers, my mother would explain, had to defend people whether they were
guilty or not, while politicians, my father would say, were all crooks. A doctor helped everybody, rich and poor, white and black. If I became a doctor,
I could study hay fever and find a cure for it, my godmother would say.
Also, I could take care of my parents when they were old. I liked the idea
of helping, and for nineteen years my sole ambition was to study medicine.

My house had books, not many, but my parents encouraged me to read. 9
As I became a good reader they bought books for me and never refused me
money for their purchase. My father once built a bookcase for me. It was an

important moment, for I had always believed that my father was not too happy about my being a bookworm. The atmosphere at home was always warm. We seemed to be a popular family. We entertained frequently, with two standing parties a year—at Christmas and for my birthday. Parties were always large. My father would dismantle the beds and move all the furniture so that the full two rooms could be used for dancing. My mother would cook up a storm, particularly at Christmas. *Pasteles, lechon asado, arroz con gan-dules,* and a lot of *coquito* to drink (meat-stuffed plantain, roast pork, rice with pigeon peas, and coconut nog). My father always brought in a band. They played without compensation and were guests at the party. They ate and drank and danced while a victrola covered the intermissions. One year my father brought home a whole pig and hung it in the foyer doorway. He and my mother prepared it by rubbing it down with oil, oregano, and garlic. After preparation, the pig was taken down and carried over to a local bakery where it was cooked and returned home. Parties always went on till day-break, and in addition to the band, there were always volunteers to sing and declaim poetry.

My mother kept an immaculate household. Bedspreads (chenille [10] seemed to be very in) and lace curtains, washed at home like everything else, were hung up on huge racks with rows of tight nails. The racks were assembled in the living room, and the moisture from the wet bedspreads would fill the apartment. In a sense, that seems to be the lasting image of that period of my life. The house was clean. The neighbors were clean. The streets, with few cars, were clean. The buildings were clean and uncluttered with people on the stoops. The park was clean. The visitors to my house were clean, and the relationships that my family had with other Puerto Rican families, and the Italian families that my father had met through baseball and my mother through the garment center, were clean. Second Avenue was clean and most of the apartment windows had awnings. There was always music, there seemed to be no rain, and snow did not become slush. School was fun, we wrote essays about how grand America was, we put up hunchbacked cats at Halloween, we believed Santa Claus visited everyone. I believed everyone was Catholic. I grew up with dogs, nightingales, my godmother's guitar, rocking chair, cat, guppies, my father's occasional roosters, kept in a cage on the fire escape. Laundry delivered and collected by horse and wagon, fruits and vegetables sold the same way, windowsill refrigeration in winter, iceman and box in summer. The police my friends, likewise the teachers.

In short, the first seven or so years of my life were not too great a vari- [11] ation on Dick and Jane, the school book figures who, if my memory serves me correctly, were blond Anglo-Saxons, not immigrants, not migrants like the Puerto Ricans, and not the children of either immigrants or migrants.

My family moved in 1941 to Lexington Avenue into a larger apartment [12] where I could have my own room. It was a light, sunny, railroad flat on the top floor of a well-kept building. I transferred to a new school, and whereas before my classmates had been mostly black, the new school had few blacks. The classes were made up of Italians, Irish, Jews, and a sprinkling of Puerto Ricans. My block was populated by Jews, Italians, and Puerto Ricans.

And then a whole series of different events began. I went to junior high   13
school. We played in the backyards, where we tore down fences to build fires to cook stolen potatoes. We tore up whole hedges, because the green tender limbs would not burn when they were peeled, and thus made perfect skewers for our stolen "mickies." We played tag in the abandoned buildings, tearing the plaster off the walls, tearing the wire lath off the wooden slats, tearing the wooden slats themselves, good for fires, for kites, for sword fighting. We ran up and down the fire escapes playing tag and over and across many rooftops. The war ended and the heavy Puerto Rican migration began. The Irish and the Jews disappeared from the neighborhood. The Italians tried to consolidate east of Third Avenue.

What caused the clean and open world to end? Many things. Into an   14
ancient neighborhood came pouring four to five times more people than it had been designed to hold. Men who came running at the promise of jobs were jobless as the war ended. They were confused. They could not see the economic forces that ruled their lives as they drank beer on the corners, reassuring themselves of good times to come while they were hell-bent toward alcoholism. The sudden surge in numbers caused new resentments, and prejudice was intensified. Some were forced to live in cellars, and were then characterized as cave dwellers. Kids came who were confused by the new surroundings; their Puerto Ricanness forced us against a mirror asking, "If they are Puerto Ricans, what are we?" and thus they confused us. In our confusion we were sometimes pathetically reaching out, sometimes pathologically striking out. Gangs. Drugs. Wine. Smoking. Girls. Dances and slow-drag music. Mambo. Spics, Spooks, and Wops. Territories, brother gangs, and war councils establishing rules for right of way on blocks and avenues and for seating in the local theater. Pegged pants and zip guns. Slang.

Dick and Jane were dead, man. Education collapsed. Every classroom   15
had ten kids who spoke no English. Black, Italian, Puerto Rican relations in the classroom were good, but we all knew we couldn't visit one another's neighborhoods. Sometimes we could not move too freely within our own blocks. On 109th, from the lamp post west, the Latin Aces, and from the lamp post east, the Senecas, the "club" I belonged to. The kids who spoke no English became known as Marine Tigers, picked up from a popular Spanish song. (The *Marine Tiger* and the *Marine Shark* were two ships that sailed from San Juan to New York and brought over many, many migrants from the island.)

The neighborhood had its boundaries. Third Avenue and east, Italian.   16
Fifth Avenue and west, black. South, there was a hill on 103rd Street known
locally as Cooney's Hill. When you got to the top of the hill, something
strange happened: America began, because from the hill south was where
the "Americans" lived. Dick and Jane were not dead; they were alive and
well in a better neighborhood.

When, as a group of Puerto Rican kids, we decided to go swimming to   17
Jefferson Park Pool, we knew we risked a fight and a beating from the Italians. And when we went to La Milagrosa Church in Harlem, we knew we
risked a fight and a beating from the blacks. But when we went over Cooney's Hill, we risked dirty looks, disapproving looks, and questions from the
police like, "What are you doing in this neighborhood?" and "Why don't
you kids go back where you belong?"

Where we belonged! Man, I had written compositions about America.   18
Didn't I belong on the Central Park tennis courts, even if I didn't know how
to play? Couldn't I watch Dick play? Weren't these policemen working for
me too?

Junior high school was a waste. I can say with 90 per cent accuracy that   19
I learned nothing. The woodshop was used to manufacture stocks for "home-
mades" after Macy's stopped selling zipguns. We went from classroom to
classroom answering "here," and trying to be "good." The math class was
generally permitted to go to the gym after roll call. English was still a good
class. Partly because of a damn good, tough teacher named Miss Beck, and
partly because of the grade-number system (7-1 the smartest seventh grade
and 7-12, the dumbest). Books were left in school, there was little or no
homework, and the whole thing seemed to be a holding operation until high
school. Somehow or other, I passed the entrance exam to Brooklyn Technical
High School. But I couldn't cut the mustard, either academically or with the
"American" kids. After one semester, I came back to PS 83, waited a semester, and went on to Benjamin Franklin High School.

I still wanted to study medicine and excelled in biology. English was   20
always an interesting subject, and I still enjoyed writing compositions and
reading. In the neighborhood it was becoming a problem being categorized
as a bookworm and as one who used "Sunday words," or "big words." I dug
school, but I wanted to be one of the boys more. I think the boys respected
my intelligence, despite their ribbing. Besides which, I belonged to a club
with a number of members who were interested in going to college, and so
I wasn't so far out.

My introduction to marijuana was in junior high school in 1948. A kid   21
named Dixie from 124th Street brought a pack of joints to school and taught
about twelve guys to smoke. He told us we could buy joints at a quarter each
or five for a dollar. Bombers, or thicker cigarettes, were thiry-five cents each

or three for a dollar. There were a lot of experimenters, but not too many buyers. Actually, among the boys there was a strong taboo on drugs, and the Spanish word *"motto"* was a term of disparagement. Many clubs would kick out members who were known to use drugs. Heroin was easily available, and in those days came packaged in capsules or "caps" which sold for fifty cents each. Method of use was inhalation through the nose, or "sniffing," or "snorting."

I still remember vividly the first kid I ever saw who was mainlining.   22
Prior to this encounter, I had known of "skin-popping," or subcutaneous injection, but not of mainlining. Most of the sniffers were afraid of skin-popping because they knew of the danger of addiction. They seemed to think that you could not become addicted by sniffing.

I went over to 108th Street and Madison where we played softball on   23
an empty lot. This kid came over who was maybe sixteen or seventeen and asked us if we wanted to buy Horse. He started telling us about shooting up and showed me his arms. He had tracks, big black marks on the inside of his arm from the inner joint of the elbow down to his wrist and then over onto the back of his hand. I was stunned. Then he said, "That's nothing, man. I ain't hooked, and I ain't no junky. I can stop anytime I want to." I believe that he believed what he was saying. Invariably the kids talking about their drug experiences would say over and over, "I ain't hooked. I can stop anytime."

But they didn't stop; and the drug traffic grew greater and more open.   24
Kids were smoking on the corners and on the stoops. Deals were made on the street, and you knew fifteen places within a block radius where you could buy anything you wanted. Cocaine never seemed to catch on although it was readily available. In the beginning, the kids seemed to be able to get the money for stuff easily. As the number of shooters grew and the prices went up, the kids got more desperate and apartment robbing became a real problem.

More of the boys began to leave school. We didn't use the term drop   25
out; rather, a guy would say one day, after forty-three truancies, "I'm quitting school." And so he would. It was an irony, for what was really happening was that after many years of being rejected, ignored, and shuffled around by the school, the kid wanted to quit. Only you can't quit something you were never a part of, nor can you drop out if you were never in.

Some kids lied about their age and joined the army. Most just hung   26
around. Not drifting to drugs or crime or to work either. They used to talk about going back at night and getting the diploma. I believe that they did not believe they could get their diplomas. They knew that the schools had abandoned them a long time ago—that to get the diploma meant starting all

over again and that was impossible. Besides, day or night, it was the same school, the same staff, the same shit. But what do you say when you are powerless to get what you want, and what do you say when the other side has all the cards and writes all the rules? You say, "Tennis is for fags," and "School is for fags."

My mother leads me by the hand and carries a plain brown shopping   27
bag. We enter an immense airplane hangar. Structural steel crisscrosses on the ceiling and walls; large round and square rivets look like buttons or bubbles of air trapped in the girders. There are long metallic counters with people bustling behind them. It smells of C.N. disinfectant. Many people stand on many lines up to these counters; there are many conversations going on simultaneously. The huge space plays tricks with voices and a very eerie combination of sounds results. A white cabbage is rolled down a counter at us. We retaliate by throwing down stamps.

For years I thought that sequence happened in a dream. The rolling   28
cabbage rolled in my head, and little unrelated incidents seemed to bring it to the surface of my mind. I could not understand why I remembered a once-dreamt dream so vividly. I was sixteen when I picked up and read Freud's *The Interpretation of Dreams*. One part I understood immediately and well, sex and symbolism. In no time, I had hung my shingle; Streetcorner Analyst. My friends would tell me their dreams and with the most outrageous sexual explanations we laughed whole evenings away. But the rolling cabbage could not be stopped and neither quack analysis nor serious thought could explain it away. One day I asked my mother if she knew anything about it.

"That was home relief, 1937 or 1938. You were no more than four years   29
old then. Your father had been working at a restaurant and I had a job downtown. I used to take you every morning to Dona Eduvije who cared for you all day. She loved you very much, and she was very clean and neat, but I used to cry on my way to work, wishing I could stay home with my son and bring him up like a proper mother would. But I guess I was fated to be a workhorse. When I was pregnant, I would get on the crowded subway and go to work. I would get on a crowded elevator up. Then down. Then back on the subway. Every day I was afraid that the crowd would hurt me, that I would lose my baby. But I had to work. I worked for the WPA right into my ninth month."

My mother was telling it "like it was," and I sat stupefied, for I could   30
not believe that what she said applied to the time I thought of as open and clean. I had been existing in my life like a small plant in a bell jar, my parents defining my awareness. There were things all around me I could not see.

"When you were born we had been living as boarders. It was hard to   31
find an apartment, even in Harlem. You saw signs that said 'No Renting to
Colored or Spanish.' That meant Puerto Ricans. We used to say, 'This is supposed to be such a great country?' But with a new baby we were determined
not to be boarders and we took an apartment on 111th Street. Soon after we
moved, I lost my job because my factory closed down. Your father was making seven or eight dollars a week in a terrible job in a carpet factory. They
used to clean rugs, and your father's hands were always in strong chemicals.
You know how funny some of his fingernails are? It was from that factory.
He came home one night and he was looking at his fingers, and he started
saying that he didn't come to this country to lose his hands. He wanted to
hold a bat and play ball and he wanted to work—but he didn't want to lose
his hands. So he quit the job and went to a restaurant for less pay. With me
out of work, a new apartment and therefore higher rent, we couldn't manage. Your father was furious when I mentioned home relief. He said he
would rather starve than go on relief. But I went and filled out the papers
and answered all the questions and swallowed my pride when they treated
me like an intruder. I used to say to them, 'Find me a job—get my husband
a better job—we don't want home relief.' But we had to take it. And all that
mess with the stamps in exchange for food. And they used to have weekly
'specials' sort of—but a lot of things were useless—because they were American food. I don't remember if we went once a week or once every two
weeks. You were so small I don't know how you remember that place and
the long lines. It didn't last long because your father had everybody trying
to find him a better job and finally somebody did. Pretty soon I went into
the WPA and thank God, we never had to deal with those people again. I
don't know how you remember that place, but I wish you didn't. I wish I
could forget that home relief thing myself. It was the worst time for your
father and me. He still hates it.

(He still hates it and so do many people. The expression, "I'd rather   32
starve than go on welfare" is common in the Puerto Rican community. This
characteristic pride is well chronicled throughout Spanish literature. For
example, one episode of *Lazarillo del Tormes*, the sixteenth-century pica-
resque novel, tells of a squire who struts around all day with his shiny sword
and pressed cape. At night the squire takes food from the boy, Lazarillo—
who has begged or stolen it—explaining that it is not proper for a squire to
beg or steal, or even to work! Without Lazarillo to feed him, the squire would
probably starve.)

"You don't know how hard it was being married to your father then.   33
He was young and very strong and very active and he wanted to work. Welfare deeply disturbed him, and I was afraid that he would actually get very

violent if an investigator came to the house. They had a terrible way with people, like throwing that cabbage, that was the way they gave you everything, the way we used to throw the kitchen slop to the pigs in Puerto Rico. Some giving! Your father was, is, *muy macho,* and I used to worry if anybody says anything or gives him that why-do-you-people-come-here-to-ruin-things look he'll be in jail for thirty years. He almost got arrested once when you were just a baby. We went to a hospital clinic—I don't remember now if it was Sydenham or Harlem Hospital—you had a swelling around your throat—and the doctor told me, 'Put on cold compresses.' I said I did that and it didn't help. The doctor said, 'Then put hot compresses.' Your father blew up. In his broken English, he asked the doctor to do that to his mother, and then invited him to transfer over to the stable on 104th Street. 'You do better with horses—maybe they don't care what kind of compresses they get.'

    "One morning your father tells me, 'I got a new job. I start today driving a truck delivering soft drinks.' That night I ask him about the job—he says, 'I quit—bunch of Mafia—I went to the first four places on my list and each storeowner said, "I didn't order any soda." So I got the idea real fast. The Mafia was going to leave soda in each place and then make the guys buy from them only. As soon as I figured it out, I took the truck back, left it parked where I got it, and didn't even say good-bye.' The restaurant took him back. They liked him. The chef used to give him eggs and meats; it was very important to us. Your father never could keep still (still can't), so he was loved wherever he worked. I feel sorry for people on welfare—forget about the cabbage—I never should have taken you there."

    My father and I are walking through East Harlem, south down Lexington from 112th toward 110th, in 1952. Saturday in late spring, I am eighteen years old, sun brilliant on the streets, people running back and forth on household errands. My father is telling me a story about how back in nineteen thirty something, we were very poor and Con Ed light meters were in every apartment. "The Puerto Ricans, maybe everybody else, would hook up a shunt wire around the meter, specially in the evenings when the use was heavy—that way you didn't pay for all the electric you used. We called it *'pillo'* (thief)."

    We arrive at 110th Street and all the cart vendors are there peddling plantains, avocados, yams, various subtropical roots. I make a casual remark about how foolish it all seemed, and my father catches that I am looking down on them. "Are they stealing?" he asks. "Are they selling people colored water? Aren't they working honestly? Are they any different from a bank president? Aren't they hung like you and me? They are *machos*, and to be respected. Don't let college go to your head. You think a Ph.D is automatically better than a peddler? Remember where you come from—poor people. I mopped floors for people and I wasn't ashamed, but I never let them look down on me. Don't you look down on anybody."

We walk for a way in silence, I am mortified, but he is not angry. "One day I decide to play a joke on your mother. I come home a little early and knock. When she says 'Who?' I say 'Edison man.' Well, there is this long silence and then a scream. I open the door and run in. Your mother's on a chair, in tears, her right arm black from pinky to elbow. She ran to take the *pillo* out, but in her nervousness she got a very slight shock, the black from the spark. She never has forgiven me. After that, I always thought through my jokes."

We walk some more and he says, "I'll tell you another story. This one on me. I was twenty-five years old and was married to your mother. I took her down to Puerto Rico to meet Papa and Mama. We were sitting in the living room, and I remember it like it happened this morning. The room had rattan furniture very popular in that time. Papa had climbed in rank back to captain and had a new house. The living room had double doors which opened onto a large *balcon*. At the other end of the room you could see the dining table with a beautiful white handmade needlework cloth. We were sitting and talking and I took out a cigarette. I was smoking Chesterfields then. No sooner had I lit up than Papa got up, came over, and smacked me in the face. 'You haven't received my permission to smoke,' he said. Can you imagine how I felt?" So my father dealt with his love for me through lateral actions: building bookcases, and through tales of how he got his wounds, he anointed mine.

What is a migration? What does it happen to? Why are the Eskimos still dark after living in that snow all these centuries? Why don't they have a word for snow? What things are around me with such high saturation that I have not named them? What is a migration? If you rob my purse, are you really a fool? Can a poor boy really be president? In America? Of anything? If he is not white? Should one man's achievement fulfill one million people? Will you let us come near your new machine: after all, there is no more ditch digging? What is a migration? What does it happen to?

The most closely watched migrants of this world are birds. Birds migrate because they get bored singing in the same place to the same people. And they see that the environment gets hostile. Men move for the same reasons. When a Puerto Rican comes to America, he comes looking for a job. He takes the cold as one of a negative series of givens. The mad hustle, the filthy city, filthy air, filthy housing, sardine transportation, are in the series.

He knows life will be tough and dangerous. But he thinks he can make a buck. And in his mind, there is only one tableau: himself retired, owner of his home in Puerto Rico, chickens cackling in the back yard.

It startles me still, though it has been five years since my parents went back to the island. I never believed them. My father, driving around New York for the Housing Authority, knowing more streets in more boroughs than I do, and my mother, curious in her later years about museums and theaters, and reading my books as fast as I would put them down, then giving me cryptic reviews. Salinger is really silly *(Catcher in the Rye)*, but entertaining. That evil man deserved to die *(Moby Dick)*. He's too much (Dostoevski in *Crime and Punishment)*. I read this when I was a little girl in school (*Hamlet* and *Macbeth)*. It's too sad for me *(Cry, the Beloved Country)*.

My father, intrigued by the thought of passing the foreman's exam, sitting down with a couple of arithmetic books, and teaching himself at age fifty-five to do work problems and mixture problems and fractions and decimals, and going into the civil service exam and scoring a seventy-four and waiting up one night for me to show me three poems he had written. These two cosmopolites, gladiators without skills or language, battling hostile environments and prejudiced people and systems, had graduated from Harlem to the Bronx, had risen into America's dream-cherished lower middle class, and then put it down for Puerto Rico after thirty plus years.

What is a migration, when is it not just a long visit?

I was born in Harlem, and I live downtown. And I am a migrant, for if a migration is anything, it is a state of mind. I have known those Eskimos who lived in America twenty and thirty years and never voted, never attended a community meeting, never filed a complaint against a landlord, never informed the police when they were robbed or swindled, or when their daughters were molested. Never appeared at the State or City Commission on Human Rights, never reported a business fraud, never, in other words, saw the snow.

And I am very much a migrant because I am still not quite at home in America. Always there are hills; on the other side—people inclined to throwing cabbages. I cannot "earn and return"—there is no position for me in my father's tableau.

However, I approach the future with optimism. Fewer Puerto Ricans like Eskimos, a larger number of leaders like myself, trained in the university, tempered in the ghetto, and with a vision of America moving from its unexecuted policy to a society open and clean, accessible to anyone.

Dick and Jane? They, too, were tripped by the society, and in our several ways, we are all still migrating.

QUESTIONS

Words to Know

Harlem (paragraph 1), evacuate (1), Victorian (2), Louis XIV furniture (5), Van Gogh (5), Canaletto (5), compensation (9), foyer (9), immaculate (10), Anglo-Saxon (11), railroad flat (12), pathologically (14), disparagement (21), subcutaneous (22), immense (27), stupefied (30), mortified (37), lateral (38), anointed (38), migration (39), saturation (39), tableau (40), cryptic (41), cosmopolities (42), gladiators (42).

Some of the Issues

1. The first seven paragraphs describe Agueros' first house: its layout, its furnishings, and decorations. What impression does Agueros' description give you? Cite details that contribute to this impression.
2. In paragraph 4 Agueros lists the activities of his father in the home. In paragraph 10 he does the same for his mother's work. How do their roles differ? Are these differences similar to those in homes you know?
3. What is the key word in paragraph 10? How does it contribute to the impression the author gives of his childhood?
4. In paragraph 11 Agueros sums up his feelings about his childhood. How do the preceding paragraphs, and paragraph 10 in particular, justify that conclusion?
5. Compare the early experiences of Agueros, as he remembers them, with his experiences in junior high. "What caused the clean and open world to end?"
6. Explain what Agueros means when he says "Their Puerto Ricanness forced us against a mirror, asking, "If they are Puerto Rican, what are we?"
7. Paragraphs 13 through 26 describe the author's progression through junior high and high school. What changes does he record? What are the way stations?
8. During the Depression of the 1930s Agueros' family went on relief. Much later he finds out about that time from his mother when he learns that the story of the cabbage (27) was not a dream. Compare that adult experience with his recollection of childhood in paragraph 10. Which is the real dream world?
9. In paragraphs 35 through 38 Agueros describes a talk with his father. What do we learn from their conversation?

10. In the last part of the essay Agueros repeatedly asks, "What is a migration?" What does he mean by that question? In what ways has he remained a migrant? What is he trying to tell the reader about migration?
11. Which family is more distant, in your opinion, from "mainstream" America: Agueros' or Kingston's? Explain.

The Way We Are Told

12. Find the various references to Dick and Jane in the text. How does the author use them to express his theme? What does the essay's title mean?
13. How does paragraph 13 serve as a transition?
14. Note the last few lines of paragraph 14 and the opening sentence of paragraph 15. What is their effect? How has the language changed since paragraph 10?
15. Why does Agueros change to the present tense for paragraph 27? (He reverts to the past tense in paragraph 28.)
16. Agueros tells of the talk with his father (paragraphs 35 through 38) in the present tense as well. Are his reasons for doing so the same as in the cabbage story? Look at paragraphs 39 through 46 before you answer.

Some Subjects for Essays

17. Compare two schools you have attended and explain the differences between them. To what do you attribute these differences: your classmates, your teachers, the administration, different locations, or changes in you? Try to focus on one or two possible reasons in organizing your essay.
18. Agueros describes several objects that were important to him as a child. Describe an object that was important to you and explain its meaning. How would it affect you now?
19. "I am a migrant, for if migration is anything, it is a state of mind." (44) Describe yourself as a migrant; consider in what ways you have "moved," not necessarily physically, but mentally or emotionally.

WAR GAMES

Black Elk, as Told to John G. Neihardt

Black Elk (1863–1950) was a holy man of the Ogalala Sioux tribe. His recollections were recorded by John G. Neihardt (1881–1973), who spent several years among the Sioux early in the twentieth century. Neihardt later worked as literary editor of the *Minneapolis Tribune* and the *St. Louis Post Dispatch*. Poet, playwright, lecturer, and advocate of the Indians, Neihardt wrote several books, including *The Song of the Indian Wars* (1925) and *When the Tree Flowered: an Authentic Tale of the Old Sioux* (1951). *Black Elk Speaks*, from which this selection was taken, was published in 1932. *Wasichus* is the Ogalala word for whites.

When it was summer again we were camping on the Rosebud, and I did not [1] feel so much afraid, because the Wasichus seemed farther away and there was peace there in the valley and there was plenty of meat. But all the boys from five or six years up were playing war. The little boys would gather together from the different bands of the tribe and fight each other with mud balls that they threw with willow sticks. And the big boys played the game called Throwing-Them-Off-Their-Horses, which is a battle all but the killing; and sometimes they got hurt. The horsebacks from the different bands would line up and charge upon each other, yelling; and when the ponies came together on the run, they would rear and flounder and scream in a big dust, and the riders would seize each other, wrestling until one side had lost all its men, for those who fell upon the ground were counted dead.

When I was older, I, too, often played this game. We were always naked [2] when we played it, just as warriors are when they go into battle if it is not too cold, because they are swifter without clothes. Once I fell off on my back right in the middle of a bed of prickly pears, and it took my mother a long while to pick all the stickers out of me. I was still too little to play war that summer, but I can remember watching the other boys, and I thought that when we all grew up and were big together, maybe we could kill all the Wasichus or drive them far away from our country.

There was also a war game that we little boys played after a big hunt. [3] We went out a little way from the village and built some grass tepees, playing we were enemies and this was our village. We had an adviser, and when it got dark he would order us to go and steal some dried meat from the big people. He would hold a stick up to us and we had to bite off a piece of it.

If we bit a big piece we had to get a big piece of meat, and if we bit a little piece, we did not have to get so much. Then we started for the big people's village, crawling on our bellies, and when we got back without getting caught, we would have a big feast and a dance and make kill talks, telling of our brave deeds like warriors. Once, I remember, I had no brave deed to tell. I crawled up to a leaning tree beside a tepee and there was meat hanging on the limbs. I wanted a tongue I saw up there in the moonlight, so I climbed up. But just as I was about to reach it, the man in the tepee yelled "Ye-a-a!" He was saying this to his dog, who was stealing some meat too, but I thought the man had seen me, and I was so scared I fell out of the tree and ran away crying.

Then we used to have what we called a chapped breast dance. Our adviser would look us over to see whose breast was burned most from not having it covered with the robe we wore; and the boy chosen would lead the dance while we all sang like this:

> "*I have a chapped breast.*
> *My breast is red.*
> *My breast is yellow.*"

And we practiced endurance too. Our adviser would put dry sunflower seeds on our wrists. These were lit at the top, and we had to let them burn clear down to the skin. They hurt and made sores, but if we knocked them off or cried Owh!, we would be called women.

QUESTIONS

Some of the Issues

1. From this brief passage what can you surmise about the values of Black Elk's culture?
2. Do the games Black Elk describes emphasize competition or cooperation? In this respect, how do they compare with the games you learned as a child?
3. Black Elk's society seems to have very definite ideas about behavior appropriate to certain ages and sexes. In your opinion, is this also true of American society?

4. Some of the games that Black Elk describes might seem cruel. Are there any grounds on which that cruelty can by justified?

The Way We Are Told

5. When does Black Elk give a straight description of the games, and when does he inject some personal attitudes and feelings? Cite specific words or phrases.

Some Subjects for Essays

6. Examine a game you know well. Describe it as to one particular aspect: cruelty. Is it cruel? Can the cruelty be justified? (Remember that cruelty need not be physical only.)
7. Argue the cruelty of a game foreign to the United States, such as cock-fighting or bullfighting. Then argue the cruelty of an American sport, such as boxing or football, which people in some other cultures may consider cruel.
8. The games Black Elk describes seem to have a function as a preparation for adulthood. Describe a game or sport in your culture that serves such a purpose. What are the values it teaches?

INCIDENT

Countee Cullen

Countee Cullen (1903–1946) gained recognition for his poetry while still in high school and published his first volume of poetry at the age of 22. He attended New York University and Harvard and continued to publish poetry and fiction. "Incident" is included in *On These I Stand* (1947).

Once riding in old Baltimore
    Heart-filled, head-filled with glee,
I saw a Baltimorean
    Keep looking straight at me.

Now I was eight and very small,
    And he was no whit bigger,
And so I smiled, but he poked out
    His tongue, and called me, "Nigger."

I saw the whole of Baltimore
    From May until December;
Of all the things that happened there
    That's all that I remember.

TWO

Heritage

*E*very one of us inherits something; it may not be money or property, but something much less concrete and tangible, and we may not even be aware of it. It may be a way of doing some daily task or the way we decide some major moral problem for ourselves. It may be something important and central to our thinking, or something minor, something we proudly or nostalgically think of as "our heritage," or something we would like to ignore or forget. Heritage may therefore be a source of pride as well as a source of embarrassment, a discovery or a burden.

Heritage expresses itself in traditions, observances, and rituals. These unite families and occasionally divide them by accentuating differences between generations. They can create common bonds as well as sharp divisions, uniting groups as well as dividing them from others. The four selections included in this section examine some meanings of heritage; they exemplify the search for it, the celebration of it, and the ordinary, daily ways in which we meet it.

In the first selection, N. Scott Momaday, a Kiowa Indian, describes a return to the home of his ancestors. His account is deeply introspective, a kind of pilgrimage in search of his own feelings about being an Indian. Pride in his ancestry mingles with bitterness at the vanishing of a culture he could have called his own.

We encounter our heritage, or that of others in ordinary ways as well: in the restaurant, for example, or the grocery store. America, with its many ethnic groups, is richer, perhaps more than any other country, in the variety of its foods; they form a starting place where almost every day we encounter the diversity of heritage.

The next two selections both have ethnic food as their point of departure. Harry Golden nostalgically recalls the Lower East Side of New York early in twentieth century by describing its street foods. In the process he describes aspects of Jewish immigrant society at the turn of the century: its coherence, its upward mobility, and its ability to survive under adverse circumstances. Harry Mark Petrakis, in the third selection, describes a boy who is embarrassed by his heritage—not an unusual thing for the children of immigrants to America. He wants to be American and eat American food, and he insults the Greek grocer Barba Nikos. In the end, the older man teaches the boy to respect their common heritage through an appreciation of the foods he sells in his store. To him these foods are symbols of the 3,000-year history of the Greek people.

The last selection is much less personal and more analytical. Arthur L. Campa describes and tries to account for the major cultural differences between Anglos and Chicanos, English and Spanish-speaking North Americans.

THE WAY TO RAINY MOUNTAIN

N. Scott Momaday

N. Scott Momaday was born in Oklahoma in 1934. A Kiowa Indian, he attended schools on various reservations—Navaho, Apache, Pueblo—and took an undergraduate degree at the University of New Mexico, followed by a Ph.D at Stanford in 1960. He is now a professor of English and comparative literature. His interest in his Indian heritage is reflected in much of his work: *House Made of Dawn* (1968), which won a Pulitzer Prize for fiction, and *The Way to Rainy Mountain* (1969), a collection of Kiowa folk stories. The following selection serves as the introduction to the latter book.

A single knoll rises out of the plain in Oklahoma, north and west of the Wichita Range. For my people, the Kiowas, it is an old landmark, and they gave it the name Rainy Mountain. The hardest weather in the world is there. Winter brings blizzards, hot tornadic winds arise in the spring, and in summer the prairie is an anvil's edge. The grass turns brittle and brown, and it cracks beneath your feet. There are green belts along the rivers and creeks, linear groves of hickory and pecan, willow and witch hazel. At a distance in July or August the steaming foliage seems almost to writhe in fire. Great green and yellow grasshoppers are everywhere in the tall grass, popping up like corn to sting the flesh, and tortoises crawl about on the red earth, going nowhere in the plenty of time. Loneliness is an aspect of the land. All things in the plain are isolate; there is no confusion of objects in the eye, but *one* hill or *one* tree or *one* man. To look upon that landscape in the early morning, with the sun at your back, is to lose the sense of proportion. Your imagination comes to life, and this, you think, is where Creation was begun. 1

I returned to Rainy Mountain in July. My grandmother had died in the spring, and I wanted to be at her grave. She had lived to be very old and at last infirm. Her only living daughter was with her when she died, and I was told that in death her face was that of a child. 2

I like to think of her as a child. When she was born, the Kiowas were living the last great moment of their history. For more than a hundred years they had controlled the open range from the Smoky Hill River to the Red, from the headwaters of the Canadian to the fork of the Arkansas and Cimarron. In alliance with the Comanches, they had ruled the whole of the south- 3

49

ern Plains. War was their sacred business, and they were among the finest horsemen the world has ever known. But warfare for the Kiowas was preeminently a matter of disposition rather than of survival, and they never understood the grim, unrelenting advance of the U.S. Cavalry. When at last, divided and ill-provisioned, they were driven onto the Staked Plains in the cold rains of autumn, they fell into panic. In Palo Duro Canyon they abandoned their crucial stores to pillage and had nothing then but their lives. In order to save themselves, they surrendered to the soldiers at Fort Sill and were imprisoned in the old stone corral that now stands as a military museum. My grandmother was spared the humiliation of those high gray walls by eight or ten years, but she must have known from birth the affliction of defeat, the dark brooding of old warriors.

Her name was Aho, and she belonged to the last culture to evolve in   4 North America. Her forebears came down from the high country in western Montana nearly three centuries ago. They were a mountain people, a mysterious tribe of hunters whose language has never been positively classified in any major group. In the late seventeenth century they began a long migration to the south and east. It was a journey toward the dawn, and it led to a golden age. Along the way the Kiowas were befriended by the Crows, who gave them the culture and religion of the Plains. They acquired horses, and their ancient nomadic spirit was suddenly free of the ground. They acquired Tai-me, the sacred Sun Dance doll, from that moment the object and symbol of their worship, and so shared in the divinity of the sun. Not least, they acquired the sense of destiny, therefore courage and pride. When they entered upon the southern Plains they had been transformed. No longer were they slaves to the simple necessity of survival; they were a lordly and dangerous society of fighters and thieves, hunters and priests of the sun. According to their origin myth, they entered the world through a hollow log. From one point of view, their migration was the fruit of an old prophecy, for indeed they emerged from a sunless world.

Although my grandmother lived out her long life in the shadow of   5 Rainy Mountain, the immense landscape of the continental interior lay like memory in her blood. She could tell of the Crows, whom she had never seen, and of the Black Hills, where she had never been. I wanted to see in reality what she had seen more perfectly in the mind's eye, and traveled fifteen hundred miles to begin my pilgrimage.

Yellowstone, it seemed to me, was the top of the world, a region of deep   6 lakes and dark timber, canyons and waterfalls. But, beautiful as it is, one might have the sense of confinement there. The skyline in all directions is close at hand, the high wall of the woods and deep cleavages of shade. There is a perfect freedom in the mountains, but it belongs to the eagle and the elk, the badger and the bear. The Kiowas reckoned their stature by the distance they could see, and they were bent and blind in the wilderness.

Descending eastward, the highland meadows are a stairway to the plain. In July the inland slope of the Rockies is luxuriant with flax and buckwheat, stonecrop and larkspur. The earth unfolds and the limit of the land recedes. Clusters of trees, and animals grazing far in the distance, cause the vision to reach away and wonder to build upon the mind. The sun follows a longer course in the day, and the sky is immense beyond all comparison. The great billowing clouds that sail upon it are shadows that move upon the grain like water, dividing light. Farther down, in the land of the Crows and Blackfeet, the plain is yellow. Sweet clover takes hold of the hills and bends upon itself to cover and seal the soil. There the Kiowas paused on their way; they had come to the place where they must change their lives. The sun is at home on the plains. Precisely there does it have the certain character of a god. When the Kiowas came to the land of the Crows, they could see the dark lees of the hills at dawn across the Bighorn River, the profusion of light on the grain shelves, the oldest deity ranging after the solstices. Not yet would they veer southward to the caldron of the land that lay below; they must wean their blood from the northern winter and hold the mountains a while longer in their view. They bore Tai-me in procession to the east.

A dark mist lay over the Black Hills, and the land was like iron. At the top of a ridge I caught sight of Devil's Tower upthrust against the gray sky as if in the birth of time the core of the earth had broken through its crust and the motion of the world was begun. There are things in nature that engender an awful quiet in the heart of man; Devil's Tower is one of them. Two centuries ago, because they could not do otherwise, the Kiowas made a legend at the base of the rock. My grandmother said:

Eight children were there at play, seven sisters and their brother. Suddenly the boy was struck dumb; he trembled and began to run upon his hands and feet. His fingers became claws, and his body was covered with fur. Directly there was a bear where the boy had been. The sisters were terrified; they ran, and the bear after them. They came to the stump of a great tree, and the tree spoke to them. It bade them climb upon it, and as they did so it began to rise into the air. The bear came to kill them, but they were just beyond its reach. It reared against the tree and scored the bark all around with its claws. The seven sisters were borne into the sky, and they became the stars of the Big Dipper.

From that moment, and so long as the legend lives, the Kiowas have kinsmen in the night sky. Whatever they were in the mountains, they could be no more. However tenuous their well-being, however much they had suffered and would suffer again, they had found a way out of the wilderness.

My grandmother had a reverence for the sun, a holy regard that now   11
is all but gone out of mankind. There was a wariness in her, and an ancient
awe. She was a Christian in her later years, but she had come a long way
about, and she never forgot her birthright. As a child she had been to the
Sun Dances; she had taken part in those annual rites, and by them she had
learned the restoration of her people in the presence of Tai-me. She was
about seven when the last Kiowa Sun Dance was held in 1887 on the Washita
River above Rainy Mountain Creek. The buffalo were gone. In order to consummate the ancient sacrifice—to impale the head of a buffalo bull upon the
medicine tree—a delegation of old men journeyed into Texas, there to beg
and barter for an animal from the Goodnight herd. She was ten when the
Kiowas came together for the last time as a living Sun Dance culture. They
could find no buffalo; they had to hang an old hide from the sacred tree.
Before the dance could begin, a company of soldiers rode out from Fort Sill
under orders to disperse the tribe. Forbidden without cause the essential act
of their faith, having seen the wild herds slaughtered and left to rot upon the
ground, the Kiowas backed away forever from the medicine tree. That was
July 20, 1890, at the great bend of the Washita. My grandmother was there.
Without bitterness, and for as long as she lived, she bore a vision of deicide.

Now that I can have her only in memory, I see my grandmother in the   12
several postures that were peculiar to her: standing at the wood stove on a
winter morning and turning meat in a great iron skillet; sitting at the south
window, bent above her beadwork, and afterwards, when her vision failed,
looking down for a long time into the fold of her hands; going out upon a
cane, very slowly as she did when the weight of age came upon her; praying.
I remember her most often at prayer. She made long, rambling prayers out
of suffering and hope, having seen many things. I was never sure that I had
the right to hear, so exclusive were they of all mere custom and company.
The last time I saw her she prayed standing by the side of her bed at night,
naked to the waist, the light of a kerosene lamp moving upon her dark skin.
Her long, black hair, always drawn and braided in the day, lay upon her
shoulders and against her breasts like a shawl. I do not speak Kiowa, and I
never understood her prayers, but there was something inherently sad in the
sound, some merest hesitation upon the syllables of sorrow. She began in a
high and descending pitch, exhausting her breath to silence; then again and
again—and always the same intensity of effort, of something that is, and is
not, like urgency in the human voice. Transported so in the dancing light
among the shadows of her room, she seemed beyond the reach of time. But
that was illusion; I think I knew then that I should not see her again.

Houses are like sentinels in the plain, old keepers of the weather watch.   13
There, in a very little while, wood takes on the appearance of great age. All
colors wear soon away in the wind and rain, and then the wood is burned

gray and the grain appears and the nails turn red with rust. The window-
panes are black and opaque; you imagine there is nothing within, and indeed
tbere are many ghosts, bones given up to the land. They stand here and there
against the sky, and you approach them for a longer time than you expect.
They belong in the distance; it is their domain.

Once there was a lot of sound in my grandmother's house, a lot of com-   14
ing and going, feasting and talk. The summers there were full of excitement
and reunion. The Kiowas are a summer people; they abide the cold and keep
to themselves, but when the season turns and the land becomes warm and
vital they cannot hold still; an old love of going returns upon them. The aged
visitors who came to my grandmother's house when I was a child were made
of lean and leather, and they bore themselves upright. They wore great black
hats and bright ample shirts that shook in the wind. They rubbed fat upon
their hair and wound their braids with strips of colored cloth. Some of them
painted their faces and carried the scars of old and cherished enmities. They
were an old council of warlords, come to remind and be reminded of who
they were. Their wives and daughters served them well. The women might
indulge themselves; gossip was at once the mark and compensation of their
servitude. They made loud and elaborate talk among themselves, full of jest
and gesture, fright and false alarm. They went abroad in fringed and flowered shawls, bright beadwork and German silver. They were at home in the
kitchen, and they prepared meals that were banquets.

There were frequent prayer meetings, and great nocturnal feasts. When   15
I was a child I played with my cousins outside, where the lamplight fell upon
the ground and the singing of the old people rose up around us and carried
away into the darkness. There were a lot of good things to eat, a lot of laughter and surprise. And afterwards, when the quiet returned, I lay down with
my grandmother and could hear the frogs away by the river and feel the
motion of the air.

Now there is a funeral silence in the rooms, the endless wake of some   16
final word. The walls have closed in upon my grandmother's house. When I
returned to it in mourning, I saw for the first time in my life how small it
was. It was late at night, and there was a white moon, nearly full. I sat for a
long time on the stone steps by the kitchen door. From there I could see out
across the land; I could see the long row of trees by the creek, the low light
upon the rolling plains, and the stars of the Big Dipper. Once I looked at the
moon and caught sight of a strange thing. A cricket had perched upon the
handrail, only a few inches away from me. My line of vision was such that
the creature filled the moon like a fossil. It had gone there, I thought, to live
and die, for there, of all places, was its small definition made whole and
eternal. A warm wind rose up and purled like the longing within me.

The next morning I awoke at dawn and went out on the dirt road to   17

Rainy Mountain. It was already hot, and the grasshoppers began to fill the air. Still, it was early in the morning, and the birds sang out of the shadows. The long yellow grass on the mountain shone in the bright light and a scissortail hied above the land. There, where it ought to be, at the end of a long and legendary way, was my grandmother's grave. Here and there on the dark stones were ancestral names. Looking back once, I saw the mountain and came away.

QUESTIONS

Words to Know

disposition (paragraph 3), unrelenting (3), ill-provisioned (3), affliction (3), luxuriant (7), tenuous (10), birthright (11), deicide (11), inherently (12), transported (12), sentinels (13), servitude (14), purled (16).

Some of the Issues

1. Consider Momaday's title. In what different ways can you interpret his use of "way"?
2. How does Rainy Mountain, as Momaday describes it in paragraph 1, serve as a symbol of the entire selection? What is the importance of the seasons? Consider carefully the details he gives in this first paragraph and link them to other details in his account.
3. Cite the main changes in Kiowa life that occurred during the life of the author's grandmother.
4. Look at the last sentence in paragraph 5, in which Momaday indicates the beginning of a journey. Does he emphasize the fact that he travels? What is important to him about that journey?
5. The story of the author's grandmother is mingled with the history of the Kiowas. Explain why that is the case and what effect it has.
6. Show the way in which Momaday places himself in the history of the Kiowas. What is the significance of the fact that he does not speak Kiowa?
7. Explain the following statements: " . . . she belonged to the last culture to evolve in North America." (paragraph 4, opening.) "My grandmother

had a reverence for the sun, a holy regard that now is all but gone out
of mankind." (paragraph 11, opening.)
8. In what way is the myth (paragraph 9) symbolic of Kiowa existence?

The Way We Are Told

9. Momaday frequently uses such parallel constructions as "groves of hickory and pecan. willow and witch hazel." Find additional instances.
10. In addition to the plants mentioned in paragraph 1, Momaday mentions
    many other native trees and plants. Why?
11. The first paragraph is a description of nature. What kinds of details does
    Momaday single out to describe Rainy Mountain? In what ways do these
    different details serve to characterize his people, the Kiowas, their lives,
    and their fate?
12. In looking back on the selection, try to show, concretely, by what means
    Momaday makes the reader feel loneliness and isolation.

Some Subjects for Essays

13. Do you remember a story, folk tale, or legend you were told as a child?
    If so, retell it, trying to find if it has symbolic meanings. Why do you
    think your family preserved that story?

FOR TWO CENTS PLAIN

Harry Golden

Harry Golden (1903–1981) was born in the Austro-Hungarian monarchy and came to the United States as a child. After earning a B.A. at the City College of New York, he worked as a reporter on several New York newspapers. In 1939 he moved to Charlotte, North Carolina, where he spent most of the rest of his life. He wrote numerous articles and sketches, and his books are mostly collections of these pieces. Among them are *Only in America* (1958), from which the following selection is taken, *For Two Cents Plain* (1959), and *Enjoy, Enjoy* (1960).

The rabbinical students in Europe and in America had a regular schedule of "eating days." Mondays he ate with family A; Tuesdays with B; and so forth. On the Lower East Side this system still lingered to some extent, but it usually involved a young boy who had immigrated without a family. His fellow-townsmen set up his seven eating days. Usually this was a very religious boy who would not take a chance to eat "out" or could not yet afford to buy his meals. Some of the hosts on these eating days used the fellow to check up on the melamed (Hebrew teacher). The melamed came at half past three and taught the children for a half-hour—for a twenty-five-cent fee. Learning the prayers was entirely by rote. There was no explanation or translation of the Hebrew into English or Yiddish. Once in a while the mother would ask the eating-days fellow to come a half-hour earlier. The boy came with his usual appetite, but soon learned the reason for the early appointment. The mother wanted him to test the children to see if the melamed was doing all right. The boy always gave the melamed a clean bill of health.

Sometimes the eating-days boy ate too much and in poor households this was quite a problem. But in most homes the mother saw to it that he kept packing it away, and in addition always had something wrapped up for him to take back to his room—for later. Many households had these strangers at their tables, but only the very religious boys remained, those who expected to continue their religious studies.

The others were soon gone. America was too great and too wonderful; there were too many things to see and do, and even a hot dog at a pushcart was an adventure, to say nothing of the wonderful Max's Busy Bee.

The streets were crowded with vendors with all sorts of delightful and exotic tidbits and nasherei (delicacies).

56

Across the border (the Bowery) was the Italian hot-dog man. The hot   5
plate (a coal fire) was mounted on his pushcart, and behind the stove was a
barrel of lemonade to which he added chunks of ice every few hours. The
hot dog, roll, mustard, and relish was three cents; the drink, two cents; and
it was all a memorable experience.

A few years ago I saw a fellow with a similar cart near the Battery on   6
Lower Broadway and I made a mad dash for him. The whole operation was
now fifteen cents, but it wasn't anywhere near as wonderful as it was when
I was twelve years old.

In the late fall and winter came the fellow with the haiseh arbus (hot   7
chick-peas). He started to make his rounds a few minutes before noon as the
children were leaving the schools for lunch. You sat in the classroom and
everything was quiet and dignified, and all of a sudden you heard those loud
blasts—"Haiseh arbus," "Haiseh, haiseh" (hot, hot)—and you knew it was
time to go. Sometimes he was a little early and the teacher had to close the
window. The price was one penny for a portion which the man served in a
rolled-up piece of newspaper, like the English working people buy their fish
and chips. There were also fellows with roasted sweet potatoes; two cents
each, and three cents for an extra large one. These people used a galvanized
tin contraption on wheels which looked exactly like a bedroom dresser with
three drawers. In the bottom drawer were the potatoes he was roasting, while
in the upper drawers were the two different sizes ready to serve. On the
bottom of everything, of course, was the coal-burning fire. He had a small
bag of coal attached to the front of the stove and every once in a while he
shook up the fire.

My uncle Berger once operated one of those sweet-potato pushcarts   8
with the stove on the bottom, and years later he always said that he began
life in America as an engineer. He boasted of this after he had made a million
dollars operating the Hotel Normandie on Broadway and 38th Street during
World War I.

An interesting fellow was the peddler with a red fez, a "Turk," who   9
sold an exotic sweet drink. He carried a huge bronze water container
strapped to his back. This beautiful container had a long curved spout which
came over his left shoulder. Attached to his belt, in front, was a small pail of
warm water to rinse his two glasses. The drink was one penny. You held the
glass, and he leaned toward you as the liquid came forth.

Nuts were very popular. There were pushcarts loaded down with "polly   10
seeds." I have forgotten the authentic name for this nut but the East Side
literally bathed in the stuff. "Polly seed" because it was the favorite food of
parrots—"Polly want a cracker?"

Indian nuts, little round brown nuts. The father of one of the kids on   11

the block sold Indian nuts, of all things. On his pushcart he had a huge glass
bowl the size of an army soup vat, and it was filled with Indian nuts. I had
daydreams of taking my shoes off and jumping up and down in that vat of
Indian nuts, like the French girls make champagne.

This was the era when people walked a great deal. Shoeshine parlors   12
were all over the place. On Sunday mornings you went out to get a shine
and did not mind waiting in line for it either. "We are going for a walk next
Saturday night." Sounds silly today, but it was an event, and make no mistake. And on every corner there were pushcarts selling fruit in season.
Apples, pears, peaches, and above all, grapes. A common sight was a boy and
girl eating grapes. The boy held the stem aloft as each of them pulled at the
bunch and walked along the street. The grapes were sold by weight per
bunch; the other fruits were sold individually, of course. And "in season"
there was the man or the woman with "hot corn." I did not hear the term
"corn-on-the-cob" till quite a few years later. We knew it only as "hot corn."
The vendor had boiled the ears at home and usually carried the large vat to
a convenient street corner, or he put the vat on a baby carriage and wheeled
it around the neighborhood. A lot of women were in this hot-corn business.
The hot corn was a nickel, and there was plenty of bargaining. "Throw it
back, give me that one, the one over there." We kids waited around until
the lady was all sold out, except the ones which had been thrown back, and
often we paid no more than a penny. There are two moments when it is best
to buy from a peddler, a "first" and the "close-out."

Confections of all sorts were sold, many of them famous in the Orient   13
and eastern Europe. Fellows sold candy known as "rah-hott," which sounds
Turkish or Arabic. It was beautiful to look at and there were two or three
different tastes with each bite. Halvah, of course, was the real big seller, and
the memory of this has lingered to this day. No delicatessen store today is
without halvah, although I shall not do them the injustice of comparing the
East Side halvah and the stuff they sell today. But at least you are getting a
whiff of it, which is worth anything you pay. I had a Gentile friend here who
had been courting a widow for years without any success and I gave him a
box of chocolate-covered halvah to take to her, and the next time I saw the
guy he was dancing in the streets of Charlotte. We used to eat it between
slices of rye bread, "a halvah sonavich," and it was out of this world. There
was another candy called "buckser" (St. John's bread), imported from Pal-
estine. It had a long, hard, curved shell and inside a very black seed with an
interesting taste which is hard to describe.

There were pushcarts loaded down with barrels of dill pickles and pick-   14
led tomatoes, which we called "sour tomatoes." Working people, men and
women on the way home from the needle factories, stopped off to buy a sour
tomato as a sort of appetizer for their evening meal, or perhaps to take the

edge off the appetite. These tidbits sold for two and three cents each, and you served yourself. You put your hand into the vinegar barrel and pulled one out. Years later a relative of mine asked me to accompany him to a lawyer's office "to talk for him." I met him on the old East Side and we decided to walk out of the district and into Lower Broadway.

Suddenly I noticed that he was no longer at my side. I looked back and there he was biting into one sour tomato and holding a fresh one in the other hand, all ready to go. I had become a fancy guy by then and he was afraid he would embarrass me, but my mouth was watering, Broadway and all.

And then there were the permanent vendors—the soda-water stands. On nearly every corner a soda-water stand. These were the size and shape of the average newsstand you see in most of the big cities today. There was a soda fountain behind a narrow counter, and a rack for factory-made American candy, which was becoming increasingly popular, especially the Hershey bar. The fellow also sold cigarettes. No woman was ever seen smoking a cigarette in those days. The brands were Mecca, Hassan, Helmar, Sweet Caporal (which are still sold), Egyptian Deities, Moguls, Schinasi, Fifth Avenue, and Afternoons.

My father smoked Afternoons. Half the cigarette was a hard mouth-piece, or what the advertising boys today call a filter. I bought many a box of Afternoons and they were seven cents for ten cigarettes. I also bought whiskey. There was no inhibition about it and no sense of guilt. We had no drunks down there, and a kid could buy a bottle of whiskey for his father the same as he could buy a loaf of bread. I read the label many times on the way home, "Pennsylvania Rye Whiskey; we guarantee that this whiskey has been aged in the wood twenty years before bottling; signed, Park and Tilford." Cost, $1.80 for an imperial quart. No fancy "fifth-shmifth" business.

The fellow with the stand had a small marble counter on which he served his drinks and made change for candy and cigarettes. Along the counter were jars of preserves—cherry, raspberry, mulberry—for his mixed drinks. He also had a machine to make malted milks. How the immigrants took to the malted milk!

Like the other folks, my mother pronounced it "ah molta." But, of course, the big seller was seltzer (carbonated water), either plain or with syrup. A small glass of seltzer cost a penny—"Give me a small plain." That meant no syrup. And for the large glass you said, "Give me for two cents plain." For an extra penny he ladled out a spoonful of one of his syrups and mixed it with the seltzer. Here, too, there was plenty of bargaining. A fellow said, "Give me for two cents plain," and as the man was filling the glass with seltzer the customer said, casuallike, "Put a little on the top." This meant syrup, of course, and yet it did not mean the extra penny. You did not say, "Give me a raspberry soda." It was all in the way you said it, nonchalantly and in a sort of deprecating tone, "Put a little on the top." It meant that you were saving the fellow the trouble of even stirring the glass. Well, the man had already filled the glass with seltzer and what could he do with it unless you paid for it? So he "put a little on the top" but not the next time if he could help it. Often he would take the two cents first and give you a glass of plain. "I know my customers," he'd say. The man who had the stand on our corner was an elderly gent, "Benny," and once when I was playing around his counter, one of his jars fell down and the syrup got all over me. Every time I came near Benny's stand after that he took extra precautions; "Go way hard luck," he always said to me. Benny wore a coat he had brought from Europe and it reached down to his ankles. He would take a handful of that coat, feel it a while, and tell you whether it was going to rain the next day. People came from blocks around to get a weather forecast from Benny and his coat. He rarely missed.

And so you can hardly blame the young boy, the eating-days boy, when   20
he quit the table of those home-cooked meals and went down into this world of pleasures and joys.

QUESTIONS

Some of the Issues

1. Golden reminisces about several small pleasures. How does his catalog of small events contribute to the picture of the world of his childhood?
2. To what extent are the pleasures Golden speaks of available today? Are they still appreciated?
3. In paragraph 12 Golden refers to customs which he says seem silly today. What point is he making?
4. In paragraph 19 the last and most detailed description of street food summarizes the life Golden reminisces about. Explain the different aspects of that summary.

The Way We Are Told

5. Golden begins and ends his essay with the "eating days" of rabbinical students. How does this beginning and ending provide a frame for the rest of the essay?

6. Golden's account of street food seems random and unconnected at first. How does he tie his essay together?
7. Compare Golden's style of reminiscence with Momaday's. Read Momaday's second and third paragraphs aloud and then paragraphs 6 through 8 in Golden's essay. Characterize the differences in tone.
8. Golden gives many specific details, particularly in paragraph 16 where he goes so far as to give a list of the names of cigarettes. What do these details contribute?

Some Subjects for Essays

9. Describe a childhood experience with food or with a simple purchase, trying to cite as many concrete details as possible. Try to convey the feeling the food or the purchase gave you without directly saying so, conveying your feelings through the use of details.
10. In your experience, are particular foods associated with particular events: traditional holiday meals in your family, or food associated with a reward such as an ice cream soda for being brave at the dentist, or special food you were given when recovering from an illness? To what extent does the food evoke the memory of the event? Describe.
11. Golden seems to be saying that people have forgotten how to enjoy the simple things in life. Do you agree or not? Cite reasons for your views.

BARBA NIKOS

Harry Mark Petrakis

Harry Mark Petrakis was born in St. Louis, in 1923 but has spent most of his life in and around Chicago. Petrakis is a novelist and short story writer whose books include *Pericles on 31st Street* (1965), *A Dream of Kings* (1966), and *Stelmark: A Family Recollection* (1970), from which the following selection is an excerpt.

There was one storekeeper I remember above all others in my youth. It was 1 shortly before I became ill, spending a good portion of my time with a motley group of varied ethnic ancestry. We contended with one another to deride the customs of the old country. On our Saturday forays into neighborhoods beyond our own, to prove we were really Americans, we ate hot dogs and drank Cokes. If a boy didn't have ten cents for this repast he went hungry, for he dared not bring a sandwich from home made of the spiced meats our families ate.

One of our untamed games was to seek out the owner of a pushcart or 2 a store, unmistakably an immigrant, and bedevil him with a chorus of insults and jeers. To prove allegiance to the gang it was necessary to reserve our fiercest malevolence for a storekeeper or peddler belonging to our own ethnic background.

For that reason I led a raid on the small, shabby gorcery of old Barba 3 Nikos, a short, sinewy Greek who walked with a slight limp and sported a flaring, handlebar mustache.

We stood outside his store and dared him to come out. When he 4 emerged to do battle, we plucked a few plums and peaches from the baskets on the sidewalk and retreated across the street to eat them while he watched. He waved a fist and hurled epithets at us in ornamental Greek.

Aware that my mettle was being tested, I raised my arm and threw my 5 half-eaten plum at the old man. My aim was accurate and the plum struck him on the cheek. He shuddered and put his hand to the stain. He stared at me across the street, and although I could not see his eyes, I felt them sear my flesh. He turned and walked silently back into the store. The boys slapped my shoulders in admiration, but it was a hollow victory that rested like a stone in the pit of my stomach.

At twilight when we disbanded, I passed the grocery alone on my way 6 home. There was a small light burning in the store and the shadow of the old man's body outlined against the glass. Goaded by remorse, I walked to the door and entered.

The old man moved from behind the narrow wooden counter and stared at me. I wanted to turn and flee, but by then it was too late. As he motioned for me to come closer, I braced myself for a curse or a blow. 7

"You were the one," he said, finally, in a harsh voice. 8

I nodded mutely. 9

"Why did you come back?" 10

I stood there unable to answer. 11

"What's your name?" 12

"Haralambos," I said, speaking to him in Greek. 13

He looked at me in shock. "You are Greek!" he cried. "A Greek boy attacking a Greek grocer!" He stood appalled at the immensity of my crime. "All right," he said coldly. "You are here because you wish to make amends." His great mustache bristled in concentration. "Four plums, two peaches," he said. "That makes a total of 78 cents. Call it 75. Do you have 75 cents, boy?" 14

I shook my head. 15

"Then you will work it off," he said. "Fifteen cents an hour into 75 cents makes—he paused—"five hours of work. Can you come here Saturday morning?" 16

"Yes," I said. 17

"Yes, Barba Nikos," he said sternly. "Show respect." 18

"Yes, Barba Nikos," I said. 19

"Saturday morning at eight o'clock," he said. "Now go home and say thanks in your prayers that I did not loosen your impudent head with a solid smack on the ear." I needed no further urging and fled. 20

Saturday morning, still apprehensive, I returned to the store. I began by sweeping, raising clouds of dust in dark and hidden corners. I washed the windows, whipping the squeegee swiftly up and down the glass in a fever of fear that some member of the gang would see me. When I finished I hurried back inside. 21

For the balance of the morning I stacked cans, washed the counter, and dusted bottles of yellow wine. A few customers entered, and Barba Nikos served them. A little after twelve o'clock he locked the door so he could eat lunch. He cut himself a few slices of sausage, tore a large chunk from a loaf of crisp-crusted bread, and filled a small cup with a dozen black shiny olives floating in brine. He offered me the cup. I could not help myself and grimaced. 22

"You are a stupid boy," the old man said. "You are not really Greek, are you?" 23

"Yes, I am." 24

"You might be," he admitted grudgingly. "But you do not act Greek.   25
Wrinkling your nose at these fine olives. Look around this store for a minute.
What do you see?"

"Fruits and vegetables," I said. "Cheese and olives and things like that."   26

He stared at me with a massive scorn. "That's what I mean," he said.   27
"You are a bonehead. You don't understand that a whole nation and a people
are in this store."

I looked uneasily toward the storeroom in the rear, almost expecting   28
someone to emerge.

"What about olives?" he cut the air with a sweep of his arm. "There   29
are olives of many shapes and colors. Pointed black ones from Kalamata, oval
ones from Amphissa, pickled green olives and sharp tangy yellow ones.
Achilles carried black olives to Troy and after a day of savage battle leading
his Myrmidons, he'd rest and eat cheese and ripe black olives such as these
right here. You have heard of Achilles, boy, haven't you?"

"Yes," I said.   30

"Yes, Barba Nikos."   31

"Yes, Barba Nikos," I said.   32

He motioned at the row of jars filled with varied spices. "There is ori-   33
ganon there and basilikon and daphne and sesame and miantanos, all the
marvelous flavorings that we have used in our food for thousands of years.
The men of Marathon carried small packets of these spices into battle, and
the scents reminded them of their homes, their families, and their children."

He rose and tugged his napkin free from around his throat. "Cheese,   34
you said. Cheese! Come closer, boy, and I educate your abysmal ignorance."
He motioned toward a wooden container on the counter. "That glistening
white delight is feta, made from goat's milk, packed in wooden buckets to
retain the flavor. Alexander the Great demanded it on his table with his casks
of wine when he planned his campaigns."

He walked limping from the counter to the window where the piles of   35
tomatoes, celery, and green peppers clustered. "I suppose all you see here
are some random vegetables?" He did not wait for me to answer. "You are
dumb again. These are some of the ingredients that go to make up a Greek
salad. Do you know what a Greek salad really is? A meal in itself, an experience, an emotional involvement. It is created deftly and with grace. First,
you place large lettuce leaves in a big, deep bowl." He spread his fingers and
moved them slowly, carefully, as if he were arranging the leaves. "The
remainder of the lettuce is shredded and piled in a small mound," he said.
"Then comes celery, cucumbers, tomatoes sliced lengthwise, green peppers,
origanon, green olives, feta, avocado, and anchovies. At the end you dress it
with lemon, vinegar, and pure olive oil, glinting golden in the light."

He finished with a heartfelt sigh and for a moment closed his eyes. Then   36
he opened one eye to mark me with a baleful intensity. "The story goes that
Zeus himself created the recipe and assembled and mixed the ingredients on
Mount Olympus one night when he had invited some of the other gods to
dinner."

He turned his back on me and walked slowly again across the store,   37
dragging one foot slightly behind him. I looked uneasily at the clock, which
showed that it was a few minutes past one. He turned quickly and startled
me. "And everything else in here," he said loudly. "White beans, lentils,
garlic, crisp bread, kokoretsi, meat balls, mussels and clams." He paused and
drew a deep, long breath. "And the wine," he went on, "wine from Samos,
Santorini, and Crete, retsina and mavrodaphne, a taste almost as old as water
. . . and then the fragrant melons, the pastries, yellow diples and golden lou-
koumades, the honey custard galatobouriko. Everything a part of our history,
as much a part as the exquisite sculpture in marble, the bearded warriors,
Pan and the oracles at Delphi, and the nymphs dancing in the shadowed
groves under Homer's glittering moon." He paused, out of breath again, and
coughed harshly. "Do you understand now, boy?"

He watched my face for some response and then grunted. We stood   38
silent for a moment until he cocked his head and stared at the clock. "It is
time for you to leave," he motioned brusquely toward the door. "We are
square now. Keep it that way."

I decided the old man was crazy and reached behind the counter for   39
my jacket and cap and started for the door. He called me back. From a box
he drew out several soft, yellow figs that he placed in a piece of paper. "A
bonus because you worked well," he said. "Take them. When you taste them,
maybe you will understand what I have been talking about."

I took the figs and he unlocked the door and I hurried from the store. I   40
looked back once and saw him standing in the doorway, watching me, the
swirling tendrils of food curling like mist about his head.

I ate the figs late that night. I forgot about them until I was in bed, and   41
then I rose and took the package from my jacket. I nibbled at one, then ate
them all. They broke apart between my teeth with a tangy nectar, a thick
sweetness running like honey across my tongue and into the pockets of my
cheeks. In the morning when I woke, I could still taste and inhale their
fragrance.

I never again entered Barba Nikos's store. My spell of illness, which   42
began some months later, lasted two years. When I returned to the streets I
had forgotten the old man and the grocery. Shortly afterwards my family
moved from the neighborhood.

Some twelve years later, after the war, I drove through the old neigh-   43

borhood and passed the grocery. I stopped the car and for a moment stood
before the store. The windows were stained with dust and grime, the interior
bare and desolate, a store in a decrepit group of stores marked for razing so
new structures could be built.

I have been in many Greek groceries since then and have often bought   44
the feta and Kalamata olives. I have eaten countless Greek salads and have
indeed found them a meal for the gods. On the holidays in our house, my
wife and sons and I sit down to a dinner of steaming, buttered pilaf like my
mother used to make and lemon-egg avgolemono and roast lamb richly seasoned with cloves of garlic. I drink the red and yellow wines, and for dessert
I have come to relish the delicate pastries coated with honey and powdered
sugar. Old Barba Nikos would have been pleased.

But I have never been able to recapture the halcyon flavor of those figs   45
he gave me on that day so long ago, although I have bought figs many times.
I have found them pleasant to my tongue, but there is something missing.
And to this day I am not sure whether it was the figs or the vision and passion
of the old grocer that coated the fruit so sweetly I can still recall their savor
and fragrance after almost thirty years.

QUESTIONS

Words to Know

motley (paragraph 1), deride (1), foray (1), repast (1), bedevil (2), allegiance
(2), appalled (14), immensity (14), Achilles (29), Troy (29), Myrmidons (29),
Marathon (33), Alexander the Great (34), Zeus (36), Mount Olympus (36),
Pan (37), Delphi (37), Homer (37), halcyon (45).

Some of the Issues

1. Why do the gang members attack immigrants of their own ethnic
   groups?
2. What is the first sign that the narrator will change his mind about his
   deed?

3. What is the boy's first reaction to the olives? How does it set the scene for later reactions?
4. What does Barba Nikos mean when he says, "a whole nation and a people are in this store"?

The Way We Are Told

5. In the first four paragraphs the author uses a number of rather unusual words and phrases for simple events: motley, repast, untamed, bedevil, malevolence, to do battle. What effect is achieved by this choice?
6. Contrast the tone of the narrative frame at the beginning and end of the selection with the telling of the story through dialog in the middle. What is the effect?
7. Examine the various references to Barba Nikos throughout the selection. What impression do we have of him in the beginning? How does it change?
8. List the various references linking food and drink to mythology. What is their purpose?
9. In what way do the last two paragraphs sum up the theme of the essay?

Some Subjects for Essays

10. Describe a time when you did something against your better judgment, perhaps under pressure from friends. What exactly was the pressure that led you to it, and how did you feel afterwards?
11. In the previous selection, Harry Golden also uses descriptions of food to convey something about his ethnic heritage. Write an essay comparing and contrasting Petrakis' presentation with Golden's.

ANGLO VS. CHICANO: WHY?

Arthur L. Campa

Arthur L. Campa (1905–1978) was born to American missionary parents in Mexico. He attended the University of New Mexico and Columbia, and was professor and chairman of the Department of Modern Languages at the University of Denver. He also served as cultural attaché at several United States embassies. The following selection appeared in the *Western Review*.

The cultural differences between Hispanic and Anglo-American people have been dwelt upon by so many writers that we should all be well informed about the values of both. But audiences are usually of the same persuasion as the speakers, and those who consult published works are for the most part specialists looking for affirmation of what they believe. So, let us consider the same subject, exploring briefly some of the basic cultural differences that cause conflict in the Southwest, where Hispanic and Anglo-American cultures meet. 1

Cultural differences are implicit in the conceptual content of the languages of these two civilizations, and their value systems stem from a long series of historical circumstances. Therefore, it may be well to consider some of the English and Spanish cultural configurations before these Europeans set foot on American soil. English culture was basically insular, geographically and ideologically; was more integrated on the whole, except for some strong theological differences; and was particularly zealous of its racial purity. Spanish culture was peninsular, a geographical circumstance that made it a catch-all of Mediterranean, central European and north African peoples. The composite nature of the population produced a marked regionalism that prevented close integration, except for religion, and led to a strong sense of individualism. These differences were reflected in the colonizing enterprise of the two cultures. The English isolated themselves from the Indians physically and culturally; the Spanish, who had strong notions about *pureza de sangre* [purity of blood] among the nobility, were not collectively averse to adding one more strain to their racial cocktail. Cortés led the way by siring the first *mestizo* in North America, and the rest of the conquistadores followed suit. The ultimate products of these two orientations meet today in the Southwest. 2

68

Anglo-American culture was absolutist at the onset; that is, all the dominant values were considered identical for all, regardless of time and place. Such values as justice, charity, honesty were considered the superior social order for all men and were later embodied in the American Constitution. The Spaniard brought with him a relativistic viewpoint and saw fewer moral implications in man's actions. Values were looked upon as the result of social and economic conditions.   3

The motives that brought Spaniards and Englishmen to America also differed. The former came on an enterprise of discovery, searching for a new route to India initially, and later for new lands to conquer, the fountain of youth, minerals, the Seven Cities of Cíbola and, in the case of the missionaries, new souls to win for the Kingdom of Heaven. The English came to escape religious persecution, and once having found a haven, they settled down to cultivate the soil and establish their homes. Since the Spaniards were not seeking a refuge or running away from anything, they continued their explorations and circled the globe 25 years after the discovery of the New World.   4

This peripatetic tendency of the Spaniard may be accounted for in part by the fact that he was the product of an equestrian culture. Men on foot do not venture far into the unknown. It was almost a century after the landing on Plymouth Rock that Governor Alexander Spotswood of Virginia crossed the Blue Ridge Mountains, and it was not until the nineteenth century that the Anglo-Americans began to move west of the Mississippi.   5

The Spaniard's equestrian role meant that he was not close to the soil, as was the Anglo-American pioneer, who tilled the land and built the greatest agricultural industry in history. The Spaniard cultivated the land only when he had Indians available to do it for him. The uses to which the horse was put also varied. The Spanish horse was essentially a mount, while the more robust English horse was used in cultivating the soil. It is therefore not surprising that the viewpoints of these two cultures should differ when we consider that the pioneer is looking at the world at the level of his eyes while the *caballero* [horseman] is looking beyond and down at the rest of the world.   6

One of the most commonly quoted, and often misinterpreted, characteristics of Hispanic peoples is the deeply ingrained individualism in all walks of life. Hispanic individualism is a revolt against the incursion of collectivity, strongly asserted when it is felt that the ego is being fenced in. This attitude leads to a deficiency in those social qualities based on collective standards, an attitude that Hispanos do not consider negative because it manifests a measure of resistance to standardization in order to achieve a measure of individual freedom. Naturally, such an attitude has no *reglas fijas* [fixed rules].   7

Anglo-Americans who achieve a measure of success and security   8
through institutional guidance not only do not mind a few fixed rules but
demand them. The lack of a concerted plan of action, whether in business
or in politics, appears unreasonable to Anglo-Americans. They have a sense
of individualism, but they achieve it through action and self-determination.
Spanish individualism is based on feeling, on something that is the result not
of rules and collective standards but of a person's momentary, emotional
reaction. And it is subject to change when the mood changes. In contrast to
Spanish emotional individualism, the Anglo-American strives for objectivity
when choosing a course of action or making a decision.

The Southwestern Hispanos voiced strong objections to the lack of cour-   9
tesy of the Anglo-Americans when they first met them in the early days of
the Santa Fe trade. The same accusation is leveled at the *Americanos* today
in many quarters of the Hispanic world. Some of this results from their different conceptions of polite behavior. Here too one can say that the Spanish
have no *reglas fijas* because for them courtesy is simply an expression of the
way one person feels toward another. To some they extend the hand, to some
they bow and for the more *íntimos* there is the well-known *abrazo*. The
concepts of "good or bad" or "right and wrong" in polite behavior are moral
considerations of an absolutist culture.

Another cultural contrast appears in the way both cultures share part of   10
their material substance with others. The pragmatic Anglo-American con-
tributes regularly to such institutions as the Red Cross, the United Fund and
a myriad of associations. He also establishes foundations and quite often
leaves millions to such institutions. The Hispano prefers to give his contribution directly to the recipient so he can see the person he is helping.

A century of association has inevitably acculturated both Hispanos and   11
Anglo-Americans to some extent, but there still persist a number of culture
traits that neither group has relinquished altogether. Nothing is more dis-
quieting to an Anglo-American who believes that time is money than the
time perspective of Hispanos. They usually refer to this attitude as the "*mañ-
ana* psychology." Actually, it is more of a "today psychology," because Hispanos cultivate the present to the exclusion of the future; because the latter
has not arrived yet, it is not a reality. They are reluctant to relinquish the
present, so they hold on to it until it becomes the past. To an Hispano, nine
is nine until it is ten, so when he arrives at nine-thirty, he jubilantly exclaims:
"*¡Justo!*" [right on time]. This may be why the clock is slowed down to a
walk in Spanish while in English it runs. In the United States, our future-
oriented civilization plans our lives so far in advance that the present loses
its meaning. January magazine issues [including ID's] are out in December;
1973 cars have been out since October; cemetery plots and even funeral

arrangements are bought on the installment plan. To a person engrossed in living today the very idea of planning his funeral sounds like the tolling of the bells.

It is a natural corollary that a person who is present oriented should be   12
compensated by being good at improvising. An Anglo-American is told in advance to prepare for an "impromptu speech," but an Hispano usually can improvise a speech because *"Nosotoros lo improvisamos todo"* [we improvise everything].

Another source of cultural conflict arises from the difference between   13
being and *doing*. Even when trying to be individualistic, the Anglo-American achieves it by what he does. Today's young generation decided to be themselves, to get away from standardization, so they let their hair grow, wore ragged clothes and even went barefoot in order to be different from the Establishment. As a result they all ended up doing the same things and created another stereotype. The freedom enjoyed by the individuality of *being* makes it unnecessary for Hispanos to strive to be different.

In 1963 a team of psychologists from the University of Guadalajara in   14
Mexico and the University of Michigan compared 74 upper-middle-class students from each university. Individualism and personalism were found to be central values for the Mexican students. This was explained by saying that a Mexican's value as a person lies in his *being* rather than, as is the case of the Anglo-Americans, in concrete accomplishments. Efficiency and accomplishments are derived characteristics that do not affect worthiness in the Mexican, whereas in the American it is equated with success, a value of highest priority in the American culture. Hispanic people disassociate themselves from material things or from actions that may impugn a person's sense of being, but the Anglo-American shows great concern for material things and assumes responsibility for his actions. This is expressed in the language of each culture. In Spanish one says, *"Se me cayó la taza"* [the cup fell away from me] instead of "I dropped the cup."

In English, one speaks of money, cash and all related transactions with   15
frankness because material things of this high order do not trouble Anglo-Americans. In Spanish such materialistic concepts are circumvented by referring to cash as *efectivo* [effective] and when buying or selling as something *al contado* [counted out], and when without it by saying *No tengo fondos* [I have no funds]. This disassociation from material things is what produces *sobriedad* [sobriety] in the Spaniard according to Miguel de Unamuno, but in the Southwest the disasscciation from materialism leads to *dejadez* [lassitude] and *desprendimiento* [disinterestedness]. A man may lose his life defending his honor but is unconcerned about the lack of material things. *Desprendimiento* causes a man to spend his last cent on a friend,

which when added to lack of concern for the future may mean that tomorrow he will eat beans as a result of today's binge.

The implicit differences in words that appear to be identical in meaning are astonishing. Versatile is a compliment in English and an insult in Spanish. An Hispano student who is told to apologize cannot do it, because the word doesn't exist in Spanish. *Apología* means words in praise of a person. The Anglo-American either apologizes, which is form of retraction abhorrent in Spanish, or compromises, another concept foreign to Hispanic culture. *Compromiso* means a date, not a compromise. In colonial Mexico City, two hidalgos once entered a narrow street from opposite sides, and when they could not go around, they sat in their coaches for three days until the viceroy ordered them to back out. All this because they could not work out a compromise.

It was that way then and to some extent now. Many of today's conflicts in the Southwest have their roots in polarized cultural differences, which need not be irreconcilable when approached with mutual respect and understanding.

QUESTIONS

Words to Know

implicit (paragraph 2), conceptual (2), configuration (2), zealous (2), *mestizo*—mixed blood (2), conquistadores (2), absolutist (3), relativistic (3), peripatetic (5), equestrian (5), incursion (7), collectivity (7), *abrazo*—embrace, greeting (9), circumvented (15), versatile (16), *hidalgo*—gentleman, nobleman (16).

Some of the Issues

1. Find the sentence that most precisely states the thesis of the essay.
2. It is relatively easy to find thesis statements for the various paragraphs. Find them for paragraphs 3, 7, and 10. What is the arrangement of supporting evidence in each case?
3. Campa makes a number of assertions throughout the essay. Examine the evidence he presents for each. Which ones do you find to be strongly supported? Which are less well sustained?

4. According to Campa, individuality is a virtue in both Anglo and Hispanic cultures. How do the notions of individuality differ in the two cultures?

The Way We Are Told

5. Make an outline of the essay, showing its organizational pattern.
6. Each paragraph (or small group of paragraphs) deals with a particular contrast between Anglos and Chicanos. In your view, would the essay be more or less effective if the author had used a different pattern, that is, if he had developed the Anglo and Hispanic characteristics in two major, separate sections? Support your opinion.
7. How objective do you find Campa's article? Does the author favor one side? If you think he does, what evidence can you cite for your view?

Some Subjects for Essays

8. Write an essay comparing and contrasting two related subjects you know well: high school and college; an old home and your present one; two jobs.
9. Give your own definition of individuality and support it with examples.

THREE

Families

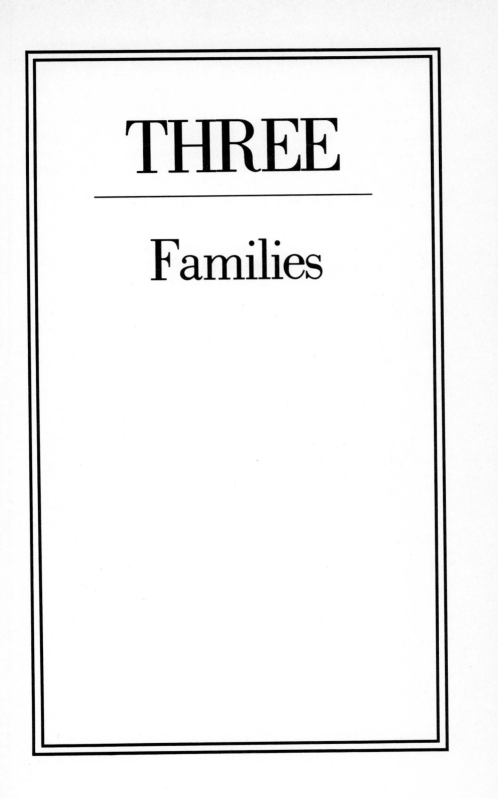

*T*here are many kinds of families. The nuclear family—two parents and their children—is the traditional model, but one which is, according to the 1980 census, no longer typical. The extended family, which adds grandparents, uncles, aunts, and cousins to the nucleus, is much more common throughout the world and in some communities in the United States. The census also shows that there has been a rapid rise in families in which the nucleus consists of only one parent living with children. Furthermore, households functioning as families may consist of two or more individuals, unrelated by blood or marriage, living with or without children.

Part Three begins with an essay by Jane Howard in which she describes the characteristics of good families. She includes not only the families into which we are born but families we choose to make ourselves part of through friendship. Birth and marriage, she says, are not the only way to get a family, "if we're going to go around devising new ones, we might as well have the luxury of picking their members ourselves."

The other selections are personal accounts, reflecting the diversity of families and family life. Alfred Kazin, in recollecting his childhood in the Jewish ghetto of New York, describes his family: poor, closely knit, bent on work. Its center—one might say its life—is the mother.

Willa Cather's description of an encounter of two families is an excerpt from her novel *My Ántonia*. The American family, established in rural Nebraska and including the young narrator of the episode, meets the new arrivals from Bohemia, a patriarchal Old World family painfully trying to adjust to a new life.

Helen Sekaquaptewa, a Hopi Indian, describes the central event of establishing a new family: marriage. The traditional ceremonies of the Hopi depend on the participation not only of the couples' extended families but of the whole village.

Finally, Carolina Maria de Jesus' diary records her struggles, day-in, day-out, to feed, clothe, and raise her children under almost impossible circumstances, and to maintain them and herself as a family.

FAMILIES

Jane Howard

Jane Howard, born in Springfield, Illinois, in 1935, is a reporter, editor, and writer. Among her books are *Please Touch: A Guided Tour of the Human Potential Movement* (1970), the autobiographical *A Different Woman* (1973), and *Families* (1978). She has also taught at several universities.

Each of us is born into one family not of our choosing. If we're going to go around devising new ones, we might as well have the luxury of picking their members ourselves. Clever picking might result in new families whose benefits would surpass or at least equal those of the old. The new ones by definition cannot spawn us—as soon as they do that, they stop being new—but there is plenty they can do. I have seen them work wonders. As a member in reasonable standing of six or seven tribes in addition to the one I was born to, I have been trying to figure which earmarks are common to both kinds of families: 1

(1) Good families have a chief, or a heroine, or a founder—someone around whom others cluster, whose achievements as the Yiddish word has it, let them *kvell*, and whose example spurs them on to like feats. Some blood dynasties produce such figures regularly; others languish for as many as five generations between demigods, wondering with each new pregnancy whether this, at last, might be the messianic baby who will redeem us. Look, is there not something gubernatorial about her footstep, or musical about the way he bangs with his spoon on his cup? All clans, of all kinds, need such a figure now and then. Sometimes clans based on water rather than blood harbor several such personages at one time. The Bloomsbury Group in London six decades ago was not much hampered by its lack of a temporal history. 2

(2) Good families have a switchboard operator—someone like my mother who cannot help but keep track of what all the others are up to, who plays Houston Mission Control to everyone else's Apollo. This role, like the foregoing one, is assumed rather than assigned. Someone always volunteers for it. That person often also has the instincts of an archivist, and feels driven to keep scrapbooks and photograph albums up to date, so that the clan can see proof of its own continuity. 3

(3) Good families are much to all their members, but everything to none. Good families are fortresses with many windows and doors to the outer world. The blood clans I feel most drawn to were founded by parents who are nearly as devoted to whatever it is they do outside as they are to each 4

other and their children. Their curiosity and passion are contagious. Everybody, where they live, is busy. Paint is spattered on eyeglasses. Mud lurks under fingernails. Person-to-person calls come in the middle of the night from Tokyo and Brussels. Catchers' mitts, ballet slippers, overdue library books and other signs of extrafamilial concerns are everywhere.

(4) Good families are hospitable. Knowing that hosts need guests as much as guests need hosts, they are generous with honorary memberships for friends, whom they urge to come early and often and to stay late. Such clans exude a vivid sense of surrounding rings of relatives, neighbors, teachers, students and godparents, any of whom at any time might break or slide into the inner circle. Inside that circle a wholesome, tacit emotional feudalism develops: you give me protection, I'll give you fealty. Such treaties begin with, but soon go far beyond, the jolly exchange of pie at Thanksgiving for cake on birthdays. It means you can ask me to supervise your children for the fortnight you will be in the hospital, and that however inconvenient this might be for me, I shall manage to. It means I can phone you on what for me is a dreary, wretched Sunday afternoon and for you is the eve of a deadline, knowing you will tell me to come right over, if only to watch you type. It means we need not dissemble. ("To yield to seeming," as Buber wrote, "is man's essential cowardice, to resist it is his essential courage . . . one must at times pay dearly for life lived from the being, but it is never too dear.")

(5) Good families deal squarely with direness. Pity the tribe that doesn't have, and cherish, at least one flamboyant eccentric. Pity too the one that supposes it can avoid for long the woes to which all flesh is heir. Lunacy, bankruptcy, suicide and other unthinkable fates sooner or later afflict the noblest of clans with an undertow of gloom. Family life is a set of givens, someone once told me, and it takes courage to see certain givens as blessings rather than as curses. Contradictions and inconsistencies are givens, too. So is the war against what the Oregon patriarch Kenneth Babbs calls malarkey. "There's always malarkey lurking, bubbles in the cesspool, fetid bubbles that pop and smell. But I don't put up with malarkey, between my step-kids and my natural ones or anywhere else in the family."

(6) Good families prize their rituals. Nothing welds a family more than these. Rituals are vital especially for clans without histories, because they evoke a past, imply a future, and hint at continuity. No line in the Seder service at Passover reassures more than the last: "Next year in Jerusalem!" A clan becomes more of a clan each time it gathers to observe a fixed ritual (Christmas, birthdays, Thanksgiving, and so on), grieve at a funeral (anyone may come to most funerals; those who do declare their tribalness), and devises a new rite of its own. Equinox breakfasts and all-white dinners can be at least as welding as Memorial Day parades. Several of us in the old *Life*

magazine years used to meet for lunch every Pearl Harbor Day, preferably to eat some politically neutral fare like smorgasbord, to "forgive" our only ancestrally Japanese colleague Irene Kubota Neves. For that and other reasons we became, and remain, a sort of family.

"Rituals," a California friend of mine said, "aren't just externals and 8 holidays. They are the performances of our lives. They are a kind of shorthand. They can't be decreed. My mother used to try to decree them. She'd make such a goddamn fuss over what we talked about at dinner, aiming at Topics of Common Interest, topics that celebrated our cohesion as a family. These performances were always hollow, because the phenomenology of the moment got sacrificed for the *idea* of the moment. Real rituals are discovered in retrospect. They emerge around constitutive moments, moments that only happen once, around whose memory meanings cluster. You don't choose those moments. They choose themselves." A lucky clan includes a born mythologizer, like my blood sister, who has the gift of apprehending such a moment when she sees it, and who cannot help but invent new rituals everywhere soe goes.

(7) Good families are affectionate. This of course is a matter of style. I 9 know clans whose members greet each other with gingerly handshakes or, in what pass for kisses, with hurried brushes of side jawbones, as if the object were to touch not the lips but the ears. I don't see how such people manage. "The tribe that does not hug," as someone who has been part of many *ad hoc* families recently wrote to me, "is no tribe at all. More and more I realize that everybody, regardless of age, needs to be hugged and comforted in a brotherly or sisterly way now and then. Preferably now."

(8) Good families have a sense of place, which these days is not achieved 10 easily. As Susanne Langer wrote in 1957, "Most people have no home that is a symbol of their childhood, not even a definite memory of one place to serve that purpose . . . all the old symbols are gone." Once I asked a roomful of supper guests who, if anyone, felt any strong pull to any certain spot on the face of the earth. Everyone was silent, except for a visitor from Bavaria. The rest of us seemed to know all too well what Walker Percy means in *The Moviegoer* when he tells of the "genie-soul of the place which every place has or else is not a place [and which] wherever you go, you must meet and master or else be met and mastered." All that meeting and mastering saps plenty of strength. It also underscores our need for tribal bases of the sort which soaring real estate taxes and splintering families have made all but obsolete.

So what are we to do, those of us whose habit and pleasure and doom 11 is our tendency, as a Georgia lady put it, to "fly off at every other whipstitch?" Think in terms of movable feasts, for a start. Live here, wherever here may be, as if we were going to belong here for the rest of our lives. Learn to hallow whatever ground we happen to stand on or land on. Like medieval knights who took their tapestries along on Crusades, like modern Afghanis with their yurts, we must pack such totems and icons as we can to make short-term quarters feel like home. Pillows, small rugs, watercolors can dispel much of the chilling anonymity of a sublet apartment or motel room. When we can, we should live in rooms with stoves or fireplaces or anyway candlelight. The ancient saying still is true: Extinguished hearth, extinguished family. Round tables help, too, and as a friend of mine once put it, so do "too many comfortable chairs, with surfaces to put feet on, arranged so as to encourage a maximum of eye contact." Such rooms inspire good talk, of which good clans can never have enough.

(9) Good families, not just the blood kind, find some way to connect with posterity. "To forge a link in the humble chain of being, encircling heirs to ancestors," as Michael Novak has written, "is to walk within a circle of magic as primitive as humans knew in caves." He is talking of course about babies, feeling them leap in wombs, giving them suck. Parenthood, however, is a state which some miss by chance and others by design, and a vocation to which not all are called. Some of us, like the novelist Richard P. Brickner, "look on as others name their children who in turn name their own lives, devising their own flags from their parents' cloth." What are we who lack children to do? Build houses? Plant trees? Write books or symphonies or laws? Perhaps, but even if we do these things, there still should be children on the sidelines, if not at the center, of our lives. It is a sadly impoverished tribe that does not allow access to, and make much of, some children. Not too much, of course: it has truly been said that never in history have so many educated people devoted so much attention to so few children. Attention, in excess, can turn to fawning, which isn't much better than neglect. Still, if we don't regularly see and talk to and laugh with people who can expect to outlive us by twenty years or so, we had better get busy and find some.

(10) Good families also honor their elders. The wider the age range, the stronger the tribe. Jean-Paul Sartre and Margaret Mead, to name two spectacularly confident former children, have both remarked on the central importance of grandparents in their own early lives. Grandparents now are in much more abundant supply than they were a generation or two ago when old age was more rare. If actual grandparents are not at hand, no family should have too hard a time finding substitute ones to whom to give unfeigned homage. The Soviet Union's enchantment with day care centers, I have heard, stems at least in part from the state's eagerness to keep children away from their presumably subversive grandparents. Let that be a lesson to clans based on interest as well as to those based on genes.

QUESTIONS

Words to Know

messianic (paragraph 2), Bloomsbury Group (2), temporal (2), exude (5), feudalism (5), fortnight (5), direness (6), flamboyant (6), inconsistencies (6), Passover (7), Equinox (7), smorgasgord (7), decreed (8), constitutive (8), whipstitch (11), Crusades (11), anonymity (11), posterity (12), fawning (12), Jean-Paul Sartre (13), Margaret Mead (13).

Some of the Issues

1. In paragraph 1, and elsewhere in her book *Families*, Howard suggests that people should build their own families, "devising new ones" with friends, supplementing (or replacing?) natural families. What do you think of her idea?
2. In offering her ten "earmarks . . . common to both kinds of families" does she distinguish at any time between "natural" and "new" families? If so, in what way?
3. Look at each of the ten points, and consider if each one is convincing. If you agree, try to add evidence from your own experience. If you disagree, try to develop counterarguments.
4. Read Alfred Kazin's "The Kitchen." Which of the ten points fit that family and why?

The Way We Are Told

5. Each of the ten points begins in exactly the same way. What is the effect of this repetition?
6. Describe how each of the points is constructed. How is the content arranged? How consistent is the arrangement?
7. Howard frequently uses what one can call "the part for the whole"; examples are the last two sentences of point 3; or, in point 4, "you can ask me to supervise your children for the fortnight you will be in the hospital." Find other examples. What is their effect?

Some Subjects for Essays

8. Select a topic similar to Howard's, for example, "The good citizen," or "An educated person," or "an effective teacher." Then treat it as Howard might, developing the points one by one that together constitute a series of definitions of the subject.

9. Consider your own family or families, if you think you have both of Howard's kinds. Describe any person, event, or occasion that fits any of her ten points.

10. Are gangs families? Argue for or against that proposition.

11. Howard's definitions are implicitly based on mainstream American culture. On the basis of your experience or reading, would you say that her definitions hold for families in another culture?

THE KITCHEN

Alfred Kazin

Alfred Kazin, born in New York in 1915, has taught at several universities, most recently at the City University of New York. He has held
several distinguished fellowships and is a member of the American
Academy of Arts and Sciences. His books include *On Native Grounds*
(1942), *The Inmost Leaf* (1955), *A Walker in the City* (1957), *Starting
Out in the Thirties* (1965), and *New York Jew* (1978). The following
selection is from *A Walker in the City.*

In Brownsville tenements the kitchen is always the largest room and the center of the household. As a child I felt that we lived in a kitchen to which four
other rooms were annexed. My mother, a "home" dressmaker, had her workshop in the kitchen. She told me once that she had begun dressmaking in
Poland at thirteen; as far back as I can remember, she was always making
dresses for the local women. She had an innate sense of design, a quick eye
for all the subtleties in the latest fashions, even when she despised them, and
great boldness. For three or four dollars she would study the fashion magazines with a customer, go with the customer to the remnants store on Bel-
mont Avenue to pick out the material, argue the owner down—all remnants
stores, for some reason, were supposed to be shady, as if the owners dealt in
stolen goods—and then for days would patiently fit and baste and sew and
fit again. Our apartment was always full of women in their housedresses sitting around the kitchen table waiting for a fitting. My little bedroom next to
the kitchen was the fitting room. The sewing machine, an old nut-brown
Singer with golden scrolls painted along the black arm and engraved along
the two tiers of little drawers massed with needles and thread on each side
of the treadle, stood next to the window and the great coal-black stove which
up to my last year in college was our main source of heat. By December the
two outer bedrooms were closed off, and used to chill bottles of milk and
cream, cold borscht and jellied calves' feet.

The kitchen held our lives together. My mother worked in it all day
long, we ate in it almost all meals except the Passover *seder*, I did my homework and first writing at the kitchen table, and in winter I often had a bed
made up for me on three kitchen chairs near the stove. On the wall just over
the table hung a long horizontal mirror that sloped to a ship's prow at each
end and was lined in cherry wood. It took up the whole wall, and drew every
object in the kitchen to itself. The walls were a fiercely stippled whitewash,

83

so often rewhitened by my father in slack seasons that the paint looked as if it had been squeezed and cracked into the walls. A large electric bulb hung down the center of the kitchen at the end of a chain that had been hooked into the ceiling; the old gas ring and key still jutted out of the wall like antlers. In the corner next to the toilet was the sink at which we washed, and the square tub in which my mother did our clothes. Above it, tacked to the shelf on which were pleasantly ranged square, blue-bordered white sugar and spice jars, hung calendars from the Public National Bank on Pitkin Avenue and the Minsker Progressive Branch of the Workman's Circle; receipts for the payment of insurance premiums, and household bills on a spindle; two little boxes engraved with Hebrew letters. One of these was for the poor, the other to buy back the Land of Israel. Each spring a bearded little man would suddenly appear in our kitchen, salute us with a hurried Hebrew blessing, empty the boxes (sometimes with a sidelong look of disdain if they were not full), hurriedly bless us again for remembering our less fortunate Jewish brothers and sisters, and so take his departure until the next spring, after vainly trying to persuade my mother to take still another box. We did occasionally remember to drop coins in the boxes, but this was usually only on the dreaded morning of "midterms" and final examinations, because my mother thought it would bring me luck. She was extremely superstitious, but embarrassed about it, and always laughed at herself whenever, on the morning of an examination, she counseled me to leave the house on my right foot. "I know it's silly," her smile seemed to say, "but what harm can it do? It may calm God down."

The kitchen gave a special character to our lives; my mother's character. 3 All my memories of that kitchen are dominated by the nearness of my mother sitting all day long at her sewing machine, by the clacking of the treadle against the linoleum floor, by the patient twist of her right shoulder as she automatically pushed at the wheel with one hand or lifted the foot to free the needle where it had got stuck in a thick piece of material. The kitchen was her life. Year by year, as I began to take in her fantastic capacity for labor and her anxious zeal, I realized it was ourselves she kept stitched together. I can never remember a time when she was not working. She worked because the law of her life was work, work and anxiety; she worked because she would have found life meaningless without work. She read almost no English; she could read the Yiddish paper, but never felt she had time to. We were always talking of a time when I would teach her how to read, but somehow there was never time. When I awoke in the morning she was already at her machine, or in the great morning crowd of housewives at the grocery getting fresh rolls for breakfast. When I returned from school she was at her machine, or conferring over *McCall's* with some neighborhood woman who had come in pointing hopefully to an illustration—"Mrs. Kazin! Mrs. Kazin! Make me a dress like it shows here in the picture!" When my father came home from work she had somehow mysteriously interrupted herself to make supper for us, and the dishes cleared and washed, was back at her machine. When I went to bed at night, often she was still there, pounding away at the treadle, hunched over the wheel, her hands steering a piece of gauze under the needle with a finesse that always contrasted sharply with her swollen hands and broken nails. Her left hand had been pierced through when as a girl she had worked in the infamous Triangle Shirtwaist Factory on the East Side. A needle had gone straight through the palm, severing a large vein. They had sewn it up for her so clumsily that a tuft of flesh always lay folded over the palm.

The kitchen was the great machine that set our lives running; it whirred   4
down a little only on Saturdays and holy days. From my mother's kitchen I gained my first picture of life as a white, overheated, starkly lit workshop redolent with Jewish cooking, crowded with women in housedresses, strewn with fashion magazines, patterns, dress material, spools of thread—and at whose center, so lashed to her machine that bolts of energy seemed to dance out of her hands and feet as she worked, my mother stamped the treadle hard against the floor, hard, hard, and silently, grimly at war, beat out the first rhythm of the world for me.

QUESTIONS

Words to Know

tenement (paragraph 1), innate (1), Passover *seder* (2), stippled (2), Triangle Shirtwaist Factory (3).

Some of the Issues

1. Kazin writes about the kitchen in his childhood home. Is he writing from the point of view of a child or an adult? What indications do you have of one or the other?
2. In speaking of his mother, Kazin says "The law of her life was work, work and anxiety." In an age of self-fulfillment this does not seem to be

a happy life. Can you find any evidence as to whether Mrs. Kazin was happy or unhappy? What pleasures did she have?

3. What is the meaning of the first sentence in paragraph 4? Why does Kazin call the kitchen "the great machine"?

4. Read N. Scott Momaday's "The Way to Rainy Mountain." Both Kazin and he describe a person and a place in relation to each other. How do the two descriptions differ? How do the descriptions of person and place reinforce each other in each case?

The Way We Are Told

5. Read the first sentence of each paragraph. What conclusions as to Kazin's purpose in the essay can you draw from them?

6. Compare the first two paragraphs. How do they differ from each other in content and in the way they are written?

7. Kazin talks about the kitchen of his childhood home but does not describe it until the second paragraph. What would be the effect if he had started with that description?

8. Reread the second paragraph. What details does Kazin give? How are they arranged—in which kind of order? Could an artist draw a picture on the basis of Kazin's description? Could an architect draw a plan from it?

9. Kazin describes several items in detail—the sewing machine, aspects of the kitchen itself, and his mother's work. Find some adjectives that stand out because they are unusual or that add precision or feeling to his descriptions.

Some Subjects for Essays

10. Write a paragraph about a place of significance for you, using Kazin's second paragraph as your model. Try to show its significance by the way you describe it.

11. Consider the role of work in the life of Kazin's mother. If you know someone whose life seems completely tied up with some specific activity, describe that person through his or her activity.

ANTONIA

Willa Cather

Willa Cather (1876–1947) was born in Virginia but moved to Red
Cloud, Nebraska, with her family as a child. She grew up among the
immigrant farmers described in her novel *My Ántonia* (1918) from
which the following excerpt is taken. After graduating from the University of Nebraska, she moved to New York where she became managing editor of a magazine but soon turned to the writing of fiction.
Her novels are mostly concerned with the traits of pioneer settlers,
family loyalties, and the struggle with nature. Often set in the Midwest
or Southwest, they include, in addition to *My Ántonia*, *O Pioneers*
(1913), *The Professor's House* (1925), and *Death Comes to the Arch-
bishop* (1927).

On Sunday morning Otto Fuchs was to drive us over to make the acquaint- 1
ance of our new Bohemian neighbours. We were taking them some provisions, as they had come to live on a wild place where there was no garden
or chicken-house, and very little broken land. Fuchs brought up a sack of
potatoes and a piece of cured pork from the cellar, and grandmother packed
some loaves of Saturday's bread, a jar of butter, and several pumpkin pies in
the straw of the wagon-box. We clambered up to the front seat and jolted
off past the little pond and along the road that climbed to the big cornfield.

I could hardly wait to see what lay beyond that cornfield; but there was 2
only red grass like ours, and nothing else, though from the high wagon-seat
one could look off a long way. The road ran about like a wild thing, avoiding
the deep draws, crossing them where they were wide and shallow. And all
along it, wherever it looped or ran, the sunflowers grew; some of them were
as big as little trees, with great rough leaves and many branches which bore
dozens of blossoms. They made a gold ribbon across the prairie. Occasionally
one of the horses would tear off with his teeth a plant full of blossoms, and
walk along munching it, the flowers nodding in time to his bites as he ate
down toward them.

The Bohemian family, grandmother told me as we drove along, had 3
bought the homestead of a fellow countryman, Peter Krajiek, and had paid
him more than it was worth. Their agreement with him was made before
they left the old country, through a cousin of his, who was also a relative of
Mrs. Shimerda. The Shimerdas were the first Bohemian family to come to
this part of the country. Krajiek was their only interpreter, and could tell
them anything he chose. They could not speak enough English to ask for

87

advice, or even to make their most pressing wants known. One son, Fuchs said, was well-grown, and strong enough to work the land; but the father was old and frail and knew nothing about farming. He was a weaver by trade; had been a skilled workman on tapestries and upholstery materials. He had brought his fiddle with him, which wouldn't be of much use here, though he used to pick up money by it at home.

'If they're nice people, I hate to think of them spending the winter in that cave of Krajiek's,' said grandmother. 'It's no better than a badger hole; no proper dugout at all. And I hear he's made them pay twenty dollars for his old cookstove that ain't worth ten.'   4

'Yes'm,' said Otto; 'and he's sold 'em his oxen and his two bony old horses for the price of good work-teams. I'd have interfered about the horses—the old man can understand some German—if I'd 'a' thought it would do any good. But Bohemians has a natural distrust of Austrians.'   5

Grandmother looked interested. 'Now, why is that, Otto?'   6

Fuchs wrinkled his brow and nose. 'Well, ma'm, it's politics. It would take me a long while to explain.'

The land was growing rougher; I was told that we were approaching Squaw Creek, which cut up the west half of the Shimerdas' place and made the land of little value for farming. Soon we could see the broken, grassy clay cliffs which indicated the windings of the stream, and the glittering tops of the cottonwoods and ash trees that grew down in the ravine. Some of the cottonwoods had already turned, and the yellow leaves and shining white bark made them look like the gold and silver trees in fairy tales.   8

As we approached the Shimerdas' dwelling, I could still see nothing but rough red hillocks, and draws with shelving banks and long roots hanging out where the earth had crumbled away. Presently, against one of those banks, I saw a sort of shed, thatched with the same wine-coloured grass that grew everywhere. Near it tilted a shattered windmill frame, that had no wheel. We drove up to this skeleton to tie our horses, and then I saw a door and window sunk deep in the drawbank. The door stood open, and a woman and a girl of fourteen ran out and looked up at us hopefully. A little girl trailed along behind them. The woman had on her head the same embroidered shawl with silk fringes that she wore when she had alighted from the train at Black Hawk. She was not old, but she was certainly not young. Her face was alert and lively, with a sharp chin and shrewd little eyes. She shook grandmother's hand energetically.   9

'Very glad, very glad!' she ejaculated. Immediately she pointed to the bank out of which she had emerged and said, 'House no good, house no good!'   10

Grandmother nodded consolingly. 'You'll get fixed up comfortable after while, Mrs. Shimerda; make good house.'   11

My grandmother always spoke in a very loud tone to foreigners, as if   12
they were deaf. She made Mrs. Shimerda understand the friendly intention
of our visit, and the Boheniam woman handled the loaves of bread and even
smelled them, and examined the pies with lively curiosity, exclaiming,
'Much good, much thank!'—and again she wrung grandmother's hand.

The oldest son, Ambrož—they called it Ambrosch—came out of the   13
cave and stood beside his mother. He was nineteen years old, short and
broad-backed, with a close-cropped, flat head, and a wide, flat face. His hazel
eyes were little and shrewd, like his mother's, but more sly and suspicious;
they fairly snapped at the food. The family had been living on corncakes
and sorghum molasses for three days.

The little girl was pretty, but Án-tonia—they accented the name thus,   14
strongly, when they spoke to her—was still prettier. I remembered what the
conductor had said about her eyes. They were big and warm and full of light,
like the sun shining on brown pools in the wood. Her skin was brown, too,
and in her cheeks she had a glow of rich, dark colour. Her brown hair was
curly and wild-looking. The little sister, whom they called Yulka (Julka), was
fair, and seemed mild and obedient. While I stood awkwardly confronting
the two girls, Krajiek came up from the barn to see what was going on. With
him was another Shimerda son. Even from a distance one could see that
there was something strange about this boy. As he approached us, he began
to make uncouth noises, and held up his hands to show us his fingers, which
were webbed to the first knuckle, like a duck's foot. When he saw me draw
back, he began to crow delightedly, 'Hoo, hoo-hoo, hoo-hoo!' like a rooster.
His mother scowled and said sternly, 'Marek!' then spoke rapidly to Krajiek
in Bohemian.

'She wants me to tell you he won't hurt nobody, Mrs. Burden. He was   15
born like that. The others are smart. Ambrosch, he make good farmer.' He
struck Ambrosch on the back, and the boy smiled knowingly.

At that moment the father came out of the hole in the bank. He wore   16
no hat, and his thick, iron-grey hair was brushed straight back from his forehead. It was so long that it brushed out behind his ears, and made him look
like the old portraits I remembered in Virginia. He was tall and slender, and
his thin shoulders stooped. He looked at us understandingly, then took grandmother's hand and bent over it. I noticed how white and well-shaped his
own hands were. They looked calm, somehow, and skilled. His eyes were
melancholy, and were set back deep under his brow. His face was ruggedly
formed, but it looked like ashes—like something from which all the warmth
and light had died out. Everything about this old man was in keeping with
his dignified manner. He was neatly dressed. Under his coat he wore a knit-
ted grey vest, and, instead of a collar, a silk scarf of a dark bronze-green,
carefully crossed and held together by a red coral pin. While Krajiek was

translating for Mr. Shimerda, Ántonia came up to me and held out her hand coaxingly. In a moment we were running up the steel drawside together, Yulka trotting after us.

When we reached the level and could see the gold tree-tops, I pointed toward them, and Ántonia laughed and squeezed my hand as if to tell me how glad she was I had come. We raced off toward Squaw Creek and did not stop until the ground itself stopped—fell away before us so abruptly that the next step would have been out into the tree-tops. We stood panting on the edge of the ravine, looking down at the trees and bushes that grew below us. The wind was so strong that I had to hold my hat on, and the girls' skirts were blown out before them. Ántonia seemed to like it; she held her little sister by the hand and chattered away in that language which seemed to me spoken so much more rapidly than mine. She looked at me, her eyes fairly blazing with things she could not say.   17

'Name? What name?' she asked, touching me on the shoulder. I told her my name, and she repeated it after me and made Yulka say it. She pointed into the gold cottonwood tree behind whose top we stood and said again, 'What name?'   18

We sat down and made a nest in the long red grass. Yulka curled up like a baby rabbit and played with a grasshopper. Ántonia pointed up to the sky and questioned me with her glance. I gave her the word, but she was not satisfied and pointed to my eyes. I told her, and she repeated the word, making it sound like 'ice.' She pointed up to the sky, then to my eyes, then back to the sky, with movements so quick and impulsive that she distracted me, and I had no idea what she wanted. She got up on her knees and wrung her hands. She pointed to her own eyes and shook her head, then to mine and to the sky, nodding violently.   19

'Oh,' I exclaimed, 'blue, blue sky.'   20

She clapped her hands and murmured, 'Blue sky, blue eyes,' as if it amused her. While we snuggled down there out of the wind, she learned a score of words. She was quick, and very eager. We were so deep in the grass that we could see nothing but the blue sky over us and the gold tree in front of us. It was wonderfully pleasant. After Ántonia had said the new words over and over, she wanted to give me a little chased silver ring she wore on her middle finger. When she coaxed and insisted, I repulsed her quite sternly. I didn't want her ring, and I felt there was something reckless and extravagant about her wishing to give it away to a boy she had never seen before. No wonder Krajiek got the better of these people, if this was how they behaved.   21

While we were disputing about the ring, I heard a mournful voice calling, 'Án-tonia, Án-tonia!' She sprang up like a hare. '*Tatinek! Tatinek!*' she   22 shouted, and we ran to meet the old man who was coming toward us. Ántonia reached him first, took his hand and kissed it. When I came up, he touched my shoulder and looked searchingly down into my face for several seconds. I became somewhat embarrassed, for I was used to being taken for granted by my elders.

We went with Mr. Shimerda back to the dugout, where grandmother was waiting for me. Before I got into the wagon, he took a book out of his pocket, opened it, and showed me a page with two alphabets, one English and the other Bohemian. He placed this book in my grandmother's hands, looked at her entreatingly, and said, with an earnestness which I shall never forget, 'Te-e-ach, te-e-ach my Án-tonia!'

QUESTIONS

Words to Know

Bohemian (paragraph 1), clambered (1), draws (2), frail (3), thatched (9), uncouth (14), ravine (17), entreatingly (23).

Some of the Issues

1. What particular hardships or difficulties do the Shimerdas encounter in their new country?
2. The narrator is a young boy. How does this affect the story? How would it change if the narrator were Otto Fuchs? The grandmother?
3. What criticism of the Shimerdas is implied in the conversation between Fuchs and the grandmother (paragraphs 4 through 7)? Why doesn't Fuchs interfere when he sees the Shimerdas being cheated? Is his own explanation for his refusal to do so satisfactory?
4. Mr. Shimerda is the one who is described in greatest detail (paragraph 16). Why?
5. Explain the episode of the ring (paragraph 21). What is its meaning, and how does it contribute to our understanding of the Shimerdas? Of the narrator?
6. How are we shown, step by step, that the Shimerdas are different? Which differences are personal? Which are more the result of the fam-

ily's newness in the country? Which are what one might call cultural differences?

7. Though neither Fuchs nor the grandmother may be conscious of it, they seem to feel superior to the Shimerdas. How does Cather make that clear?

The Way We Are Told

8. How does Willa Cather prepare us for the Shimerdas and for the conditions in which they live? How does she build our knowledge? What would be the effect if she started her description with the narrator's arrival at the Shimerdas' home?
9. Throughout the selection the problem of communication, or miscommunication, is very prominent, involving, at one time or another, all nine of the characters. Select examples of how Cather emphasizes its crucial importance.

Some Ideas for Essays

10. Rewrite the scene of the visit from Ántonia's point of view.
11. Describe a first encounter with a person you had previously heard about. Explain your expectations and then relate the reality of the encounter. What were the differences?

MARRIAGE

Helen Sekaquaptewa

Helen Sekaquaptewa was born in the early years of the twentieth century in Oraibi, one of the 11 Hopi villages in the arid plateau country of northeastern Arizona. She was raised there in the traditions of the Hopi. In later years, when she was living in Phoenix and taking care of her grandchildren, she met Louise Udall and had long talks with her. From these talks developed the idea that she tell the story of her life to Ms. Udall who would then write what eventually became the book, *Me and Mine* (1969), from which the following excerpt is taken.

THE HOME OF THE bridegroom is the center of activity in a Hopi wedding. When a couple decides to marry, the father of the groom takes over. He furnishes everything—cotton for the weaving and food to feed the workers during the time the weaving is in progress. Each household keeps a supply of cotton on hand against the time when a son may marry. 1

In Emory's case there was a problem. His parents had separated years before and his mother had remarried and lived in Oraibi. Emory lived with his mother during his childhood; Wickvaya, Emory's grandfather, also lived in the same household. This is why Wickvaya took his grandson to school at Keams Canyon and brought him back in the spring. Emory's father was among the men sent to the Indian School at Carlisle in Pennsylvania for five years, in 1906. When he returned he went to Hotevilla to live, and in due-time remarried. Emory had never lived with his father. 2

Emory's mother wanted us to come to her home in Oraibi, but Emory had been away at school so many years that it wasn't really home to him. As he grew older he had lived in Bacabi, with his cousin Susie and her husband, who was his godfather, during the summers that he was home, helping in whatever way he could. Susie invited us to come to her home, and Emory's uncles and cousins all helped put in for the cotton and food and were the hosts for us. 3

After we decided to get married, I spent every minute that I could grinding in preparation for feeding the wedding guests. Women and girls of my relatives who wanted to help started grinding too. When my sister Verlie walked with me to Bacabi to Susie's house, I carried a big pan full of fine white cornmeal. I never left Susie's house for the entire period (about a month) and was under her watchful care, even slept with her the first three nights. 4

93

As a bride I was considered sacred the first few days, being in a room   5
with the shades on the windows, talking to no one. All this time I was steadily
grinding corn which was brought in by Emory's kinswomen. Each brought,
say, a quart of corn in a basket or on a plaque to be passed in to me to be
ground, each lot separately. After the first grinding I handed the corn out
and waited while it was roasted and passed back to me to be ground real
fine. As each lot was finished, I put it back into its own container, lining it
up along the wall with others. When the aunts came back in the evening to
get their corn there was food on the table and they ate. White corn was the
grist the first day, blue corn on the second and third days. At the end of each
day Susie gave me a relaxing rubdown.

Early each morning of the first three days, Cousin Susie went with me   6
to the east edge of the mesa, and there, facing the rising sun, we bowed our
heads and each offered a silent prayer for a happy married life. Our days
began with the rising of the sun and ended with its setting, because there
was no artificial light for night working.

The fourth day is the actual wedding day. Everyone of the relatives is   7
up when the cock crows, to participate in the marriage ritual, the hair washing. Suds are made from the tuber of the yucca root, pounded into a pulp,
put into two basins of water, and worked with the hands until the pan is
filled with foamy suds.

Two pans were placed side by side on the floor, where Susie and my   8
sister Verlie prepared the suds. Usually the mothers of the bride and groom
do this. Susie and Verlie acted for our mothers. While Susie washed my hair,
Verlie washed Emory's. Then each took a strand of hair and twisted them
together hard and tight as a symbol of acceptance of the new in-law into the
clan (family) and also to bind the marriage contract, as they said, "Now you
are united, never to go apart."

Next Emory was taken outside and stripped to the waist by the women   9
of my family. Each had brought her small container of water which she
poured over his shoulders as he knelt over a tub. They splashed the water
over him with their hands. It was still dark, so they could not see him; they
put a blanket around him, and he came back into the house to get warm
from that icy bath.

Now, with our hair still wet and hanging loose, Emory and I walked   10
together to the eastern edge of the village and once more faced the rising
sun, and with bowed heads we prayed in silence for a long time; for a good
life together, for children, and to be together all of our lives and never stray
from each other.

After my hair was dry on this day, they combed it up like a married   11
woman, never to be worn in maiden style again. Married women parted
their hair from the center in the front to the nape of the neck. Each side was

folded over the hand until it reached nearly to the ear where it was bound with a cord made from hair and a little yarn, leaving a soft puff at the ends. The hair in front of the ears was cut into sideburns about two inches long.

The making of the robes begins on the morning of the nuptial hair washing. The father or uncle of the groom (in our case Susie's father) took a bag of cotton and, passing through the village, stopped at each house. He was expected, and each housewife opened her door and extended a plaque to receive some cotton (everyone was required to wash his hands before touching the cotton). Immediately all hands went to work cleaning the cotton of seeds, burrs, and little sticks. It was all cleaned that same day. 12

In the evening the uncles, godfather, and men who wished to help, gathered at the groom's house to card the cotton. The cards were a pair of flat, wire-toothed brushes, four by twelve inches, with wooden handles at a slight angle, on the long side. They were bought from the trader and used for both wool and cotton. I watched my father and my grandfather use them in my time. A small handful of cotton was spread over all the teeth of one card; with the second card, the cotton was combed back and forth until all the lumps were out and it became fluffy. Another motion made it into a strip as long as the card, which strip was put aside and another one started. The men worked late carding big piles of white cotton. Coal-oil lamps lighted their work. During this time the men told stories, with the bride sitting nearby, along with the kinswomen. From time to time the bride thanked the workers for their service. Everyone enjoyed the stories, and before they realized it, it was midnight and quitting time. The men were served refreshments and everyone went home to bed. It took several nights to do the carding. 13

All the men in the village worked to spin this cotton into thread in one day. Food was obtained and prepared to feed the whole village. Ten or fifteen sheep were required. If the host didn't have sheep of his own, he bought them. One or two might be donated by someone. Wood had to be brought in for the cooking and to heat the kivas. 14

At sunrise on spinning day the custodian of each kiva went early to clean up his kiva and start the fire and get it warm. The women were busy too, putting the big kettles on the fire and adding ingredients for the stew, making ready every plaque and basket. 15

After his breakfast, each man went to his kiva, taking his spindle (every adult male owns one). Emory's uncle came around early to deliver to each kiva the carded cotton to be spun. In Bacabi there were three kivas. Soon all spindles were humming away. Emory's uncle checked the kivas from time to time to keep them all supplied with carded cotton. Dinner would be late, so they were served a snack at noon in the kiva. The spun cotton was made 16 into skeins; the warp thread was finer than the woof. The pile of light, fluffy hanks of warp and woof thread was beautiful.

In the meantime the women were getting the food and tables ready. 17 My relatives and myself were served earlier so we could be free to serve the community dinner. However, the bride did not serve but mingled with the other women. They teased me as all made merry and had a happy time. The men were served at the tables in Susie's house and neighboring houses as needed, and then the women and children of the village ate. Whatever food was left, especially the stew, was divided among the people.

The weaving took about two weeks, and it began a few days after the 18 spinning was finished. One sheep was butchered this time, and the other foods were made ready for the first day of the weaving. At dawn and before breakfast the three special looms used in wedding weaving were brought out from their storage place to the kiva (one kiva) where they were untied and spread out on the floor. Two or three men at a time worked at the long and tedious job of stringing each loom, rolling the warp back and forth to each other, over the notches close together on the two end poles.

The bridal clothing consisted of a robe six by eight feet, a second one 19 about four by six feet to cover the shoulders, and a girdle about ten inches wide and eight feet long, which is tied around the waist. The moccasins had leggings made of white buckskin. Then there is the reed roll, which is a sort of suitcase in which to wrap and carry extra gifts. Emory gathered the reed from the edge of the wash, cut them into uniform lengths and tied them together with cord like a bamboo window blind.

The threaded looms were hung from loops in the ceiling beams and 20 fastened to loops on the floor and stretched tight, and the weaving began, the best weavers taking turns during the day. The belt is braided rather than woven.

At noon, food was brought to the kiva by relatives. After dinner a man 21 took his place at each loom and worked until evening. The host did not weave all the time, but he stayed with them at all times. In the evening each man carried the loom he had worked on to Susie's house, where I received them and put them away in a back room for safekeeping. The men sat down to eat of piki and beans and leftover food from dinner and somviki, which is tamales made from finely ground blue corn, sweetened and wrapped in corn husks, and tied with yucca strips and then boiled, and made by the bride every evening. As the weavers left after supper, I gave each of them a few tamales on top of a folded piki. Each morning the weaving continued. Only one man could work on each loom at a time, but the best weavers came and took turns during the day. Other men came, bringing their spinning or knitting, or just sat and visited and listened as the older men retold the traditional stories. Sometimes they all sang together.

About halfway through the rites, our consciences troubled us, because   22
we felt the Hopi way was not quite right. We decided to get a license and
be married legally. Emory told his folks what we wanted to do. He made
application to the agency at Keams Canyon, and a marriage license was
obtained by mail from Holbrook, the nearest county seat. It took about a
week. In the afternoon that the license came, I went to my father's house in
Hotevilla; Emory went with me. I just walked in and told my father that I
was going to be married by license that night and had come to get my
clothes. I could feel the disapproval of my father and my sister as I gathered
the things I was going to wear. I just could not stay there and get dressed. I
took my clothes and went to one of the school teachers, and she let me dress
in her house.

I was married in a white batiste dress, which was my pride and joy. I   23
had earned the money and bought the material and made the dress in
domestic art class in the Phoenix school. It had lace insertion set in bow knots
around the gathered skirt, on the flared sleeves, and on the collar. My teacher
had entered it in the State Fair, and I got second prize on it. I wore it once
to a party and then decided it was too nice to wear and put it away in a box.

Later I made this dress into two little dresses for my first baby, our little   24
girl "Joy." About the second time that I hung these dresses out on the clothes-
line to dry, one of them disappeared. Two years later I was getting water at
the spring one day, and there was a little two-year-old girl playing around,
wearing that dress. I took her by the hand, led her to my house, and took off
the dress (it was too little for her anyway). I put a nice colorful gingham
dress on her, and gave her some bread and jam. She was pleased with it all,
as I opened the door and sent her home. I heard no more on that. My babies
wore out those dresses.

We were married in the evening on February 14, 1919, in the living   25
room of the home of Mr. Anderson, principal of the school in Hotevilla, by
Reverend Dirkson of the Mennonite Mission. Emory's people, including
some of his cousins, came to the ceremony. The teachers served some refreshments and gave us some little presents and a room where we could spend
the night. In the morning they served a wedding breakfast, and then we
went back to finish the tribal wedding rites at Bacabi.

Emory was working at the school and had to be on the job, so he wasn't   26
able to participate in the weaving during the daytime. The activity died
down after the first few days anyway, the weavers carrying on until everything was done. I helped with the grinding and cooking until the outfit was
completed.

When the weaving was finished the men took the robes from the looms   27
and brought them into the house to be tried on. A border of sixteen running

stitches in red was embroidered in the two corners, suggesting a limit of sixteen children, the most a person should have, and four stitches in each of the other two corners in orange, suggesting a minimum number of children. The white moccasins with leggings in one piece were finished just in time to be put on with the rest of the outfit. It was by then evening; food was placed before the guests and everyone ate again. (Hopis do not invite you to eat. They set the food before you, and the food invites.)

The next morning before sunup, Susie led the others in clothing me, first washing my hair. Everyone admired the bride, and I was now ready to go back to my father's house. A line of white cornmeal was sprinkled on the ground, pointing the way. There was a lot of snow on the ground, so they wrapped rags over my white moccasins so I wouldn't get them wet or muddy. Emory's people went with me out of the village and over the little hill back to my home in Hotevilla. Emory did not go with me this time. How I wished that my own dear mother could be there to meet me. The sun was just coming up when we got to my father's house. Verlie opened the door, and my father thanked them for the beautiful bridal apparel that would make his daughter eligible to enter the world of the hereafter. Thus ends the wedding ritual. 28

I went inside and removed the wedding apparel and spread it out on the bed. Then all the clan women came in and admired and tried on the robes. Then everything was rolled up and stored away. After a period of time these may be used as needed, even cut into kilts for men to wear or to make bags to carry packs on burros. 29

A bride of the village who has been married in the preceding year should dress in her complete bridal attire and go into the plaza at the time of the Home Dance, accompanied by her mother-in-law, and show herself to the kachinas during their last round of the day, thus establishing her status as a married woman in their eyes. We had gone to Idaho but were back by the Home Dance in July. My father had shown his disapproval of me by cutting up my big robe and making little kilts out of it. I had taken the small robe with me. I had my moccasins and did make this appearance, accompanied by Susie. 30

Miss Abbott came to see me once during the thirty days of the tribal ceremony. She said she did not want to embarrass me, but she whispered in my ear, "You have never looked better in your life. You look healthy and happy. You have rosy cheeks. This has done you good." 31

The groom may follow the bride to her home as soon as he likes. Some go right away, some wait a long time before claiming their brides. Emory came over after a few days and stayed a couple of nights, but I could see 32 that the tension and hostility was hard on him; too many children, too little room, not even a room to ourselves. After my going through all that ceremony just to please my family, my sister was still so hostile that I felt neither wanted nor welcome.

One day, about a month after we were married, when no one was at home, I felt that I could not stand it another minute. I gathered and packed my belongings, as many as I could carry, returning later for the rest of them, and went to the house where Emory lived near the school. He was at his work teaching shop when I got there. I cleaned up the house and had a meal cooked when he came home, and we were real happy. Soon afterward I got a job teaching beginners in the school. It was hard to get teachers there because it was so isolated.

QUESTIONS

Words to Know

kinswomen (paragraph 5), grist (5), mesa (6), tuber (7), nape (11), nuptial (12), carding (13), kiva (14), warp (16), rites (22), kachina (30).

Some of the Issues

1. What does the first paragraph tell the reader about Hopi weddings? How do the practices it describes differ from the general Western view regarding weddings?
2. Which is the actual wedding day? What does the wedding consist of? What is its symbolic meaning?
3. In a Hopi marriage women's work and men's work are clearly separate. How would you characterize the duties of each sex?
4. There are practical as well as symbolic aspects to the complex of ceremonies and activities that make up a Hopi marriage ceremony. What is practical about the activities?
5. Helen's father disapproves of her (paragraph 22). How does he manifest his disapproval?
6. Are there are indications of the influence of white society on Hopi customs?

The Way We Are Told

7. Helen Sekaquaptewa tells her story in a very straightforward way, with short, declarative sentences. At a few points she modifies her description by talking about about feelings. Give some examples.

Some Subjects for Essays

8. Describe a ceremony you participated in—for example, a graduation—concentrating on the accuracy of the description and keeping the expression of your feelings and attitudes to a minimum.
9. Describe an event—a journey, an accident, a party—in the same manner.
10. Compare the symbolism of a Hopi wedding to that of another traditional wedding ceremony you are familiar with. What are the symbols used in each tradition and what do they mean? In particular, select several Hopi symbols and determine what some appropriate complementary symbols would be in the ceremony you have chosen to describe.

DIARY

Carolina Maria de Jesus

Carolina Maria de Jesus, the child of illiterate Brazilian farm workers, was born in 1913. She learned to read in the space of three months but had altogether no more than two years of schooling. In her youth she worked at various jobs until her first pregnancy forced her to give up regular work and, like thousands of other penniless people, build her own shack of boards and tin cans in one of Brazil's *favelas*, or slums. She bore seven children, only three of whom survived infancy. She kept a diary which a news reporter discovered and persuaded her to publish. It appeared in book form in 1960, became Brazil's all-time best-seller, and was instrumental in promoting some reforms in the slums that surround Brazil's major cities.

July 15, 1955 The birthday of my daughter Vera Eunice. I wanted to buy a pair of shoes for her, but the price of food keeps us from realizing our desires. Actually we are slaves to the cost of living. I found a pair of shoes in the garbage, washed them, and patched them for her to wear.

I didn't have one cent to buy bread. So I washed three bottles and traded them to Arnaldo. He kept the bottles and gave me bread. Then I went to sell my paper. I received 65 cruzeiros. I spent 20 cruzeiros for meat. I got one kilo of ham and one kilo of sugar and spent six cruzeiros on cheese. And the money was gone.

I was ill all day. I thought I had a cold. At night my chest pained me. I started to cough. I decided not to go out at night to look for paper. I searched for my son João. He was at Felisberto de Carvalho Street near the market. A bus had knocked a boy into the sidewalk and a crowd gathered. João was in the middle of it all. I poked him a couple of times and within five minutes he was home.

I washed the children, put them to bed, then washed myself and went to bed. I waited until 11:00 for a certain someone. He didn't come. I took an aspirin and laid down again. When I awoke the sun was sliding in space. My daughter Vera Eunice said: "Go get some water, Mother!"

July 16 I got up and obeyed Vera Eunice. I went to get the water. I made coffee. I told the children that I didn't have any bread, that they would have to drink their coffee plain and eat meat with *farinha*. I was feeling ill and decided to cure myself. I stuck my finger down my throat twice, vomited, and knew I was under the evil eye. The upset feeling left and I went to Senhor Manuel, carrying some cans to sell. Everything that I find in the

101

garbage I sell. He gave me 13 cruzeiros. I kept thinking that I had to buy bread, soap, and milk for Vera Eunice. The 13 cruzeiros wouldn't make it. I returned home, or rather to my shack, nervous and exhausted. I thought of the worrisome life that I led. Carrying paper, washing clothes for the children, staying in the street all day long. Yet I'm always lacking things, Vera doesn't have shoes and she doesn't like to go barefoot. For at least two years I've wanted to buy a meat grinder. And a sewing machine.

I came home and made lunch for the two boys. Rice, beans, and meat, and I'm going out to look for paper. I left the children, told them to play in the yard and not go into the street, because the terrible neighbors I have won't leave my children alone. I was feeling ill and wished I could lie down. But the poor don't rest nor are they permitted the pleasure of relaxation. I was nervous inside, cursing my luck. I collected two sacks full of paper. Afterward I went back and gathered up some scrap metal, some cans, and some kindling wood. As I walked I thought—when I return to the favela there is going to be something new. Maybe Dona Rosa or the insolent Angel Mary fought with my children. I found Vera Eunice sleeping and the boys playing in the street. I thought: it's 2:00. Maybe I'm going to get through this day without anything happening. João told me that the truck that gives out money was here to give out food. I took a sack and hurried out. It was the leader of the Spiritist Center at 103 Vergueiro Street. I got two kilos of rice, two of beans, and two kilos of macaroni. I was happy. The truck went away. The nervousness that I had inside left me. I took advantage of my calmness to read. I picked up a magazine and sat on the grass, letting the rays of the sun warm me as I read a story. I wrote a note and gave it to my boy João to take to Senhor Arnaldo to buy soap, two aspirins, and some bread. Then I put water on the stove to make coffee. João came back saying he had lost the aspirins. I went back with him to look. We didn't find them.

When I came home there was a crowd at my door. Children and women claiming José Carlos had thrown stones at their houses. They wanted me to punish him.

July 17   Sunday   A marvelous day. The sky was blue without one cloud. The sun was warm. I got out of bed at 6:30 and went to get water. I only had one piece of bread and three cruzeiros. I gave a small piece to each child and put the beans, that I got yesterday from the Spiritist Center, on the fire. Then I went to wash clothes. When I returned from the river the beans were cooked. The children asked for bread. I gave the three cruzeiros to João to go and buy some. Today it was Nair Mathias who started an argument with my children. Silvia and her husband have begun an open-air spectacle. He is hitting her and I'm disgusted because the children are present.

They heard words of the lowest kind. Oh, if I could move from here to a more decent neighborhood!

I went to Dona Florela to ask for a piece of garlic. I went to Dona Analia   9
and got exactly what I expected:

"I don't have any!"   10

I went to collect my clothes. Dona Aparecida asked me: 11

"Are you pregnant?"   12

"No, Senhora," I replied gently.   13

I cursed her under my breath. If I am pregnant it's not your business. I   14
can't stand these favela women, they want to know everything. Their
tongues are like chicken feet. Scratching at everything. The rumor is circu-
lating that I am pregnant! If I am, I don't know about it!

I went out at night to look for paper. When I was passing the São Paulo   15
football stadium many people were coming out. All of them were white and
only one black. And the black started to insult me:

"Are you looking for paper, auntie? Watch your step, auntie dear!"   16

I was ill and wanted to lie down, but I went on. I met several friends   17
and stopped to talk to them. When I was going up Tiradentes Avenue I met
some women. One of them asked me:

"Are your legs healed?"   18

After I was operated on, I got better, thanks to God. I could even dance   19
at Carnival in my feather costume. Dr. José Torres Netto was who operated
on me. A good doctor. And we spoke of politics. When a woman asked me
what I thought of Carlos Lacerda [President of Brazil from 1956 to 1961], I
replied truthfully:

"He is very intelligent, but he doesn't have an education. He is a slum   20
politician. He likes intrigues, to agitate."

One woman said it was a pity, that the bullet that got the major didn't   21
get Carlos Lacerda.

"But his day . . . it's coming," commented another.   22

Many people had gathered and I was the center of attention. I was   23
embarrassed because I was looking for paper and dressed in rags. I didn't
want to talk to anyone, because I had to collect paper. I needed the money.
There was none in the house to buy bread. I worked until 11:30. When I
returned home it was midnight. I warmed up some food, gave some to Vera
Eunice, ate and laid down. When I awoke the rays of the sun were coming
through the gaps of the shack.

QUESTIONS

Words to Know

cruzeiro—unit of Brazilian currency (paragraph 2), kilo (2), *farinha*—coarse wheat flour (5).

Some of the Issues

1. Carolina Maria de Jesus records events of her daily existence. What makes them interesting?
2. Occasionally de Jesus interrupts her record of events for a comment. Find several of these and try to show how they relate to the details she gives.
3. How does de Jesus separate herself from the other women in the *favela?*

The Way We Are Told

4. Some of the reasons for the effectiveness of the de Jesus diary are the absence of self-pity and her way of understating the hardships of her existence. Find and analyze two or three examples of each.
5. The usual account we read of slum life is written by a social scientist or journalist—an outsider. De Jesus' account differs in telling the story from the inside. Find several elements in the diary that indicate that difference.

Some Subjects For Essays

6. Keep a journal for three days—three entries at least—and record what happens to you, nothing else.
7. Then keep a journal for a week, recording the events of your life, together with some of your reactions to them and your thoughts about them.

FOUR

Encounters

*The word ghetto is of Italian origin, although the first compulsory ghet-
tos were probably in Spain and Portugal as early as the fourteenth
century. Ghettos have always been overcrowded, unsanitary, depressing
places in which a majority segregates a minority: Jews in Europe, Blacks
in America. In former times official rules limited the access of these segregated people to the rest of the city, through numerical restrictions, cur-
fews, and the like. Later, as for example in America, there were no such
rules and the inhabitants of the ghetto could leave it, although often at
their own peril. In any case, clear lines could be drawn on a map to show
where certain people lived or were forced to live. Encounters between them
and the rest of the population were thereby limited, and mutual ignorance,
breeding distrust and hate, was intensified.*

*In a country as diverse in racial, ethnic, religious, and cultural com-
position as the United States, the lines of segregation that can be drawn
on the maps of its urban areas tell only part of the story. In America, one
might say, there are ghettos of the mind as well as of the body, and cross-
cultural contacts—or noncontacts—are of a complexity and sometimes of
an explosiveness that culturally homogeneous countries do not experience.*

*The first selection describes such an explosive encounter. The year was
1906. Walter White lived with his large family in Atlanta near the line
that separated the white community from his own. In September of that
year White's family was swept up in an historical event: the race riot which
he describes in this excerpt from his autobiography.*

*Piri Thomas describes a more common occurrence, one that many
young people have experienced: being the new kid on the block. Changing
neighborhoods or cities and going to a new school are likely to produce
anxiety. Piri Thomas had more reason than most to be nervous when his
family moved just a few blocks from his old home in New York City; he is
a Puerto Rican, and the block to which he moved was solidly Italian. He
describes what happened there.*

*With the Houstons' "Arrival at Manzanar," we turn once more to a
story of people who were caught up in an historical event. In the early
months of 1942, with the United States still in retreat after the Japanese
attack on Pearl Harbor, fear and anger turned popular feeling against Japanese-Americans, especially on the West Coast. On government orders,
thousands of these American citizens of Japanese descent—men, women,
and children—were rounded up and put in hastily constructed internment
camps where most of them had to spend the war years. They were deprived
of their businesses and belongings, which they either had to sell for next to
nothing or abandon completely. Jeanne Houston tells that it took her 30
years to be able to talk about her family's internment.*

*In the next two selections, members of two other minorities, a native
American and a Chinese-American, express their anger with bitter humor.
Vine Deloria, a Sioux, compares the treatment of Indians and Blacks. He*

accounts for the differences in how the dominant society treated them, sarcastically explaining why and how it suited the majority to make those distinctions.

In "Confessions of a Number One Son," Frank Chin, a playwright and Hollywood scriptwriter, parodies the stereotype of the Chinese in American films. He describes the hypocrisy behind the image that Hollywood filmmakers have created.

Directly or by implication, the accusations leveled by all these writers are against an unnamed majority. Who is this majority? That it is white one can assume, but upon closer examination we find that it in turn consists of groups that see themselves as the objects of discrimination and that the stereotypes of them are just as untrue as those of Indians, Blacks, or Chinese. Michael Novak attacks the discrimination that is practiced, he asserts, against "white ethnics": largely working class, Catholic, patriotic, hard working, socially conservative, and frequently accused of racial prejudice. He explains their origins, their struggles, and their resentment that they, unlike Blacks or Indians, have never received the compassion of that undefined majority that all these writers have talked about.

Who, then, is left? Only the WASPS—the White, Anglo-Saxon Protestants who, as Robert Claiborne says in their defense, are themselves a minority. Although he grants that in some respects they have a more favorable position than other groups, he asserts that they deserve credit for the development of representative government and for that freedom of expression which enables the other groups to complain about them.

Three pieces of satire conclude these encounters. Two are prose pieces: one American and one British (or Irish), one modern, one old. Jerry Gambill, a Mohawk Indian, outlines 21 ways to steal human rights. Jonathan Swift, writing more than 250 years ago, makes a proposal, which he calls modest, to solve the problems of starvation in Ireland.

The last selection is a poem by Eve Merriam, "A Wasp Hymn," that addresses the basic complaints of all of the others.

I LEARN WHAT I AM

Walter White

Walter White was born in Atlanta, Georgia, in 1893. He joined the NAACP early in its development and served as its head from 1931 until his death in 1955. The following excerpt is taken from his autobiography, *A Man Called White* (1948).

There were nine light-skinned Negroes in my family: mother, father, five sisters, an older brother, George, and myself. The house in which I discovered what it meant to be a Negro was located on Houston Street, three blocks from the Candler Building, Atlanta's first skyscraper, which bore the name of the ex-drug clerk who had become a millionaire from the sale of Coca-Cola. Below us lived none but Negroes; toward town all but a very few were white. Ours was an eight room, two-story frame house which stood out in its surroundings not because of its opulence but by contrast with the drabness and unpaintedness of the other dwellings in a deteriorating neighborhood.

Only Father kept his house painted, the picket fence repaired, the board fence separating our place from those on either side whitewashed, the grass neatly trimmed, and flower beds abloom. Mother's passion for neatness was even more pronounced and it seemed to me that I was always the victim of her determination to see no single blade of grass longer than the others or any one of the pickets in the front fence less shiny with paint than its mates. This spic-and-spanness became increasingly apparent as the rest of the neighborhood became more down-at-heel, and resulted, as we were to learn, in sullen envy among some of our white neighbors. It was the violent expression of that resentment against a Negro family neater than themselves which set the pattern of our lives.

On a day in September 1906, when I was thirteen, we were taught that there is no isolation from life. The unseasonably oppressive heat of an Indian summer day hung like a steaming blanket over Atlanta. My sisters and I had casually commented upon the unusual quietness. It seemed to stay Mother's volubility and reduced Father, who was more taciturn, to monosyllables. But, as I remember it, no other sense of impending trouble impinged upon our consciousness.

I had read the inflammatory headlines in the *Atlanta News* and the more restrained ones in the *Atlanta Constitution* which reported alleged rapes and other crimes committed by Negroes. But these were so standard and familiar that they made—as I look back on it now—little impression.

The stories were more frequent, however, and consisted of eight-column streamers instead of the usual two- or four-column ones.

Father was a mail collector. His tour of duty was from three to eleven 5 P.M. He made his rounds in a little cart into which one climbed from a step in the rear. I used to drive the cart for him from two until seven, leaving him at the point nearest our home on Houston Street, to return home either for study or sleep. That day Father decided that I should not go with him. I appealed to Mother, who thought it might be all right, provided Father sent me home before dark because, she said, "I don't think they would dare start anything before nightfall." Father told me as we made the rounds that ominous rumors of a race riot that night were sweeping the town. But I was too young that morning to understand the background of the riot. I became much older during the next thirty-six hours, under circumstances which I now recognize as the inevitable outcome of what had preceded. . . .

During the afternoon preceding the riot little bands of sullen, evil-look- 6 ing men talked excitedly on street corners all over downtown Atlanta. Around seven o'clock my father and I were driving toward a mail box at the corner of Peachtree and Houston Streets when there came from near-by Pryor Street a roar the like of which I had never heard before, but which sent a sensation of mingled fear and excitement coursing through my body. I asked permission of Father to go and see what the trouble was. He bluntly ordered me to stay in the cart. A little later we drove down Atlanta's main business thoroughfare, Peachtree Street. Again we heard the terrifying cries, this time near at hand and coming toward us. We saw a lame Negro boot-black from Herndon's barber shop pathetically trying to outrun a mob of whites. Less than a hundred yards from us the chase ended. We saw clubs and fists descending to the accompaniment of savage shouting and cursing. Suddenly a voice cried, "There goes another nigger!" Its work done, the mob went after the new prey. The body with the withered foot lay dead in a pool of blood on the street.

Father's apprehension and mine steadily increased during the evening, 7 although the fact that our skins were white kept us from attack. Another circumstance favored us—the mob had not yet grown violent enough to attack United States government property. But I could see Father's relief when he punched the time clock at eleven P.M. and got into the cart to go home. He wanted to go the back way down Forsyth Street, but I begged him, in my childish excitement and ignorance, to drive down Marietta to Five Points, the heart of Atlanta's business district, where the crowds were densest and the yells loudest. No sooner had we turned into Marietta Street, however, than we saw careening toward us an undertaker's barouche. Crouched in the rear of the vehicle were three Negroes clinging to the sides of the carriage as it lunged and swerved. On the driver's seat crouched a white man, the reins held taut in his left hand. A huge whip was gripped in his right. Alternately he lashed the horses and, without looking backward, swung the whip in savage swoops in the faces of members of the mob as they lunged at the carriage determined to seize the three Negroes.

There was no time for us to get out of its path, so sudden and swift was the appearance of the vehicle. The hub cap of the right rear wheel of the barouche hit the right side of our much lighter wagon. Father and I instinctively threw our weight and kept the cart from turning completely over. Our mare was a Texas mustang which, frightened by the sudden blow, lunged in the air as Father clung to the reins. Good fortune was with us. The cart settled back on its four wheels as Father said in a voice which brooked no dissent, "We are going home the back way and not down Marietta." 8

But again on Pryor Street we heard the cry of the mob. Close to us and in our direction ran a stout and elderly woman who cooked at a downtown white hotel. Fifty yards behind, a mob which filled the street from curb to curb was closing in. Father handed the reins to me and, though he was of slight stature, reached down and lifted the woman into the cart. I did not need to be told to lash the mare to the fastest speed she could muster. 9

The church bells tolled the next morning for Sunday service. But no one in Atlanta believed for a moment that the hatred and lust for blood had been appeased. Like skulls on a cannibal's hut the hats and caps of victims of the mob of the night before had been hung on the iron hooks of telegraph poles. None could tell whether each hat represented a dead Negro. But we knew that some of those who had worn the hats would never again wear any. 10

Late in the afternoon friends of my father's came to warn of more trouble that night. They told us that plans had been perfected for a mob to form on Peachtree Street just after nightfall to march down Houston Street to what the white people called "Darktown," three blocks or so below our house, to "clean out the niggers." There had never been a firearm in our house before that day. Father was reluctant even in those circumstances to violate the law, but he at last gave in at Mother's insistence. 11

We turned out the lights early, as did all our neighbors. No one removed his clothes or thought of sleep. Apprehension was tangible. We could almost touch its cold and clammy surface. Toward midnight the unnatural quiet was broken by a roar that grew steadily in volume. Even today I grow tense in remembering it. 12

Father told Mother to take my sisters, the youngest of them only six, to the rear of the house, which offered more protection from stones and bullets. My brother George was away, so Father and I, the only males in the house, took our places at the front windows of the parlor. The windows opened on 13 a porch along the front side of the house, which in turn gave onto a narrow lawn that sloped down to the street and a picket fence. There was a crash as Negroes smashed the street lamp at the corner of Houston and Piedmont Avenue down the street. In a very few minutes the vanguard of the mob, some of them bearing torches, appeared. A voice which we recognized as that of the son of the grocer with whom we had traded for many years yelled, "That's where that nigger mail carrier lives! Let's burn it down! It's too nice for a nigger to live in!" In the eerie light Father turned his drawn face toward me. In a voice as quiet as though he were asking me to pass him the sugar at the breakfast table, he said, "Son, don't shoot until the first man puts his foot on the lawn and then—don't you miss!"

In the flickering light the mob swayed, paused, and began to flow   14
toward us. In that instant there opened up within me a great awareness; I knew then who I was. I was a Negro, a human being with an invisible pigmentation which marked me a person to be hunted, hanged, abused, discriminated against, kept in poverty and ignorance, in order that those whose skin was white would have readily at hand a proof of their superiority, a proof patent and inclusive, accessible to the moron and the idiot as well as to the wise man and the genius. No matter how low a white man fell, he could always hold fast to the smug conviction that he was superior to two-thirds of the world's population, for those two-thirds were not white.

It made no difference how intelligent or talented my millions of broth-   15
ers and I were, or how virtuously we lived. A curse like that of Judas was upon us, a mark of degradation fashioned with heavenly authority. There were white men who said Negroes had no souls, and who proved it by the Bible. Some of these now were approaching us, intent upon burning our house.

Theirs was a world of contrasts in values: superior and inferior, profit   16
and loss, cooperative and noncooperative, civilized and aboriginal, white and black. If you were on the wrong end of the comparison, if you were inferior, if you were noncooperative, if you were aboriginal, if you were black, then you were marked for excision, expulsion, or extinction. I was a Negro; I was therefore that part of history which opposed the good, the just, and the enlightened. I was a Persian, falling before the hordes of Alexander. I was a Carthaginian, extinguished by the Legions of Rome. I was a Frenchman at Waterloo, an Anglo-Saxon at Hastings, a Confederate at Vicksburg. I was the defeated, wherever and whenever there was a defeat.

Yet as a boy there in the darkness amid the tightening fright, I knew   17
the inexplicable thing—that my skin was as white as the skin of those who were coming at me.

The mob moved toward the lawn. I tried to aim my gun, wondering   18

what it would feel like to kill a man. Suddenly there was a volley of shots.
The mob hesitated, stopped. Some friends of my father's had barricaded
themselves in a two-story brick building just below our house. It was they
who had fired. Some of the mobsmen, still bloodthirsty, shouted, "Let's go
get the nigger." Others, afraid now for their safety, held back. Our friends,
noting the hesitation, fired another volley. The mob broke and retreated up
Houston Street.

In the quiet that followed I put my gun aside and tried to relax. But a   19
tension different from anything I had ever known possessed me. I was
gripped by the knowledge of my identity, and in the depths of my soul I
was vaguely aware that I was glad of it. I was sick with loathing for the
hatred which had flared before me that night and come so close to making
me a killer; but I was glad I was not one of those who hated; I was glad I
was not one of those made sick and murderous by pride. I was glad I was
not one of those whose story is in the history of the world, a record of blood-
shed, rapine, and pillage. I was glad my mind and spirit were part of the
races that had not fully awakened, and who therefore had still before them
the opportunity to write a record of virtue as a memorandum to
Armageddon.

It was all just a feeling then, inarticulate and melancholy, yet reassuring   20
in the way that death and sleep are reassuring, and I have clung to it now
for nearly half a century.

QUESTIONS

Words to KNow

opulence (paragraph 1), volubility (3), taciturn (3), impinged (3), apprehension (7), patent (14), degradation (15), enlightened (16), Carthaginian (16),
Waterloo (16), Hastings (16), Armageddon (19).

Some of the Issues

1. What phrase in paragraph 1 points to some of the events White will
   describe?
2. In paragraph 1 White refers to the Candler Building and digresses to

speak of "the ex-drug clerk who had become a millionaire from the sale of Coca-Cola." What is the meaning of this interruption?

3. What does White mean when he says in paragraph 3, "we were taught that there is no isolation from life"?

4. What is the difference between the two days of rioting?

The Way We Are Told

5. Why does White give his description of home and neighborhood in two paragraphs (1 and 2)? How do the paragraphs differ?

6. How does White begin to build suspense in paragraph 3? How do paragraphs 4 and 5 also prepare the reader for what is to come?

7. Paragraph 6 gives the first description of a specific event, using several words and phrases that have emotional impact. Cite four or five of these.

8. In paragraph 9 White describes another episode of rescue. See if there are any words here, like those in paragraph 6, that have emotional connotations.

9. How does White heighten the suspense in the final paragraphs of the essay?

Some Subjects for Essays

10. Have you ever felt yourself in real danger? If so, try to describe the circumstances in two ways: give an objective description of the events and then rewrite your essay, trying to heighten the effect by the careful use of emotionally effective words and phrases. (You will find that the overuse of emotional words diminishes rather than enhances the effect.)

11. White describes his experience in the Atlanta riots as a turning point in his life. Describe an experience in your own life that profoundly changed your values.

12. Read Lillian Smith's "When I Was a Child." Then write a paragraph giving your view of what Smith's parents' attitude would likely have been toward the riots and the rioters. Explain what made you reach your conclusions.

ALIEN TURF

Piri Thomas

Piri Thomas was born in Spanish Harlem in 1928 and grew up in its
world of gangs, drugs, and petty crime. In his teens he became an
addict, was convicted of attempted armed robbery, and served six
years of a 15-year sentence. After his release, he began to work for drug
rehabilitation programs in New York and Puerto Rico and developed
a career as a writer. The autobiographical *Down These Mean Streets*
(1967), from which the following selection is taken, was his first book.
A sequel, *Savior, Savior, Hold My Hand*, was published in 1972.

Sometimes you don't fit in. Like if you're a Puerto Rican on an Italian block. 1
After my new baby brother, Ricardo, died of some kind of germs, Poppa
moved us from 111th Street to Italian turf on 114th Street between Second
and Third Avenue. I guess Poppa wanted to get Momma away from the hard
memories of the old pad.

I sure missed 111th Street, where everybody acted, walked, and talked 2
like me. But on 114th Street everything went all right for a while. There
were a few dirty looks from the spaghetti-an'-sauce cats, but no big sweat.
Till that one day I was on my way home from school and almost had reached
my stoop when someone called: "Hey, you dirty fuckin' spic."

The words hit my ears and almost made me curse Poppa at the same 3
time. I turned around real slow and found my face pushing in the finger of
an Italian kid about my age. He had five or six of his friends with him.

"Hey, you," he said, "What nationality are ya?" 4

I looked at him and wondered which nationality to pick. And one of his 5
friends said, "Ah, Rocky, he's black enuff to be a nigger. Ain't that what you
is, kid?"

My voice was almost shy in its anger. "I'm Puerto Rican," I said. "I was 6
born here." I wanted to shout it, but it came out like a whisper.

"Right here inna street?" Rocky sneered. "Ya mean right here inna 7
middle of da street?"

They all laughed. I hated them. I shook my head slowly from side to 8
side.

"Uh-uh," I said softly. "I was born inna hospital—inna bed." 9

"Umm, *paisan*—born inna bed," Rocky said. 10

I didn't like Rocky Italiano's voice. "Inna hospital," I whispered, and all 11
the time my eyes were trying to cut down the long distance from this trouble

to my stoop. But it was no good; I was hemmed in by Rocky's friends. I couldn't help thinking about kids getting wasted for moving into a block belonging to other people.

"What hospital, *paisan?*" Bad Rocky pushed.   12

"Harlem Hospital," I answered, wishing like all hell that it was 5 o'clock   13
instead of just 3 o'clock, 'cause Poppa came home at 5. I looked around for some friendly faces belonging to grown-up people, but the elders were all busy yakking away in Italian. I couldn't help thinking how much like Spanish it sounded. Shit, that should make us something like relatives.

"Harlem Hospital?" said a voice. "I knew he was a nigger."   14

"Yeah," said another voice from an expert on color. "That's the hospital   15
where all them black bastards get born at."

I dug three Italian elders looking at us from across the street and I felt   16
saved. But that went out the window when they just smiled and went on talking. I couldn't decide whether they had smiled because this new whatever-he-was was gonna get his ass kicked or because they were pleased that their kids were welcoming a new kid to their country. An older man nodded his head at Rocky, who smiled back. I wondered if that was a signal for my funeral to begin.

"Ain't that right, kid?" Rocky pressed. "Ain't that where all black peo-   17
ple get born?"

I dug some of Rocky's boys grinding and pushing and punching closed   18
fists against open hands. I figured they were looking to shake me up, so I straightened up my humble voice and made like proud. "There's all kinds of people born there. Colored people, Puerto Ricans like me, an'—even spaghetti-benders like you."

"That's a dirty fuckin' lie"—*bash*, I felt Rocky's fist smack into my   19
mouth—"you dirty fuckin' spic."

I got dizzy and then more dizzy when fists started to fly from every-   20
where and only toward me. I swung back, *splat*, *bish*—my fist hit some face and I wished I hadn't, 'cause then I started getting kicked.

I heard people yelling in Italian and English and I wondered if maybe   21
it was 'cause I hadn't fought fair in having hit that one guy. But it wasn't. The voices were trying to help me.

"Whas'sa matta, you no-good kids, leeva da kid alone," a man said. I   22
looked through a swelling eye and dug some Italians pushing their kids off me with slaps. One even kicked a kid in the ass. I could have loved them if I didn't hate them so fuckin' much.

"You all right, kiddo?" asked the man.   23

"Where you live, boy?" said another one.   24

"Is the *bambino* hurt?" asked a woman.   25

I didn't look at any of them. I felt dizzy. I didn't want to open my 26
mouth to talk, 'cause I was fighting to keep from puking up. I just hoped my
face was cool-looking. I walked away from the group of strangers. I reached
my stoop and started to climb the steps.

"Hey, spic," came a shout from across the street. I started to turn to the 27
voice and changed my mind. "Spic" wasn't my name. I knew that voice,
though. It was Rocky's. "We'll see ya again, spic," he said.

I wanted to do something tough, like spitting in their direction. But you 28
gotta have spit in your mouth in order to spit, and my mouth was hurt dry.
I just stood there with my back to them.

"Hey, your old man just better be the janitor in that fuckin' building." 29

Another voice added, "Hey, you got any pretty sisters? We might let 30
ya stay onna block."

Another voice mocked, "Aw, fer Chrissake, where ya ever hear of one 31
of them black broads being pretty?"

I heard the laughter. I turned around and looked at them. Rocky made 32
some kind of dirty sign by putting his left hand in the crook of his right arm
while twisting his closed fist in the air.

Another voice said, "Fuck it, we'll just cover the bitch's face with the 33
flag an' fuck er for old glory."

All I could think of was how I'd like to kill each of them two or three 34
times. I found some spit in my mouth and splattered it in their direction and
went inside.

Momma was cooking, and the smell of rice and beans was beating the 35
smell of Parmesan cheese from the other apartments. I let myself into our
new pad. I tried to walk fast past Momma so I could wash up, but she saw
me.

"My God, Piri, what happened?" she cried. 36

"Just a little fight in school, Momma. You know how it is, Momma, I'm 37
new in school an' . . ." I made myself laugh. Then I made myself say, "But
Moms, I whipped the living ———outta two guys, an' one was bigger'n
me."

"*Bendito*, Piri, I raise this family in Christian way. Not to fight. Christ 38
says to turn the other cheek."

"Sure, Momma." I smiled and went and showered, feeling sore at Poppa 39
for bringing us into spaghetti country. I felt my face with easy fingers and
thought about all the running back and forth from school that was in store
for me.

I sat down to dinner and listened to Momma talk about Christian living 40
without really hearing her. All I could think of was that I hadda go out in
that street again. I made up my mind to go out right after I finished eating.
I had to, shook up or not; cats like me had to show heart.

"Be back, Moms," I said after dinner, "I'm going out on the stoop." I   41
got halfway to the stoop and turned and went back to our apartment. I
knocked.

"Who is it?" Momma asked.   42

"Me, Momma."   43

She opened the door. "*Qué pasa?*" she asked.   44

"Nothing, Momma, I just forgot something," I said. I went into the bed-   45
room and fiddled around and finally copped a funny book and walked out
the door again. But this time I made sure the switch on the lock was open,
just in case I had to get back real quick. I walked out on that stoop as cool
as could be, feeling braver with the lock open.

There was no sign of Rocky and his killers. After awhile I saw Poppa   46
coming down the street. He walked like beat tired. Poppa hated his pick-
and-shovel job with the WPA. He couldn't even hear the name WPA without
getting a fever. *Funny,* I thought, *Poppa's the same like me, a stone Puerto
Rican, and nobody in this block even pays him a mind. Maybe older people
get along better'n us kids.*

Poppa was climbing the stoop. "Hi, Poppa," I said.   47

"How's it going, son? Hey, you sure look a little lumped up. What   48
happened?"

I looked at Poppa and started to talk it outta me all at once and stopped,   49
'cause I heard my voice start to sound scared, and that was no good.

"Slow down, son," Poppa said. "Take it easy." He sat down on the stoop   50
and made a motion for me to do the same. He listened and I talked. I gained
confidence. I went from a tone of being shook up by the Italians to a tone of
being a better fighter than Joe Louis and Pedro Montanez lumped together,
with Kid Chocolate thrown in for extra.

"So that's what happened," I concluded. "And it looks like only the   51
beginning. Man, I ain't scared, Poppa, but like there's nothin' but Italianos
on this block and there's no me's like me except me an' our family."

Poppa looked tight. He shook his head from side to side and mumbled   52
something about another Puerto Rican family that lived a coupla doors down
from us.

I thought, *What good would that do me, unless they prayed over my*   53
dead body in Spanish? But I said, "Man! That's great. Before ya know it,
there'll be a whole bunch of us moving in, huh?"

Poppa grunted something and got up. "Staying out here, son?"   54

"Yeah, Poppa, for a little while longer."   55

From that day on I grew eyes all over my head. Anytime I hit that street   56
for anything, I looked straight ahead, behind me and from side to side all at
the same time. Sometimes I ran into Rocky and his boys—that cat was never
without his boys—but they never made a move to snag me. They just

grinned at me like a bunch of hungry alley cats that could get to their mouse anytime they wanted. That's what they made me feel like—a mouse. Not like a smart house mouse but like a white house pet that ain't got no business in the middle of cat country but don't know better 'cause he grew up thinking he was a cat—which wasn't far from wrong 'cause he'd end up as part of the inside of some cat.

Rocky and his fellas got to playing a way-out game with me called "One-finger-across-the-neck-inna-slicing-motion," followed by such gentle words as "It won't be long, spico." I just looked at them blank and made it to wherever I was going.   57

I kept wishing those cats went to the same school I went to, a school that was on the border between their country and mine, and I had *amigos* there—and there I could count on them. But I couldn't ask two or three *amigos* to break into Rocky's block and help me mess up his boys. I knew 'cause I had asked them already. They had turned me down fast, and I couldn't blame them. It would have been murder, and I guess they figured one murder would be better than four.   58

I got through the days trying to play it cool and walk on by Rocky and his boys like they weren't there. One day I passed them and nothing was said. I started to let out my breath. I felt great; I hadn't been seen. Then someone yelled in a high, girlish voice, "Yoo-hoo . . . Hey, *paisan* . . . we see yoo . . ." And right behind that voice came a can of evaporated milk— whoosh, clatter. I walked cool for ten steps then started running like mad.   59

This crap kept up for a month. They tried to shake me up. Every time they threw something at me, it was just to see me jump. I decided that the next fucking time they threw something at me I was gonna play bad-o and not run. That next time came about a week later. Momma sent me off the stoop to the Italian market on 115th Street and First Avenue, deep in Italian country. Man, that was stompin' territory. But I went, walking in the style which I had copped from the colored cats I had seen, a swinging and stepping down hard at every step. Those cats were so down and cool that just walking made a way-out sound.   60

Ten minutes later I was on my way back with Momma's stuff. I got to the corner of First Avenue and 114th Street and crushed myself right into Rocky and his fellas.   61

"Well-l, fellas," Rocky said. "Lookee who's here."   62

I didn't like the sounds coming out of Rocky's fat mouth. And I didn't like the sameness of the shitty grins spreading all over the boys' faces. But I thought, *No more! No more! I ain't gonna run no more.* Even so, I looked around, like for some kind of Jesus miracle to happen. I was always looking for miracles to happen.   63

"Say, *paisan*," one guy said, "you even buying from us *paisans*, eh?   64
Man, you must wantta be Italian."

Before I could bite that dopey tongue of mine, I said, "I wouldn't be a   65
guinea on a motherfucking bet."

"Wha-at?" said Rocky, really surprised. I didn't blame him; I was sur-   66
prised myself. His finger began digging a hole in his ear, like he hadn't heard
me right. "Wha-at? Say that again?"

I could feel a thin hot wetness cutting itself down my leg. I had been so   67
ashamed of being so damned scared that I had peed on myself. And then I
wasn't scared any more; I felt a fuck-it-all attitude. I looked real bad at
Rocky and said, "Ya heard me. I wouldn't be a guinea on a bet."

"Ya little sonavabitch, we'll kick the shit outta ya," said one guy, Tony,   68
who had made a habit of asking me if I had any sen-your-ritas for sisters.

"Kick the shit outta me yourself if you got any heart, you motherfuckin'   69
fucker," I screamed at him. I felt kind of happy, the kind of feeling that you
get only when you got heart.

Big-mouth Tony just swung out, and I swung back and heard all of   70
Momma's stuff plopping all over the street. My fist hit Tony smack dead in
the mouth. He was so mad he threw a fist at me from about three feet away.
I faked and jabbed and did fancy dance steps. Big-mouth put a stop to all
that with a punch in my mouth. I heard the home cheers of "Yea, yea, bust
that spic wide open!" Then I bloodied Tony's nose. He blinked and sniffed
without putting his hands to his nose, and I remembered Poppa telling me,
"Son, if you're ever fighting somebody an' you punch him in the nose, and
he just blinks an' sniffs without holding his nose, you can do one of two
things: fight like hell or run like hell—'cause that cat's a fighter."

Big-mouth came at me and we grabbed each other and pushed and   71
pulled and shoved. *Poppa*, I thought, *I ain't gonna cop out. I'm a fighter,
too*. I pulled away from Tony and blew my fist into his belly. He puffed and
butted my nose with his head. I sniffed back. *Poppa, I didn't put my hands
to my nose*. I hit Tony again in that same weak spot. He bent over in the
middle and went down to his knees.

Big-mouth got up as fast as he could, and I was thinking how much   72
heart he had. But I ran toward him like my life depended on it; I wanted to
cool him. Too late. I saw his hand grab a fistful of ground asphalt which had
been piled nearby to fix a pothole in the street. I tried to duck; I should have
closed my eyes instead. The shitty-gritty stuff hit my face, and I felt the
scrappy pain make itself a part of my eyes. I screamed and grabbed for two
eyes with one hand, while the other I beat some kind of helpless tune on air
that just couldn't be hurt. I heard Rocky's voice shouting, "Ya scum bag, ya
didn't have to fight the spic dirty; you could've fucked him up fair and

square!" I couldn't see. I heard a fist hit a face, then Big-mouth's voice: "Whatta ya hittin' me for?" and then Rocky's voice: "*Putana!* I ought ta knock all your fuckin' teeth out."

I felt hands grabbing at me between my screams. I punched out. *I'm* 73
gonna get killed, I thought. Then I heard many voices: "Hold it, kid." "We ain't gonna hurt ya." "Je-*sus*, don't rub your eyes." "ooooohhhh, shit, his eyes is fulla that shit."

You're fuckin' right, I thought, *and it hurts like* coño. 74

I heard a woman's voice now: "Take him to a hospital." And an old 75
man asked: "How did it happen?"

"Momma, Momma," I cried. 76

"Comon, kid," Rocky said, taking my hand. "Lemme take ya home." I 77
fought for the right to rub my eyes. "Grab his other hand, Vincent," Rocky said. I tried to rub my eyes with my eyelids. I could feel hurt tears cutting down my cheeks. "Come on, kid, we ain't gonna hurt ya," Rocky tried to assure me. "Swear to our mudders. We just wanna take ya home."

I made myself believe him, and trying not to make pain noises, I let 78
myself be led home. I wondered if I was gonna be blind like Mr. Silva, who went around from door to door selling dish towels and brooms, his son leading him around.

"You okay, kid?" Rocky asked. 79

"Yeah," what was left of me said. 80

"A-huh," mumbled Big-mouth. 81

"He got much heart for a nigger," somebody else said. 82

A *spic*, I thought. 83

"For anybody," Rocky said. "Here we are, kid," he added. "Watch 84
your step."

I was like carried up the steps. "What's your apartment number?" 85
Rocky asked.

"One-B—inna back—ground floor," I said, and I was led there. Some- 86
body knocked on Momma's door. Then I heard running feet and Rocky's voice yelling back, "Don't rat, huh, kid?" And I was alone.

I heard the door open and Momma say, "*Bueno*, Piri, come in." I didn't 87
move. I couldn't. There was a long pause; I could hear Momma's fright. "My God," she said finally. "What's happened?" Then she took a closer look. "Ai-eeee," she screamed. "*Dios mio!*"

"I was playing with some kids, Momma," I said, "an' I got some dirt in 88
my eyes." I tried to make my voice come out without the pain, like a man.

"*Dios eterno*—your eyes!" 89

"What's the matter? What's the matter?" Poppa called from the 90
bedroom.

"*Está ciego!*" Momma screamed. "He is blind!" 91

I heard Poppa knocking things over as he came running. Sis began to   92
cry. Blind, hurting tears were jumping out of my eyes. "Whattya mean, he's
blind?" Poppa said as he stormed into the kitchen. "What happened?" Poppa's voice was both scared and mad.

"Playing, Poppa."   93

"Whatta ya mean, 'playing'?" Poppa's English sounded different when   94
he got warm.

"Just playing, Poppa."   95

"Playing? Playing got all that dirt in your eyes? I bet my ass. Them   96
damn Ee-ta-liano kids ganged up on you again." Poppa squeezed my head
between the fingers of one hand. "That settles it—we're moving outta this
damn section, outta this damn block, outta this damn shit."

Shit, I thought, *Poppa's sure cursin' up a storm.* I could hear him slap- 97
ping the side of his leg, like he always did when he got real mad.

"Son," he said, "you're gonna point them out to me."   98

"Point who out, Poppa? I was playin' an'—"   99

"Stop talkin' to him and take him to the hospital!" Momma screamed.   100

"*Pobrecito,* poor Piri," cooed my little sister.   101

"You sure, son?" Poppa asked. "You was only playing?"   102

"Shit, Poppa, I said I was."   103

Smack—Poppa was so scared and mad, he let it out in a slap to the side 104
of my face.

"*Bestia!* ani-*mul!*" Momma cried. "He's blind, and you hit him!"   105

"I'm sorry, son, I'm sorry," Poppa said in a voice like almost crying. I 106
heard him running back into the bedroom, yelling, "Where's my pants?"

Momma grabbed away fingers that were trying to wipe away the hurt   107
in my eyes. "*Camamba,* no rub, no rub," she said, kissing me. She told Sis
to get a rag and wet it with cold water.

Poppa came running back into the kitchen. "Let's go, son, let's go. Jesus! 108
I didn't mean to smack ya, I really didn't," he said, his big hand rubbing and
grabbing my hair gently.

"Here's the rag, Momma," said Sis.   109

"What's that for?" asked Poppa.   110

"To put on his eyes," Momma said.   111

I heard the smack of a wet rag, *blapt,* against the kitchen wall. "We 112
can't put nothing on his eyes. It might make them worse. Come on, son,"
Poppa said nervously, lifting me up in his big arms. I felt like a little baby,
like I didn't hurt so bad. I wanted to stay there, but I said, "Let me down,
Poppa, I ain't no kid."

"Shut up," Poppa said softly. "I know you ain't, but it's faster this way." 113

"Which hospeetal are you taking him to?" Momma asked.   114

"Nearest one," Poppa answered as we went out the door. He carried   115 me through the hall and out into the street, where the bright sunlight made a red hurting color through the crap in my eyes. I heard voices on the stoop and on the sidewalk: "Is that the boy?"

"A-huh. He's probably blinded." [116]

"We'll get a cab, son," Poppa said. His voice loved me. I heard Rocky [117] yelling from across the street, "We're pulling for ya, kid. Remember what we . . ." The rest was lost to Poppa's long legs running down to the corner of Third Avenue. He hailed a taxi and we zoomed off toward Harlem Hospital. I felt the cab make all kinds of sudden stops and turns.

"How do you feel, *hijo?*" Poppa asked. [118]

"It burns like hell." [119]

"You'll be okay," he said, and as an afterthought added, "Don't curse, [120] son."

I heard cars honking and the Third Avenue el roaring above us. I knew [121] we were in Puerto Rican turf, 'cause I could hear our language.

"Son." [122]

"Yeah, Poppa." [123]

"Don't rub your eyes, fer Christ sake." He held my skinny wrists in his [124] one hand, and everything got quiet between us.

The cab got to Harlem Hospital. I heard change being handled and the [125] door opening and Poppa thanking the cabbie for getting here fast. "Hope the kid'll be okay," the driver said.

I *will be,* I thought. *I ain't gonna be like Mr. Silva.* [126]

Poppa took me in his arms again and started running. "Where's emer- [127] gency, mister?" he asked someone.

"To your left and straight away," said a voice. [128]

"Thanks a lot," Poppa said, and we were running again. [129]

"Emergency?" Poppa said when we stopped. [130]

"Yes, sir," said a girl's voice. "What's the matter?" [131]

"My boy's got his eyes full of ground-up tar an'—" [132]

"What the matter?" said a man's voice. [133]

"Youngster with ground tar in his eyes, doctor." [134]

"We'll take him, mister. You just put him down here and go with the [135] nurse. She'll take down the information. Uh, you the father?"

"That's right, doctor." [136]

"Okay, just put him down here." [137]

"Poppa, don't leave me," I cried. [138]

"Sh, son, I ain't leaving you. I'm just going to fill out some papers, an' I'll be right back."

I nodded my head up and down and was wheeled away. When the [139] rolling stretcher stopped, somebody stuck a needle in me and I got sleepy and started thinking about Rocky and his boys, and Poppa's slap, and how great Poppa was, and how my eyes didn't hurt no more . . .

I woke up in a room blind with darkness. The only lights were the ones inside my head. I put my fingers to my eyes and felt bandages. "Let them be, sonny," said a woman's voice. 140

I wanted to ask the voice if they had taken my eyes out, but I didn't. I was afraid the voice would say yes. 141

"Let them be, sonny," the nurse said, pulling my hand away from the bandages. "You're all right. The doctor put the bandages on to keep the light out. They'll be off real soon. Don't you worry none, sonny." 142

I wished she would stop calling me sonny. "Where's Poppa?" I asked cool like. 143

"He's outside, sonny. Would you like me to send him in?" 144

I nodded. "Yeah." I heard walking-away shoes, a door opening, a whisper, and shoes walking back toward me. "How do you feel, *hijo?*" Poppa asked. 145

"It hurts like shit, Poppa." 146

"It's just for awhile, son, and then off come the bandages. Everything's gonna be all right." 147

I thought, *Poppa didn't tell me to stop cursing.* 148

"And son, I thought I told you to stop cursing," he added. 149

I smiled. Poppa hadn't forgotten. Suddenly I realized that all I had on was a hospital gown. "Poppa, where's my clothes?" I asked. 150

"I got them. I'm taking them home an'—" 151

"Whatta ya mean, Poppa?" I said, like scared. "You ain't leavin' me here? I'll be damned if I stay." I was already sitting up and feeling my way outta bed. Poppa grabbed me and pushed me back. His voice wasn't mad or scared any more. It was happy and soft, like Momma's. 152

"Hey," he said, "get your ass back in bed or they'll have to put a bandage there too." 153

"Poppa," I pleaded. "I don't care, wallop me as much as you want, just take me home." 154

"Hey, I thought you said you wasn't no kid. Hell, you ain't scared of being alone?" 155

Inside my head there was a running of *Yeah, yeah, yeah,* but I answered, "Naw, Poppa, it's just that Momma's gonna worry and she'll get sick an' everything, and—" 156

157

"Won't work, son," Poppa broke in with a laugh. 158

I kept quiet. 159

"It's only for a couple days. We'll come and see you an' everybody'll bring you things." 160

I got interested but played it smooth. "What kinda things," Poppa?"   161

Poppa shrugged his shoulders and spread his big arms apart and   162
answered me like he was surprised that I should ask. "Uh . . . fruits and . . .
candy and ice cream. And Momma will probably bring you chicken soup."

I shook my head sadly. "Poppa, you know I don't like chicken soup."   163

"So we won't bring chicken soup. We'll bring what you like. Goddam-   164
mit, whatta ya like?"

"I'd like the first things you talked about, Poppa," I said softly. "But   165
instead of soup I'd like"—I held my breath back, then shot it out—"some
roller skates!"

Poppa let out a whistle. Roller skates were about $1.50, and that was rice   166
and beans for more than a few days. Then he said, "All right, son, soon as
you get home, you got 'em."

But he had agreed too quickly. I shook my head from side to side. Shit,   167
I was gonna push all the way for the roller skates. It wasn't every day you'd
get hurt bad enough to ask for something so little like a pair of roller skates.
I wanted them right away.

"Fer Christ sakes," Poppa protested, "you can't use 'em in here. Why,   168
some kid will probably steal 'em on you." But Poppa's voice died out slowly
in a "you win" tone as I just kept shaking my head from side to side. "Bring
'em tomorrow," he finally mumbled, "but that's it."

"Thanks, Poppa."   169

"Don't ask for no more."   170

My eyes were starting to hurt like mad again. The fun was starting to   171
go outta the game between Poppa and me. I made a face.

"Does it hurt, son?"   172

"Naw, Poppa. I can take it." I thought how I was like a cat in a movie   173
about Indians, taking it like a champ, tied to a stake and getting like burned
toast.

Poppa sounded relieved. "Yeah, it's only at first it hurts." His hand   174
touched my foot. "Well, I'll be going now . . ." Poppa rubbed my foot gently
and then slapped me the same gentle way on the side of my leg. "Be good,
son," he said and walked away. I heard the door open and the nurse telling
him about how they were gonna move me to the ward 'cause I was out of
danger. "Son," Poppa called back, "you're *un hombre.*"

I felt proud as hell.   175

"Poppa."   176

"Yeah, son?"   177

"You won't forget to bring the roller skates, huh?"   178

Poppa laughed. "Yeah, son."   179

I heard the door close.   180

QUESTIONS

Words to Know

paisan—kid, peasant (paragraph 10), *bambino*—child (25), *bendito*—stupid (38), *qué pasa*—What's going on (44), *putana*—whore (72), *Dios mío*—my God (87), *Dios eterno*—eternal God (89), *está ciego*—he's blind (91), *pobrecito*—you poor boy (101), *hijo*—son (118), *hombre*—man (173).

Some of the Issues

1. How do the first two sentences set the scene?
2. Piri wants to project a certain self-image in front of the gang. Characterize it.
3. Until the climactic fight, the cat-and-mouse game that Rocky's gang plays goes through several stages. Determine what these stages are and how Piri reacts to them.
4. How do the grown-ups (those in the street as well as Piri's parents) react to the situation at the various stages? How does Piri deal with his parents' reactions in particular?
5. How does Rocky's attitude toward Piri change after one of the gang members throws the asphalt? What causes the change?
6. Explain Piri's reaction to "Spic" and "Nigger." Is Piri's desire to be identified as a Puerto Rican a matter of pride or practicality?
7. What is the importance of being "un hombre," of having "heart?" How does Piri prove himself a man? By whose standards?

The Way We Are Told

8. There is almost no description in this selection. It is all action and dialog. Thomas nevertheless manages to convey some strong impressions of individuals and their attitudes. How does he do it? Cite some examples.
9. Both Angelou ("Graduation") and Thomas tell their stories from an adolescent's point of view. Apart from the content, how do the two stories differ? What causes the differences?

Some Subjects for Essays

10. *Rite de passage*, a French term, is usually used to indicate the ceremony marking the formal change of a young person from childhood to adulthood, such as a confirmation or *bar mitzvah*. Usually it is a religious ceremony. Write an essay arguing that Angelou's graduation and Thomas' big fight (or one or the other) were such rites of passage.
11. Write about a conflict that you have had. Set the scene and then use mostly dialog to tell your story. See if you can make the voices authentic.
12. Both Jack Agueros ("Halfway to Dick and Jane") and Thomas describe growing up Puerto Rican in New York City. Write an essay comparing and contrasting the way they talk about their childhoods.

ARRIVAL AT MANZANAR

Jeanne Wakatsuki Houston and
James D. Houston

Jeanne Wakatsuki Houston was born in California. She was seven years old when she, together with her family, was put into an internment camp in the year after the Americans entered World War II. She lived in the camp, in Manzanar, California, until age 11. After high school she studied sociology and journalism at San Jose State College where she met her husband, James D. Houston, a novelist. Together they wrote *Farewell to Manzanar*, published in 1973, as a record of life in the camp and of its impact on her and her family. The following is a selection from it.

In December of 1941 Papa's disappearance didn't bother me nearly so much as the world I soon found myself in.

He had been a jack-of-all-trades. When I was born he was farming near Inglewood. Later, when he started fishing, we moved to Ocean Park, near Santa Monica, and until they picked him up, that's where we lived, in a big frame house with a brick fireplace, a block back from the beach. We were the only Japanese family in the neighborhood. Papa liked it that way. He didn't want to be labeled or grouped by anyone. But with him gone and no way of knowing what to expect, my mother moved all of us down to Terminal Island. Woody already lived there, and one of my older sisters had married a Terminal Island boy. Mama's first concern now was to keep the family together; and once the war began, she felt safer there than isolated racially in Ocean Park. But for me, at age seven, the island was a country as foreign as India or Arabia would have been. It was the first time I had lived among other Japanese, or gone to school with them, and I was terrified all the time.

This was partly Papa's fault. One of his threats to keep us younger kids in line was "I'm going to sell you to the Chinaman." When I had entered kindergarten two years earlier, I was the only Oriental in the class. They sat me next to a Caucasian girl who happened to have very slanted eyes. I looked at her and began to scream, certain Papa had sold me out at last. My fear of her ran so deep I could not speak of it, even to Mama, couldn't explain why I was screaming. For two weeks I had nightmares about this girl, until the teachers finally moved me to the other side of the room. And it was still with me, this fear of Oriental faces, when we moved to Terminal Island.

127

In those days it was a company town, a ghetto owned and controlled by 4
the canneries. The men went after fish, and whenever the boats came back—
day or night—the women would be called to process the catch while it was
fresh. One in the afternoon or four in the morning, it made no difference.
My mother had to go to work right after we moved there. I can still hear the
whistle—two toots for French's, three for Van Camp's—and she and Chizu
would be out of bed in the middle of the night, heading for the cannery.

The house we lived in was nothing more than a shack, a barracks with 5
single plank walls and rough wooden floors, like the cheapest kind of migrant
workers' housing. The people around us were hardworking, boisterous, a little proud of their nickname, *yo-go-re*, which meant literally *uncouth one*,
or roughneck, or dead-end kid. They not only spoke Japanese exclusively,
they spoke a dialect peculiar to Kyushu, where their families had come from
in Japan, a rough, fisherman's language, full of oaths and insults. Instead of
saying *ba-ka-ta-re*, a common insult meaning *stupid*, Terminal Islanders
would say *ba-ka-ya-ro*, a coarser and exclusively masculine use of the word,
which implies gross stupidity. They would swagger and pick on outsiders and
persecute anyone who didn't speak as they did. That was what made my
own time there so hateful. I had never spoken anything but English, and the
other kids in the second grade despised me for it. They were tough and
mean, like ghetto kids anywhere. Each day after school I dreaded their
ambush. My brother Kiyo, three years older, would wait for me at the door,
where we would decide whether to run straight home together, or split up,
or try a new and unexpected route.

None of these kids ever actually attacked. It was the threat that fright- 6
ened us, their fearful looks, and the noises they would make, like miniature
Samurai, in a language we couldn't understand.

At the time it seemed we had been living under this reign of fear for 7
years. In fact, we lived there about two months. Late in February the navy
decided to clear Terminal Island completely. Even though most of us were
American-born, it was dangerous having that many Orientals so close to the
Long Beach Naval Station, on the opposite end of the island. We had known
something like this was coming. But, like Papa's arrest, not much could be
done ahead of time. There were four of us kids still young enough to be
living with Mama, plus Granny, her mother, sixty-five then, speaking no
English, and nearly blind. Mama didn't know where else she could get work,
and we had nowhere else to move *to*. On February 25 the choice was made
for us. We were given forty-eight hours to clear out.

The secondhand dealers had been prowling around for weeks, like 8
wolves, offering humiliating prices for goods and furniture they knew many
of us would have to sell sooner or later. Mama had left all but her most

valuable possessions in Ocean Park, simply because she had nowhere to put them. She had brought along her pottery, her silver, heirlooms like the kimonos Granny had brought from Japan, tea sets, lacquered tables, and one fine old set of china, blue and white porcelain, almost translucent. On the day we were leaving, Woody's car was so crammed with boxes and luggage and kids we had just run out of room. Mama had to sell this china.

One of the dealers offered her fifteen dollars for it. She said it was a full 9 setting for twelve and worth at least two hundred. He said fifteen was his top price. Mama started to quiver. Her eyes blazed up at him. She had been packing all night and trying to calm down Granny, who didn't understand why were moving again and what all the rush was about. Mama's nerves were shot, and now navy jeeps were patrolling the streets. She didn't say another word. She just glared at this man, all the rage and frustration channeled at him through her eyes.

He watched her for a moment and said he was sure he couldn't pay 10 more than seventeen fifty for that china. She reached into the red velvet case, took out a dinner plate and hurled it at the floor right in front of his feet.

The man leaped back shouting, "Hey! Hey, don't do that! Those are 11 valuable dishes!"

Mama took out another dinner plate and hurled it at the floor, then 12 another and another, never moving, never opening her mouth, just quivering and glaring at the retreating dealer, with tears streaming down her cheeks. He finally turned and scuttled out the door, heading for the next house. When he was gone she stood there smashing cups and bowls and platters until the whole set lay in scattered blue and white fragments across the wooden floor.

The name Manzanar meant nothing to us when we left Boyle Heights. 13 We didn't know where it was or what it was. We went because the government ordered us to. And, in the case of my older brothers and sisters, we went with a certain amount of relief. They had all heard stories of Japanese homes being attacked, of beatings in the streets of California towns. They were as frightened of the Caucasians as Caucasians were of us. Moving, under what appeared to be government protection, to an area less directly threatened by the war seemed not such a bad idea at all. For some it actually sounded like a fine adventure.

Our pickup point was a Buddhist church in Los Angeles. It was very 14 early, and misty, when we got there with our luggage. Mama had bought heavy coats for all of us. She grew up in eastern Washington and knew that anywhere inland in early April would be cold. I was proud of my new coat, and I remember sitting on a duffel bag trying to be friendly with the Greyhound driver. I smiled at him. He didn't smile back. He was befriending no one. Someone tied a numbered tag to my collar and to the duffel bag (each family was given a number, and that became our official designation until the camps were closed), someone else passed out box lunches for the trip, and we climbed aboard.

I had never been outside Los Angeles County, never traveled more than ten miles from the coast, had never even ridden on a bus. I was full of excitement, the way any kid would be, and wanted to look out the window. But for the first few hours the shades were drawn. Around me other people played cards, read magazines, dozed, waiting. I settled back, waiting too, and finally fell asleep. The bus felt very secure to me. Almost half its passengers were immediate relatives. Mama and my older brothers had succeeded in keeping most of us together, on the same bus, headed for the same camp. I didn't realize until much later what a job that was. The strategy had been, first, to have everyone living in the same district when the evacuation began, and then to get all of us included under the same family number, even though names had been changed by marriage. Many families weren't as lucky as ours and suffered months of anguish while trying to arrange transfers from one camp to another.   15

We rode all day. By the time we reached our destination, the shades were up. It was late afternoon. The first thing I saw was a yellow swirl across a blurred, reddish setting sun. The bus was being pelted by what sounded like splattering rain. It wasn't rain. This was my first look at something I would soon know very well, a billowing flurry of dust and sand churned up by the wind through Owens Valley.   16

We drove past a barbed-wire fence, through a gate, and into an open space where trunks and sacks and packages had been dumped from the baggage trucks that drove out ahead of us. I could see a few tents set up, the first rows of black barracks, and beyond them, blurred by sand, rows of barracks that seemed to spread for miles across this plain. People were sitting on cartons or milling around, with their backs to the wind, waiting to see which friends or relatives might be on this bus. As we approached, they turned or stood up, and some moved toward us expectantly. But inside the bus no one stirred. No one waved or spoke. They just stared out the windows, ominously silent. I didn't understand this. Hadn't we finally arrived, our whole family intact? I opened a window, leaned out, and yelled happily. "Hey! This whole bus is full of Wakatsukis!"   17

Outside, the greeters smiled. Inside there was an explosion of laughter, hysterical, tension-breaking laughter that left my brothers choking and whacking each other across the shoulders.   18

We had pulled up just in time for dinner. The mess halls weren't completed yet. An outdoor chow line snaked around a half-finished building that   19 broke a good part of the wind. They issued us army mess kits, the round metal kind that fold over, and plopped in scoops of canned Vienna sausage, canned string beans, steamed rice that had been cooked too long, and on top of the rice a serving of canned apricots. The Caucasian servers were thinking the fruit poured over rice would make a good dessert. Among the Japanese, of course, rice is never eaten with sweet foods, only with salty or savory foods. Few of us could eat such a mixture. But at this point no one dared protest. It would have been impolite. I was horrified when I saw the apricot syrup seeping through my little mound of rice. I opened my mouth to complain. My mother jabbed me in the back to keep quiet. We moved on through the line and joined the others squatting in the lee of half-raised walls, dabbing courteously at what was, for almost everyone there, an inedible concoction.

After dinner we were taken to Block 16, a cluster of fifteen barracks   20 that had just been finished a day or so earlier—although finished was hardly the word for it. The shacks were built of one thickness of pine planking covered with tarpaper. They sat on concrete footings, with about two feet of open space between the floorboards and the ground. Gaps showed between the planks, and as the weeks passed and the green wood dried out, the gaps widened. Knotholes gaped in the uncovered floor.

Each barracks was divided into six units, sixteen by twenty feet, about   21 the size of a living room, with one bare bulb hanging from the ceiling and an oil stove for heat. We were assigned two of these for the twelve people in our family group; and our official family "number" was enlarged by three digits—16 plus the number of this barracks. We were issued steel army cots, two brown army blankets each, and some mattress covers, which my brothers stuffed with straw.

The first task was to divide up what space we had for sleeping. Bill and   22 Woody contributed a blanket each and partitioned off the first room: one side for Bill and Tomi, one side for Woody and Chizu and their baby girl. Woody also got the stove, for heating formulas.

The people who had it hardest during the first few months were young   23 couples like these, many of whom had married just before the evacuation began, in order not to be separated and sent to different camps. Our two rooms were crowded, but at least it was all in the family. My oldest sister and her husband were shoved into one of those sixteen-by-twenty-foot compartments with six people they had never seen before—two other couples, one recently married like themselves, the other with two teenage boys. Partitioning off a room like that wasn't easy. It was bitter cold when we arrived, and the wind did not abate. All they had to use for room dividers were those army blankets, two of which were barely enough to keep one person warm. They argued over whose blanket should be sacrificed and later argued about noise at night—the parents wanted their boys asleep by 9:00 p.m.—and they continued arguing over matters like that for six months, until my sister and her husband left to harvest sugar beets in Idaho. It was grueling work up there, and wages were pitiful, but when the call came through camp for workers to alleviate the wartime labor shortage, it sounded better than their life at Manzanar. They knew they'd have, if nothing else, a room, perhaps a cabin of their own.

That first night in Block 16, the rest of us squeezed into the second room—Granny, Lillian, age fourteen, Ray, thirteen, May, eleven, Kiyo, ten, Mama, and me. I didn't mind this at all at the time. Being youngest meant I got to sleep with Mama. And before we went to bed I had a great time jumping up and down on the mattress. The boys had stuffed so much straw into hers, we had to flatten it some so we wouldn't slide off. I slept with her every night after that until Papa came back.   24

QUESTIONS

Words to Know

Caucasian (paragraph 3), Samurai (6), ominously (17), abate (23).

Some of the Issues

1. What do the first three paragraphs tell us about Houston's family?
2. Paragraphs 3 through 7 explain her fears. What are they? What would you imagine would be the mother's fears in this peroid?
3. Read Maxine Hong Kingston's "Girlhood Among Ghosts." Both Kingston and Houston grew up in California at about the same time. In what way are the two experiences similar to each another? How do they differ?
4. What does the story about the second-hand dealer (paragraphs 8 through 12) tell us about the situation of Japanese-Americans at that time? What does it tell us about Houston's mother?
5. Examine the actions of the camp officials. To what extent can the authorities be said to be deliberately cruel? unthoughtful? or uninformed about cultural differences? Cite specific details to support your view.

The Way We Are Told

6. In paragraphs 20 through 24 Houston gives a detailed description of the barracks. Does her description contain any words or phrases that express emotions? Justify their presence or absence.

Some Subjects for Essays

7. Jeanne Houston describes the bus ride to Manzanar from a child's point of view, as an adventure, almost fun, and not as a tragedy. Recall an incident of your childhood that would look different to you now (a fire, getting lost in a strange neighborhood). Describe it from a child's point of view and end with a paragraph explaining how you view the same incident as an adult.

CUSTER DIED FOR YOUR SINS

Vine Deloria Jr.

Vine Deloria Jr. is a Sioux Indian born on the Pine Ridge Reservation
in South Dakota. A lawyer, he is active in the struggle for Indian rights
and served as executive director of the National Congress of American
Indians. His books include *We Talk, You Listen* (1970), *God is Red*
(1973), and *Custer Died for Your Sins* (1969), from which the following selection is taken.

One of the finest things about being an Indian is that people are always 1
interested in you and your "plight." Other groups have difficulties, predic-
aments, quandaries, problems, or troubles. Traditionally we Indians have had
a "plight."

Our foremost plight is our transparency. People can tell just be looking 2
at us what we want, what should be done to help us, how we feel, and what
a "real" Indian is really like. Indian life, as it relates to the real world, is a
continuous attempt not to disappoint people who know us. Unfulfilled expectations cause grief and we have already had our share.

Because people can see right through us, it becomes impossible to tell 3
truth from fiction or fact from mythology. Experts paint us as they would
like us to be. Often we paint ourselves as we wish we were or as we might
have been.

The more we try to be ourselves the more we are forced to defend what 4
we have never been. The American public feels most comfortable with the
mythical Indians of stereotype-land who were always THERE. These Indians are fierce, they wear feathers and grunt. Most of us don't fit this idealized
figure since we grunt only when overeating, which is seldom.

Indians reactions are sudden and surprising. One day at a conference 5
we were singing "My Country 'Tis of Thee" and we came across the part
that goes:

> Land where our fathers died
> Land of the Pilgrims' pride . . .

Some of us broke out laughing when we realized that our fathers undoubtedly died trying to keep those Pilgrims from stealing our land. In fact, many
of our fathers died because the Pilgrims killed them as witches. We didn't
feel much kinship with those Pilgrims, regardless of who they did in.

We often hear "give it back to the Indians" when a gadget fails to work. 6
It's a terrible thing for a people to realize that society has set aside all non-
working gadgets for their exclusive use.

American blacks had become recognized as a species of human being 7
by amendments to the Constitution shortly after the Civil War. Prior to
emancipation they had been counted as three-fifths of a person in determining population for representation in the House of Representatives. Early
Civil Rights bills nebulously state that other people shall have the same rights
as "white people," indicating there *were* "other people." But Civil Rights
bills passed during and after the Civil War systematically excluded Indian
people. For a long time an Indian was not presumed capable of initiating an
action in a court of law, of owning property, or of giving testimony against
whites in court. Nor could an Indian vote or leave his reservation. Indians
were America's captive people without any defined rights whatsoever.

Then one day the white man discovered that the Indian tribes still 8
owned some 135 million acres of land. To his horror he learned that much
of it was very valuable. Some was good grazing land, some was farm land,
some mining land, and some covered with timber.

Animals could be herded together on a piece of land, but they could 9
not sell it. Therefore it took no time at all to discover that Indians were really
people and should have the right to sell their lands. Land was the means of
recognizing the Indian as a human being. It was the method whereby land
could be stolen legally and not blatantly.

Once the Indian was thus acknowledged, it was fairly simple to deter- 10
mine what his goals were. If, thinking went, the Indian was just like the
white, he must have the same outlook as the white. So the future was planned
for the Indian people in public and private life. First in order was allotting
them reservations so that they could sell their lands. God's foreordained plan
to repopulate the continent fit exactly with the goals of the tribes as they
were defined by their white friends.

It is fortunate that we were never slaves. We gave up land instead of 11
life and labor. Because the Negro labored, he was considered a draft animal.
Because the Indian occupied large areas of land, he was considered a wild
animal. Had we given up anything else, or had anything else to give up, it
is certain that we would have been considered some other thing.

Whites have had different attitudes toward the Indians and the blacks 12
since the Republic was founded. Whites have always refused to give non-
whites the respect which they have been found to legally possess. Instead
there has always been a contemptuous attitude that although the law says
one thing, "we all know better."

Thus whites steadfastly refused to allow blacks to enjoy the fruits of full 13 citizenship. They systematically closed schools, churches, stores, restaurants, and public places to blacks or made insulting provisions for them. For one hundred years every program of public and private white America was devoted to the exclusion of the black. It was, perhaps, embarrassing to be rubbing shoulders with one who had not so long before been defined as a field animal.

The Indian suffered the reverse treatment. Law after law was passed   14
requiring him to conform to white institutions. Indian children were kidnapped and forced into boarding schools thousands of miles from their homes to learn the white man's ways. Reservations were turned over to different Christian denominations for governing. Reservations were for a long time church operated. Everything possible was done to ensure that Indians were forced into American life. The wild animal was made into a household pet whether or not he wanted to be one.

QUESTIONS

Words to Know

plight (paragraph 1), quandary (1), allotting (10), foreordained (10), draft animal (11).

Some of the Issues

1. What is the point Deloria makes about Indians' "transparency"?
2. Characterize the "mythical Indian" by adding details to what Deloria says. Where do these details come from?
3. What are to Deloria the differences in the way that whites have looked at the Blacks and the Indians? What are the causes of these differences?

The Way We Are Told

4. How does Deloria support his assertions?
5. Who would you say is Deloria's audience?
6. Find examples of irony in the article.

Some Subjects for Essays

7. Find one common stereotype in the media that bothers you, for example: the Archie Bunker type, the dumb secretary, the housewife worried about waxy buildup on the kitchen floor or about the whiteness of her neighbor's laundry. Describe the stereotyped role, trying to use a satirical tone.
8. Examine advertisements in several magazines. Find one that makes use of a stereotype. Describe the advertisement and its effect.
9. Why, in your opinion, are stereotypes formed?

CONFESSIONS OF A NUMBER ONE SON

Frank Chin

Frank Chin, born in Berkeley, California, is the author of numerous film scripts and several plays, including *The Year of the Dragon* which premiered in New York in 1974 and was also televised. He has also edited *Aiiieeeee*, an anthology of Asian-American writing. The following essay deals with the image of the Chinese in American films.

I was born and last seen being carried off by alleycats into a dark neighborhood. William Bendix found me in the rubble of a village during a Japanese air raid at my dead momma's withered tit wailing hoarsely. The movie was *China.* I was the symbol of helpless, struggling China in the arms of William Bendix. He named me "Donald Duck." 1

The wail went from movie to movie. The Japs have tortured me into giving up the secret position and are driving the little life of me left in my little battered body in a truck full of Jap soldiers out to get the jump on John Wayne and my missionary teacher from Indiana and all my friends. I grabbed the wheel of the truck and pulled that truck right off the world and sent it down the darkness. My body rolled out of the burning truck to the feet of John Wayne and all my surprised friends working their stealthy way through the jungle. America saw my face by the flamelight of the burning truck full of Japs. They saw me trying not to cry out in pain while tears streamed down my cheeks. 2

"Don't try to talk," John Wayne said softly. And John Wayne and the missionary teacher who'd failed to teach me how to properly spell A-M-E-R-I-C-A instead of A-M-E-L-L-I-C-A exchanged looks and sadly shook their heads. And all the soldiers and all my friends were getting down on their knees around me. "I failed," I said. "I guess I'll never be promoted to sergeant now," and my eyes began to roll back into my skull and my breath, a quiet shriek from my lungs, was the sound of metal scraped with a long file. Now and then I coughed and blood rosebudded out of my mouth. John Wayne took the colonel's bird off his collar and pinned it on me. 3

By the light of burning Japs sputtering and sizzling in the background, women in the shopper's matinees with their paper sacks and red meat tokens saw tears in John Wayne's eyes. "You didn't fail," he said to me and had to gulp something back before he could say, "He-yeck! You got that promotion! 4

138

I got orders from the President himself to promote you all the way to colonel." And the women in the shopper's matinee sighed at the vision of my face filling the darkness. My eyes opened up big and buzzed with an orchestra playing the *Battle Hymn of the Republic*. And the missionary teacher from Indiana put her ear to my mouth as I agonized out my last words, "Ayeeee! Emmmm!" My eyes came open, shining gleaming silver like something crazy. She wiped the blood from my lips, from my eyes, and arranged my hair a bit at a time. "Eee," I continued. "Easy, champ," John Wayne said. He shrugged violently, suddenly, and looked into the flames of the burning truckful of Japs. "Ell! Ell!" I screamed. "Eye! See! Ayy! AMEL-LICA!" I cried struggling up to my elbows suddenly. The missionary teacher screamed. John Wayne said, "At ease, colonel," and I fell back into a shot of John Wayne with his mouth open and was dead in his arms.

One summer vacation from college I was Frank Sinatra's gunbearer in the jungle south of the Chinese border in World War II. The Japs ambushed us, wiped out the field hospital and Frank Sinatra stuck his gun out to me while continuing to glare off after the direction of the runoff Japs.

5

And his arm stayed out there awhile until he got the idea something was wrong. I hadn't taken the gun from him. He turned around to see I wasn't there. I was on the ground awhile back, been blinking sweat out of my eyes a long time now, on my back with a twenty-two pound Browning Automatic Rifle and bipod, a six pound M-1 Garand rifle, a Thompson machine gun with a drum magazine and sack of hand grenades, spare parts and extra Zippo lighters. "I have failed you," I said. "Don't talk now," Frank Sinatra said. Then they were all around my cot. The doctor and Sinatra exchanged looks and shook their heads no at each other. I'm shuddering, trying not to cry. In this movie I'm as tall as Frank Sinatra. Breath comes whinneying from my lungs. Frank Sinatra draws his Colt forty-five and chambers a round. He tells everyone to leave the tent. "You can't do it!" someone says. "It's murder!"

6

"It's either this way, quick, or letting him scream all night," Sinatra said. "You wouldn't let a dog suffer like that." I was never heard from again in that movie. From the time I was born screaming in a bombed-out railroad station in Shanghai through the days I was known on the lot as America's most loyal Chinese American, because the Japs I came up with on the screen were fouler than even the white man imagined, I always get killed. I'm known in the industry as "The Chinese who dies." So I ask the question: Why me?

7

The answer is Charlie Chan of the movies. Our Father Which art in Hollywood, Charlie Chan be Thy Name. Amen. Everybody took to Charlie

8

Chan, knew he was only passing but saw him as the real image of Chinamen anyway. That was in 1925. By 1936 the success of the Charlie Chan image filtered to the top, well-fixed in the minds of the finest people, including the first official Chinatown spokesman: Leong Gor Yun—a fake Chinatown author with a fake Chinese name, who wrote a fake book "Chinatown Inside Out."

America in its sinister wisdom invented a different movie form to irritate and mess on the minds of each of its minorities individually. For Indians it was the Western. The black movie was the courtroom drama where a black man would be accused of crime and then sit in a courtroom and listen to two white men discuss Abraham Lincoln and Karl Marx. The Chinese movie was the Charlie Chan movie and the road movie. Whites like Gary Cooper in *The General Died at Dawn*, Barbara Stanwyck in *The Bitter Tea of General Yen*, Alan Ladd in *China*, and James Stewart in *The Mountain Road* came to China out of Hollywood to get on a Chinese road over some mountains and discover that this road through China, bumping into love and hate, birth and death, is the road of life and runs into roadblocks, sideroads, and wham, a crossroads! But the beginning is Charlie Chan.   9

In the beginning there was Earl Derr Biggers, mild-mannered hack writer with a gift for cliches. In Hawaii, laying out on the lanai, sipping his Mai Tai and listening to the happy kanakas crooning harmoniously in the fields as they chopped the sugarcane, Derr Biggers was the picture of a contented Southern colonel sipping a julep on the verandah. He read about a Chinese detective before. And out of the void of this white man's mind, Charlie Chan was born.   10

In the tradition of 2100 feature films and stage productions with Chinese character leads, no Chinaman's ever played the role of Charlie Chan. Two Japanese in the early days when the Chan part was so small it was at the small print end of the credits, but no Chinaman. Not even when the old men of Fox and Monogram's 44 features had passed. Warner Oland and Sidney Toler were both dead and Roland Winters retired from playing out the last days of his career as someone's grandfather in James Garner and Jerry Lewis movies. All the classic Chans are gone and NBC and Universal Studios did prophesy Chan's second coming in color and sent NBC vice-president David Tebet out into the world saying he was looking for an "Oriental actor who spoke English in an accent understandable to U.S. audiences." Not even when they promised it out of the trade papers, gossip columns, and wire services did a Chinaman ever play Charlie Chan.   11

Keye Luke, the original Number One Son and still active in the post-midnight talk shows doing his Lionel Barrymore imitation, still looks in his forties and now and then shows up as a blind priest of Chinese mysticism   12 who's overcome his handicap by reciting the drabber quotations of Kahlil Gibran on ABC's *Kung Fu*.

Keye spoke English in an accent good enough to be understood playing [13] fools, converts to Catholicism and Oxford all with that same stiff, studied ineptitude of his Number One Son for over 40 years and was last seen renewing an old friendship with Gregory Peck that led directly to his being trampled to death by the Red Guard in *The Chairman*. Keye took a chance and auditioned for the part of his own father. He also had an idea of his own about playing Number One Son grown up. Keye Luke envisioned a television series featuring the adventures of Charlie Chan's Number One Son all grown up. A hip and modern Chinese American tough who might have been an all-American quarterback before a few years as a special agent of the F.B.I. "Charlie Chan worked for the police department," Keye notes. "This will be different. I will be a private detective." Keye Luke didn't get the part of Charlie Chan. And the Derr Biggers estate that owned Charlie Chan demanded the new Chan be just like the old ones. Keye's registered with Medicare now. Number One Son's in his sixties and still dreaming of going into private practice.

Victor Sen Yung, Number Two Son, was Chinatown San Francisco born [14] and raised himself up through high school as a live-in houseboy for a white uptown family where he learned to speak English like he was born in Chicago, Illinois. He's the most talented Asian-American actor there ever was. He stole the show from Bette Davis in *The Letter*, and drove the censors at Paramount nuts with his ability to make anything he said to Loretta Young, in *China*, sound lecherous and aggressive. Scenes between him and Alan Ladd were cut from the finished film because Victor's hornrimmed glasses, skinny, smartass Chinese student was too much for Alan Ladd, who was on the road of life. Among the Yellow actors in Hollywood, Victor Sen Yung is remembered for being moody, pushy, totally out of his mind. He's thought of as being jinxed. I got the impression people were avoiding him. The lines yellow actors are given to speak have been pretty much the same for fifty years. But with Victor Sen Yung's ability to talk any kind of white American and European accent and give it a twirl and a question mark at the end of every phrase and pass it off as a Chinese accent, the lines took on some class.

Soon after Pearl Harbor, the United States Government in the form of [15] the Office of War Information (OWI) notified Hollywood that Charlie Chan movies were now official anti-Jap propaganda. To signal the fact righteously to the Japs, Hollywood produced a grotesque parody of the Chan movies involving a Charlie Chan and his Number One Son who go from comic and lovable clowns to pitiful and loathsome reptiles, from comforting to sinister merely by going from Chinese to Japanese in *Across the Pacific*, John Huston's first big film after his smash *The Maltese Falcon*.

Sydney Greenstreet was a white man who's Jap at heart in Charlie   16
Chan's white suit and white snapbrim . . . unsnapped. And Victor Sen Yung
was the gunzel Joe Tatsuiko. He was to parody himself.

As Charlie Chan's Number Two Son he dressed in the latest fads—   17
pleated pants and two-tone shoes. He took double, wham wham with his eyes
back on white girls, and be bop baree bopped all kinds of American slang
all ineptly, making Americans laugh. They admired the dumb son of Charlie
Chan for wanting to be like them. With instinctive genius Victor Sen Yung
produced a most distasteful and sinister Joe Tatsuiko merely by doing what
Number Two Son did badly for comic relief, but doing it well, so well that,
except for the eyes, the skin and hair, he was immaculately, perfectly American.
Whites couldn't stand it. The sincere fumbling Number Two Son who
was so shy he was rarely seen talking to anyone other than his father or the
black chauffeur was now cocky, backslapping Joe Tatsuiko, looking Humphrey
Bogart in the eye and saying, "Boy, it's good to find someone on this
boat who speaks my language!" He was the first one Bogart shot and killed
in the climactic scenes.

When NBC was sniffing the watering holes of the world for an Oriental   18
actor to play an Oriental role, Victor Sen Yung was showing up as Hop Sing,
the Cartwright boys' cook on TV's *Bonanza*. Benson Fong, Charlie Chan's
Number Three Son, used to be so young, with such a sincere, trusting, handsome
face that he got viciously shot up by the Japs in almost every movie he
was in outside of the Charlie Chan movies. Today Benson Fong runs a string
of sweet'n'sour joints and boasts of buying a new Cadillac every two years.
He still gets killed in most of his movies and was last seen going to his maker
in ABC's *Kung Fu*.

Benson Fong, Victor Sen Yung, and Keye Luke were all in Ross Hunt-   19
er's 1961 production of *Flower Drum Song*. The film's director, Henry Koster,
told me that musicals were usually the costliest form of Hollywood movie
to make, because of the high salaries commanded by stars who were both
actors and song and dance people. But *Flower Drum Song* didn't cost very
much to make, Koster said, because "You don't have to pay Oriental actors
as much as you do regular actors."

NBC and Universal didn't cast a yellow lead in the role of Charlie Chan   20
because they hadn't found an Oriental actor that was "dynamic," had "charisma"
and "star quality"—in other words, "balls"—enough to play the part
of Charlie Chan: . . . a decrepit, hunched over, mealy mouthed, sycophantic
clumsy, more-than-slightly-effeminate, limp-wristed, bucktoothed detective
you could tell was Chinese because he never used first-person pronouns "I,"

"Me," or "We" in the presence of whites. And to compound the offense, NBC trotted out their only black vice-president, Stan Robertson, to say, "We don't think it's offensive," telling us what white men used to tell blacks a generation ago, "We wanted to cast an Oriental, and we looked here and in London and in Hong Kong. Unfortunately, we never found an Oriental actor who could carry the movie."

Stan Robertson was Birmingham's revenge. The Chan movies of the   21
Forties and Fifties were on-screen off-screen double-visioned parables of rac- ist order with whites on top, blacks on the bottom, and two kinds of Chinese in between. "I'm sure that any intelligent and proud Chinese would more or less resent the whole idea of Chan," Roland Winters, the last Chan, said. "Not so much Chan, because he wasn't too bad, but his, you know, the silly kids that did stupid things."

The Chinese and the silly kids that did stupid things had a servant, Bir-   22
mingham. Birmingham was black—lowest fool on the totem pole and played by Mantan Moreland, last seen doing the same vaudeville routine he brought to the Chan films, in a Midas muffler commercial. Now in 1972, a black man speaking for NBC told us that being told not one of us was dynamic enough to play sleepy old Charlie Chan wasn't offensive.

Whites all over America weren't surprised to see a Chinaman with a   23
black servant and talking nasty into the face of people like Willy Best in *Charlie Chan at the Race Track*. A film that featured Charlie Chan saying, "Murder without blood, like Amos without Andy." But it didn't look right to me. Word got around Hollywood that I was a troublemaker. A picture of Stepin Fetchit basking by his pool in Beverly Hills had Chinese servants in Mandarin collars serving him drinks. I sensed a primitive message running to the blacks out of the Charlie Chan movies.

It's no secret that Charlie Chan was official U.S. Government propa-   24
ganda controlled by the Office of War Information during WW2. In the ten Chan films made in the war years, Charlie Chan and his sons weren't busy smashing Jap spy rings or even obviously involved in the war effort. He con- tinued solving high-society murders. His effectiveness as an anti-Japanese tool depended not on his exploits but his being visibly and actively not Jap- anese with all his heart and soul. The lives of Chinese and Chinese-Ameri- cans on and off the screen were pushed by American pop culture as images of the ideal American minority. Our mere and very being encouraged Amer- icans to hate Japanese. We wore buttons that read "I am a loyal Chinese- American."

Later, as one of history's little ironies would have it, Chinamen and Japs   25
were one in Hollywood's mind, and Chinese- and Japanese-Americans were

used against the blacks now the way Chinese-Americans had been used against Japanese-Americans. *U.S. News and World Report* threw us at the blacks with "Success Story of One Minority Group in U.S." "Still being taught," they wrote, "is the old idea that people should depend on their own efforts—not a welfare check—in order to reach America's 'promised land.'" There are those in Chinatown who say the date of that story, December 26, 1966, was the day the San Francisco papers started their run of Negro gunman kills Chinese grocer stories. And with amazingly similar language, *Newsweek*, on June 21, 1971, ran a two-page spread headlined, *The Japanese American Success Story: Outwhiting the Whites*. Tom Wolfe said in *Esquire* that a Chinaman who was "loud, violent, sexually aggressive," was imitating blacks because "loud, violent, sexually aggressive," was "stuff that really stunned most Chinese." David Hilliard of the Black Panthers told the people of Chinatown they were "the Uncle Toms of the non-white peoples."

For the Charlie Chan of the '70s NBC and Universal Studios preserved   26
a white racist tradition. Ross Martin, a white actor best known for playing grotesques on TV's *Wild Wild West*, became the fourth white man to play Charlie Chan in 40 years . . . the fifth, if you count the short-lived TV series that starred J. Carroll Nash as Chan.

None of the Sons got the job as pop, and far from being bitter, Victor   27
Sen Yung blames the blacks for the present scarcity of jobs for yellow actors and objects to Asian-Americans protesting against the casting practice because he fears white backlash in the form of no jobs at all for any yellow actor. Benson Fong doesn't talk about politics or religion or race. And the original Number One Son, Keye Luke, reveals that he has become resigned to white supremacy as a fact of life when he says, "There is one consideration that overrides all others, and that's box office. After all, this is not Oriental theatre, it's a white man's theatre. You have to cater to that."

When I wasn't Charlie Chan's son I was the Chinese who always dies.   28
I died with funny last words, like looking at Alan Ladd and calling him Brother Number Four on my dying breath. "Goodbye. . . . Brother Number Fourererer . . ." I said and went limp, and slipped off the raft into the river. This Spencer Tracy movie was the first movie in which I died off screen. I'd never been *found* dead in a movie before. I'd never died alone without a scene before. Always before I passed and went limp as a movie star was pinning a medal to my bloody shirt, or was shot in the head by the star. I always have a relationship with the star. Like my best friend, Steve McQueen in *The Sand Pebbles*, shooting off the top of my head with his Springfield rifle. Or sometimes I'd die shouting something paradoxical. "The river does not contend against the willow, yet the doorknob still turns," I'd say, and

crash, I was dead. I've never been cut up by a boozer who wore a surgical mask made from one cup of a Chinese nurse's bra. He's sniffed the insides of the nurse's bras before boiling them, and the audience had laughed, as if the sniffing of a sock pulled off a Chinese tit had been sneaked in the movie. The audience laughed when he sniffed round and round the stitching down inside the cup of one large bra, moved to boil it, then did a double take with his nose and sniffed a long hissing sniff of something that made him groan. And he sighed and said, "This fits my face perfectly," bringing the audience out of the dark laughing. I'd never been treated like that in a movie before. I'd never been left alone in a movie, to die away from the Yanks. For me, William Bendix had pulled the pin on a hand grenade, laid his arms out back behind his head, and on the throw shouted, "This is for Donald Duck!"

My only consolation was that someday, all of them, Keye Luke, Victor 29 Sen Yung, Benson Fong, Richard Loo, all of them will find themselves in a movie, dying without a scene and end up like me, seen fit only as a fanatically faithful Chinese-Catholic convert, cooking and dusting for Humphrey Bogart passing himself off as a priest, at an out-of-the-way Chinese village on the road of life. In a scene with a beautiful woman horny for Bogart, Bogart said I was like a woman to him. He said I took care of him "like a good wife." Whatever it was I'd done, Hollywood hadn't forgiven me or forgotten. I stood up in the middle of the movies out of the seating section and asked the stars why I had to die and why they had to make me smile when Bogart likened me to a woman in front of a beautiful woman. I try to talk them out of leaving me alone to die. I'll die, but why do I have to be alone? If I could only be out of the room when Bogart likens me to a woman, or if I didn't understand English in this movie. And the people in the audience wait for Spencer Tracy and the airmen to leave me behind, see it becoming inevitable and weep for me, and they wait for the woman to knock on Bogart's door and come in and laugh.

QUESTIONS

Words to Know

cliché (paragraph 10), *lanai*—verandah (10, *kanakas*—South Sea Islanders (10), mysticism (12), grotesque (15), sycophantic (20), parable (21).

Some of the Issues

1. Who is the "I" in the first seven and last two paragraphs of Chin's essay?
2. How is Charlie Chan characterized? Why, according to Chin, has no Chinese ever acted that role?
3. In paragraph 11 Chin quotes an NBC vice-president. What is the point of the quotation?
4. What does Chin mean when he says, "America in its sinister wisdom invented a different movie form to irritate and mess on the minds of each of its minorities individually" (paragraph 9)? Do you agree with his examples? Can you think of others?
5. Reread the last sentence of paragraph 19. What is your reaction to that statement?
6. In paragraph 20 Chin cites another NBC vice-president. In paragraph 21, why does he call him "Birmingham's revenge"?
7. What is the "primitive message" Chin senses in paragraph 23, and how is the message sent?
8. Explain the irony Chin finds in post-World War II attitudes toward both Chinese and Japanese (paragraph 25).

The Way We Are Told

9. The first seven and last two paragraphs are constructed differently from the others. What is their effect?
10. Chin uses imagined, overdramatized dialog from American movies. How does he make it funny?

Some Subjects for Essays

11. In an essay explain what image of Chinese in American movies Chin most resents.
12. In the 1970s a new type of film involving Chinese characters became

popular: Kung Fu, particularly the films of Bruce Lee. Write an essay in which you argue either one of two theses: that these more recent films represent a stereotype of the Chinese that is essentially not different from those satirized by Frank Chin; or, alternately, that these films add a new dimension to the characterization of Chinese, one that contrasts or contradicts Frank Chin's analysis.

13. Read Vine Deloria's "Custer Died for Your Sins." Both Chin and Deloria attack the stereotyping of their people. In an essay compare and contrast the stereotypes of American Indians and Chinese as the two authors describe them.

IN ETHNIC AMERICA

Michael Novak

Michael Novak, an American of Slovak descent, was born in Johnstown, Pennsylvania. A professor at the State University of New York in Old Westbury, he is the author of several books and articles, most notably *The Rise of the Unmeltable Ethnics* (1972), a defense of the cultural role of southern and eastern European immigrants and their descendants. The selection here comes from that book.

More recently Novak has written *The American Vision* (1978), and *The Spirit of Democratic Capitalism* (1982).

Growing up in America has been an assault upon my sense of worthiness. It has also been a kind of liberation and delight. 1

There must be countless women in America who have known for years that something is peculiarly unfair, yet who only recently have found it possible, because of Women's Liberation, to give tongue to their pain. In recent months I have experienced a similar inner thaw, a gradual relaxation, a willingness to think about feelings heretofore shepherded out of sight. 2

I am born of PIGS—those Poles, Italians, Greeks, and Slavs, those non-English-speaking immigrants numbered so heavily among the workingmen of this nation. Not particularly liberal or radical; born into a history not white Anglo-Saxon and not Jewish; born outside what, in America, is considered the intellectual mainstream—and thus privy to neither power nor status nor intellectual voice. 3

Those Poles of Buffalo and Milwaukee—so notoriously taciturn, sullen, nearly speechless. Who has ever understood them? It is not that Poles do not feel emotion—what is their history if not dark passion, romanticism, betrayal, courage, blood? But where in America is there anywhere a language for voicing what a Christian Pole in this nation feels? He has no Polish culture left him, no Polish tongue. Yet Polish feelings do not go easily into the idiom of happy America, the America of the Anglo-Saxons and yes, in the arts, the Jews. (The Jews have long been a culture of the word, accustomed to exile, skilled in scholarship and in reflection. The Christian Poles are largely of peasant origin, free men for hardly more than a hundred years.) Of what shall the young man of Lackawanna think on his way to work in the mills, departing his relatively dreary home and street? What roots does he have? What language of the heart is available to him? 4

The PIGS are not silent willingly. The silence burns like hidden coals in the chest. 5

148

All four of my grandparents, unknown to one another, arrived in America from the same county in Slovakia. My grandfather had a small farm in Pennsylvania; his wife died in a wagon accident. Meanwhile, Johanna, fifteen, arrived on Ellis Island, dizzy from witnessing births and deaths and illnesses aboard the crowded ship. She had a sign around her neck lettered PASSAIC. There an aunt told her of a man who had lost his wife in Pennsylvania. She went. They were married. She inherited his three children.

Each year for five years Grandma had a child of her own. She was among the lucky; only one died. When she was twenty-two and the mother of seven (my father was the last), her husband died. "Grandma Novak," as I came to know her many years later, resumed the work she had begun in Slovakia at the town home of a man known to my father only as "the Professor"; she housecleaned and she laundered.

I heard this story only weeks ago. Strange that I had not asked insistently before. Odd that I should have such shallow knowledge of my roots. Amazing to me that I do not know what my family suffered, endured, learned, and hoped these last six or seven generations. It is as if there were no project in which we all have been involved, as if history in some way began with my father and with me.

The estrangement I have come to feel derives not only from lack of family history. Early in life, I was made to feel a slight uneasiness when I said my name. When I was very young, the "American" kids still made something out of names unlike their own, and their earnest, ambitious mothers thought long thoughts when I introduced myself.

Under challenge in grammar school concerning my nationality, I had been instructed by my father to announce proudly: "American." When my family moved from the Slovak ghetto of Johnstown to the WASP suburb on the hill, my mother impressed upon us how well we must be dressed, and show good manners, and behave—people think of us as "different" and we mustn't give them any cause. "Whatever you do, marry a Slovak girl," was other advice to a similar end: "They cook. They clean. They take good care of you. For your own good." I was taught to be proud of being Slovak, but to recognize that others wouldn't know what it meant, or care.

Nowhere in my schooling do I recall any attempt to put me in touch with my own history. The strategy was clearly to make an American of me. English literature, American literature, and even the history books, as I recall them, were peopled mainly by Anglo-Saxons from Boston (where most historians seemed to live). Not even my native Pennsylvania, let alone my Slovak forebears, counted for very many paragraphs. (We did have something called "Pennsylvania History" somewhere; I seem to remember its puffs for industry. It could have been written by a Mellon.) I don't remember feeling envy or regret: a feeling, perhaps, of unimportance, of remoteness, of not having heft enough to count.

The fact that I was born a Catholic also complicated life. What is a Catholic but what everybody else is in reaction against? Protestants reformed "the whore of Babylon." Others were "enlightened" from it, and Jews had reason to help Catholicism and the social structure it was rooted in fall apart. The history books and the whole of education hummed in upon that point (for during crucial years I attended a public school): to be modern is decidedly not to be medieval; to be reasonable is not to be dogmatic; to be free is clearly not to live under ecclesiastical authority; to be scientific is not to attend ancient rituals, cherish irrational symbols, indulge in mythic practices. It is hard to grow up Catholic in America without becoming defensive, perhaps a little paranoid, feeling forced to divide the world between "us" and "them."

We had a special language all our own, our own pronunciation for words we shared in common with others (Augústine, contémplative), sights and sounds and smells in which few others participated (incense at Benediction of the Most Blessed Sacrament, Forty Hours, wakes, and altar bells at the silent consecration of the Host); and we had our own politics and slant on world affairs. Since earliest childhood, I have known about a "power elite" that runs America: the boys from the Ivy League in the State Department as opposed to the Catholic boys in Hoover's FBI who (as Daniel Moynihan once put it), keep watch on them. And on a whole host of issues, my people have been, though largely Democratic, conservative: on censorship, on communism, on abortion, on religious schools, etc. "Harvard" and "Yale" long meant "them" to us.

We did not feel this country belonged to us. We felt fierce pride in it, more loyalty than anyone could know. But we felt blocked at every turn. There were not many intellectuals among us, not even very many professional men. Laborers mostly. Small businessmen, agents for corporations perhaps. Content with a little, yes, modest in expectation, and content. But somehow feeling cheated. For a thousand years the Slovaks survived Hungarian hegemony and our strategy here remained the same: endurance and steady work. Slowly, one day, we would overcome.

A special word is required about a complicated symbol: sex. To this day my mother finds it hard to spell the word intact, preferring to write "s--." Not that much was made of sex in our environment. And that's the point: silence. Demonstrative affection, emotive dances, an exuberance Anglo-Saxons seldom seem to share; but on the realities of sex, discretion. Reverence, perhaps; seriousness, surely. On intimacies, it was as though our tongues had been stolen, as though in peasant life for a thousand years—as in the novels of Tolstoi, Sholokhov, and even Kosinski—the context had been otherwise. Passion, certainly; romance, yes; family and children, certainly; but sex rather a minor if explosive part of life.

Imagine, then, the conflict in the generation of my brothers, sister, and [16] myself. Suddenly, what for a thousand years was minor becomes an all-absorbing investigation. Some view it as a drama of "liberation" when the ruling classes (subscribers to the *New Yorker*, I suppose) move progressively, generation by generation since Sigmund Freud, toward concentration upon genital stimulation, and latterly toward consciousness-raising sessions in Clit. Lib. But it is rather a different drama when we stumble suddenly upon mores staggering any expectation our grandparents ever cherished.

Yet more significant in the ethnic experience in America is the intellec- [17] tual world one meets: the definition of values, ideas, and purposes emanating from universities, books, magazines, radio, and television. One hears one's own voice echoed back neither by spokesmen of "middle America" (so complacent, smug, nativist, and Protestant), nor by the "intellectuals." Almost unavoidably, perhaps, education in America leads the student who entrusts his soul to it in a direction which, lacking a better word, we might call liberal: respect for individual conscience, a sense of social responsibility, trust in the free exchange of ideas and procedures of dissent, a certain confidence in the ability of men to "reason together" and adjudicate their differences, a frank recognition of the vitality of the unconscious, a willingness to protect workers and the poor against the vast economic power of industrial corporations, and the like.

On the other hand, the liberal imagination has appeared to be astonish- [18] ingly universalist and relentlessly missionary. Perhaps the metaphor "enlightenment" offers a key. One is *initiated into light*. Liberal education tends to separate children from their parents, from their roots, from their history, in the cause of a universal and superior religion.

In particular, I have regretted and keenly felt the absence of that sym- [19] pathy for PIGS which simple human feeling might have prodded intelligence to muster, that same sympathy which the educated find so easy to conjure up for black culture, Chicano culture, Indian culture, and other cultures of the poor. In such cases one finds the universalist pretensions of liberal culture suspended; some groups, at least, are entitled to be both different and respected. Why do the educated classes find it so difficult to want to understand the man who drives a beer truck, or the fellow with a helmet working on a site across the street with plumbers and electricians, while their sensitivities race easily to Mississippi or even Bedford-Stuyvesant?

There are deep secrets here, no doubt, unvoiced fantasies and scarcely [20] admitted historical resentments. Few persons in describing "middle Americans," "the silent majority," or Scammon and Wattenberg's "typical American voter" distinguish clearly enough between the nativist American and the ethnic American. The first is likely to be Protestant, the second Catholic. Both may be, in various ways, conservative, loyalist, and unenlightened. Each has his own agonies, fears, betrayed expectations. Neither is ready, quite, to become an ally of the other. Neither has the same history behind him here. Neither has the same hopes. Neither lives out the same psychic voyage, shares the same symbols, has the same sense of reality. The rhetoric and metaphors proper to each differ from those of the other.

There is overlap, of course. But country music is not a polka; a successful   21
politician in a Chicago ward needs a very different "common touch" from the one needed by the county clerk in Normal. The urban experience of immigration lacks that mellifluous, optimistic, biblical vision of the good America which springs naturally to the lips of politicians from the Bible Belt. The nativist tends to believe with Richard Nixon that he "knows America, and the American heart is good." The ethnic tends to believe that every American who preceded him has an angle, and that he, by God, will some day find one, too. (Often, ethnics complain that by working hard, obeying the law, trusting their political leaders, and relying upon the American dream, they now have only their own naiveté to blame for rising no higher than they have.)

Unfortunately, it seems, the ethnics erred in attempting to Americanize   22
themselves before clearing the project with the educated classes. They learned to wave the flag and to send their sons to war. They learned to support their President—an easy task, after all, for those accustomed to obeying authority. And where would they have been if Franklin Roosevelt had not sided with them against established interests? They knew a little about communism—the radicals among them in one way, and by far the larger number of conservatives in another. To this day not a few exchange letters with cousins and uncles who did not leave for America when they might have, whose lot is demonstrably harder than their own and less than free.

Finally, the ethnics do not like, or trust, or even understand the intel-   23
lectuals. It is not easy to feel uncomplicated affection for those who call you "pig," "fascist," "racist." One had not yet grown accustomed to not hearing "hunkie," "Polack," "spic," "mick," "dago," and the rest.

At no little sacrifice, one had apologized for foods that smelled too   24
strong for Anglo-Saxon noses; moderated the wide swings of Slavic and Italian emotion; learned decorum; given onself to education, American style; tried to learn tolerance and assimilation. Each generation criticized the earlier for its authoritarian and European and old-fashioned ways. "Up-to-date" was a moral lever. And now when the process nears completion, when a generation appears that speaks without accent and goes to college, still you are considered "pigs," "fascists," and "racists." Racists? Our ancestors owned

no slaves. Most of us ceased being serfs only in the last two hundred years—
the Russians in 1861. . . .

Whereas the Anglo-Saxon model appears to be a system of atomic indi-   25
viduals and high mobility, our model has tended to stress communities of our
own, attachment to family and relatives, stability, and roots. Ethnics tend to
have a fierce sense of attachment to their homes, having been homeowners
for less than three generations: a home is almost fulfillment enough for one
man's life. Some groups save arduously in a passion to *own;* others rent. We
have most ambivalent feelings about suburban assimilation and mobility.
The melting pot is a kind of homogenized soup, and its mores only partly
appeal to ethnics: to some, yes, and to others, no.

It must be said that ethnics think they are better people than the blacks.   26
Smarter, tougher, harder working, stronger in their families. But maybe
many are not sure. Maybe many are uneasy. Emotions here are delicate; one
can understand the immensely more difficult circumstances under which the
blacks have suffered; and one is not unaware of peculiar forms of fear, envy,
and suspicion across color lines. How much of this we learned in America by
being made conscious of our olive skin, brawny backs, accents, names, and
cultural quirks is not plain to us. Racism is not our invention; we did not
bring it with us; we had prejudices enough and would gladly have been
spared new ones. Especially regarding people who suffer more than we.

QUESTIONS

Words to Know

assault (paragraph 1), privy (3), taciturn (4), WASP (10), Mellon (11), ecclesiastical (12), ritual (12), mythic (12), Augústine (13), contémplative (13),
hegemony (14), Tolstoi (15), Sholokhov (15), Kosinski (15), nativist (17), adjudicate (17), unconscious (17), Bedford-Stuyvesant (19), mellifluous (21),
authoritarian (24).

Some of the Issues

1. Explain the meaning of the first paragraph after you have read the third.
   What aspects of his own background does Novak single out? How do
   they relate to his opening statement?

2. Novak refers to his background in paragraph 3 and returns to his family history in paragraphs 6 through 8. What is his reason for inserting paragraphs 4 and 5 in between?

3. How does Novak's family history reflect the silence of the ethnics to which he refers?

4. In paragraph 14, Novak says, "We did not feel this country belonged to us." What has he said in the preceding part of the essay to substantiate that assertion?

5. Explain the anger Novak reflects in discussing sex (paragraphs 15 and 16).

6. Show the points Novak makes to contrast the ethnic and liberal outlook on life in America.

7. What reasons does Novak give for the liberal, intellectual sympathy for Blacks, Chicanos, or Indians, but not for ethnics?

The Way We Are Told

8. Why does Novak make the analogy between Women's Liberation and his own "inner thaw" (paragraph 2)?

9. In paragraphs 4 and 5 Novak uses emotional terms to characterize ethnics. Find some of them, and then contrast them to the language of paragraphs 6 and 7. Can you explain the reasons for the difference between the two sets of paragraphs?

10. In paragraph 10 Novak refers to his people as "different." Different from whom? How does he show that difference? What do his comments imply about Americans?

11. On a few occasions Novak uses sarcasm, or satirizes the people he considers anti-ethnic, the "them" at the end of paragraph 12. Find some examples of satiric statements.

12. Look at the last sentence of paragraph 14. Do you hear any echoes?

Some Subjects For Essays

13. In paragraph 1 Novak refers to growing up in America as "an assault upon my sense of worthiness" as well as "a kind of liberation and delight." In an essay explain how Novak's experience could be both of these.

14. "We did not feel this country belonged to us" (paragraph 14). Novak echoes here many other writers in this anthology. Whom does the country belong to? Try to write a realistic appraisal. (It is easy to say "to all of us," but hardly an answer to the results of cultural difference.)
15. In an essay determine Novak's intended audience. Is it PIGS, for example? Liberals? Argue from the contents of the essay and the way it is written.

A WASP STINGS BACK

Robert Claiborne

Born in England, Robert Claiborne has spent much of his adult life in the United States. His professional activities have largely been concerned with making science understandable to general audiences, as associate editor of *The Scientific American*, editor of the Life Science Library, and the author of a number of books, including *Climate, Man and History* (1970), *The First Americans* (1973), *God or Beast: Evolution and Human Nature* (1974), and *Astronomy for Absolute Beginners* (1975). He has also written many articles for *Harper's*, *The Nation*, *The New York Times*, and other publications. The following selection was published in the "My Turn" section of *Newsweek*.

Over the past few years, American pop culture has acquired a new folk antihero: the Wasp. One slick magazine tells us that the White Anglo-Saxon Protestants rule New York City, while other media gurus credit (or discredit) them with ruling the country—and, by inference, ruining it. A Polish-American declares in a leading newspaper that Wasps have "no sense of honor." NEWSWEEK patronizingly describes Chautauqua as a citadel of "Wasp values," while other folklorists characterize these values more explicitly as a compulsive commitment to the work ethic, emotional uptightness and sexual inhibition. The Wasps, in fact, are rapidly becoming the one minority that every other ethnic group—blacks, Italians, chicanos, Jews, Poles and all the rest—feels absolutely free to dump on. I have not yet had a friend greet me with "Did you hear the one about the two Wasps who . . . ?"—but any day now! 1

I come of a long line of Wasps; if you disregard my French great-great-grandmother and a couple of putatively Irish ancestors of the same vintage, a rather pure line. My mother has long been one of the Colonial Dames, an organization some of whose members consider the Daughters of the American Revolution rather parvenu. My umpty-umpth Wasp great-grandfather, William Claiborne, founded the first European settlement in what is now Maryland (his farm and trading post were later ripped off by the Catholic Lord Baltimore, Maryland politics being much the same then as now). 2

As a Wasp, the mildest thing I can say about the stereotype emerging from the current wave of anti-Wasp chic is that I don't recognize myself. As regards emotional uptightness and sexual inhibition, modesty forbids comment—though I dare say various friends and lovers of mine could testify on these points if they cared to. I will admit to enjoying work—because I am 3

156

lucky enough to be able to work at what I enjoy—but not, I think, to the point of compulsiveness. And so far as ruling America, or even New York, is concerned, I can say flatly that (a) it's a damn lie because (b) if I *did* rule them, both would be in better shape than they are. Indeed I and all my Wasp relatives, taken in a lump, have far less clout with the powers that run this country than any one of the Buckleys or Kennedys (Irish Catholic), the Sulzbergers or Guggenheims (Jewish), or the late A. P. Giannini (Italian) of the Bank of America.

Admittedly, both corporate and (to a lesser extent) political America are 4 dominated by Wasps—just as (let us say) the garment industry is dominated by Jews, and organized crime by Italians. But to conclude from this that The Wasps are the American elite is as silly as to say that The Jews are cloak-and-suiters or The Italians are gangsters. Wasps, like other ethnics, come in all varieties, including criminals—political, corporate and otherwise.

More seriously, I would like to say a word for the maligned "Wasp val- 5 ues," one of them in particular. As a matter of historical fact, it was we Wasps—by which I mean here the English-speaking peoples—who invented the idea of *limited governments:* that there are some things that no king, President or other official is allowed to do. It began more than seven centuries ago, with Magna Carta, and continued (to cite only the high spots) through the wrangles between Parliament and the Stuart kings, the Puritan Revolution of 1640, the English Bill of Rights of 1688, the American Revolution and our own Bill of Rights and Constitution.

The Wasp principle of limited government emerged through protracted 6 struggle with the much older principle of unlimited government. This latter was never more cogently expressed than at the trial of Charles I, when the hapless monarch informed his judges that, as an anointed king, he was not accountable to any court in the land. A not dissimilar position was taken more recently by another Wasp head of state—and with no more success; Executive privilege went over no better in 1974 than divine right did in 1649. The notion that a king, a President or any other official can do as he damn well pleases has never played in Peoria—or Liverpool or Glasgow, Melbourne or Toronto. For more than 300 years, no Wasp nation has endured an absolute monarchy, dictatorship or any other form of unlimited government—which is something no Frenchman, Italian, German, Pole, Russian or Hispanic can say.

It is perfectly true, of course, that we Wasps have on occasion imposed 7 unlimited governments on other (usually darker) peoples. We have, that is, acted in much the same way as have most other nations that possessed the requisite power and opportunity—including many Third World nations whose leaders delight in lecturing us on political morality (for recent information on this point, consult the files on Biafra, Bangladesh and Brazil, Indian tribes of). Yet even here, Wasp values have played an honorable part. When you start with the idea that Englishmen are entitled to self-government, you end by conceding the same right to Africans and Indians. If you begin by declaring that all (white) men are created equal, you must sooner or later face up to the fact that blacks are also men—and conform your conduct, however reluctantly, to your values.

Keeping the Wasp faith hasn't always been easy. We Wasps, like other people, don't always live up to our own principles, and those of us who don't, if occupying positions of power, can pose formidable problems to the rest of us. Time after time, in the name of anti-Communism, peace with honor or some other slippery shibboleth, we have been conned or bullied into tolerating government interference with our liberties and privacy in all sorts of covert—and sometimes overt—ways; time after time we have had to relearn the lesson that eternal vigilance is the price of liberty.

It was a Wasp who uttered that last thought. And it was a congress of Wasps who, about the same time, denounced the executive privileges of George III and committed to the cause of liberty their lives, their fortunes and—*pace* my Polish-American compatriot—their sacred honor.

QUESTIONS

Words to Know

Wasp (title), parvenu (paragraph 2), maligned (5), Magna Carta (5), Stuart kings (5), Charles I (6), Biafra (7), shibboleth (8).

Some of the Issues

1. Find the topic sentence of paragraph 1.
2. What is the point Claiborne makes about ethnic jokes (paragraph 1)?
3. In what way does Claiborne establish his credentials?
4. In paragraph 3 Claiborne says that "it's a damn lie" that he rules New York, let alone America. In paragraph 4, however, he says "Admittedly, both corporate and (to a lesser extent) political America are dominated by Wasps." Is he contradicting himself in these two paragraphs?

5. Paragraph 5 changes the tone. How does Claiborne move from defense of Wasps (paragraphs 1 through 4) to a counterattack? What is the main point of that counterattack?
6. What is the reference to "Executive privilege" in 1974? How justified is the analogy between it and the fate of King Charles I in 1649 (paragraph 6)?
7. Consider the last sentence of paragraph 6 and the first of paragraph 7. Does Claiborne feel he has to defend the Wasp role further?
8. What is the topic of the last sentence of paragraph 7? Is it true historically as well as logically?
9. What does Claiborne mean by "slippery shibboleth" (paragraph 8)?

The Way We Are Told

10. Find words and phrases in paragraph 1 that Claiborne uses to lay the groundwork for his defense of Wasps, or for his counterattack.
11. Find the main thesis that Claiborne advances and show how he supports and defends it. Make an outline of his essay for this purpose.
12. Show how, in paragraph 5, Claiborne builds to his major point.

Some Subjects for Essays

13. In an essay advance the thesis that the knowledge of history is important in developing national, ethnic, racial, or religious pride and coherence. Develop your thesis through the use of logical argument and examples.
14. If you feel that your nationality (ethnicity, race, religion) has been, as Claiborne puts it, "dumped on," explain the dumping and write a defense.

ON THE ART OF STEALING HUMAN RIGHTS

Rarihokwats (Jerry Gambill)

Rarihokwats is a Mohawk Indian scholar and former editor of *Akwasasne Notes*. This satirical essay was originally presented as a speech before a human rights conference at the Tobique Reserve in New Brunswick, Canada, in the summer of 1968.

The art of denying Indians their human rights has been refined to a science. The following list of commonly used techniques will be helpful in "burglarproofing" your reserves and *your rights*.

GAIN THE INDIANS' CO-OPERATION—It is much easier to steal someone's human rights if you can do it with his OWN co-operation. SO. . . .

1. Make him a non-person. Human rights are for people. Convince Indians their ancestors were savages, that they were pagan, that Indians are drunkards. Make them wards of the government. Make a legal distinction, as in the Indian Act, between Indians and persons. Write history books that tell half the story.

2. Convince the Indian that he should be patient, that these things take time. Tell him that we are making progress, and that progress takes time.

3. Make him believe that things are being done for his own good. Tell him that you're sure that after he has experienced your laws and actions that he will realize how good they have been. Tell the Indian he has to take a little of the bad in order to enjoy the benefits you are conferring on him.

4. Get some Indian people to do the dirty work. There are always those who will act for you to the disadvantage of their own people. Just give them a little honor and praise. This is generally the function of band councils, chiefs, and advisory councils: They have little legal power, but can handle the tough decisions such as welfare, allocation of housing, etc.

5. Consult the Indian, but do not act on the basis of what you hear. Tell the Indian he has a voice and go through the motions of listening. Then interpret what you have heard to suit your own needs.

6. Insist that the Indian "GOES THROUGH THE PROPER CHANNELS." Make

160

the channels and the procedures so difficult that he won't bother to do anything. When he discovers what the proper channels are and becomes profi-
cient at the procedures, change them.

7. Make the Indian believe that you are working hard for him, putting   9
in much overtime and at a great sacrifice, and imply that he should be appre-
ciative. This is the ultimate in skills in stealing human rights: When you
obtain the thanks of your victim.

8. Allow a few individuals to "MAKE THE GRADE" and then point to them   10
as examples. Say that the "HARDWORKERS" and the "GOOD" Indians have
made it, and that therefore it is a person's own fault if he doesn't succeed.

9. Appeal to the Indian's sense of fairness, and tell him that, even though   11
things are pretty bad, it is not right for him to make strong protests. Keep
the argument going on his form of protest and avoid talking about the real
issue. Refuse to deal with him while he is protesting. Take all the fire out of
his efforts.

10. Encourage the Indian to take his case to court. This is very expen-   12
sive, takes lots of time and energy, and is very safe because the laws are
stacked against him. The court's ruling will defeat the Indian's cause, but
makes him think he has obtained justice.

11. Make the Indian believe that things could be worse, and that instead   13
of complaining about the loss of human rights, to be grateful for the human
rights we do have. In fact, convince him that to attempt to regain a right he
has lost is likely to jeopardize the rights that he still has.

12. Set yourself up as the protector of the Indian's human rights, and   14
then you can choose to act on only those violations you wish to act upon. By
getting successful action on a few minor violations of human rights, you can
point to these as examples of your devotion to his cause. The burglar who is
also the doorman is the perfect combination.

13. Pretend that the reason for the loss of human rights is for some other   15
reason than that the person is an Indian. Tell him some of your best friends
are Indians, and that his loss of rights is because of his housekeeping, his
drinking, his clothing. If he improves in these areas, it will be necessary for
you to adopt another technique of stealing his rights.

14. Make the situation more complicated than is necessary. Tell the   16
Indian you will have to take a survey to find out just how many other Indians
are being discriminated against. Hire a group of professors to make a year-
long research project.

15. Insist on unanimity. Let the Indian know that when all the Indians   17
in Canada can make up their minds about just what they want as a group,
then you will act. Play one group's special situation against another group's
wishes.

16. Select very limited alternatives, neither of which has much merit, and then tell the Indian that he indeed has a choice. Ask, for instance, if he could or would rather have council elections in June or December, instead of asking if he wants them at all. 18

17. Convince the Indian that the leaders who are the most beneficial and powerful are dangerous and not to be trusted. Or simply lock them up on some charge like driving with no lights. Or refuse to listen to the real leaders and spend much time with the weak ones. Keep the people split from their leaders by sowing rumor. Attempt to get the best leaders into high-paying jobs where they have to keep quiet to keep their paycheck coming in. 19

18. Speak of the common good. Tell the Indian that you can't consider yourselves when there is the whole nation to think of. Tell him that he can't think only of himself. For instance, in regard to hunting rights, tell him we have to think of all the hunters, or the sporting-goods industry. 20

19. Remove rights so gradually that people don't realize what has happened until it is too late. Again, in regard to hunting rights, first restrict the geographical area where hunting is permitted, then cut the season to certain times of the year, then cut the limits down gradually, then insist on licensing, and then Indians will be on the same grounds as white sportsmen. 21

20. Rely on reason and logic (your reason and logic) instead of rightness and morality. Give thousands of reasons for things, but do not get trapped into arguments about what is right. 22

21. Hold a conference on HUMAN RIGHTS, have everyone blow off steam and tension, and go home feeling that things are well in hand. 23

QUESTIONS

Some of the Issues

1. What is Gambill's thesis?
2. Can you sum up Gambill's argument in fewer points? Which ones could be grouped together?
3. Examine Gambill's 21 points one by one. Which are more convincing, in your opinion? Where possible, either add additional examples or counter-examples to support or contradict his points.

The Way We Are Told

4. Gambill uses satire. Try to define it (after looking it up in a dictionary, if necessary) by citing instances of its use in the 21 points.
5. Each of Gambill's 21 arguments begins with a verb in the imperative form. What is the effect of this repetition?
6. Who is Gambill's audience? Indians? Non-Indians? Argue your opinion.

Some Subjects for Essays

7. Write your own satirical essay modeled on Gambill's. Topics may be The Art of Stealing Students' Rights Women's Rights, Worker's Rights, Children's Rights, or Senior Citizen's Rights.

A MODEST PROPOSAL

Jonathan Swift

Jonathan Swift (1667–1745) is the author of *Gulliver's Travels* (1726). Born in Dublin of a Protestant family in a Catholic country, he was educated at Trinity College, Dublin, and at Oxford University. He took orders in the Anglican Church and eventually became Dean of St. Patrick's Cathedral in Dublin. One of the great satirists of English literature, he attacked religious as well as social and educational corruption in his books, *A Tale of a Tub* and *Gulliver's Travels*. In his "Modest Proposal" Swift addresses himself to the English absentee rulers of Ireland

"This great town" in the first paragraph refers to Dublin. The last sentence of paragraph 1 refers to the practice of poor people committing themselves, usually for a fixed number of years, to service in a military enterprise or in a colony (including the American colonies).

A MODEST PROPOSAL

*For Preventing the Children of Poor People in Ireland
from Being a Burden to Their Parents or Country,
and for Making Them Beneficial to the Public*

It is a melancholy object to those who walk through this great town or travel in the country, when they see the streets, the roads, and cabin doors, crowded with beggars of the female sex, followed by three, four, or six children, all in rags and importuning every passenger for an alms. These mothers, instead of being able to work for their honest livelihood, are forced to employ all their time in strolling to beg sustenance for their helpless infants, who, as they grow up, either turn thieves for want of work, or leave their dear native country to fight for the Pretender in Spain, or sell themselves to the Barbadoes.

I think it is agreed by all parties that this prodigious number of children in the arms, or on the backs, or at the heels of their mothers, and frequently of their fathers, is in the present deplorable state of the kingdom a very great additional grievance; and therefore whoever could find out a fair, cheap, and easy method of making these children sound, useful members of the commonwealth would deserve so well of the public as to have his statue set up for a preserver of the nation.

But my intention is very far from being confined to provide only for the children of professed beggars; it is of a much greater extent, and shall

164

take in the whole number of infants at a certain age who are born of parents in effect as little able to support them as those who demand our charity in the streets.

As to my own part, having turned my thoughts for many years upon this important subject, and maturely weighed the several schemes of other projectors, I have always found them grossly mistaken in their computation. It is true, a child just dropped from its dam may be supported by her milk for a solar year, with little other nourishment; at most not above the value of two shillings, which the mother may certainly get, or the value in scraps, by her lawful occupation of begging; and it is exactly at one year old that I propose to provide for them in such a manner as instead of being a charge upon their parents or the parish, or wanting food and raiment for the rest of their lives, they shall on the contrary contribute to the feeding, and partly to the clothing, of many thousands. 4

There is likewise another great advantage in my scheme, that it will prevent those voluntary abortions, and that horrid practice of women murdering their bastard children, alas, too frequent among us, sacrificing the poor innocent babes, I doubt, more to avoid the expense than the shame, which would move tears and pity in the most savage and inhuman breast. 5

The number of souls in this kingdom being usually reckoned one million and a half, of these I calculate there may be about two hundred thousand couples whose wives are breeders; from which number I subtract thirty thousand couples who are able to maintain their own children, although I apprehend there cannot be so many under the present distress of the kingdom; but this being granted, there will remain an hundred and seventy thousand breeders. I again subtract fifty thousand for those women who miscarry, or whose children die by accident or disease within the year. There only remain an hundred and twenty thousand children of poor parents annually born. The question therefore is, how this number shall be reared and provided for, which, as I have already said, under the present situation of affairs, is utterly impossible by all the methods hitherto proposed. For we can neither employ them in handicraft nor agriculture; we neither build houses (I mean in the country) nor cultivate land. They can very seldom pick up a livelihood by stealing till they arrive at six years old, except where they are of towardly parts; although I confess they learn the rudiments much earlier, during which time they can however be looked upon only as probationers, as I have been informed by a principal gentleman in the country of Cavan, who protested to me that he never knew above one or two instances under the age of six, even in a part of the kingdom so renowned for the quickest proficiency in that art. 6

I am assured by our merchants that a boy or a girl before twelve years 7

old is no salable commodity; and even when they come to this age, they will
not yield above three pounds, or three pounds and half a crown at most on
the Exchange; which cannot turn to account either to the parents or the kingdom, the charge of nutriment and rags having been at least four times that
value.

I shall now therefore humbly propose my own thoughts, which I hope   8
will not be liable to the least objection.

I have been assured by a very knowing American of my acquaintance   9
in London, that a young healthy child well nursed is at a year old a most
delicious, nourishing, and wholesome food, whether stewed, roasted, baked,
or boiled; and I make no doubt that it will equally serve in a fricassee or a
ragout.

I do therefore humbly offer it to public consideration that of the   10
hundred and twenty thousand children, already computed, twenty thousand
may be reserved for breed, whereof only one fourth part to be males, which
is more than we allow to sheep, black cattle, or swine; and my reason is that
these children are seldom the fruits of marriage, a circumstance not much
regarded by our savages, therefore one male will be sufficient to serve four
females. That the remaining hundred thousand may at a year old be offered
in sale to the persons of quality and fortune through the kingdom, always
advising the mother to let them suck plentifully in the last month, so as to
render them plump and fat for a good table. A child will make two dishes
at an entertainment for friends; and when the family dines alone, the fore
or hind quarter will make a reasonable dish, and seasoned with a little pepper or salt will be very good boiled on the fourth day, especially in winter.

I have reckoned upon a medium that a child just born will weigh twelve   11
pounds, and in a solar year if tolerably nursed increaseth to twenty-eight
pounds.

I grant this food will be somewhat dear, and therefore very proper for   12
landlords, who, as they have already devoured most of the parents, seem to
have the best title to the children.

Infant's flesh will be in season throughout the year, but more plentiful   13
in March, and a little before and after. For we are told by a grave author,
an eminent French physician, that fish being a prolific diet, there are more
children born in Roman Catholic countries about nine months after Lent,
than at any other season; therefore, reckoning a year after Lent, the markets
will be more glutted than usual, because the number of popish infants is at
least three to one in this kingdom; and therefore it will have one other collateral advantage, by lessening the number of Papists among us.

I have already computed the charge of nursing a beggar's child (in   14
which list I reckon all cottagers, laborers, and four fifths of the farmers) to

be about two shillings per annum, rags included; and I believe no gentleman would repine to give ten shillings for the carcass of a good fat child, which, as I have said, will make four dishes of excellent nutritive meat, when he hath only some particular friend or his own family to dine with him. Thus the squire will learn to be a good landlord, and grow popular among the tenants; the mother will have eight shillings net profit, and be fit for work till she produces another child.

Those who are more thrifty (as I must confess the times require) may flay the carcass; the skin of which artificially dressed will make admirable gloves for ladies, and summer boots for fine gentlemen.   15

As to our city of Dublin, shambles may be appointed for this purpose in the most convenient parts of it, and butchers we may be assured will not be wanting; although I rather recommend buying the children alive, and dressing them hot from the knife as we do roasting pigs.   16

A very worthy person, a true lover of his country, and whose virtues I highly esteem, was lately pleased in discoursing on this matter to offer a refinement upon my scheme. He said that many gentlemen of his kingdom, having of late destroyed their deer, he conceived that the want of venison might be well supplied by the bodies of young lads and maidens, not exceeding fourteen years of age nor under twelve, so great a number of both sexes in every county being now ready to starve for want of work and service; and these to be disposed of by their parents, if alive, or otherwise by their nearest relations. But with due deference to so excellent a friend and so deserving a patriot, I cannot be altogether in his sentiments; for as to the males, my American acquaintance assured me from frequent experience that their flesh was generally tough and lean, like that of our schoolboys, by continual exercise, and their taste disagreeable; and to fatten them would not answer the charge. Then as to the females, it would, I think with humble submission, be a loss to the public, because they soon would become breeders themselves; and besides, it is not improbable that some scrupulous people might be apt to censure such a practice (although indeed very unjustly) as a little bordering upon cruelty; which, I confess, hath always been with me the strongest objection against any project, how well soever intended.   17

But in order to justify my friend, he confessed that this expedient was put into his head by the famous Psalmanazar, a native of the island Formosa, who came from thence to London above twenty years ago, and in conversation told my friend that in his country when any young person happened to be put to death, the executioner sold the carcass to the persons of quality as a prime dainty; and that in his time the body of a plump girl of fifteen, who was crucified for an attempt to poison the emperor, was sold to his Imperial Majesty's prime minister of state, and other great mandarins of the   18 court, in joints from the gibbet, at four hundred crowns. Neither indeed can I deny that if the same use were made of several plump young girls in this town, who without one single groat to their fortunes cannot stir abroad without a chair, and appear at the playhouse and assemblies in foreign fineries which they never will pay for, the kingdom would not be the worse.

Some persons of a desponding spirit are in great concern about that vast 19 number of poor people who are aged, diseased, or maimed, and I have been desired to employ my thoughts what course may be taken to ease the nation of so grievous an encumbrance. But I am not in the least pain upon that matter, because it is very well known that they are every day dying and rotting by cold and famine, and filth and vermin, as fast as can be reasonably expected. And as to the younger laborers, they are now in almost as hopeful a condition. They cannot get work, and consequently pine away for want of nourishment to a degree that if any time they are accidentally hired to common labor, they have not strength to perform it; and thus the country and themselves are happily delivered from the evils to come.

I have too long digressed, and therefore shall return to my subject. I 20 think the advantages by the proposal which I have made are obvious and many, as well as of the highest importance.

For first, as I have already observed, it would greatly lessen the number 21 of Papists, with whom we are yearly overrun, being the principal breeders of the nation as well as our most dangerous enemies; and who stay at home on purpose to deliver the kingdom to the Pretender, hoping to take their advantage by the absence of so many good Protestants, who have chosen rather to leave their country than to stay at home and pay tithes against their conscience to an Episcopal curate.

Secondly, the poorer tenants will have something valuable of their own, 22 which by law may be made liable to distress, and help to pay their landlord's rent, their corn and cattle being already seized and money a thing unknown.

Thirdly, whereas the maintenance of an hundred thousand children, 23 from two years old and upwards, cannot be computed at less than ten shillings a piece per annum, the nation's stock will be thereby increased fifty thousand pounds per annum, besides the profit of a new dish introduced to the tables of all gentlemen of fortune in the kingdom who have any refinement in taste. And the money will circulate among ourselves, the goods being entirely of our own growth and manufacture.

Fourthly, the constant breeders, besides the gain of eight shillings sterling per annum by the sale of their children, will be rid of the charge for 24 maintaining them after the first year.

Fifthly, this food would likewise bring great custom to taverns, where 25 the vintners will certainly be so prudent as to procure the best receipts for dressing it to perfection, and consequently have their houses frequented by all the fine gentlemen, who justly value themselves upon their knowledge in good eating; and a skillful cook, who understands how to oblige his guests, will contrive to make it as expensive as they please.

Sixthly, this would be a great inducement to marriage, which all wise 26 nations have either encouraged by rewards or enforced by laws and penalties. It would increase the care and tenderness of mothers toward their children, when they were sure of a settlement for life to the poor babes, provided in some sort by the public, to their annual profit instead of expense. We should see an honest emulation among the married women, which of them could bring the fattest child to the market. Men would become as fond of their wives during the time of their pregnancy as they are now of their mares in foal, their cows in calf, or sows when they are ready to farrow; nor offer to beat or kick them (as is too frequent a practice) for fear of a miscarriage.

Many other advantages might be enumerated. For instance, the addi- 27 tion of some thousand carcasses in our exportation of barreled beef, the propagation of swine's flesh, and improvements in the art of making good bacon, so much wanted among us by the great destruction of pigs, too frequent at our tables, which are no way comparable in taste or magnificence to a well-grown, fat, yearling child, which roasted whole will make a considerable figure at a lord mayor's feast or any other public entertainment. But this and many others I omit, being studious of brevity.

Supposing that one thousand families in this city would be constant cus- 28 tomers for infants' flesh, besides others who might have it at merry meetings, particularly weddings and christenings, I compute that Dublin would take off annually about twenty thousand carcasses, and the rest of the kingdom (where probably they will be sold somewhat cheaper) the remaining eighty thousand.

I can think of no one objection that will possibly be raised against this 29 proposal, unless it should be urged that the number of people will be thereby much lessened in the kingdom. This I freely own, and it was indeed one principal design in offering it to the world. I desire the reader will observe, that I calculate my remedy for this one individual kingdom of Ireland and for no other that ever was, is, or I think ever can be upon earth. Therefore, let no man talk to me of other expedients: of taxing our absentees at five shillings a pound: of using neither clothes nor household furniture except what is of our own growth and manufacture: of utterly rejecting the materials and instruments that promote foreign luxury: of curing the expensiveness of pride, vanity, idleness, and gaming in our women: of introducing a vein of parsimony, prudence, and temperance: of learning to love our country, in the want of which we differ even from Laplanders and the inhabitants of Topinamboo: of quitting our animosities and factions, nor acting any longer like the Jews, who were murdering one another at the very moment their city was taken: of being a little cautious not to sell our country and conscience for nothing: of teaching landlords to have at least one degree of mercy toward their tenants: lastly, of putting a spirit of honesty, industry, and skill into our shopkeepers; who, if a resolution could now be taken to buy only our native goods, would immediately unite to cheat and exact upon us in the price, the measure, and the goodness, nor could ever yet be brought to make one fair proposal of just dealing, though often and earnestly invited to it.

Therefore, I repeat, let no man talk to me of these and the like expedients, till he hath at least some glimpse of hope that there will ever be some hearty and sincere attempt to put them in practice. 30

But as to myself, having been wearied out for many years with offering vain, idle, visionary thoughts, and at length utterly despairing of success, I fortunately fell upon this proposal, which, as it is wholly new, so it hath something solid and real, of no expense and little trouble, full in our own power, and whereby we can incur no danger in disobliging England. For this kind of commodity will not bear exportation, the flesh being of too tender a consistence to admit a long continuance in salt, although perhaps I could name a country which would be glad to eat up our whole nation without it. 31

After all, I am not so violently bent upon my own opinion as to reject any offer proposed by wise men, which shall be found equally innocent, cheap, easy, and effectual. But before something of that kind shall be advanced in contradiction to my scheme, and offering a better, I desire the author or authors will be pleased maturely to consider two points. First, as things now stand, how they will be able to find food and raiment for an hundred thousand useless mouths and backs. And secondly, there being a round million of creatures in human figure throughout this kingdom, whose sole subsistence put into a common stock would leave them in debt two millions of pounds sterling, adding those who are beggars by profession to the bulk of farmers, cottagers, and laborers, with their wives and children who are beggars in effect; I desire those politicians who dislike my overture, and may perhaps be so bold to attempt an answer, that they will first ask the parents of these mortals whether they would not at this day think it a great happiness to have been sold for food at a year old in this manner I prescribe, and thereby have avoided such a perpetual scene of misfortunes as they have since gone through by the oppression of landlords, the impossibility of paying rent without money or trade, the want of common sustenance, with neither house nor clothes to cover them from the inclemencies of the weather, and the most inevitable prospect of entailing the like or greater miseries upon their breed forever. 32

I profess, in the sincerity of my heart, that I have not the least personal 33 interest in endeavoring to promote this necessary work, having no other motive than the public good of my country, by advancing our trade, providing for infants, relieving the poor, and giving some pleasure to the rich. I have no children by which I can propose to get a single penny; the youngest being nine years old, and my wife past childbearing.

QUESTIONS

Words to Know

object (paragraph 1), importuning (1), alms (1), sustenance (1), Pretender (1), prodigious (2), dam (4), raiment (4), towardly parts (6), rudiments (6), probationer (6), commodity (7), nutriment (7), fricassee (9), ragout (9), quality (10), fortune (10), popish (13), collateral (13), Papist (13), repine (14), shambles (16), deference (17), scrupulous (17), censure (17), expedient (18), gibbet (18), groat (18), assemblies (18), desponding (19), maimed (19), encumbrance (19), vermin (19), digressed (20), prudent (25), receipts (25), propagation (27), gaming (29), parsimony (29), inclemencies (32).

Some of the Issues

1. Paragraphs 1 through 6 are an introduction. What is the main point the author wants to make?
2. Paragraph 7 is a transition. Before you have read the the rest, what might it foretell?
3. The short paragraph 8 is the beginning of the real proposal and paragraph 9, its central idea. Explain that idea.
4. Paragraph 10 expands the proposal in 9. It relates in particular to paragraph 6. Why are all these statistical calculations important? What do they contribute to the impact of the essay?
5. Look back to paragraph 5. What hints of the ideas to come do you now find in it?
6. Paragraphs 15 through 17 offer refinements on the main theme. What are they?
7. Examine the logic of each of the advantages of the proposal, as listed in

paragraphs 21 through 26. Why is the lessening of the number of Papists a particular advantage?

8. In paragraph 29, when the essay turns to possible objections, which are the ones that are omitted completely? Why? Why does the narrator so vehemently concentrate on Ireland in this paragraph?

9. In paragraph 29 other remedies are also proposed for solving the plight of Ireland. What distinguishes them from the one the narrator is advocating?

The Way We Are Told

10. Swift creates a narrator whose modest proposal this is. Try to imagine him: what kind of person might he be? What might be his profession? Consider some of the phrases he uses, his obsession with statistics and the financial aspects of the problem, and his attention to detail.

11. In paragraph 4, in the narrator's choice of words, you find the first hint of what is to come. Locate it. Do you find an echo in paragraph 6?

12. Having made his proposal boldly in paragraph 9, the narrator develops it in paragraphs 10 through 14. Paragraphs 15 through 17 heighten the effect. Consider the choice of images in these paragraphs.

Some Subjects for Essays

13. Do you have any modest proposals as to what to do with teachers, younger brothers or sisters, former boyfriends or girlfriends, or anyone else?

A WASP HYMN

Eve Merriam

Eve Merriam, a poet, playwright, and teacher, has published more than 40 books. Her plays include *The Club,* in which women impersonate men, and *And I Ain't Finished Yet,* produced off-Broadway in 1981. Merriam's poetry, often humorous and satirical, at times treats feminist themes. Her poetry collections include *The Double Bed from the Feminine Side* (1958), *Mommies at Work* (1961), *Growing up Female in America* (1971), and *The Birthday Cow* (1978). "A Wasp Hymn" was published in *The New Republic* in 1969.

All men are brothers:
White Anglo-Saxon Protestants and others.

All God's children are blessed:
White Anglo-Saxon Protestants and the rest.

We are all one in His sight:
White Anglo-Saxon Protestants and those whom the census designates as non-white.

To each of us His grace is willed:
White Anglo-Saxon Protestants and the traditionally unskilled.

His love is ever seeking
White Anglo-Saxon Protestants and the non-English speaking.

His amplitude embraces
White Anglo-Saxon Protestants and municipal welfare cases.

Divinely He inspires
White Anglo-Saxon Protestants and low-income-housing-project qualifiers.

A single Omnipotence rules
White Anglo-Saxon Protestants and vocational guidance schools.

One Godhead hath created
White Anglo-Saxon Protestants and the limited credit-rated.

173

United we all hearken to His almighty heeding:
White Anglo-Saxon Protestants   and   those in need of remedial
                                                                 reading.

His great beneficence imbues
White Anglo-Saxon Protestants   and   those with sublimated I.Q.s.

Yes, his total glory doth infuse
White Anglo-Saxon Protestants   and   those who do not belong to
                                                                 and therefore who do not have
                                                                 to pay any country club dues.

Then praise Him who fathers all believers:
White Anglo-Saxon Protestants   and   socio-economico-culturally
                                                                    disadvantaged underachievers.

For the good Lord hath us all begot:
White Anglo-Saxon Protestants   and   not!

FIVE

Identities

*O*ne of the ways in which American society has traditionally been described is by the image of the melting pot. For many, it has been the right image. Millions came to this continent, the "huddled masses yearning to breathe free" in the line from Emma Lazarus' poem that is inscribed on the base of the Statue of Liberty. They traveled in steerage, they passed through the ordeal of Ellis Island, they worked and struggled, they moved up in the world (and out to the suburbs), and melted into the mainstream of America.

Not all did, or could, or wanted to. Emma Lazarus' poem, after all, did not take account of those who came in chains, or those, not much better off, who came as indentured labor. And even for those who wanted to come, the new life could be a wrenching experience, an unsettling change of identity.

The selections in this part of the anthology offer some examples of the process and problem of adjustment, whether to a new country, a different social class, or a dominant group.

Mary Antin came to America at the turn of the twentieth century from a small town in Russia. She came at the height of mass immigration from Europe, when as many as a million newcomers arrived annually. She had experienced persecution; her father had come ahead to establish himself and make a home; and now she arrived, a child with her mother, sisters, and brother, to start a new life in the Promised Land or, to be more precise, in a tenement flat in a shabby alley of a Boston slum. Yet, it was all new, glorious, and promising to her, especially the prospect of a free education.

Norman Podhoretz was the recipient of that free education at a much later date. His story differs from Antin's. She came to America eager to assume whatever changed identity the new land would bestow on her. Podhoretz resisted the process that was to turn the "dirty slum child" into a Harvard swan. In the end, the new identity wins out in the "brutal bargain" he describes, but it is a wrenching process of gain and loss.

The story of Frank Rissarro, a case history recorded by Richard Sennett and Jonathan Cobb, involves a change of identity in a different sphere. Rissarro, a third-generation Italian-American of working class background, rises into the middle class with a suburban home and a steady office job, but he never feels entirely comfortable in his new role. His change is also a process of gain and loss, like Podhoretz', but he is much less aware of its impact on him.

Ernesto Galarza experienced acculturation in yet another way. As a Mexican immigrant to a California city, he describes the differences in daily living between the Mexican-American and Anglo communities and his own role as emissary between the two cultures.

Malcolm X, in a brief excerpt from his autobiography, describes how, *as a teen-ager, he put himself through the painful and ultimately degrading process of "conking": straightening his hair with a lye solution to make it look like a white man's. He bitterly describes that incident in his youth to show how far someone might go in trying to become part of the majority.*

The last selection is a poem by Gwendolyn Brooks, a short, succinct view of a group that remains outside.

THE PROMISED LAND

Mary Antin

"I was born, I have lived, and I have been made over." So begins the
autobiography of Mary Antin (1881–1949), significantly called *The
Promised Land* (1912). It describes her childhood in "the Pale," that
part of Czarist Russia in which Jews were allowed to live—more or
less. It tells the story of her family's departure from Russia, of the long
journey in steerage to America, of her fright and bewilderment, and
the rush of new, startling experiences. In particular, she describes her
adaptation to American life and the impact of American education.

Anybody who knows Boston knows that the West and North Ends are the 1
wrong ends of that city. They form the tenement district, or, in the newer
phrase, the slums of Boston. Anybody who is acquainted with the slums of
any American metropolis knows that that is the quarter where poor immigrants foregather, to live, for the most part, as unkempt, half-washed, toiling,
unaspiring foreigners; pitiful in the eyes of social missionaries, the despair of
boards of health, the hope of ward politicians, the touchstone of American
democracy. The well-versed metropolitan knows the slums as a sort of house
of detention for poor aliens, where they live on probation till they can show
a certificate of good citizenship.

He may know all this and yet not guess how Wall Street, in the West 2
End, appears in the eyes of a little immigrant from Polotzk. What would the
sophisticated sight-seer say about Union Place, off Wall Street, where my
new home waited for me? He would say that it is no place at all, but a short
box of an alley. Two rows of three-story tenements are its sides, a stingy strip
of sky is its lid, a littered pavement is the floor, and a narrow mouth its exit.

But I saw a very different picture on my introduction to Union Place. I 3
saw two imposing rows of brick buildings, loftier than any dwelling I had
ever lived in. Brick was even on the ground for me to tread on, instead of
common earth or boards. Many friendly windows stood open, filled with
uncovered heads of women and children. I thought the people were interested in us, which was very neighborly. I looked up to the topmost row of
windows, and my eyes were filled with the May blue of an American sky!

In our days of affluence in Russia we had been accustomed to uphol- 4
stered parlors, embroidered linen, silver spoons and candlesticks, goblets of
gold, kitchen shelves shining with copper and brass. We had featherbeds
heaped halfway to the ceiling; we had clothes presses dusky with velvet and

silk and fine woollen. The three small rooms into which my father now ushered us, up one flight of stairs, contained only the necessary beds, with lean mattresses; a few wooden chairs; a table or two; a mysterious iron structure, which later turned out to be a stove; a couple of unornamental kerosene lamps; and a scanty array of cooking-utensils and crockery. And yet we were all impressed with our new home and its furniture. It was not only because we had just passed through our seven lean years, cooking in earthen vessels, eating black bread on holidays and wearing cotton; it was chiefly because these wooden chairs and tin pans were American chairs and pans that they shone glorious in our eyes. And if there was anything lacking for comfort or decoration we expected it to be presently supplied—at least, we children did. Perhaps my mother alone, of us newcomers, appreciated the shabbiness of the little apartment, and realized that for her there was as yet no laying down of the burden of poverty.

Our initiation into American ways began with the first step on the new   5
soil. My father found occasion to instruct or correct us even on the way from the pier to Wall Street, which journey we made crowded together in a rickety cab. He told us not to lean out of the windows, not to point, and explained the word "greenhorn." We did not want to be "greenhorns," and gave the strictest attention to my father's instructions. I do not know when my parents found opportunity to review together the history of Polotzk in the three years past, for we children had no patience with the subject; my mother's narrative was constantly interrupted by irrelevant questions, interjections, and explanations.

The first meal was an object lesson of much variety. My father produced   6
several kinds of food, ready to eat, without any cooking, from little tin cans that had printing all over them. He attempted to introduce us to a queer, slippery kind of fruit, which he called "banana," but had to give it up for the time being. After the meal, he had better luck with a curious piece of furniture on runners, which he called "rocking-chair." There were five of us newcomers, and we found five different ways of getting into the American machine of perpetual motion, and as many ways of getting out of it. One born and bred to the use of a rocking-chair cannot imagine how ludicrous people can make themselves when attempting to use it for the first time. We laughed immoderately over our various experiments with the novelty, which was a wholesome way of letting off steam after the unusual excitement of the day.

In our flat we did not think of such a thing as storing the coal in the   7
bathtub. There was no bathtub. So in the evening of the first day my father conducted us to the public baths. As we moved along in a little procession, I was delighted with the illumination of the streets. So many lamps, and they

burned until morning, my father said, and so people did not need to carry lanterns. In America, then, everything was free, as we had heard in Russia. Light was free; the streets were as bright as a synagogue on a holy day. Music was free; we had been serenaded, to our gaping delight, by a brass band of many pieces, soon after our installation on Union Place.

Education was free. That subject my father had written about repeat-   8
edly, as comprising his chief hope for us children, the essence of American opportunity, the treasure that no thief could touch, not even misfortune or poverty. It was the one thing that he was able to promise us when he sent for us; surer, safer than bread or shelter. On our second day I was thrilled with the realization of what this freedom of education meant. A little girl from across the alley came and offered to conduct us to school. My father was out, but we five between us had a few words of English by this time. We knew the word school. We understood. This child, who had never seen us till yesterday, who could not pronounce our names, who was not much better dressed than we, was able to offer us the freedom of the schools of Boston! No application made, no questions asked, no examinations, rulings, exclusions; no machinations, no fees. The doors stood open for every one of us. The smallest child could show us the way.

This incident impressed me more than anything I had heard in advance   9
of the freedom of education in America. It was a concrete proof—almost the thing itself. One had to experience it to understand it.

It was a great disappointment to be told by my father that we were not   10
to enter upon our school career at once. It was too near the end of the term, he said, and we were going to move to Crescent Beach in a week or so. We had to wait until the opening of the schools in September. What a loss of precious time—from May till September!

Not that the time was really lost. Even the interval on Union Place was   11
crowded with lessons and experiences. We had to visit the stores and be dressed from head to foot in American clothing; we had to learn the mys-teries of the iron stove, the washboard, and the speaking-tube; we had to learn to trade with the fruit peddler through the window, and not to be afraid of the policeman; and, above all, we had to learn English.

The kind people who assisted us in these important matters form a   12
group by themselves in the gallery of my friends. If I had never seen them from those early days till now, I should still have remembered them with gratitude. When I enumerate the long list of my American teachers, I must begin with those who came to us on Wall Street and taught us our first steps. To my mother, in her perplexity over the cookstove, the woman who showed her how to make the fire was an angel of deliverance. A fairy godmother to us children was she who led us to a wonderful country called "uptown,"

where, in a dazzlingly beautiful palace called a "department store," we exchanged our hateful homemade European costumes, which pointed us out as "greenhorns" to the children on the street, for real American machine-made garments, and issued forth glorified in each other's eyes.

With our despised immigrant clothing we shed also our impossible 13 Hebrew names. A committee of our friends, several years ahead of us in American experience, put their heads together and concocted American names for us all. Those of our real names that had no pleasing American equivalents they ruthlessly discarded, content if they retained the initials. My mother, possessing a name that was not easily translatable, was punished with the undignified nickname of Annie. Fetchke, Joseph, and Deborah issued as Frieda, Joseph, and Dora, respectively. As for poor me, I was simply cheated. The name they gave me was hardly new. My Hebrew name being Maryashe in full, Mashke for short, Russianized into Marya *(Mar-ya)*, my friends said that it would hold good in English as *Mary:* which was very disappointing, as I longed to possess a strange-sounding American name like the others.

I am forgetting the consolation I had, in this matter of names, from the 14 use of my surname, which I have had no occasion to mention until now. I found on my arrival that my father was "Mr. Antin" on the slightest prov-ocation, and not, as in Polotzk, on state occasions alone. And so I was "Mary Antin," and I felt very important to answer to such a dignified title. It was just like America that even plain people should wear their surnames on week days.

As a family we were so diligent under instruction, so adaptable, and so 15 clever in hiding our deficiencies, that when we made the journey to Crescent Beach, in the wake of our small wagon-load of household goods, my father had very little occasion to admonish us on the way, and I am sure he was not ashamed of us. So much we had achieved toward our Americanization dur-ing the two weeks since our landing.

QUESTIONS

Words to Know

metropolis (paragraph 1), foregather (1), unkempt (1), toiling (1), touchstone (1), detention (1), probation (1), loftier (3), affluence (4), goblets (4), dusky (4), scanty (4), array (4), crockery (4), initiation (5), greenhorn (5), irrelevant

(5), perpetual motion (6), ludicrous (6), illumination (7), essence (8), machination (8), enumerate (12), perplexity (12), concocted (13), provocation (14), admonish (15).

Some of the Issues

1. Why does Antin characterize the new immigrants as "the hope of ward politicians, the touchstone of American democracy" (paragraph 1)?
2. In the first three paragraphs Antin gives the reader two contrasting views of her new neighborhood in Boston. What are they?
3. Why was Antin so intent on not being a "greenhorn" (paragraph 5)?
4. What is the promise of a free education? Why is it so strongly emphasized? Compare Antin's attitude to Frank Rissarro's in the essay "Third Generation" and to Ivan Illich's "Effects of Development."
5. Antin seems to shed her "despised immigrant clothing" and her Hebrew name without the slightest regret. Can you explain this? Do you find it surprising?

The Way We Are Told

6. Antin seems to use different voices, so to speak: those of the "greenhorn," the child, and the adult accustomed to American ways. Find examples of each. Why does she use these different voices?
7. Antin records her first days in America as something of a dream world. Find examples of words and phrases that help to create that impression.

Some Subjects For Essays

8. Describe your arrival at a new place: a strange city, a new home, a school. Try to recapture the first sensations, the first sensory impressions. Try to let the reader see and feel them by means of your description.
9. Antin believes that education is the key to a better life. Write an argument for or against that view, trying to be as specific as possible.
10. "What's in a name?" Shakespeare asks. Write about a name, yours or someone else's. Has it any positive or negative significance? How are you affected by people's names? Your own?

THE BRUTAL BARGAIN

Norman Podhoretz

Norman Podhoretz, who describes some of the events of his earlier life
in the selection here, received his B.A. degree from Columbia University in 1950, at the age of 20, and a further B.A. from Cambridge University in England in 1952. He is the editor-in-chief of *Commentary*
and the author of, among other works, *Breaking Ranks* (1979), *The
Present Danger* (1980), *Why We Were in Viet-Nam* (1982), and *Making It* (1964), from which the following selection is taken.

One of the longest journeys in the world is the journey from Brooklyn to   1
Manhattan—or at least from certain neighborhoods in Brooklyn to certain
parts of Manhattan. I have made that journey, but it is not from the experience of having made it that I know how very great the distance is, for I
started on the road many years before I realized what I was doing, and by
the time I did realize it I was for all practical purposes already there. At so
imperceptible a pace did I travel, and with so little awareness, that I never
felt footsore or out of breath or weary at the thought of how far I still had
to go. Yet whenever anyone who has remained back there where I started—
remained not physically but socially and culturally, for the neighborhood is
now a Negro ghetto and the Jews who have "remained" in it mostly reside
in the less affluent areas of Long Island—whenever anyone like that happens
into the world in which I now live with such perfect ease, I can see that in
his eyes I have become a fully acculturated citizen of a country as foreign to
him as China and infinitely more frightening.

That country is sometimes called the upper middle class; and indeed I   2
am a member of that class, less by virtue of my income than by virtue of the
way my speech is accented, the way I dress, the way I furnish my home, the
way I entertain and am entertained, the way I educate my children—the
way, quite simply, I look and I live. It appalls me to think what an immense
transformation I had to work on myself in order to become what I have
become: if I had known what I was doing I would surely not have been able
to do it, I would surely not have wanted to. No wonder the choice had to be
blind; there was a kind of treason in it: treason toward my family, treason
toward my friends. In choosing the road I chose, I was pronouncing a judgment upon them, and the fact that they themselves concurred in the judgment makes the whole thing sadder but no less cruel.

When I say that the choice was blind, I mean that I was never aware—   3

183

obviously not as a small child, certainly not as an adolescent, and not even as a young man already writing for publication and working on the staff of an important intellectual magazine in New York—how inextricably my "noblest" ambitions were tied to the vulgar desire to rise above the class into which I was born; nor did I understand to what an astonishing extent these ambitions were shaped and defined by the standards and values and tastes of the class into which I did not know I wanted to move. It is not that I was or am a social climber as that term is commonly used. High society interests me, if at all, only as a curiosity; I do not wish to be a member of it; and in any case, it is not, as I have learned from a small experience of contact with the very rich and fashionable, my "scene." Yet precisely because social climbing is not one of my vices (unless what might be called celebrity climbing, which very definitely *is* one of my vices, can be considered the contemporary variant of social climbing), I think there may be more than a merely personal significance in the fact that class has played so large a part both in my life and in my career.

But whether or not the significance is there, I feel certain that my long-time blindness to the part class was playing in my life was not altogether idiosyncratic. "Privilege," Robert L. Heilbroner has shrewdly observed in *The Limits of American Capitalism*, "is not an attribute we are accustomed to stress when we consider the construction of *our* social order." For a variety of reasons, says Heilbroner, "privilege under capitalism is much less 'visible,' especially to the favored groups, than privilege under other systems" like feudalism. This "invisibility" extends in America to class as well.

No one, of course, is so naïve as to believe that America is a classless society or that the force of egalitarianism, powerful as it has been in some respects, has ever been powerful enough to wipe out class distinctions altogether. There was a moment during the 1950's, to be sure, when social thought hovered on the brink of saying that the country had to all intents and purposes become a wholly middle-class society. But the emergence of the civil-rights movement in the 1960's and the concomitant discovery of the poor—to whom, in helping to discover them, Michael Harrington interestingly enough applied, in *The Other America*, the very word ("invisible") that Heilbroner later used with reference to the rich—has put at least a temporary end to that kind of talk. And yet if class has become visible again, it is only in its grossest outlines—mainly, that is, in terms of income levels—and to the degree that manners and style of life are perceived as relevant at all, it is generally in the crudest of terms. There is something in us, it would seem, which resists the idea of class. Even our novelists, working in a genre for which class has traditionally been a supreme reality, are largely indifferent to it—which is to say, blind to its importance as a factor in the life of the individual.

In my own case, the blindness to class always expressed itself in an out-   6
right and very often belligerent refusal to believe that it had anything to do
with me at all. I no longer remember when or in what form I first discovered
that there was such a thing as class, but whenever it was and whatever form
the discovery took, it could only have coincided with the recognition that
criteria existed by which I and everyone I knew were stamped as inferior:
we were in the *lower* class. This was not a proposition I was willing to accept,
and my way of not accepting it was to dismiss the whole idea of class as a
prissy triviality.

Given the fact that I had literary ambitions even as a small boy, it was   7
inevitable that the issue of class would sooner or later arise for me with a
sharpness it would never acquire for most of my friends. But given the fact
also that I was on the whole very happy to be growing up where I was, that
I was fiercely patriotic about Brownsville (the spawning-ground of so many
famous athletes and gangsters), and that I felt genuinely patronizing toward
other neighborhoods, especially the "better" ones like Crown Heights and
East Flatbush which seemed by comparison colorless and unexciting—given
the fact, in other words, that I was not, for all that I wrote poetry and read
books, an "alienated" boy dreaming of escape—my confrontation with the
issue of class would probably have come later rather than sooner if not for
an English teacher in high school who decided that I was a gem in the rough
and who took it upon herself to polish me to as high a sheen as she could
manage and I would permit.

I resisted—far less effectively, I can see now, than I then thought,   8
though even then I knew that she was wearing me down far more than I
would ever give her the satisfaction of admitting. Famous throughout the
school for her altogether outspoken snobbery, which stopped short by only a
hair, and sometimes did not stop short at all, of an old-fashioned kind of
patrician anti-Semitism, Mrs. K. was also famous for being an extremely
good teacher; indeed, I am sure that she saw no distinction between the
hopeless task of teaching the proper use of English to the young Jewish barbarians whom fate had so unkindly deposited into her charge and the equally
hopeless task of teaching them the proper "manners." (There were as many
young Negro barbarians in her charge as Jewish ones, but I doubt that she
could ever bring herself to pay very much attention to them. As she never
hesitated to make clear, it was punishment enough for a woman of her background—her family was old-Brooklyn and, she would have us understand,
extremely distinguished—to have fallen among the sons of East European
immigrant Jews.)

For three years, from the age of thirteen to the age of sixteen, I was her   9
special pet, though that word is scarcely adequate to suggest the intensity of
the relationship which developed between us. It was a relationship right out

of *The Corn Is Green,* which may, for all I know, have served as her model; at any rate, her objective was much the same as the Welsh teacher's in that play: she was determined that I should win a scholarship to Harvard. But whereas (an irony much to the point here) the problem the teacher had in *The Corn Is Green* with her coal-miner pupil in the traditional class society of Edwardian England was strictly academic, Mrs. K.'s problem with me in the putatively egalitarian society of New Deal America was strictly social. My grades were very high and would obviously remain so, but what would they avail me if I continued to go about looking and sounding like a "filthy little slum child" (the epithet she would invariably hurl at me whenever we had an argument about "manners")?

Childless herself, she worked on me like a dementedly ambitious   10
mother with a somewhat recalcitrant son; married to a solemn and elderly man (she was then in her early forties or thereabouts), she treated me like a callous, ungrateful adolescent lover on whom she had humiliatingly bestowed her favors. She flirted with me and flattered me, she scolded me and insulted me. Slum child, filthy little slum child, so beautiful a mind and so vulgar a personality, so exquisite in sensibility and so coarse in manner. What would she do with me, what would become of me if I persisted out of stubborness and perversity in the disgusting ways they had taught me at home and on the streets?

To her the most offensive of these ways was the style in which I dressed: 11
a tee shirt, tightly pegged pants, and a red satin jacket with the legend "Cherokees, S.A.C." (social-athletic club) stitched in large white letters across the back. This was bad enough, but when on certain days I would appear in school wearing, as a particular ceremonial occasion required, a suit and tie, the sight of those immense padded shoulders and my white-on-white shirt would drive her to even greater heights of contempt and even lower depths of loving despair than usual. *Slum child, filthy little slum child.* I was beyond saving; I deserved no better than to wind up with all the other horrible little Jewboys in the gutter (by which she meant Brooklyn College). If only I would listen to her, the whole world could be mine: I could win a scholarship to Harvard, I could get to know the best people, I could grow up into a life of elegance and refinement and taste. Why was I so stupid as not to understand?

In those days it was very unusual, and possibly even against the rules,   12
for teachers in public high schools to associate with their students after hours. Nevertheless, Mrs. K. sometimes invited me to her home, a beautiful old brownstone located in what was perhaps the only section in the whole of Brooklyn fashionable enough to be intimidating. I would read her my poems and she would tell me about her family, about the schools she had gone to,

about Vassar, about writers she had met, while her husband, of whom I was frightened to death and who to my utter astonishment turned out to be Jewish (but not, as Mrs. K. quite unnecessarily hastened to inform me, *my* kind of Jewish), sat stiffly and silently in an armchair across the room, squinting at his newspaper through the first *pince-nez* I had ever seen outside the movies. He spoke to me but once, and that was after I had read Mrs. K. my tearful editorial for the school newspaper on the death of Roosevelt—an effusion which provoked him into a full five-minute harangue whose blasphemous contents would certainly have shocked me into insensibility if I had not been even more shocked to discover that he actually had a voice.

But Mrs. K. not only had me to her house; she also—what was even   13
more unusual—took me out a few times, to the Frick Gallery and the Metropolitan Museum, and once to the theater, where we saw a dramatization of *The Late George Apley*, a play I imagine she deliberately chose with the not wholly mistaken idea that it would impress upon me the glories of aristocratic Boston.

One of our excursions into Manhattan I remember with particular viv-   14
idness because she used it to bring the struggle between us to rather a dramatic head. The familiar argument began this time on the subway. Why, knowing that we would be spending the afternoon together "in public," had I come to school that morning improperly dressed? (I was, as usual, wearing my red satin club jacket over a white tee shirt.) She realized, of course, that I owned only one suit (this said not in compassion but in derision) and that my poor parents had, God only knew where, picked up the idea that it was too precious to be worn except at one of those bar mitzvahs I was always going to. Though why, if my parents were so worried about clothes, they had permitted me to buy a suit which made me look like a young hoodlum she found it very difficult to imagine. Still, much as she would have been embarrassed to be seen in public with a boy whose parents allowed him to wear a zoot suit, she would have been somewhat less embarrassed than she was now by the ridiculous costume I had on. Had I no consideration for her? Had I no consideration for myself? Did I want everyone who laid eyes on me to think that I was nothing but an ill-bred little slum child?

My standard ploy in these arguments was to take the position that such   15
things were of no concern to me: I was a poet and I had more important matters to think about than clothes. Besides, I would feel silly coming to school on an ordinary day dressed in a suit. Did Mrs. K. want me to look like one of those "creeps" from Crown Heights who were all going to become doctors? This was usually an effective counter, since Mrs. K. despised her middle-class Jewish students even more than she did the "slum children," but probably because she was growing desperate at the thought of how I

would strike a Harvard interviewer (it was my senior year), she did not respond according to form on that particular occasion. "At least," she snapped, "they reflect well on their parents."

I was accustomed to her bantering gibes at my parents, and sensing,   16
probably, that they arose out of jealousy, I was rarely troubled by them. But this one bothered me; it went beyond banter and I did not know how to deal with it. I remember flushing, but I cannot remember what if anything I said in protest. It was the beginning of a very bad afternoon for both of us.

We had been heading for the Museum of Modern Art, but as we got off   17
the subway, Mrs. K. announced that she had changed her mind about the museum. She was going to show me something else instead, just down the street on Fifth Avenue. This mysterious "something else" to which we proceeded in silence turned out to be the college department of an expensive clothing store, de Pinna. I do not exaggerate when I say that an actual physical dread seized me as I followed her into the store. I had never been inside such a store; it was not a store, it was enemy territory, every inch of it mined with humiliations. "I am," Mrs. K. declared in the coldest human voice I hope I shall ever hear, "going to buy you a suit that you will be able to wear at your Harvard interview." I had guessed, of course, that this was what she had in mind, and even at fifteen I understood what a fantastic act of aggression she was planning to commit against my parents and asking me to participate in. Oh no, I said in a panic (suddenly realizing that I *wanted* her to buy me that suit), I can't, my mother wouldn't like it. "You can tell her it's a birthday present. Or else I will tell her. If I tell her, I'm sure she won't object." The idea of Mrs. K. meeting my mother was more than I could bear: my mother, who spoke with a Yiddish accent and of whom, until that sickening moment, I had never known I was ashamed and so ready to betray.

To my immense relief and my equally immense disappointment, we   18
left the store, finally, without buying a suit, but it was not to be the end of clothing or "manners" for me that day—not yet. There was still the ordeal of a restaurant to go through. Where I came from, people rarely ate in restaurants, not so much because most of them were too poor to afford such a luxury—although most of them certainly were—as because eating in restaurants was not regarded as a luxury at all; it was, rather, a necessity to which bachelors were pitiably condemned. A home-cooked meal was assumed to be better than anything one could possibly get in a restaurant, and considering the class of restaurants in question (they were really diners or luncheonettes), the assumption was probably correct. In the case of my own family, myself included until my late teens, the business of going to restaurants was complicated by the fact that we observed the Jewish dietary laws, and except in certain neighborhoods, few places could be found which served

kosher food; in midtown Manhattan in the 1940's, I believe there were only two and both were relatively expensive. All this is by way of explaining why I had had so little experience of restaurants up to the age of fifteen and why I grew apprehensive once more when Mrs. K. decided after we left de Pinna that we should have something to eat.

The restaurant she chose was not at all an elegant one—I have, like a criminal, revisited it since—but it seemed very elegant indeed to me: enemy territory again, and this time a mine exploded in my face the minute I set foot through the door. The hostess was very sorry, but she could not seat the young gentleman without a coat and tie. If the lady wished, however, something could be arranged. The lady (visibly pleased by this unexpected—or was it expected?—object lesson) did wish, and the so recently defiant but by now utterly docile young gentleman was forthwith divested of his so recently beloved but by now thoroughly loathsome red satin jacket and provided with a much oversized white waiter's coat and a tie—which, there being no collar to a tee shirt, had to be worn around his bare neck. Thus attired, and with his face supplying the touch of red which had moments earlier been supplied by his jacket, he was led into the dining room, there to be taught the importance of proper table manners through the same pedagogic instrumentality that had worked so well in impressing him with the importance of proper dress.

Like any other pedagogic technique, however, humiliation has its limits, and Mrs. K. was to make no further progress with it that day. For I had had enough, and I was not about to risk stepping on another mine. Knowing she would subject me to still more ridicule if I made a point of my revulsion at the prospect of eating nonkosher food, I resolved to let her order for me and then to feign lack of appetite or possibly even illness when the meal was served. She did order—duck for both of us, undoubtedly because it would be a hard dish for me to manage without using my fingers.

The two portions came in deep oval-shaped dishes, swimming in a brown sauce and each with a sprig of parsley sitting on top. I had not the faintest idea of what to do—should the food be eaten directly from the oval dish or not?—nor which of the many implements on the table to do it with. But remembering that Mrs. K. herself had once advised me to watch my hostess in such a situation and then to do exactly as she did, I sat perfectly still and waited for her to make the first move. Unfortunately, Mrs. K. also remembered having taught me that trick, and determined as she was that I should be given a lesson that would force me to mend my ways, she waited too. And so we both waited, chatting amiably, pretending not to notice the food while it sat there getting colder and colder by the minute. Thanks partly to the fact that I would probably have gagged on the duck if I had tried to eat it—dietary taboos are very powerful if one has been conditioned to them—I was prepared to wait forever. And in fact it was Mrs. K. who broke first.

"Why aren't you eating?" she suddenly said after something like fifteen   22
minutes had passed. "Aren't you hungry?" Not very, I answered. "Well," she said, "I think we'd better eat. The food is getting cold." Whereupon, as I watched with great fascination, she deftly captured the sprig of parsley between the prongs of her serving fork, set it aside, took up her serving spoon and delicately used those two esoteric implements to transfer a piece of duck from the oval dish to her plate. I imitated the whole operation as best I could, but not well enough to avoid splattering some partly congealed sauce onto my borrowed coat in the process. Still, things could have been worse, and having more or less successfully negotiated my way around that particular mine, I now had to cope with the problem of how to get out of eating the duck. But I need not have worried. Mrs. K. took one bite, pronounced it inedible (it must have been frozen by then), and called in quiet fury for the check.

Several months later, wearing an altered but respectably conservative   23
suit which had been handed down to me in good condition by a bachelor uncle, I presented myself on two different occasions before interviewers from Harvard and from the Pulitzer Scholarship Committee. Some months after that, Mrs. K. had her triumph: I won the Harvard scholarship on which her heart had been so passionately set. It was not, however, large enough to cover all expenses, and since my parents could not afford to make up the difference, I was unable to accept it. My parents felt wretched but not, I think, quite as wretched as Mrs. K. For a while it looked as though I would wind up in the "gutter" of Brooklyn College after all, but then the news arrived that I had also won a Pulitzer Scholarship which paid full tuition if used at Columbia and a small stipend besides. Everyone was consoled, even Mrs. K.: Columbia was at least in the Ivy League.

The last time I saw her was shortly before my graduation from Colum-   24
bia and just after a story had appeared in the *Times* announcing that I had been awarded a fellowship which was to send me to Cambridge University. Mrs. K. had passionately wanted to see me in Cambridge, Massachusetts, but Cambridge, England was even better. We met somewhere near Columbia for a drink, and her happiness over my fellowship, it seemed to me, was if anything exceeded by her delight at discovering that I now knew enough to know that the right thing to order in a cocktail lounge was a very dry martini with lemon peel, please.

QUESTIONS

Words to Know

imperceptible (paragraph 1), acculturated (1), idiosyncratic (4), attribute (4), egalitarianism (5), genre (5), triviality (6), alienated (7), patrician (8), dementedly (10), recalcitrant (10), intimidating (12), *pince-nez* (12), effusion (12), harangue (12), blasphemous (12), insensibility (12), derision (14), zoot suit (14), bantering (16), gibes (16), pitiably (18), divested (19), pedagogic (19), instrumentality (19).

Some of the Issues

1. Explain what kind of "journey" Podhoretz refers to in paragraph 1.
2. In paragraph 2 Podhoretz refers to his journey as "a kind of treason." What does he mean?
3. In Podhoretz's view, America is not a classless society (paragraph 5), but seems so at times because both the poor and the rich seem invisible. (See Harrington's "The Invisible Poor" in Part Six.) What would you say is the meaning of class in America? On what grounds do you place people in this class structure?
4. Reread the first sentence of paragraph 7; why is a link between class and literary ambition "inevitable"?
5. Where and how does Podhoretz make the transition from his general observations to the particular story he wants to tell?
6. Beginning with paragraph 14, Podhoretz focuses on one particular day he spent with Mrs. K. How exactly do these episodes show what Mrs. K wants to change in Podhoretz?
7. Consider the title of the selection: "The Brutal Bargain." How does Podhoretz's story relate to that title?
8. In the struggle between Podhoretz and Mrs. K., who wins the battle? Who wins the war?

The Way We Are Told

9. Podhoretz opens his essay with the image of a journey. Examine how he uses that analogy in paragraphs 1 and 2.
10. When Podhoretz introduces Mrs. K., he widens the analogy of the jour-

ney; it becomes a journey into battle. Paragraphs 8 through 11 contain words and phrases that introduce the idea of combat. Find them.

11. In paragraph 14 Podhoretz begins his climactic, detailed story about the store and the restaurant. Show how he continues to develop his analogy of the journey here, both the journey into a new class and the journey into battle.

Some Subjects for Essays

12. Try to describe some basic change in your life, using a controlling image such as one of those Podhoretz uses: a journey, a series of battles, or a treasonable activity, or another image appropriate to your story. Subjects might be the changing or dropping of friends, going off to college, leaving a job.

13. Read Sennett's and Cobb's "Third Generation." Frank Rissarro also has moved from one class to another. Compare and contrast the attitudes of Podhoretz and Rissarro, and try to explain the differences.

THIRD GENERATION

Richard Sennett and Jonathan Cobb

Richard Sennett teaches sociology at New York University. Among his books are *The Uses of Disorder* and *Families Against the City*. Jonathan Cobb works for the Center for the Study of Public Policy in Cambridge, Massachusetts. *The Hidden Injuries of Class* (1972), from which the following selection is taken, is primarily the result of in-depth interviews conducted by the authors and a staff of researchers. Frank Rissarro, the subject of the interview reprinted here, is a pseudonym.

Frank Rissarro, a third-generation Italian-American, forty-four years old when we talked with him, had worked his way up from being a shoeshine boy at the age of nine to classifying loan applications in a bank. He makes $10,000 a year, owns a suburban home, and every August rents a small cottage in the country. He is a man who at first glance appears satisfied—"I know I did a good job in my life"—and yet he is also a man who feels defensive about his honor, fearing that people secretly do not respect him; he feels threatened by his children, who are "turning out just the way I want them to be," and he runs his home in a dictatorial manner.

Rissarro was born in 1925, the second-eldest child and only son of parents who lived in a predominantly Italian section of Boston. His father, an uneducated day laborer, worked hard, drank hard, and beat his wife and children often. As a young boy, Rissarro was not interested in school—his life was passed in constant fear of his father's violence. He was regarded by his family as a spoiled brat, with no brains and no common sense. His sisters and cousins did better than he scholastically, all finishing high school. Yet even as a child, Rissarro worked nights and weekends helping to support his family. At sixteen he quit school, feeling incapable of doing the work and out of place. After two years in the military, he worked as a meat-cutter for nearly twenty years.

Rissaro was and is a man of ambition. The affluence spreading across America in the decades following the Second World War made him restless—he wanted to either get a butcher shop of his own or get out. The capital for a small business being beyond his reach, he had a friend introduce him to the branch manager of a bank setting up a new office in his neighborhood. He won a job processing loans for people who come in off the street; he helps them fill out the forms, though he is still too low-level to have the power to approve or disapprove the loans themselves.

193

A success story: from chaos in the Depression, from twenty years of hacking away at sides of beef, Rissarro now wears a suit to work and has a stable home in respectable surroundings. Yes, it is a success story—except that *he* does not read it that way.

As we explored with Rissarro the reasons why these good things have come to him, we found the declarations of self-satisfaction almost instantly giving way to a view of himself as a passive agent in his own life, a man who has been on the receiving end of events rather than their cause: "I was just at the right place at the right time," he says again and again. "I was lucky," he claims, in describing how he emotionally withstood the terrors of his father's home.

Is this modesty? Not for him. He feels passive in the midst of his success because he feels illegitimate, a pushy intruder, in his entrance to the middle-class world of neat suburban lawns, peaceable families, happy friendships. Despite the fact that he has gained entrée, he doesn't believe he deserves to be respected. In discussing, for instance, his marriage—to a woman somewhat more educated than he, from an Italian background equivalent to "lace-curtain Irish"—Rissarro told us something impossible to believe, considering his ungrammatical speech, his obession with his childhood, his mannerisms and gestures: "My wife didn't know that I had no background to speak of, or else she would never have married me." The possibility that she accepted him for himself, and never made an issue of where he came from, he simply cannot accept.

Sociologists have a neat formula to explain the discontent caused by upward mobility; they call Frank's malaise a product of "status incongruity": Because Frank does not yet know the rules of his new position, because he is caught between two worlds, he feels something is wrong with him. This formula falls back on an image of the antithesis between working-class struggle and educated, "higher" culture.

The trouble here, however, is that Frank *doesn't* feel caught between two worlds. He knows what the rules of middle-class life are, he has played at them now for some years; furthermore, he is not in any way ashamed of his working-class past. Indeed, he is proud of it, he thinks it makes him a more honest person at work:

"I'm working, like I said, with fellows that are educated, college boys, in that office. I'm about the only one in there in any straits to say I'm educated. I'm enjoying this job, I'm going in with the big shots. I go in at nine, I come out at five. *The other fellows, because they got an education, sneaks out early and comes in late.* The boss knows I'm there, a reliable worker. 'Cause I've had the factory life, I know what it is. I mean, a man deserves— the least you can do is put your hours in and do your job. I'm a good employee. I know I am because I see others who are educated."

In fact, toward educated white-collar work itself, beyond all its symbolic   10
connotations of success, Frank Rissaro harbors an innate disrespect: "These
jobs aren't real work where you make something—it's just pushing papers."

Then why has he striven so hard to be upwardly mobile? One ready   11
answer is that he wanted the house, the suit, the cottage in the country. And
Rissarro himself gives that answer at first. After a few hours of talk, however,
he conveys a more complicated and difficult set of feelings.

The poverty of his childhood he speaks about as something shameful,   12
not because there was a lack of things, but rather because the people who
had nothing acted like animals. He remembers this particularly in terms of
his father—his father's poverty and his drunken brutality toward Frank and
Frank's mother are interwoven in Frank's memory. Other images in his conversation concerning the poor, both white and black, similarly fuse material
deprivation with chaotic, arbitrary, and unpredictable behavior; he sees poverty, in other words, as depriving men of the capacity to act rationally, to
exercise self-control. A poor man, therefore, *has* to want upward mobility in
order to establish dignity in his own life, and dignity means, specifically,
moving toward a position in which he deals with the world in some controlled, emotionally restrained way. People who have been educated, on the
other hand, are supposed to already possess this capacity. They are supposed
to have developed skills for taming the world without force or passion.

Frank feels that it is such people on whom he ought to model the   13
changes he wants in his own life. And yet, paradoxically, he doesn't respect
the content of their powers: just as intellect gives a man respect in the world,
the educated do nothing worth respecting; their status means they can cheat.
In a further twist, Rissarro then proceeds to turn the paradox into a terrible
accusation against himself: "As far as I'm concerned, I got through life by
always trying to depend on the other guy to do my work. But when it came
to my hands, I could do all the work myself."

Capturing respect in the larger America, then, means to Frank getting   14
into an educated position; but capturing that respect means that he no longer
respects himself. This contradiction ran through every discussion we held, as
an image either of what people felt compelled to do with their own lives or
of what they sought for their sons. If the boys could get educated, anybody
in America would respect them; and yet, as we shall see, the fathers felt
education would lead the young into work not as "real" as their own.

Yet, why should Frank Rissaro be worrying about his legitimacy? And   15
why has he chosen as a "prestige model" a kind of work activity he despises?

This paradox might, of course, be read simply as a conflict in the indi-   16
vidual personalities of men like Frank Rissaro. It is more accurate, however,
to see it as an issue introduced into their lives by the America outside the
urban village. The story these workingmen have to tell is not just who they

are but what are the contradictory codes of respect in the America of their generation.

Frank Rissarro did not so much grant an interview as give a confession. The 17 interviewer began by asking a neutral question, something about what Rissarro remembered of Boston while he was growing up. He replied by talking with little interruption for more than three hours about intimate feelings and experiences to this stranger whom he had never met before. Rissarro talked to the interviewer in a peculiar way: he treated him as an emissary from a different way of life, as a representative of a higher, more educated class, before whom he spread a justification of his entire life. At various points where he spoke of situations where he felt powerless and the interviewer sympathized, Rissarro would suddenly respond to him as simply a human being, not as an emissary sent in judgment; but then, as he returned to the story of his life, which he seemed to live through again as he described it, the interviewer once again became a representative of a class of people who could do what they wanted and who made him feel inadequate. It was Rissarro's chief concern throughout to show why circumstances had not permitted him to take charge of his life in the same way.

Yet this man is someone who feels he has done a good job in establishing 18 a stable family and margin of security in contrast to the life of poverty and turmoil he knew as a child during the Depression. Why then is he so defensive?

The word "educated" as used by Rissarro, and by other men and 19 women we talked to, is what psychologists call a "cover term"; that is, it stands for a whole range of experiences and feelings that may in fact have little to do with formal schooling. Education covers, at the most abstract level, the development of capacities within a human being. At the most concrete level, education meant to the people we interviewed getting certificates for social mobility and job choice, and they felt that American society parcels out the certificates very unequally and unfairly, so that middle-class people have more of a chance to become educated than themselves. But if the abstract is connected to the concrete, this means middle-class people have more of a chance than workers to escape from becoming creatures of circumstance, more chance to develop the defenses, the tools of personal, rational control that "education" gives. Why should one class of human beings get a chance to develop the weapons of self more than another? And yet, if that class difference is a *fait accompli*, what has a man without education got inside himself to defend against this superior power?

Rissarro believes people of a higher class have a power to judge him 20 because they seem internally more developed human beings; and he is afraid, because they are better armed, that they will not respect him. He feels compelled to justify his own position, and in his life he has felt compelled to put himself up on their level in order to earn respect. All of this, in turn—when he thinks just of himself and *is not comparing himself* to his image of people in a higher class—all of this is set against a revulsion against the work of educated people in the bank, and a feeling that manual labor has more dignity.

What does he make of this contradiction in his life? That he is an impostor—but more, that the sheer fact that he is troubled must prove he really is inadequate. After all, he has played by the rules, he has gained the outward signs of material respectability; if, then, he still feels defenseless, something must be wrong with *him:* his unhappiness seems to him a sign that he simply cannot become the kind of person other people can respect. 21

This tangle of feelings appeared again and again as we talked to people who started life as poor, ethnically isolated laboring families, and have been successful in making the sort of material gains that are supposed to "melt" people into the American middle class. 22

QUESTIONS

Words to Know

upward mobility (paragraph 7), malaise (7), antithesis (7), legitimacy (15), paradox (16), emissary (17).

Some of the Issues

1. The title of the book from which this excerpt is taken is *The Hidden Injuries of Class.* In what way would you say Frank Rissarro has been injured? How are these injuries hidden from him?
2. As in the case of Podhoretz ("The Brutal Bargain"), the difficulties of Frank Rissarro are class-based, not ethnic. Why is that important? Do we sometimes mistake the one kind of difficulty for the other? Can you think of examples?
3. Outwardly, Rissarro is content; he has "arrived" at relative affluence and middle-class status. Inwardly, he has his doubts. How do Sennett and Cobb explain this?

4. On the one hand, Rissarro feels insecure with his more highly educated co-workers. On the other, he feels superior to them. How do the authors account for that paradox?
5. What, in Rissarro's view, earns him respect or should supposedly earn him respect? Does he think he has it?
6. What is his "prestige model" (paragraph 15)? How does he feel about it, and why?
7. Compare Rissarro's "prestige model" to the one implied in Podhoretz's "The Brutal Bargain." Are they similar?
8. Compare Rissarro's and Podhoretz's attitudes toward their respective backgrounds. How do they differ?

The Way We Are Told

9. To what extent do Sennett and Cobb prove their assertions about Rissarro? Are you given evidence or do you have to take their views on faith?
10. Rissaro plays a role, like most of us much of the time. How do the authors show that he is not comfortable in this role?
11. Frank Rissarro's story is a case history, the result of an interview. Compare it to an autobiographical account—Antin's "The Promised Land" or any of those in Part One. Can you characterize the ways in which these accounts differ from Sennett's and Cobb's?

Some Ideas for Essays

12. In his great funeral oration for Julius Ceasar, Mark Antony cites as the main accusation leveled against Ceasar the fact that he was supposedly "ambitious." Yet, today we often think of ambition as an asset rather than a liability. In an essay, try to examine the toll that ambition may take of a person. You can use Frank Rissarro as an example, or a friend, or a family member, or yourself. Try not to exaggerate—that is easy in this case—but examine the particular situation dispassionately, as if you were analyzing it from the outside.
13. "Know Thyself." What does it mean to know oneself? Try to explain it by means of an extended example, perhaps by telling of an experience that contributed to your own self-knowledge.
14. Examine a role that you play: as a student, a worker, a son or daughter, a lover. To what extent does the role (rather than anything else) determine your behavior?

THE BARRIO

Ernesto Galarza

Born in Tepic, Mexico, in 1905, Ernesto Galarza moved to California as a child. His life before and after that move is described in the autobiographical *Barrio Boy* (1971), from which this selection is taken.

With degrees from Occidental College and Stanford and Columbia Universities, Galarza's early career centered on Latin American research projects for the Foreign Policy Association. Later his interests turned to labor relations, particularly the exploitation of Mexican workers in the United States. His books in this area include *Merchants of Labor: The Mexican Bracero Story* (1964), and *Spiders in the House and Workers in the Field* (1970).

We found the Americans as strange in their customs as they probably found   1
us. Immediately we discovered that there were no *mercados* and that when shopping you did not put the groceries in a *chiquihuite*. Instead everything was in cans or in cardboard boxes or each item was put in a brown paper bag. There were neighborhood grocery stores at the corners and some big ones uptown, but no *mercado*. The grocers did not give children a *pilón*, they did not stand at the door and coax you to come in and buy, as they did in Mazatlán. The fruits and vegetables were displayed on counters instead of being piled up on the floor. The stores smelled of fly spray and oiled floors, not of fresh pineapple and limes.

Neither was there a plaza, only parks which had no bandstands, no con-   2
certs every Thursday, no Judases exploding on Holy Week, and no promenades of boys going one way and girls the other. There were no parks in the *barrio;* and the ones uptown were cold and rainy in winter, and in summer there was no place to sit except on the grass. When there were celebrations nobody set off rockets in the parks, much less on the street in front of your house to announce to the neighborhood that a wedding or a baptism was taking place. Sacramento did not have a *mercado* and a plaza with the cathedral to one side and the Palacio de Gobierno on another to make it obvious that there and nowhere else was the center of the town.

It was just as puzzling that the Americans did not live in *vecindades*,   3
like our block on Leandro Valle. Even in the alleys, where people knew one another better, the houses were fenced apart, without central courts to wash clothes, talk and play with the other children. Like the city, the Sacramento *barrio* did not have a place which was the middle of things for everyone.

199

In more personal ways we had to get used to the Americans. They did   4
not listen if you did not speak loudly, as they always did. In the Mexican
style, people would know that you were enjoying their jokes tremendously if
you merely smiled and shook a little, as if you were trying to swallow your
mirth. In the American style there was little difference between a laugh and
a roar, and until you got used to them you could hardly tell whether the
boisterous Americans were roaring mad or roaring happy.

The older people of the *barrio*, except in those things which they had   5
to do like the Americans because they had no choice, remained Mexican.
Their language at home was Spanish. They were continuously taking up collections to pay somebody's funeral expenses or to help someone who had had
a serious accident. Cards were sent to you to attend a burial where you would
throw a handful of dirt on top of the coffin and listen to tearful speeches at
the graveside. At every baptism a new *compadre* and a new *comadre* joined
the family circle. New Year greeting cards were exchanged, showing angels
and cherubs in bright colors sprinkled with grains of mica so that they glis-
tened like gold dust. At the family parties the huge pot of steaming tamales
was still the center of attention, the *atole* served on the side with chunks of
brown sugar for sucking and crunching. If the party lasted long enough,
someone produced a guitar, the men took over and the singing of *corridos*
began.

In the *barrio* there were no individuals who had offical titles or who   6
were otherwise recognized by everybody as important people. The reason
must have been that there was no place in the public business of the city of
Sacramento for the Mexican immigrants. We only rented a corner of the city
and as long as we paid the rent on time everything else was decided at City
Hall or the County Court House, where Mexicans went only when they were
in trouble. Nobody from the *barrio* ever ran for mayor or city councilman.
For us the most important public officials were the policemen who walked
their beats, stopped fights, and hauled drunks to jail in a paddy wagon we
called *La Julia*.

The one institution we had that gave the *colonia* some kind of image   7
was the *Comisión Honorífica*, a committee picked by the Mexican Consul
in San Francisco to organize the celebration of the *Cinco de Mayo* and the
Sixteenth of September, the anniversaries of the battle of Puebla and the
beginning of our War of Independence. These were the two events which
stirred everyone in the *barrio*, for what we were celebrating was not only
the heroes of Mexico but also the feeling that we were still Mexicans ourselves. On these occasions there was a dance preceded by speeches and a
concert. For both the *cinco* and the sixteenth queens were elected to preside
over the ceremonies.

Between celebrations neither the politicians uptown nor the *Comisión*   8
Honorífica attended to the daily needs of the *barrio*. This was done by volunteers—the ones who knew enough English to interpret in court, on a visit
to the doctor, a call at the county hospital, and who could help make out a
postal money order. By the time I had finished the third grade at the Lincoln
School I was one of these volunteers. My services were not professional but
they were free, except for the IOU's I accumulated from families who always
thanked me with "God will pay you for it."

My clients were not *pochos*, Mexicans who had grown up in California,   9
probably had even been born in the United States. They had learned to speak
English of sorts and could still speak Spanish, also of sorts. They knew much
more about the Americans than we did, and much less about us. The *chicanos* and the *pochos* had certain feelings about one another. Concerning
the *pochos*, the *chicanos* suspected that they considered themselves too good
for the *barrio* but were not, for some reason, good enough for the Americans.
Toward the *chicanos*, the *pochos* acted superior, amused at our confusions
but not especially interested in explaining them to us. In our family when I
forgot my manners, my mother would ask me if I was turning *pochito*.

Turning *pocho* was a half-step toward turning American. And America   10
was all around us, in and out of the *barrio*. Abruptly we had to forget the
ways of shopping in a *mercado* and learn those of shopping in a corner grocery or in a department store. The Americans paid no attention to the Sixteenth of September, but they made a great commotion about the Fourth of
July. In Mazatlán Don Salvador had told us, saluting and marching as he
talked to our class, that the *Cinco de Mayo* was the most glorious date in
human history. The Americans had not even heard about it.

QUESTIONS

Words to Know

mercado—marketplace (paragraph 1), *chiquihuite*—a wicker shopping basket (1), *pilón*—a bonus or small gift from a merchant to children (1), *barrio*—neighborhood (2), Palacio de Gobierno—government headquarters (2),
vecindad—neighborhood (3), *compadre*—godfather (5), *atole*—corn mush
(5), *corrido*—ballad (5), *Cinco de Mayo*—May 5 (7).

Some of the Issues

1. In the first four paragraphs Galarza cites specific differences between the daily lives of Mexicans and North Americans. What are they?
2. Galarza describes the differences between the older and younger generations of Mexican-Americans. What are they?
3. What does Galarza tell us about the power relations between the *barrio* and the city of Sacramento?
4. How does Galarza describe the differences between a *pocho* and a *chicano*? From his description, do you sense any tension between the two groups?
5. Read Antin's "The Promised Land" and compare her account of assimilation to Galarza's. How do they differ? Which one is more in favor of melting in? Why do you think so?
6. What is the point made by Galarza regarding national holidays? Why mention them?

The Way We Are Told

7. Do you find the use of Spanish words in this selection useful, appropriate? What is their use intended to contribute?

Some Subjects for Essays

8. Describe in detail a section of a neighborhood you know well, such as your own block or the street you grew up on. Use telling details that make the reader see the area as you want him or her to see it. Plan the arrangement of your information; possibilities include from wide-angle focusing down to a close-up, or walking down the street.
9. Describe a holiday that is important to you. Try to explain it as if you were writing it for someone whose culture does not include it (for example: Thanksgiving to a Frenchman, or Christmas to a Muslim.)

HAIR

Malcolm X

Malcolm X, born in Omaha, Nebraska, in 1925, changed his name from Malcolm Little when he joined Elijah Muhammad's Black Muslims, in which he eventually moved up to become second in command. He broke with the Muslims because of major differences in policy and established an organization of his own. Soon after that he was assassinated at a public meeting, on February 21, 1965. *The Autobiography of Malcolm X*, written with the help of Alex Haley (later more widely known as the author of *Roots*), was published in 1964. The selection reprinted here is from one of the early parts of the book and records an experience during his junior high school years in Michigan, in 1941.

1   Shorty soon decided that my hair was finally long enough to be conked. He had promised to school me in how to beat the barbershops' three- and four-dollar price by making up congolene, and then conking ourselves.

2   I took the little list of ingredients he had printed out for me, and went to a grocery store, where I got a can of Red Devil lye, two eggs, and two medium-sized white potatoes. Then at a drugstore near the poolroom, I asked for a large jar of vaseline, a large bar of soap, a large-toothed comb and a fine-toothed comb, one of those rubber hoses with a metal spray-head, a rubber apron and a pair of gloves.

3   "Going to lay on that first conk?" the drugstore man asked me. I proudly told him, grinning, "Right!"

4   Shorty paid six dollars a week for a room in his cousin's shabby apartment. His cousin wasn't at home. "It's like the pad's mine, he spends so much time with his woman," Shorty said. "Now, you watch me—"

5   He peeled the potatoes and thin-sliced them into a quart-sized Mason fruit jar, then started stirring them with a wooden spoon as he gradually poured in a little over half the can of lye. "Never use a metal spoon; the lye will turn it black," he told me.

6   A jelly-like, starchy-looking glop resulted from the lye and potatoes, and Shorty broke in the two eggs, stirring real fast—his own conk and dark face bent down close. The congolene turned pale-yellowish. "Feel the jar," Shorty said. I cupped my hand against the outside, and snatched it away. "Damn right, it's hot, that's the lye." he said. "So you know it's going to burn when I comb it in—it burns *bad*. But the longer you can stand it, the straighter the hair."

7   He made me sit down, and he tied the string of the new rubber apron tightly around my neck, and combed up my bush of hair. Then, from the

203

big vaseline jar, he took a handful and massaged it hard all through my hair and into the scalp. He also thickly vaselined my neck, ears and forehead. "When I get to washing out your head, be sure to tell me anywhere you feel any little stinging," Shorty warned me, washing his hands, then pulling on the rubber gloves, and trying on his own rubber apron. "You always got to remember that any congolene left in burns a sore into your head."

The congolene just felt warm when Shorty started combing it in. But then my head caught fire. 8

I gritted my teeth and tried to pull the sides of the kitchen table together. The comb felt as if it was raking my skin off. 9

My eyes watered, my nose was running. I couldn't stand it any longer; I bolted to the washbasin. I was cursing Shorty with every name I could think of when he got the spray going and started soap-lathering my head. 10

He lathered and spray-rinsed, lathered and spray-rinsed, maybe ten or twelve times, each time gradually closing the hot-water faucet, until the rinse was cold, and that helped some. 11

"You feel any stinging spots?" 12

"No," I managed to say. My knees were trembling. 13

"Sit back down, then. I think we got it all out okay." 14

The flame came back as Shorty, with a thick towel, started drying my head, rubbing hard. *"Easy, man, easy!"* I kept shouting. 15

"The first time's always worst. You get used to it better before long. You took it real good, homeboy. You got a good conk." 16

When Shorty let me stand up and see in the mirror, my hair hung down in limp, damp strings. My scalp still flamed, but not as badly; I could bear it. He draped the towel around my shoulders, over my rubber apron, and began again vaselining my hair. 17

I could feel him combing, straight back, first the big comb, then the fine-tooth one. 18

Then, he was using a razor, very delicately, on the back of my neck. Then, finally, shaping the sideburns. 19

My first view in the mirror blotted out the hurting. I'd seen some pretty conks, but when it's the first time, on your *own* head, the transformation, after the lifetime of kinks, is staggering. 20

The mirror reflected Shorty behind me. We both were grinning and sweating. And on top of my head was this thick, smooth sheen of shining red hair—real red—as straight as any white man's. 21

How ridiculous I was! Stupid enough to stand there simply lost in admiration of my hair now looking "white," reflected in the mirror in Shorty's room. I vowed that I'd never again be without a conk, and I never was for many years. 22

This was my first really big step toward self-degradation: when I   23
endured all of that pain, literally burning my flesh to have it look like a white
man's hair. I had joined that multitude of Negro men and women in America
who are brainwashed into believing that the black people are "inferior"—
and white people "superior"—that they will even violate and mutilate their
God-created bodies to try to look "pretty" by white standards.

QUESTIONS

Some of the Issues

1. What is a conk and why did Malcolm X want it?
2. Why does Malcolm X describe the process of buying the ingredients and
   of applying them in such detail?
3. What is the thesis of this short selection? With what arguments, information, or assertions does Malcolm X support his thesis?

The Way We Are Told

4. The selection divides into two very different parts. What are they? How
   do they differ?
5. The main part of the selection is a description of a process. How is it
   arranged? What qualities of instruction, even of a recipe, has it? How and
   where does it differ from a recipe?

Some Subjects for Essays

6. Malcolm X describes a process that shows, among other things, that people will go to great lengths to conform. Develop a short essay describing,
   in a straightforward, neutral manner, some example of how people will
   subject themselves to pain, inconvenience, and embarrassment to conform
   to some fashion or idea.
7. Rewrite your previous essay, but take a strong stand indicating approval
   or disapproval of the process.

8. Write an essay examining the rewards American society offers for conforming, or the penalties for not conforming. In addition to Malcolm X,
   you might read Sennett's and Cobb's "Third Generation" and Podhoretz's
   "The Brutal Bargain."

WE REAL COOL

Gwendolyn Brooks

Gwendolyn Brooks was born in Kansas but has spent most of her life
in Chicago. Her first volume of poetry, *A Street in Bronzeville*, was
published in 1945. Many of her poems concern conditions in the Black
community, its feelings, and attitudes. In 1950 she won the Pulitzer
Prize for poetry. The poem reprinted here is from *Selected Poems*
(1959).

The Pool Players
Seven at the Golden Shovel

We real cool. We
Left school. We

Lurk late. We
Strike straight. We

Sing sin. We
Thin gin. We

Jazz June. We
Die soon.

SIX

Defining America

*P*erhaps more than any other people, Americans are conscious of their diversity as a nation. Most Americans' roots in another culture usually do not date from the distant past, but are recent enough to influence their lives. Even for those whose ancestry on this continent stretches into pre-history, diversity is a factor. Native Americans will tell you that there is no such person as an "Indian": there are Sioux or Mohawks or Kiowas. We have Black Americans and hyphenated Americans, and every group is in some sense a minority. America is defined, or rather exemplified here, through views of Americans and their institutions that reach back into the past and also address the present.

The opening selection is a well-known statement in praise of the New World and its people: Michel Guillaume St. Jean de Crèvecoeur, a Frenchman who farmed in Vermont at the time of the American Revolution, defines what is best in the America of his day, contrasting it with Europe, the Old World with its engrained class structure where a man is born to wealth and high status or to poverty and drudgery without being able to change his lot. Crèvecoeur sees America as a prosperous, mobile, agricultural society, virtually classless, in which every person can reach whatever position in life his abilities allow. He sees great virtue in the cultural diversity of America, the easy mixture of people of different ethnic origins.

A century separates Crèvecoeur's definition from the next one, taken from the novel The American by Henry James. In the intervening century America had become a separate nation, the Civil War had been fought, and industrialization had begun to change the face of the country. James's American, as defined here, is rich, a leisurely traveler, visiting Paris, and contemplating the treasures of the Old World.

A century once more separates James's American from Joan Didion's "Norteamericana." In that century America had fought two world wars, had come to fear the coming of a third, and had become a superpower. Didion's woman of our time is a somewhat satirical portrait of a member of the affluent society, a casual world traveler.

These fictional portraits, one from the 1870s and one from the 1970s, are of Americans whose wealth permits them to range far and wide. The next selection, in contrast, describes a very different America. Michael Harrington's subject is poverty. He explains why the poor are, as he puts it, invisible in America and what that lack of visibility means.

The last three selections form a group. They describe two uniquely American institutions that have spread from here to many parts of the world: the soap opera and the fast-food chain. James Thurber discusses the soaps in their heyday on radio in the 1930s and 1940s. An excerpt from Newsweek describes the TV soaps of the early 1980s. In combination, the two selections show, and to an extent explain, changes in American social attitudes over the last half century.

Last, the anthropologist Conrad Phillip Kottak discusses the fast-food business, specifically McDonald's, as an American ritual.

WHAT IS AN AMERICAN?

Michel Guillaume St. Jean de Crèvecoeur

Michel Guillaume St. Jean de Crèvecoeur (1735–1813) came as a young man to the New World, settling at first in the French colony of *Louisiane*, which at that time stretched from the mouth of the St. Lawrence River in the north to the mouth of the Mississippi in the south. In the Seven Years War, called the French and Indian Wars in America, he fought under Montcalm against the British. When the colonies passed into British hands, he remained and settled as a farmer in Vermont. The Revolutionary War found him on the side of the loyalists. His *Letters from an American Farmer*, written in French, were published in 1782 and are among the earliest descriptions of life in America. Crèvecoeur returned to France permanently in 1790.

I wish I could be acquainted with the feelings and thoughts which must agitate the heart and present themselves to the mind of an enlightened Englishman, when he first lands on this continent. He must greatly rejoice, that he lived at a time to see this fair country discovered and settled; he must necessarily feel a share of national pride, when he views the chain of settlements which embellishes these extended shores. When he says to himself, this is the work of my countrymen, who, when convulsed by factions, afflicted by a variety of miseries and wants, restless and impatient, took refuge here. They brought along with them their national genius, to which they principally owe what liberty they enjoy, and what substance they possess. Here he sees the industry of his native country, displayed in a new manner, and traces in their works the embryos of all the arts, sciences, and ingenuity which flourish in Europe. Here he beholds fair cities, substantial villages, extensive fields, an immense country filled with decent houses, good roads, orchards, meadows, and bridges, where an hundred years ago all was wild, woody, and uncultivated!

What a train of pleasing ideas this fair spectacle must suggest! It is a prospect which must inspire a good citizen with the most heartfelt pleasure. The difficulty consists in the manner of viewing so extensive a scene. He is arrived on a new continent; a modern society offers itself to his contemplation, different from what he had hitherto seen. It is not composed, as in Europe, of great lords who possess every thing, and of a herd of people who have nothing. Here are no aristocratical families, no courts, no kings, no bishops, no ecclesiastical dominion, no invisible power giving to a few a very visible one; no great manufacturers employing thousands, no great refinements of luxury. The rich and the poor are not so far removed from each other as they are in Europe.

Some few towns excepted, we are all tillers of the earth, from Nova 3 Scotia to West Florida. We are a people of cultivators, scattered over an immense territory, communicating with each other by means of good roads and navigable rivers, united by the silken bands of mild government, all respecting the laws without dreading their power, because they are equitable. We are all animated with the spirit of industry, which is unfettered, and unrestrained, because each person works for himself. If he travels through our rural districts, he views not the hostile castle, and the haughty mansion, contrasted with the clay-built hut and miserable cabin, where cattle and men help to keep each other warm, and dwell in meanness, smoke, and indigence. A pleasing uniformity of decent competence appears throughout our habitations. The meanest of our log-houses is a dry and comfortable habitation. Lawyer or merchant are the fairest titles our towns afford; that of a farmer is the only appellation of the rural inhabitants of our country. It must take some time ere he can reconcile himself to our dictionary, which is but short in words of dignity, and names of honour. There, on a Sunday, he sees a congregation of respectable farmers and their wives, all clad in neat homespun, well mounted, or riding in their own humble waggons. There is not among them an esquire, saving the unlettered magistrate. There he sees a parson as simple as his flock, a farmer who does not riot on the labour of others. We have no princes, for whom we toil, starve, and bleed: we are the most perfect society now existing in the world. Here man is free as he ought to be; nor is this pleasing equality so transitory as many others are. Many ages will not see the shores of our great lakes replenished with inland nations, nor the unknown bounds of North America entirely peopled. Who can tell how far it extends? Who can tell the millions of men whom it will feed and contain? for no European foot has as yet travelled half the extent of this mighty continent!

The next wish of this traveller will be to know whence came all these 4 people? They are a mixtue of English, Scotch, Irish, Dutch, Germans, and Swedes. From this promiscuous breed, the race now called Americans have arisen. The eastern provinces must indeed be excepted, as being the unmixed descendants of Englishmen. I have heard many wish they had been more intermixed also: for my part, I am no wisher; and think it much better as it has happened. They exhibit a most conspicuous figure in this great and variegated picture; they too enter for a great share in the pleasing perspective displayed in these thirteen provinces. I know it is fashionable to reflect on them; but I respect them for what they have done; for the accuracy and wisdom with which they have settled their territory; for the decency of their manners; for their early love of letters; their ancient college, the first in this hemisphere; for their industry, which to me, who am but a farmer, is the criterion of every thing. There never was a people, situated as they are, who, with so ungrateful a soil, have done more in so short a time. Do you think that the monarchical ingredients which are more prevalent in other governments, have purged them from all foul stains? Their histories assert the contrary.

In this great American asylum, the poor of Europe have by some means 5 met together, and in consequence of various causes; to what purpose should they ask one another, what countrymen they are? Alas, two thirds of them had no country. Can a wretch who wanders about, who works and starves, whose life is a continual scene of sore affliction of pinching penury; can that man call England or any other kindgom his country? A country that had no bread for him, whose fields procured him no harvest, who met with nothing but the frowns of the rich, the severity of the laws, with jails and punishments; who owned not a single foot of the extensive surface of this planet? No! Urged by a variety of motives, here they came. Everything has tended to regenerate them; new laws, a new mode of living, a new social system; here they are become men: in Europe they were as so many useless plants, wanting vegetative mould, and refreshing showers; they withered, and were mowed down by want, hunger, and war: but now, by the power of transplantation, like all other plants, they have taken root and flourished! Formerly they were not numbered in any civil list of their country, except in those of the poor; here they rank as citizens. By what invisible power has this surprizing metamorphosis been performed? By that of the laws and that of their industry. The laws, the indulgent laws, protect them as they arrive, stamping on them the symbol of adoption; they receive ample rewards for their labours; these accumulated rewards procure them lands; those lands confer on them the title of freemen; and to that title every benefit is affixed which men can possibly require. This is the great operation daily performed by our laws. From whence proceed these laws? From our government. Whence that government? It is derived from the original genius and strong desire of the people, ratified and confirmed by government. This is the great chain which links us all, this is the picture which every province exhibits.

What attachment can a poor European emigrant have for a country 6 where he had nothing? The knowledge of the language, the love of a few kindred as poor as himself, were the only cords that tied him: his country is now that which gives him land, bread, protection, and consequence: *Ubi panis ibi patria*, is the motto of all emigrants. What then is the American, this new man? He is either an European, or the descendant of an European; hence that strange mixture of blood, which you will find in no other country.

I could point out to you a man, whose grandfather was an Englishman, whose wife was Dutch, whose son married a French woman, and whose present four sons have now four wives of different nations. *He* is an American, who, leaving behind him all his ancient prejudices and manners, receives new ones from the new mode of life he has embraced, the new government he obeys, and the new rank he holds. He becomes an American by being received in the broad lap of our great *Alma Mater*.

Here individuals of all nations are melted into a new race of men, whose labours and posterity will one day cause great change in the world. Americans are the western pilgrims, who are carrying along with them that great mass of arts, sciences, vigour, and industry, which began long since in the east; they will finish the great circle. The Americans were once scattered all over Europe; here they are incorporated into one of the finest systems of population which has ever appeared, and which will hereafter become distinct by the power of the different climates they inhabit. The American ought, therefore, to love this country much better than that wherein either he or his forefathers were born. Here the rewards of his industry follow with equal steps the progress of his labour; his labour is founded on the basis of nature, *self-interest;* can it want a stronger allurement? Wives and children, who before in vain demanded of him a morsel of bread, now, fat and frolicsome, gladly help their father to clear those fields whence exuberant crops are to arise to feed and to clothe them all; without any part being claimed, either by a despotic prince, a rich abbot, or a mighty lord. Here religion demands but little of him; a small voluntary salary to the minister, and gratitude to God; can he refuse these? The American is a new man, who acts upon new principles; he must therefore entertain new ideas, and form new opinions. From involuntary idleness, servile dependence, penury, and useless labour, he has passed to toils of a very different nature, rewarded by ample subsistence.—This is an American.

7

QUESTIONS

Words to Know

enlightened (paragraph 1), factions (1), ecclesiastical (2), dominion (2), unfettered (3), indigence (3), habitation (3), homespun (3), replenished (3), variegated (4), monarchical (4), metamorphosis (5), *ubi panis ibi patria*—where bread is, there is my country (6), frolicsome (7), exuberant (7), penury (7).

Some of the Issues

1. At the beginning of paragraph 1 Crèvecoeur refers "to the mind of an enlightened Englishman." Why does he use the word "enlightened"?
2. A few lines later he says that this Englishman "must . . . feel a share of national pride." Why a share? To what aspects of American and British history does Crèvecoeur allude in this paragraph?
3. What is the central idea of the first paragraph? Which sentence comes closest to representing it?
4. What is the central idea of the second paragraph? How does it relate to the first? How does it carry Crèvecoeur's ideas beyond the first paragraph?
5. Consider the last sentence in paragraph 2 and explain how it is expanded upon in paragraph 3.
6. Show how the last sentence of paragraph 3 leads to paragraph 4.
7. Make a list of the contrasts Crèvecoeur makes or clearly implies between Europe and America. Then attempt to organize and classify them into major groupings.
8. Crèvecoeur omits several groups of inhabitants of America. Who are they? Why do you think he omits them when he is clearly concerned about the well-being of ordinary people?

The Way We Are Told

9. Clearly, Crèvecoeur believes that the American way is superior to the European, but he does not say so directly. How does he express it in paragraph 1?
10. What details in paragraph 2 mark the distinction between Europe and America?
11. What details in paragraph 3 indicate the reasons for the American people's contentment and happiness?
12. Crèvecoeur argues for ethnic mixing. How does he demonstrate its advantages?

Some Subjects for Essays

13. Write an essay in praise of some institution that you admire. Select those aspects that seem important to you, organize them in some logical order, and write your description, stressing the favorable facts rather than giving your opinions.
14. Read Momaday's "The Way to Rainy Mountain" and then write a response by an Indian to Crèvecoeur.

THE AMERICAN

Henry James

Henry James, one of the major figures in American literature, was born in Boston in 1843 into a wealthy and distinguished family. He spent most of his adult life in England and died there in 1916. Many of his novels and short stories contain careful, in-depth examinations of Americans, usually rich Americans, placed in a European setting. His characters gravitate to France or Italy in search of culture (or, one might even say, roots). The following selection, the opening passage of James' novel *The American*, is a portrait of Christopher Newman, the hero of the novel.

On a brilliant day in May, of the year 1868, a gentleman was reclining at his ease on the great circular divan which at that period occupied the centre of the Salon Carré, in the Museum of the Louvre. This commodious ottoman has since been removed, to the extreme regret of all weak-kneed lovers of the fine arts; but our visitor had taken serene possession of its softest spot, and, with his head thrown back and his legs outstretched, was staring at Murillo's beautiful moon-borne Madonna in deep enjoyment of his posture. He had removed his hat and flung down beside him a little red guide-book and an opera-glass. The day was warm; he was heated with walking, and he repeatedly, with vague weariness, passed his handkerchief over his forehead. And yet he was evidently not a man to whom fatigue was familiar; long, lean, and muscular, he suggested an intensity of unconscious resistance. His exertions on this particular day, however, had been of an unwonted sort, and he had often performed great physical feats that left him less jaded than his quiet stroll through the Louvre. He had looked out all the pictures to which an asterisk was affixed in those formidable pages of fine print in his Bädeker; his attention had been strained and his eyes dazzled; he had sat down with an æsthetic headache. He had looked, moreover, not only at all the pictures, but at all the copies that were going forward around them in the hands of those innumerable young women in long aprons, on high stools, who devote themselves, in France, to the reproduction of masterpieces; and, if the truth must be told, he had often admired the copy much more than the original. His physiognomy would have sufficiently indicated that he was a shrewd and capable person, and in truth he had often sat up all night over a bristling bundle of accounts and heard the cock crow without a yawn. But Raphael and Titian and Rubens were a new kind of arithmetic, and they made him for the first time in his life wonder at his vaguenesses.

214

An observer with anything of an eye for local types would have had no   2
difficulty in referring this candid connoisseur to the scene of his origin, and
indeed such an observer might have made an ironic point of the almost ideal
completeness with which he filled out the mould of race. The gentleman on
the divan was the superlative American; to which affirmation of character
he was partly helped by the general easy magnificence of his manhood. He
appeared to possess that kind of health and strength which, when found in
perfection, are the most impressive—the physical tone which the owner does
nothing to "keep up." If he was a muscular Christian it was quite without
doctrine. If it was necessary to walk to a remote spot he walked, but he had
never known himself to "exercise." He had no theory with regard to cold
bathing or the use of Indian clubs; he was neither an oarsman, a rifleman nor
a fencer—he had never had time for these amusements—and he was quite
unaware that the saddle is recommended for certain forms of indigestion.
He was by inclination a temperate man; but he had supped the night before
his visit to the Louvre at the Café Anglais—some one had told him it was an
experience not to be omitted—and he had slept none the less the sleep of the
just. His usual attitude and carriage had a liberal looseness, but when, under
a special inspiration, he straightened himself he looked a grenadier on
parade. He had never tasted tobacco. He had been assured—such things are
said—that cigars are excellent for the health, and he was quite capable of
believing it; but he would no more have thought of "taking" one than of
taking a dose of medicine. His complexion was brown and the arch of his
nose bold and well-marked. His eye was of a clear, cold grey, and save for
the abundant droop of his moustache he spoke, as to cheek and chin, of the
joy of the matutinal steel. He had the flat jaw and the firm, dry neck which
are frequent in the American type; but the betrayal of native conditions is a
matter of expression even more than of feature, and it was in this respect
that our traveller's countenance was supremely eloquent. The observer we
have been supposing might, however, perfectly have measured its expres-
siveness and yet have been at a loss for names and terms to fit it. It had that
paucity of detail which is yet not emptiness, that blankness which is not simplicity, that look of being committed to nothing in particular, of standing in
a posture of general hospitality to the chances of life, of being very much at
one's own disposal, characteristic of American faces of the clear strain. It was
the eye, in this case, that chiefly told the story; an eye in which the unac-
quainted and the expert were singularly blended. It was full of contradictory
suggestions; and though it was by no means the glowing orb of a hero of
romance you could find in it almost anything you looked for. Frigid and yet
friendly, frank yet cautious, shrewd yet credulous, positive yet sceptical, confident yet shy, extremely intelligent and extremely good-humoured, there

was something vaguely defiant in its concessions and something profoundly reassuring in its reserve. The wide yet partly folded wings of this gentleman's moustache, with the two premature wrinkles in the cheek above it, and the fashion of his garments, in which an exposed shirt-front and a blue satin necktie of too light a shade played perhaps an obtrusive part, completed the elements of his identity. We have approached him perhaps at a not especially favourable moment; he is by no means sitting for his portrait. But listless as he lounges there, rather baffled on the æsthetic question and guilty of the damning fault (as we have lately discovered it to be) of confounding the aspect of the artist with that of his work (for he admires the squinting Madonna of the young lady with the hair that somehow also advertises "art," because he thinks the young lady herself uncommonly taking), he is a sufficiently promising acquaintance. Decision, salubrity, jocosity, prosperity, seem to hover within his call; he is evidently a man of business, but the term appears to confess, for his particular benefit, to undefined and mysterious boundaries which invite the imagination to bestir itself.

QUESTIONS

Words to Know

divan (paragraph 1), Louvre (1), commodious (1), ottoman (1), Murillo (1), unwonted (1), jaded (1), formidable (1), Bädeker (1), aesthetic (1), physiognomy (1), Raphael (1), Titian (1), Rubens (1), connoisseur (2), remote (2), grenadier (2), matutinal (2), countenance (2), eloquent (2), obtrusive (2), salubrity (2), jocosity (2), hover (2), bestir (2).

Some of the Issues

1. Henry James's novel opens with these two paragraphs in which he tries to establish the central character of the book. Later we learn that his name is Christopher Newman. In what way is that name appropriate? Cite specific details.
2. What particular aspects of Newman's character emerge in paragraph 1?
3. Would you consider Newman an art lover who regularly visits museums and galleries? In your answer give evidence to support your conclusions.

4. James describes Newman both as a "typical" American and as an individual. What parts of the description relate to the former? The latter?
5. James portrays an American of 100 years ago. Would you say that his portrait would also describe an American of our time? Why, or why not?

The Way We Are Told

6. James uses two lengthy paragraphs for his description. How do they differ from each other?
7. What is the topic sentence of Paragraph 2?
8. In paragraph 2 James pairs several contradictory qualities, for example, "frigid yet friendly." Find additional examples and explain how they help to define "an American."
9. What would you say is James's attitude toward the character he describes? Is he neutral? Justify your answer with specific references to words and phrases.

Some Subjects for Essays

10. Write an essay defining the typical contemporary American (or member of another national group). Or argue that such a creature does not exist.
11. Write a detailed physical description of someone you have observed, using James's style as your model. Try for some of the same richness of detail that James has, even if the result seems exaggerated to you. Don't forget to include clothing, posture, movement, and gestures.

NORTEAMERICANA

Joan Didion

Joan Didion, a Californian, is a writer who has also worked as an editor for such magazines as *Vogue, The National Review*, and *Esquire*. Her essays have appeared in a number of national magazines and were collected in *Slouching Toward Bethlehem* (1968), and *The White Album* (1979). She is the author of several screenplays including *A Star Is Born* (1979). Her novels include *Run, River* (1963), *Play It As It Lays* (1970), and *The Book of Common Prayer* (1976), from which this description of Charlotte, its main character, is taken.

Three or four things I do know about Charlotte. 1

As a child of comfortable family in the temperate zone she had been as 2 a matter of course provided with clean sheets, orthodontia, lamb chops, living grandparents, attentive godparents, one brother named Dickie, ballet lessons, and casual timely information about menstruation and the care of flat silver, as well as with a small wooden angel, carved in Austria, to sit on her bed table and listen to her prayers. In these prayers the child Charlotte routinely asked that "it" turn out all right, "it" being unspecified and all-inclusive, and she had been an adult for some years before the possibility occurred to her that "it" might not. She had put this doubt from her mind. As a child of the western United States she had been provided as well with faith in the value of certain frontiers on which her family had lived, in the virtues of cleared and irrigated land, of high-yield crops, of thrift, industry and the judicial system, of progress and education, and in the generally upward spiral of history. She was a *norteamericana*.

She was immaculate of history, innocent of politics. There were startling 3 vacuums in her store of common knowledge. During the two years she spent at Berkeley before she ran away to New York with an untenured instructor named Warren Bogart, she had read mainly the Brontës and *Vogue*, bought a loom, gone home to Hollister on weekends and slept a great deal during the week. In those two years she had entered the main library once, during a traveling exhibition of the glass flowers from Harvard. She recalled having liked the glass flowers. From books Warren Bogart gave her to read when she was twenty Charlotte learned for the first time about the Spanish Civil War, memorized the ideological distinctions among the various PSUC brigades and POUM militia, but until she was twenty-two and Warren Bogart divined and corrected her misapprehension she believed that World War II

had begun at Pearl Harbor. From Leonard Douglas she had absorbed a passing fluency in Third World power, had learned what the initials meant in
Algeria and Indochina and the Caribbean, but on a blank map of the world
she could not actually place the countries where the initials were in conflict.
She considered the conflict dubious in any case. She understood that something was always going on in the world but believed that it would turn out
all right. She believed the world to be peopled with others like herself. She
associated the word "revolution" with the Boston Tea Party, one of the few
events in the history of the United States prior to the westward expansion to
have come to her attention. She also associated it with events in France and
Russia that had probably turned out all right, otherwise why had they
happened.

> A not atypical *norteamericana*.   4
> Of her time and place.   5

QUESTIONS

Words to Know

immaculate (paragraph 3), untenured (3), Brontë (3), ideological (3), divined
(3), misapprehension (3).

Some of the Issues

1. Didion describes Charlotte as "immaculate of history." What events of
   the American past are referred to in this selection? What other historical
   events?
2. What does college "do" for Charlotte? What does Charlotte's experience
   in college tell us about her?
3. What does Didion imply about Charlotte's upbringing by some of the
   items she puts next to each other, such as "clean sheets, orthodontia, lamb
   chops" or "casual, timely information about menstruation and the care of
   flat silver"? What does this imply about her family, or about families of
   her particular background?
4. What, in paragraph 2, is implied about Charlotte's expectations of life?

The Way We Are Told

5. Look at the first sentence of paragraph 2 and explain how the rest of the paragraph relates to it. Does it repeat the assertion of that sentence, explain it, or contradict it?
6. The selection begins with one and ends with two, very short, one-sentence paragraphs. What is their effect?
7. Both Henry James, in the preceding selection, and Joan Didion describe their respective characters from the outside, as if they were butterflies pinned to a board. Compare and contrast their attitudes toward their two subjects. Cite specifics in making your comparisons.

Some Subjects for Essays

8. Try to imagine Charlotte's family. Write a description of her father and mother, and of her home.
9. At the end Didion describes Charlotte as "a not atypical Norteamericana." (Note the difference between "not atypical" and "typical.") Write an essay supporting Didion's assertion or arguing against it.

THE INVISIBLE POOR

Michael Harrington

Michael Harrington is a professor of political science at Queens College, New York. He served as associate editor of *The Catholic Worker* in the early 1950s and is a member of the Executive Committee of the Socialist Party. His books of social criticism include *The Accidental Century* (1965), *Toward a Democratic Left* (1968), *The Vast Majority: A Journey to the World's Poor* (1977), *The Next America: The Decline and Rise of the United States* (1981), and *The Other America* (1963), from which this selection is taken.

The millions who are poor in the United States tend to become increasingly invisible. Here is a great mass of people, yet it takes an effort of the intellect and will even to see them.

I discovered this personally in a curious way. After I wrote my first article on poverty in America, I had all the statistics down on paper. I had proved to my satisfaction that there were around 50,000,000 poor in this country. Yet, I realized I did not believe my own figures. The poor existed in the Government reports; they were percentages and numbers in long, close columns, but they were not part of my experience. I could prove that the other America existed, but I had never been there.

There are perennial reasons that make the other America an invisible land.

Poverty is often off the beaten track. It always has been. The ordinary tourist never left the main highway, and today he rides interstate turnpikes. He does not go into the valleys of Pennsylvania where the towns look like movie sets of Wales in the thirties. He does not see the company houses in rows, the rutted roads (the poor always have bad roads whether they live in the city, in towns, or on farms), and everything is black and dirty. And even if he were to pass through such a place by accident, the tourist would not meet the unemployed men in the bar or the women coming home from a runaway sweatshop.

Then, too, beauty and myths are perennial masks of poverty. The traveler comes to the Appalachians in the lovely season. He sees the hills, the streams, the foliage—but not the poor. Or perhaps he looks at a run-down mountain house and, remembering Rousseau rather than seeing with his eyes, decides that 'those people' are truly fortunate to be living the way they are and that they are lucky to be exempt from the strains and tensions of the middle class. The only problem is that 'those people,' the quaint inhabitants of those hills, are undereducated, underprivileged, lack medical care, and are in the process of being forced from the land into a life in the cities, where they are misfits.

These are normal and obvious causes of the invisibility of the poor. They 6 operated a generation ago; they will be functioning a generation hence. It is more important to understand that the very development of American society is creating a new kind of blindness about poverty. The poor are increasingly slipping out of the very experience and consciousness of the nation.

If the middle class never did like ugliness and poverty, it was at least 7 aware of them. 'Across the tracks' was not a very long way to go. There were forays into the slums at Christmas time; there were charitable organizations that brought contact with the poor. Occasionally, almost everyone passed through the Negro ghetto or the blocks of tenements, if only to get downtown to work or to entertainment.

Now the American city has been transformed. The poor still inhabit the 8 miserable housing in the central area, but they are increasingly isolated from contact with, or sight of, anybody else. Middle-class women coming in from Suburbia on a rare trip may catch the merest glimpse of the other America on the way to an evening at the theater, but their children are segregated in suburban schools. The business or professional man may drive along the fringes of slums in a car or bus, but it is not an important experience to him. The failures, the unskilled, the disabled, the aged, and the minorities are right there, across the tracks, where they have always been. But hardly anyone else is.

In short, the very development of the American city has removed poverty 9 from the living, emotional experience of millions upon millions of middle-class Americans. Living out in the suburbs, it is easy to assume that ours is, indeed, an affluent society.

This new segregation of poverty is compounded by a well-meaning 10 ignorance. A good many concerned and sympathetic Americans are aware that there is much discussion of urban renewal. Suddenly, driving through the city, they notice that a familiar slum has been torn down and that there are towering, modern buildings where once there had been tenements or hovels. There is a warm feeling of satisfaction, of pride in the way things are working out: the poor, it is obvious, are being taken care of.

The irony in this . . . is that the truth is nearly the exact opposite to the 11 impression. The total impact of the various housing programs in postwar America has been to squeeze more and more people into existing slums. . . . Clothes make the poor invisible too: America has the best-dressed poverty the world has ever known. For a variety of reasons, the benefits of mass production have been spread much more evenly in this area than in many others. It is much easier in the United States to be decently dressed than it is to be decently housed, fed, or doctored. Even people with terribly depressed incomes can look prosperous.

This is an extremely important factor in defining our emotional and existential ignorance of poverty. In Detroit the existence of social classes became much more difficult to discern the day the companies put lockers in the plants. From that moment on, one did not see men in work clothes on the way to the factory, but citizens in slacks and white shirts. This process has been magnified with the poor throughout the country. There are tens of thousands of Americans in the big cities who are wearing shoes, perhaps even a stylishly cut suit or dress, and yet are hungry. It is not a matter of planning, though it almost seems as if the affluent society had given out costumes to the poor so that they would not offend the rest of society with the sight of rags. 12

Then, many of the poor are the wrong age to be seen. A good number of them (over 8,000,000) are sixty-five years of age or better; an even larger number are under eighteen. The aged members of the other America are often sick, and they cannot move. Another group of them live out their lives in loneliness and frustration: they sit in rented rooms, or else they stay close to a house in a neighborhood that has completely changed from the old days. Indeed, one of the worst aspects of poverty among the aged is that these people are out of sight and out of mind, and alone. 13

The young are somewhat more visible, yet they too stay close to their neighborhoods. Sometimes they advertise their poverty through a lurid tabloid story about a gang killing. But generally they do not disturb the quiet streets of the middle class. 14

And finally, the poor are politically invisible. It is one of the cruelest ironies of social life in advanced countries that the dispossessed at the bottom of society are unable to speak for themselves. The people of the other America do not, by far and large, belong to unions, to fraternal organizations, or to political parties. They are without lobbies of their own; they put forward no legislative program. As a group, they are atomized. They have no face; they have no voice. 15

Thus, there is not even a cynical political motive for caring about the poor, as in the old days. Because the slums are no longer centers of powerful political organizations, the politicians need not really care about their inhabitants. The slums are no longer visible to the middle class, so much of the idealistic urge to fight for those who need help is gone. Only the social agencies have a really direct involvement with the other America, and they are without any great political power. 16

To the extent that the poor have a spokesman in American life, that role   17
is played by the labor movement. The unions have their own particular ide-
alism, an ideology of concern. More than that, they realize that the existence
of a reservoir of cheap, unorganized labor is a menace to wages and working
conditions throughout the entire economy. Thus, many union legislative proposals—to extend the coverage of minimum wage and social security, to
organize migrant farm laborers—articulate the needs of the poor.

That the poor are invisible is one of the most important things about   18
them. They are not simply neglected and forgotten as in the old rhetoric of
reform; what is much worse, they are not seen.

QUESTIONS

Words to Know

rutted (paragraph 4), sweatshop (4), myth (5), perennial (5), Rousseau (5),
quaint (5), forays (7), affluent (9), compounded (10), existential (12), cynical
(16), reservoir (17), articulate (17), rhetoric (18).

Some of the Issues

1. In order to establish that the poor are invisible, Harrington needs to
   establish first that poverty continues to exist in America. How does he
   do that?
2. In what way is rural poverty invisible?
3. What reasons does Harrington give for the invisibility of the urban poor?
4. How has the development of the American city increased the invisibility
   of the poor?
5. How has mass production affected that invisibility?

The Way We Are Told

6. In paragraph 2 Harrington uses the first person singular. Why does he
   refer to himself here but not elsewhere?
7. Paragraph 3 consists of one sentence. What is its function with respect
   to the organization of the selection? What is its effect?

8. Discuss the structure of paragraphs 4 and 5. How is their content developed? Find additional paragraphs that show the same structure.
9. Examine the order of Harrington's arguments, beginning with paragraph 4. Try to establish if they are in any logical sequence.

Some Subjects for Essays

10. Select a topic you feel competent to argue for, such as American (foreign) cars are a better buy than foreign (American) ones; private (public) colleges are preferable to public (private) ones; or city (suburban) living is preferable to suburban (city) living. Then make a list of all the arguments for your case you can think of. Next, sort your arguments into logical groups, subordinating items as needed. Arrange your groups in logical order. Finally, write your essay.
11. In paragraph 6 Harrington says that the causes of the invisibility of the poor "operated a generation ago: they will be functioning a generation hence." Harrington's book was published in the early 1960s and some of the circumstances he cites may now be different. Do you think his basic thesis still holds?

IVORYTOWN, RINSOVILLE, ANACINBURG, AND CRISCO CORNERS

James Thurber

James Thurber (1894–1961), one of America's foremost humorists and essayists, spent most of his working life associated with *The New Yorker* magazine. His books include *Is Sex Necesessary?* (1929, with E. B. White), *My World—And Welcome to It* (1942), and many others. *The Beast in Me, and Other Animals*, from which the following essay is taken, appeared in 1948. This essay is a lighthearted analysis of the radio soap operas of the time, and can be compared with the *Newsweek* article which follows it and discusses the TV soaps of the 1980s.

The last time I checked up on the locales of the thirty-six radio daytime serials, better known as soap operas, that are broadcast from New York five days a week to a mass audience of twenty million listeners, the score was Small Towns 24, Big Cities 12. I say "score" advisedly, for the heavy predominance of small towns in Soapland is a contrived and often-emphasized victory for good, clean little communities over cold, cruel metropolitan centers. Thus, daytime radio perpetuates the ancient American myth of the small town, idealized in novels, comedies, and melodramas at the turn of the century and before, supported by Thornton Wilder in "Our Town," and undisturbed by the scandalous revelations of such irreverent gossips as Sherwood Anderson and Edgar Lee Masters. Soapland shares with the United States at least five actual cities—New York, Chicago, Boston, Washington, and Los Angeles—but its small towns are as misty and unreal as Brigadoon. They have such names as Hartville, Dickston, Simpsonville, Three Oaks. Great Falls, Beauregard, Elmwood, Oakdale, Rushville Center, and Homeville. "Our Gal Sunday" is set in Virginia, but no states are mentioned for the towns in the other serials.

A soap opera deals with the plights and problems brought about in the lives of its permanent principal characters by the advent and interference of one group of individuals after another. Thus, a soap opera is an endless sequence of narratives whose only cohesive element is the eternal presence of its bedevilled and beleaguered principal characters. A narrative, or story sequence, may run from eight weeks to several months. The ending of one plot is always hooked up with the beginning of the next, but the connection is unimportant and soon forgotten. Almost all the villains in the small-town daytime serials are émigrés from the cities—gangsters, white-collar criminals, designing women, unnatural mothers, cold wives, and selfish, ruthless, and just plain cussed rich men. They always come up against a shrewdness that outwits them or destroys them, or a kindness that wins them over to the good way of life.

The fact that there are only two or three citizens for the villains to get   3
entangled with reduces the small town to a wood-and-canvas set with painted doors and windows. Many a soap town appears to have no policemen, mailmen, milkmen, storekeepers, lawyers, ministers, or even neighbors. The people live their continuously troubled lives within a socio-economic structure that only faintly resembles our own. Since the problems of the characters are predominantly personal, emotional, and private, affecting the activities of only five or six persons at a time, the basic setting of soap opera is the living room. But even the living room lacks the pulse of life; rarely are heard the ticking of clocks, the tinkling of glasses, the squeaking of chairs, or the creaking of floor boards. Now and then, the listener does hear *about* a hospital, a courtroom, a confectionery, a drugstore, a bank, or a hotel in the town, or a roadhouse or a large, gloomy estate outside the town limits, but in most small-town serials there are no signs or sounds of community life—no footsteps of passers-by, no traffic noises, no shouting of children, no barking of dogs, no calling of friend to friend, no newsboys to plump the evening papers against front doors. A few writers try from time to time to animate the streets of these silent towns, but in general Ivorytown and Rinsoville and Anacinburg are dead.

If the towns in Soapland are not developed as realistic communities,   4
neither are the characters—except in rare instances—developed as authentic human beings. The reason for this is that the listening housewives are believed to be interested only in problems similar to their own, and it is one of the basic tenets of soap opera that the women characters who solve these problems must be flawless projections of the housewife's ideal woman. It is assumed that the housewife identifies herself with the characters who are most put-upon, most noble, most righteous, and hence most dehumanized. Proceeding on this theory, serial producers oppose the creation of any three-dimensional character who shows signs of rising above this strange standard. Advertising agencies claim—and the record would appear to sustain them—

that a realistically written leading woman would cause the audience rating
of the show to drop.

The principal complaint of audience mail in the early days of the serials   5
was that they moved so swiftly they were hard to follow. Surveys showed
that the housewife listens, on an average, to not more than half the broadcasts
of any given serial. Plot recapitulation, familiarly called "recap," was devised
to slow down the progress of serials. "We told them what was going to happen, we told them it was happening, and we told them it had happened,"
says Robert D. Andrews. The listeners continued to complain, and action was
retarded still further, with the result that time in a soap opera is now an
amazing technique of slow motion. Compared to the swift flow of time in
the real world, it is a glacier movement. It took one male character in a soap
opera three days to get an answer to the simple question "Where have you
been?" If, in "When a Girl Marries," you missed an automobile accident that
occurred on a Monday broadcast, you could pick it up the following Thursday and find the leading woman character still unconscious and her husband
still moaning over her beside the wrecked car. In one sequence of "Just Plain
Bill," the barber of Hartville said, "It doesn't seem possible to me that Ralph
Wilde arrived here only yesterday." It didn't seem possible to me, either,
since Ralph Wilde had arrived, as mortal time goes, thirteen days before.
Bill recently required four days to shave a man in the living room of the
man's house. A basin of hot water Bill had placed on a table Monday (our
time) was still hot on Thursday, when his customer stopped talking and the
barber went to work.

Soap-opera time, by an easy miracle, always manages to coincide with   6
mortal time in the case of holidays. Memorial Day in Hartville, for example,
is Memorial Day in New York. Every year, on that day, Bill Davidson, Hartville's leading citizen, makes the Memorial Day address, a simple, cagey
arrangement of words in praise of God and the Republic. One serial writer
tells me that the word "republic" has been slyly suggested as preferable to
"democracy," apparently because "democracy" has become a provocative,
flaming torch of a word in our time. For Soapland, you see, is a peaceful
world, a political and economic Utopia, free of international unrest, the menace of fission, the threat of inflation, depression, general unemployment, the
infiltration of Communists, and the problems of racism. Except for a maid
or two, there are no colored people in the World of Soap. Papa David, in
"Life Can Be Beautiful," is the only Jew I have run into on the daytime air
since "The Goldbergs" was discontinued. (Procter & Gamble sponsored "The
Goldbergs" for many years, and the race question did not enter into its ter-
mination.) Lynn Stone and Addy Richton, who have written several serials,
were once told by a sponsor's representative to eliminate a Jewish woman

from one of their shows. "We don't want to antagonize the anti-Semites," the gentleman casually explained. They had to take out the character.

A study of the social stratification of Soapland, if I may use so elegant a term, reveals about half a dozen highly specialized groups. There are the important homely philosophers, male and female. This stratum runs through "Just Plain Bill," "Ma Perkins," "David Harum," "Life Can Be Beautiful," and "Editor's Daughter," a soap opera not heard in the East but extremely popular in the Middle West, whose male protagonist enunciates a gem of friendly wisdom at the end of every program. ("Life Can Be Beautiful," by the way, is known to the trade as "Elsie Beebe." You figure it out. I had to.) Then, there are the Cinderellas, the beautiful or talented young women of lowly estate who have married or are about to marry into social circles far above those of their hard-working and usually illiterate mothers. (Their fathers, as a rule, are happily dead.) On this wide level are Nana, daughter of Hamburger Katie; Laurel, daughter of Stella Dallas; and my special pet, Sunday, of "Our Gal Sunday," who started life as a foundling dumped in the laps of two old Western miners and is now the proud and badgered wife of Lord Henry Brinthrop, "England's wealthiest and handsomest young nobleman." Christopher Morley's famous Cinderella, Kitty Foyle, also lived in Soapland for some years. Mr. Morley was charmed by the actors and actresses who played in "Kitty," but he says that he never quite gathered what the radio prolongation of the story was about. Kitty eventually packed up and moved out of Soapland. The late Laurette Taylor received many offers for the serial rights to "Peg o' My Heart," which was written by her husband, J. Hartley Manners, but it is said that she rejected them all with the agonized cry "Oh, God, no! Not that!" On a special and very broad social stratum of Soapland live scores of doctors and nurses. You find scarcely anyone else in "Woman in White," "Road of Life," and "Joyce Jordan, M.D." The heroes of "Young Dr. Malone," "Big Sister," and "Young Widder Brown" are doctors, and medical men flit in and out of all other serials. The predominance of doctors may be accounted for by the fact that radio surveys have frequently disclosed that the practice of medicine is at the top of the list of professions popular with the American housewife.

A fourth and highly important group, since it dominates large areas of Soapland, consists of young women, single, widowed, or divorced, whose purpose in life seems to be to avoid marriage by straight-arming their suitors year after year on one pretext or another. Among the most distinguished members of this group are Joyce Jordan, who is a doctor when she gets around to it; Helen Trent, a dress designer; Ellen Brown, who runs a tea-room; Ruth Wayne, a nurse; and a number of actresses and secretaries. For some years, Portia, the woman lawyer of "Portia Faces Life," belonged to this class, but several years ago she married Walter Manning, a journalist, and became an eminent figure in perhaps the most important group of all, the devoted and long-suffering wives whose marriages have, every hour of their lives, the immediacy of a toothache and the urgency of a telegram. The husbands of these women spend most of their time trying in vain to keep their brave, high-minded wives out of one plot entanglement after another.

All men in Soapland must be able to drop whatever they are doing and 9 hurry to this living room or that at the plaint or command of a feminine voice on the phone. Bill Davidson's one-chair barbershop has not had a dozen customers in a dozen years, since the exigencies of his life keep him out of the shop most of every day. In eight months, by my official count, Kerry Donovan visited his law office only three times. He has no partners or assistants, but, like Bill, he somehow prospers. The rich men, bad and good, who descend on the small town for plot's sake never define the industries they leave behind them in New York or Chicago for months at a time. Their businesses miraculously run without the exertion of control or the need for contact. Now and then, a newspaper publisher, a factory owner, or a superintendent of schools, usually up to no good, appears briefly on the Soapland scene, but mayors, governors, and the like are almost never heard of. "The Story of Mary Marlin," just to be different, had a President of the United States, but, just to be the same, he was made heavily dependent on the intuitive political vision of his aged mother, who, in 1943, remained alive to baffle the doctors and preserve, by guiding her son's policies, the security of the Republic.

The people of Soapland, as Rudolf Arnheim, professor of psychology at 10 Sarah Lawrence, has pointed out, consist of three moral types: the good, the bad, and the weak. Good women dominate most soap operas. They are conventional figures, turned out of a simple mold. Their invariably strong character, high fortitude, and unfailing capability must have been originally intended to present them as women of a warm, dedicated selflessness, but they emerge, instead, as ladies of frigid aggressiveness. The writers are not to blame for this metamorphosis, for they are hampered by several formidable inhibitions, including what is officially called "daytime morality," the strangest phenomenon in a world of phenomena. The good people, both men and women, cannot smoke cigarettes or touch alcoholic beverages, even beer or sherry. In a moment of tragedy or emotional tension, the good people turn to tea or coffee, iced or hot. It has been estimated that the three chief characters of "Just Plain Bill" have consumed several hundred gallons of iced tea since this program began, in 1932. Furthermore, the good women must float like maiden schoolteachers above what Evangeline Adams used to call "the slime"; that is, the passionate expression of sexual love. The ban against spir-

ituous and amorous indulgence came into sharp focus once in "Just Plain
Bill" when the plot called for one Graham Steele to be caught in a posture
of apparent intimacy with the virtuous Nancy Donovan. He had carelessly
upset a glass of iced tea into the lady's lap and was kneeling and dabbing at
her dress with his handkerchief—a compromising situation indeed in Soapland—when her jealous husband arrived and suspected the worst.

The paternalistic Procter & Gamble, famous for their managerial policy   11
of "We're just one big family of good, clean folks," do not permit the smoking of cigarettes at their plants during working hours except in the case of
executives with private offices. This may have brought about the anti-ciga-
rette phase of daytime morality, but I can adduce no evidence to support
the theory. The supervision of Procter & Gamble's eleven soap operas is in
the tolerant hands of the quiet, amiable William Ramsey, who smokes Marlboros. In daytime radio, the cigarette has come to be a sign and stigma of
evil that ranks with the mark of the cloven hoof, the scarlet letter, and the
brand of the fleur-de-lis. The married woman who smokes a cigarette pro-
claims herself a bad wife or an unnatural mother or an adventuress. The
male cigarette smoker is either a gangster or a cold, calculating white-collar
criminal. The good men may smoke pipes or cigars. A man who called on
the hero of "Young Dr. Malone" brought him some excellent pipe tobacco
and announced that he himself would smoke a fine cigar. As if to take the
edge off this suggestion of wanton sensual abandon, a good woman hastily
said to the caller, "Don't you want a nice, cold glass of ice water?" "Splen-
did!" cried the gentleman. "How many cubes?" she asked. "Two, thank
you," said the visitor, and the virtue of the household was reëstablished.

Clean-living, letter-writing busybodies are unquestionably to blame for   12
prohibition in Soapland. When Mrs. Elaine Carrington, the author of "Pepper Young's Family," had somebody serve beer on that serial one hot afternoon, she received twenty indignant complaints. It wasn't many, when you
consider that "Pepper" has six million listeners, but it was enough. The latest
violation of radio's liquor law I know of occurred in "Ma Perkins," when a
bad woman was given a double Scotch-and-soda to loosen her tongue. Letters
of protest flooded in. The bad people and the weak people are known to
drink and to smoke cigarettes, but their vices in this regard are almost always
just talked about, with proper disapproval, and not often actually depicted.

As for the sexual aspect of daytime morality, a man who had a lot to do   13
with serials in the nineteen-thirties assures me that at that time there were
"hot clinches" burning up and down the daytime dial. If this is so, there has
been a profound cooling off, for my persistent eavesdropping has detected
nothing but coy and impregnable chastity in the good women, nobly abetted
by a kind of Freudian censor who knocks on doors or rings phones at crucial

moments. Young Widder Brown has kept a doctor dangling for years without benefit of her embraces, on the ground that it would upset her children if she married again. Helen Trent, who found that she could recapture romance after the age of thirty-five, has been tantalizing a series of suitors since 1933. (She would be going on fifty if she were a mortal, but, owing to the molasses flow of soap-opera time, she is not yet forty.) Helen is soap opera's No. 1 tormentor of men, all in the virtuous name of indecision, provoked and prolonged by plot device. One suitor said to her, "After all, you have never been in my arms"—as daring an advance as any of her dejected swains has ever made in my presence. Helen thereupon went into a frosty routine about marriage being a working partnership, mental stimulation, and, last and least, "emotional understanding." "Emotional understanding," a term I have heard on serials several times, seems to be the official circumlocution for the awful word "sex." The chill Miss Trent has her men frustrated to a point at which a mortal male would smack her little mouth, so smooth, so firm, so free of nicotine, alcohol, and emotion. Suitors in Soapland are usually weak, and Helen's frustration of them is aimed to gratify the listening housewives, brought up in the great American tradition of female domination. Snivelled one of the cold lady's suitors, "I'm not strong, incorruptible, stalwart. I'm weak." Helen purred that she would help him find himself. The weak men continually confess their weakness to the good women, who usually manage to turn them into stable citizens by some vague and soapy magic. The weak men and the good men often confess to one another their dependence on the good women. In one serial, a weak man said to a good man, "My strength is in Irma now." To which the good man replied, "As mine is in Joan, Steve." As this exchange indicates, it is not always easy to tell the weak from the good, but on the whole the weak men are sadder but less stuffy than the good men. The bad men, God save us all, are likely to be the most endurable of the males in Soapland.

The people of Soapland are subject to a set of special ills. Temporary blindness, preceded by dizzy spells and headaches, is a common affliction of Soapland people. The condition usually clears up in six or eight weeks, but once in a while it develops into brain tumor and the patient dies. One script writer, apparently forgetting that General Mills was the sponsor of his serial, had one of his women characters go temporarily blind because of an allergy to chocolate cake. There was hell to pay, and the writer had to make tbe doctor in charge of the patient hastily change his diagnosis. Amnesia strikes almost as often in Soapland as the common cold in our world. There have been as many as eight or nine amnesia cases on the air at one time. The hero of "Rosemary" stumbled around in a daze for months last year. When he regained his memory, he found that in his wanderings he had been lucky enough to marry a true-blue sweetie. The third major disease is paralysis of the legs. This scourge usually attacks the good males. Like mysterious blindness, loss of the use of the legs may be either temporary or permanent. The hero of "Life Can Be Beautiful" was confined to a wheel chair until his death last March, but young Dr. Malone, who was stricken with paralysis a year ago, is up and around again. I came upon only one crippled villain in 1947: Spencer Hart rolled through a three-month sequence of "Just Plain Bill" in a wheel chair. When their men are stricken, the good women become nobler than ever. A disabled hero is likely to lament his fate and indulge in self-pity now and then, but his wife or sweetheart never complains. She is capable of twice as much work, sacrifice, fortitude, endurance, ingenuity, and love as before. Joyce Jordan, M.D., had no interest in a certain male until he lost the use of both legs and took to a wheel chair. Then love began to bloom in her heart. The man in the wheel chair has come to be the standard Soapland symbol of the American male's subordination to the female and his dependence on her greater strength of heart and soul.

The children of the soap towns are subject to pneumonia and strange 15 fevers, during which their temperatures run to 105 or 106. Several youngsters are killed every year in automobile accidents or die of mysterious illnesses. Infantile paralysis and cancer are never mentioned in serials, but Starr, the fretful and errant wife in "Ma Perkins," died of tuberculosis in March as punishment for her sins. There are a number of Soapland ailments that are never named or are vaguely identified by the doctors as "island fever" or "mountain rash." A variety of special maladies affect the glands in curious ways. At least three Ivorytown and Rinsoville doctors are baffled for several months every year by strange seizures and unique symptoms.

Next to physical ills, the commonest misfortune in the world of soap is 16 false accusation of murder. At least two-thirds of the good male characters have been indicted and tried for murder since soap opera began. Last year, the heroes of "Lone Journey," "Our Gal Sunday," and "Young Dr. Malone" all went through this ordeal. They were acquitted, as the good men always are. There were also murder trials involving subsidiary characters in "Portia Faces Life," "Right to Happiness," and "Life Can Be Beautiful." I had not listened to "Happiness" for several months when I tuned in one day just in time to hear one character say, "Do you know Mrs. Cramer?", and another reply, "Yes, we met on the day of the shooting." Dr. Jerry Malone, by the way, won my True Christian Martyr Award for 1947 by being tried for murder and confined to a wheel chair at the same time. In March of this year, the poor fellow came full Soapland circle by suffering an attack of amnesia.

The most awkward cog in the machinery of serial technique is the sol- 17 emn, glib narrator. The more ingenious writers cut his intrusions down to a minimum, but the less skillful craftsmen lean upon him heavily. Most soap-opera broadcasts begin with the narrator's "lead-in," or summary of what has gone before, and end with his brief résumé of the situation and a few speculations on what may happen the following day. The voice of the narrator also breaks in from time to time to tell the listeners what the actors are doing, where they are going, where they have been, what they are thinking or planning, and, on the worst programs, what manner of men and women they are: "So the restless, intolerant, unneighborly Norma, left alone by the friendly, forgiving, but puzzled Joseph . . ."

Another clumsy expedient of soap opera is the soliloquy. The people of   18
Soapland are constantly talking to themselves. I timed one lady's chat with herself in "Woman in White" at five minutes. The soap people also think aloud a great deal of the time, and this usually is dintinguished from straight soliloquy by being spoken into a filter, a device that lends a hollow, resonant tone to the mental voice of the thinker.

In many soap operas, a permanent question is either implied or actually   19
posed every day by the serial narrators. These questions are usually expressed in terms of doubt, indecision, or inner struggle. Which is more important, a woman's heart or a mother's duty? Could a woman be happy with a man fifteen years older than herself? Should a mother tell her daughter that the father of the rich man she loves ruined the fortunes of the daughter's father? Should a mother tell her son that his father, long believed dead, is alive, well, and a criminal? Can a good, clean Iowa girl find happiness as the wife of New York's most famous matinée idol? Can a beautiful young stepmother, can a widow with two children, can a restless woman married to a preoccupied doctor, can a mountain girl in love with a millionaire, can a woman married to a hopeless cripple, can a girl who married an amnesia case—can they find soap-opera happiness and the good, soap-opera way of life? No, they can't—not, at least, in your time and mine. The characters in Soapland and their unsolvable perplexities will be marking time on the air long after you and I are gone, for we must grow old and die, whereas the people of Soapland have a magic immunity to age, like Peter Pan and the Katzenjammer Kids. When you and I are in Heaven with the angels, the troubled people of Ivorytown, Rinsoville, Anacinburg, and Crisco Corners, forever young or forever middle-aged, will still be up to their ears in inner struggle, soul searching, and everlasting frustration.

QUESTIONS

Words to Know

locales (paragraph 1), *Our Town* (1), Brigadoon (1), émigrés (2), authentic (4), slyly (6), provocative (6), Utopia (6), social stratification (7), homely (7), stratum (7), protagonist (7), enunciates (7), foundling (7), prolongation (7), exigencies (9), intuitive (9), fortitude (10), metamorphosis (10), formidable (10), phenomenon (10), paternalistic (11), swains (13), glib (17), soliloquy (18).

Some of the Issues

1. Thurber asserts in the first paragraph that the soap opera "perpetuates the ancient American myth of the small town." How would you define "myth"? Why does Thurber call it that?
2. Paragraph 2 defines the content of soap operas. What, according to Thurber, are their chief characteristics?
3. Paragraph 3 discusses the setting or background of a typical soap. Paragraph 4 begins the discussion of the characters. What, according to Thurber, have setting and characters in common?
4. Thurber describes real time in relation to soap time. In what respects do they differ, and in what respects are they the same? Account for the reasons.
5. Thurber says that "the problems of the characters are predominantly personal, emotional, and private." What, according to Thurber, are the implications of this?
6. Paragraph 8 describes a group of women that "dominate large areas of Soapland." Who are they? Why are they important and useful to the makers of soap operas?
7. Why do women, as Thurber presents them, generally seem to be the stronger sex?

The Way We Are Told

8. What is Thurber's attitude toward housewives? Cite words and phrases that illustrate his attitude.
9. How does Thurber make clear what he thinks of the sponsors of soaps? Cite some specifics.

10. Drinking, smoking, and sex were frowned upon in radio soaps. How does Thurber manage to make fun of these taboos? Examine his use of examples and of language.
11. Consider the final word in the essay: *frustration*. In what way, with what information, has Thurber led up to it? Is it justified?

Some Subjects for Essays

12. Write an essay arguing that today's soaps are more realistic—true to life—than those Thurber describes. Or argue that they are not.
13. Try to write one scene for a parody of a soap opera.

SOAPLAND TODAY

Newsweek (September 28, 1981)

Daytime TV's fervid courtship of the young stems from a dramatic shift in [1]
its balance of power. Six years ago CBS owned four of the top five soaps on
the Nielsen totem pole. Since then, ABC has emerged as the overwhelmingly
dominant force. The secret of its success: it managed to capture more young
female viewers than the other two networks combined. ABC's "General Hospital," "One Life to Live" and "All My Children" now finish win, place and
show in the ratings, while NBC's most popular soap ("Days of Our Lives")
stands no higher than a dismal ninth.

Thanks largely to the infusion of high-school and college viewers, the [2]
daytime serials are currently drawing record crowds. Nielsen reports soap
watching has become a daily habit for nearly 30 million Americans—more
than twice the combined populations of Sweden and Switzerland. What's
behind their burgeoning appeal? No one can be sure, but Kenneth Haun,
who teaches a course on soaps at New Jersey's Monmouth College, suggests
a reasonable theory. "College students usually get the habit during their
freshman year," he says. "When they're homesick and lonely, they turn on
a soap—and there are the old familiar faces to make them feel secure. As
for the high-schoolers, kids between the ages of 13 and 16 usually suffer a
communications breakdown with their parents. So they rely on the soaps as
models of ways they can cope."

As Haun suggests, the sense of continuity that soaps offer is at the heart [3]
of their appeal. Thus, though soap stories rarely advance at more than a
snail's pace, confirmed addicts hate to miss even a single episode. When they
do miss one, they can get a surrogate fix from a growing number of specialty
magazines that cater to their particular affliction. Periodicals like Soap Opera
Digest and Daytime TV provide upward of 1 million fans with detailed syn-
opses of the latest plot twists—as well as adoring portraits of their favorite
soap actors.

To the extent that some viewers look to soaps to tell them what real life [4]
is like, today's younger generation may enter adulthood with some very odd
notions about what to expect. A recent survey of soap addicts at the University of Kentucky discovered that most of them grossly overestimated the proportion of doctors and lawyers in the real world, as well as the incidence of
emotional illness and divorce. Heavy exposure to soaps may also warp adolescent sexual attitudes. According to a study conducted by a team at Michigan State, teen-age soap viewers are likely to conclude that married couples

virtually never engage in sex, while singles do almost nothing else. After watching 65 hours of serials, the researchers found that nearly 80 percent of the scenes in which intercourse was suggested occurred between unmarried lovers—and only 6 percent involved marital partners. (Not surprisingly, the soap found to contain the most sexual activity was top-rated "General Hospital.")

A less clinical examination of the genre reveals other distortions of real-   5
ity that, though harmless enough by themselves, add up to a bizarre portrait of ordinary life. With few exceptions, the inhabitants of Soapland are all upper-middle-class Wasps with homes straight out of House Beautiful. Almost all the characters are related by either marriage or blood. No one has a plain name like Jim or Jane. These people carry such monikers as Sky and Raven ("The Edge of Night"), Sebastian and Althea ("The Doctors"), Lance and Nikki ("The Young and the Restless") and Justin and Ashley ("Texas"). No one ever washes dishes, vacuums a rug, makes the beds—or watches television. No one ever swears or tells a joke. Everyone converses in Soapspeak, a language stuffed with pregnant pauses and filtered through a Cuisinart of clichés. At least once in every episode, someone is bound to blurt: "There's something I have to tell you." Answering a question with a question is a favorite device, as illustrated by a recent exchange between a divorced couple on "General Hospital":

HE: Is there a future for us?   6
SHE: What are you asking?   7
HE: I'm asking, is it too late for us?   8
SHE: What do *you* think?   9

That's not to suggest that the soaps of 1981 look and sound exactly like   10
those of a decade ago. Over the past six years nine of TV's thirteen serials have gone to a one-hour format, an expansion that has made possible far more convoluted plot permutations as well as casts as large as Army platoons. As prime time increasingly apes daytime with soaps of its own like "Dallas," "Dynasty" and "Flamingo Road," afternoon dramas are retaliating by taking on the high-gloss production values of their evening cousins. Not only have their costumes and sets become more opulent, but some soaps are breaking out of their traditional four-walled confines for location shooting in foreign climes. "Ryan's Hope" has traveled to Ireland, "One Life to Live" to Paris and "Guiding Light" to three islands in the Caribbean. This fall "Search for Tomorrow" will celebrate its 31st year on CBS by filming in Hong Kong.

The stories are still the thing, of course, and most seem to be finally   11
catching up with the times. Extramarital sex is no longer invariably punished

by pregnancy. Abortion has emerged as at least a debatable option. A few black characters now drop by on occasion, though so far none has been permitted to play musical beds like—much less with—the randy white folks. Women characters have at last been freed to have careers as well as marriages. Of the eighteen major female characters on "General Hospital," fifteen work outside the home. (Naturally, all of them are miserable.)

QUESTIONS

The questions in this section also relate to the preceding essay by James Thurber.

Some of the Issues

1. What, according to *Newsweek,* has caused the shift in audience from the housewife to "the young"? What appeal do today's soaps have to teenagers? To college students?
2. What changes in subject matter do you find between the old radio soaps and the present TV soaps?
3. Compare aspects of old and new soaps, as described by Thurber and in *Newsweek,* for example: the presence of professional people, particularly doctors; the use of time; the setting or background.
4. Thurber devotes particular attention to the presence (or absence) of smoking, drinking, and sex in the radio soaps of his day. How do present-day TV soaps compare with the radio versions in these respects?
5. What justification does *Newsweek* offer for its assertion that the soaps give a "bizarre portrait of ordinary life"?

Some Subjects for Essays

6. Write an essay on what you consider to be the most important difference in content between yesterday's radio and today's TV soaps. Support your argument with specific instances drawn from your experience and from the two selections you have read.

7. Write an essay on relations between the sexes in soap operas. Contrast the description that Thurber gives of the radio soaps of his day with that given in *Newsweek* of the TV soaps of the 1980s. You may try to explain the differences in different ways: technically—the differences between radio and TV; or socially—the changes in American attitudes over the last 40 years.

8. Write a short essay giving reasons for the prevalence of doctors in soap operas. Why are they so particularly useful?

RITUALS AT
McDONALD'S

Conrad P. Kottak

Conrad Phillip Kottak is a professor of anthropology at the University
of Michigan in Ann Arbor. He has done field work in Brazil and Mad-
agascar and has investigated life in contemporary America from an
anthropological perspective. He is editor of *Research in American
Culture* and the author of several textbooks in anthropology. The article reprinted here first appeared in *Natural History* magazine in January 1978.

The world is blessed each day, on the average, with the opening of a new   1
McDonald's restaurant. They now number more than 4,000 and dot not only
the United States but also such countries as Mexico, Japan, Australia,
England, France, Germany, and Sweden. The expansion of this international
web of franchises and company-owned outlets has been fast and efficient; a
little more than twenty years ago McDonald's was limited to a single restaurant in San Bernardino, California. Now, the number of McDonald's outlets
has far outstripped the total number of fast-food chains operative in the
United States thirty years ago.

McDonald's sales reached $1.3 billion in 1972, propelling it past Ken-   2
tucky Fried Chicken as the world's largest fast-food chain. It has kept this
position ever since. Annual sales now exceed $3 billion. McDonald's is the
nation's leading buyer of processed potatoes and fish. Three hundred thousand cattle die each year as McDonald's customers down another three bil-
lion burgers. A 1974 advertising budget of $60 million easily made the chain
one of the country's top advertisers. Ronald McDonald, our best-known purveyor of hamburgers, French fries, and milkshakes, rivals Santa Claus and
Mickey Mouse as our children's most familiar fantasy character.

How does an anthropologist, accustomed to explaining the life styles of   3
diverse cultures, interpret these peculiar developments and attractions that
influence the daily life of so many Americans? Have factors other than low
cost, taste, fast service, and cleanliness—all of which are approximated by
other chains—contributed to McDonald's success? Could it be that in consuming McDonald's products and propaganda, Americans are not just eating
and watching television but are experiencing something comparable in some
respects to a religious ritual? A brief consideration of the nature of ritual may
answer the latter question.

241

Several key features distinguish ritual from other behavior, according   4
to anthropologist Roy Rappaport. Foremost, are formal ritual events—styl-
ized, repetitive, and stereotyped. They occur in special places, at regular
times, and include liturgical orders—set sequences of words and actions laid
down by someone other than the current performer.

Rituals also convey information about participants and their cultural   5
traditions. Performed year after year, generation after generation, they
translate enduring messages, values, and sentiments into observable action.
Although some participants may be more strongly committed than others to
the beliefs on which rituals are based, all people who take part in joint public
acts signal their acceptance of an order that transcends their status as
individuals.

In the view of some anthropologists, including Rappaport himself, such   6
secular institutions as McDonald's are not comparable to rituals. They argue
that rituals involve special emotions, nonutilitarian intentions, and supernatural entities that are not characteristic of Americans' participation in
McDonald's. But other anthropologists define ritual more broadly. Writing
about football in contemporary America, William Arens (*see* "The Great
American Football Ritual," *Natural History,* October 1975) points out that
behavior can simultaneously have sacred as well as secular aspects. Thus, on
one level, football can be interpreted simply as a sport, while on another, it
can be viewed as a public ritual.

While McDonald's is definitely a mundane, secular institution—just a   7
place to eat—it also assumes some of the attributes of a sacred place. And in
the context of comparative religion, why should this be surprising? The
French sociologist Emile Durkheim long ago pointed out that some societies
worship the ridiculous as well as the sublime. The distinction between the
two does not depend on the intrinsic qualities of the sacred symbol.
Durkheim found that Australian aborigines often worshiped such humble
and non-imposing creatures as ducks, frogs, rabbits, and grubs—animals
whose inherent qualities hardly could have been the origin of the religious
sentiment they inspired. If frogs and grubs can be elevated to a sacred level,
why not McDonald's?

I frequently eat lunch—and, occasionally, breakfast and dinner—at   8
McDonald's. More than a year ago, I began to notice (and have subsequently
observed more carefully) certain ritual behavior at these fast-food restaurants. Although for natives, McDonald's seems to be just a place to eat, careful observation of what goes on in any outlet in this country reveals an astonishing degree of formality and behavioral uniformity on the part of both staff
and customers. Particularly impressive is the relative invariance in act and
utterance that has developed in the absence of a distinct theological doctrine.

Rather, the ritual aspect of McDonald's rests on twentieth-century technology—particularly automobiles, television, work locales, and the one-hour lunch.

The changes in technology and work organization that have contributed   9
to the chain's growth in the United States are now taking place in other countries. Only in a country such as France, which has an established and culturally enshrined cuisine that hamburgers and fish fillets cannot hope to displace, is McDonald's expansion likely to be retarded. Why has McDonald's been so much more successful than other businesses, than the United States Army, and even than many religious institutions in producing behavioral invariance?

Remarkably, even Americans traveling abroad in countries noted for   10
their distinctive food usually visit the local McDonald's outlet. This odd behavior is probably caused by the same factors that urge us to make yet another trip to a McDonald's here. Wherever a McDonald's may be located, it is a home away from home. At any outlet, Americans know how to behave, what to expect, what they will eat, and what they will pay. If one has been unfortunate enough to have partaken of the often indigestible pap dished out by any turnpike restaurant monopoly, the sight of a pair of McDonald's golden arches may justify a detour off the highway, even if the penalty is an extra toll.

In Paris, where the French have not been especially renowned for mak-   11
ing tourists feel at home, McDonald's offers sanctuary. It is, after all, an American institution, where only Americans, who are programmed by years of prior experience to salivate at the sight of the glorious hamburger, can feel completely at home. Americans in Paris can temporarily reverse roles with their hosts; if they cannot act like the French, neither can the French be expected to act in a culturally appropriate manner at McDonald's. Away from home, McDonald's, like a familiar church, offers not just hamburgers but comfort, security, and reassurance.

An American's devotion to McDonald's rests in part on uniformities   12
associated with almost all McDonald's: setting, architecture, food, ambience, acts, and utterances. The golden arches, for example, serve as a familiar and almost universal landmark, absent only in those areas where zoning laws prohibit garish signs. At a McDonald's near the University of Michigan campus in Ann Arbor, a small, decorous sign—golden arches encircled in wrought iron—identifies the establishment. Despite the absence of the towering arches, this McDonald's, where I have conducted much of my fieldwork, does not suffer as a ritual setting. The restaurant, a contemporary brick structure that has been nominated for a prize in architectural design, is best known for its stained-glass windows, which incorporate golden arches as their

focal point. On bright days, sunlight floods in on waiting customers through a skylight that recalls the clerestory of a Gothic cathedral. In the case of this McDonald's, the effect is to equate traditional religious symbols and golden arches. And in the view of the natives I have interviewed, the message is clear.

When Americans go to a McDonald's restaurant, they perform an ordinary, secular, biological act—they eat, usually lunch. Yet, immediately upon entering, we can tell from our surroundings that we are in a sequestered place, somehow apart from the messiness of the world outside. Except for such anomalies as the Ann Arbor campus outlet, the town house McDonald's in New York City, and the special theme McDonald's of such cities as San Francisco, Saint Paul, and Dallas, the restaurants rely on their arches, dull brown brick, plate-glass sides, and mansard roofs to create a setting as familiar as home. In some of the larger outlets, murals depicting "McDonaldland" fantasy characters, sports, outdoor activities, and landscapes surround plastic seats and tables. In this familiar setting, we do not have to consider the experience. We know what we will see, say, eat, and pay. 13

Behind the counter, McDonald's employees are differentiated into such categories as male staff, female staff, and managers. While costumes vary slightly from outlet to outlet and region to region, such apparel as McDonald's hats, ties, and shirts, along with dark pants and shining black shoes, are standard. 14

The food is also standard, again with only minor regional variations. (Some restaurants are selected to test such new menu items as "McChicken" or different milkshake flavors.) Most menus, however, from the rolling hills of Georgia to the snowy plains of Minnesota, offer the same items. The prices are also the same and the menu is usually located in the same place in every restaurant. 15

Utterances across each spotless counter are standardized. Not only are customers limited in what they can choose but also in what they can say. Each item on the menu has its appropriate McDonald's designation: "quarter pounder with cheese" or "filet-O-fish" or "large fries." The customer who asks, "What's a Big Mac?" is as out of place as a southern Baptist at a Roman Catholic Mass. 16

At the McDonald's that I frequent, the phrases uttered by the salespeople are just as standard as those of the customers. If I ask for a quarter pounder, the ritual response is "Will that be with cheese, sir?" If I do not order French fries, the agent automatically incants, "Will there be any fries today, sir?" And when I pick up my order, the agent conventionally says, "Have a nice day, sir," followed by, "Come in again." 17

Nonverbal behavior of McDonald's agents is also programmed. Prior to 18 opening the spigot of the drink machine, they fill paper cups with ice exactly to the bottom of the golden arches that decorate them. As customers request food, agents look back to see if the desired item is available. If not, they reply, "That'll be a few minutes, sir (or ma'am)," after which the order of the next customer is taken.

McDonald's lore of appropriate verbal and nonverbal behavior is even 19 taught at a "seminary," Hamburger University, located in Elk Grove Village, Illinois, near Chicago's O'Hare airport. Managers who attend choose either a two-week basic "operator's course" or an eleven-day "advanced operator's course." With a 360-page *Operations Manual* as their bible, students learn about food, equipment, and management techniques—delving into such esoteric subjects as buns, shortening, and carbonization. Filled with the spirit of McDonald's, graduates take home such degrees as bachelor or master of hamburgerology to display in their outlets. Their job is to spread the word— the secret success formula they have learned—among assistant managers and crew in their restaurants.

The total McDonald's ambience invites comparison with sacred places. 20 The chain stresses clean living and reaffirms those traditional American values that transcend McDonald's itself. Max Boas and Steve Chain, biographers of McDonald's board chairman, Ray Kroc, report that after the hundredth McDonald's opened in 1959, Kroc leased a plane to survey likely sites for the chain's expansion. McDonald's would invade the suburbs by locating its outlets near traffic intersections, shopping centers, and churches. Steeples figured prominently in Kroc's plan. He believed that suburban churchgoers would be preprogrammed consumers of the McDonald's formula—quality, service, and cleanliness.

McDonald's restaurants, nestled beneath their transcendent arches and 21 the American flag, would enclose immaculate restrooms and floors, counters and stainless steel kitchens. Agents would sparkle, radiating health and warmth. Although to a lesser extent than a decade ago, management scrutinizes employees' hair length, height, nails, teeth, and complexions. Long hair, bad breath, stained teeth, and pimples are anathema. Food containers also defy pollution; they are used only once. (In New York City, the fast-food chain Chock Full O' Nuts foreshadowed this theme long ago and took it one step further by assuring customers that their food was never touched by human hands.)

Like participation in rituals there are times when eating at McDonald's 22 is not appropriate. A meal at McDonald's is usually confined to ordinary, everyday life. Although the restaurants are open virtually every day of the year, most Americans do not go there on Thanksgiving, Easter, Passover, or other religious and quasireligious days. Our culture reserves holidays for

family and friends. Although Americans neglect McDonald's on holidays, the
chain reminds us through television that it still endures, that it will welcome
us back once our holiday is over.

The television presence of McDonald's is particularly obvious on holi-   23
days, whether it be through the McDonald's All-American Marching Band
(two clean-cut high school students from each state) in a nationally televised
Thanksgiving Day parade or through sponsorship of sports and family entertainment programs.

Although such chains as Burger King, Burger Chef, and Arby's compete   24
with McDonald's for the fast-food business, none rivals McDonald's success.
The explanation reflects not just quality, service, cleanliness, and value but,
more importantly, McDonald's advertising, which skillfully appeals to different audiences. Saturday morning television, for example, includes a steady
dose of cartoons and other children's shows sponsored by McDonald's. The
commercials feature several McDonaldland fantasy characters, headed by
the clown Ronald McDonald, and often stress the enduring aspects of
McDonald's. In one, Ronald has a time machine that enables him to introduce hamburgers to the remote past and the distant future. Anyone who
noticed the shot of the McDonald's restaurant in the Woody Allen film
Sleeper, which takes place 200 years hence, will be aware that the message
of McDonald's as eternal has gotten across. Other children's commercials
gently portray the conflict between good (Ronald) and evil (Hamburglar).
McDonaldland's bloblike Grimace is hooked on milkshakes, and Hamburglar's addiction to simple burgers regularly culminates in his confinement to
a "patty wagon," as Ronald and Big Mac restore and preserve the social
order.

Pictures of McDonaldland appear on cookie boxes and, from time to   25
time, on durable plastic cups that are given away with the purchase of a
large soft drink. According to Boas and Chain, a McDonaldland amusement
park, comparable in scale to Disneyland, is planned for Las Vegas. Even
more obvious are children's chances to meet Ronald McDonald and other
McDonaldland characters in the flesh. Actors portraying Ronald scatter their
visits, usually on Saturdays, among McDonald's outlets throughout the country. A Ronald can even be rented for a birthday party or for Halloween trick
or treating.

McDonald's adult advertising has a different, but equally effective,   26
theme. In 1976, a fresh-faced, sincere young woman invited the viewer to
try breakfast—a new meal at McDonald's—in a familiar setting. In still other
commercials, healthy, clean-living Americans gambol on ski slopes or in
mountain pastures. The single theme running throughout all the adult commercials is personalism. McDonald's, the commercials tell us, is not just a fast-

food restaurant. It is a warm, friendly place where you will be graciously welcomed. Here, you will feel at home with your family, and your children will not get into trouble. The word *you* is emphasized—"You deserve a break today"; "You, you're the one"; "We do it all for you." McDonald's commercials say that you are not simply a face in a crowd. At McDonald's, you can find respite from a hectic and impersonal society—the break you deserve.

Early in 1977, after a brief flirtation with commercials that harped on 27 the financial and gustatory benefits of eating at McDonald's, the chain introduced one of its most curious incentives—the "Big Mac attack." Like other extraordinary and irresistible food cravings, which people in many cultures attribute to demons or other spirits, a Big Mac attack could strike anyone at any time. In one commercial, passengers on a jet forced the pilot to land at the nearest McDonald's. In others, a Big Mac attack had the power to give life to an inanimate object, such as a suit of armor, or restore a mummy to life.

McDonald's advertising typically de-emphasizes the fact that the chain 28 is, after all, a profit-making organization. By stressing its program of community projects, some commercials present McDonald's as a charitable organization. During the Bicentennial year, commercials reported that McDonald's was giving 1,776 trees to every state in the union. Brochures at outlets echo the television message that, through McDonald's, one can sponsor a carnival to aid victims of muscular dystrophy. In 1976 and 1977 McDonald's managers in Ann Arbor persuaded police officers armed with metal detectors to station themselves at restaurants during Halloween to check candy and fruit for hidden pins and razor blades. Free coffee was offered to parents. In 1976, McDonald's sponsored a radio series documenting the contributions Blacks have made to American history.

McDonald's also sponsored such family television entertainment as the 29 film *The Sound of Music*, complete with a prefatory, sermonlike address by Ray Kroc. Commercials during the film showed Ronald McDonald picking up after litterbugs and continued with the theme, "We do it all for you." Other commercials told us that McDonald's supports and works to maintain the values of American family life—and went so far as to suggest a means of strengthening what most Americans conceive to be the weakest link in the nuclear family, that of father-child. "Take a father to lunch," kids were told.

Participation in McDonald's rituals involves temporary subordination of 30 individual differences in a social and cultural collectivity. By eating at McDonald's, not only do we communicate that we are hungry, enjoy hamburgers, and have inexpensive tastes but also that we are willing to adhere to a value system and a series of behaviors dictated by an exterior entity. In a land of tremendous ethnic, social, economic, and religious diversity, we proclaim that we share something with millions of other Americans.

Sociologists, cultural anthropologists, and others have shown that social   31 ties based on kinship, marriage, and community are growing weaker in the contemporary United States. Fewer and fewer people participate in traditional organized religions. By joining sects, cults, and therapy sessions, Americans seek many of the securities that formal religion gave to our ancestors. The increasing cultural, rather than just economic, significance of McDonald's, football, and similar institutions is intimately linked to these changes.

As industrial society shunts people around, church allegiance declines   32 as a unifying moral force. Other institutions are also taking over the functions of formal religions. At the same time, traditionally organized religions— Protestantism, Catholicism, and Judaism—are reorganizing themselves along business lines. With such changes, the gap between the symbolic meaning of traditional religions and the realities of modern life widens. Because of this, some sociologists have argued that the study of modern religion must merge with the study of mass culture and mass communication.

In this context, McDonald's has become one of many new and powerful   33 elements of American culture that provide common expectations, experience, and behavior—overriding region, class, formal religious affiliation, political sentiments, gender, age, ethnic group, sexual preference, and urban, suburban, or rural residence. By incorporating—wittingly or unwittingly— many of the ritual and symbolic aspects of religion, McDonald's has carved its own important niche in a changing society in which automobiles are ubiquitous and where television sets outnumber toilets.

QUESTIONS

Words to Know

franchise (paragraph 1), propelling (2), purveyor (2), fantasy (2), anthropologist (3), diverse (3), propaganda (3), ritual (3), stereotyped (4), liturgical (4), secular (6), nonutilitarian (6), supernatural (6), simultaneously (6), mundane (7), intrinsic (7), aborigines (7), inherent (7), invariance (8), utterance (8), pap (10), sanctuary (11), prior (11), salivate (11), ambience (12), decorous (12), clerestory (12), sequestered (13), anomalies (13), mansard roof (13), differentiated (14), incant (17), lore (19), esoteric (19), transcendent (21), scrutinize (21), anathema (21), foreshadowed (21), quasi-religious (22), culminate (24), gambol (26), personalism (26), respite (26), gustatory (27), incentive (27), prefatory (29), niche (33).

Some of the Issues

1. What is Kottak trying to establish in the first two paragraphs? How do the questions in paragraph 3 relate to the previous paragraphs and prepare the reader for what is to follow?
2. What is the effect of Kottak's assertion that Ronald McDonald "rivals Santa Claus and Mickey Mouse as our children's most familiar fantasy character?" Do you agree that he does? What advantages does he have over his two rivals?
3. What are the criteria that define a ritual?
4. Kottak admits that according to some definitions McDonald's cannot be classified as a ritual. How does he defend his classification?
5. In paragraphs 10 and 11 Kottak gives his reason for Americans visiting McDonald's even in countries "noted for their distinctive food." How does that reason relate to the idea of ritual?
6. In paragraph 13 Kottak stresses the physical familiarity of McDonald's, the uniformity of construction. Can you think of other enterprises that rely on a distinctive design? What do these designs contribute to the product and its sale?

The Way We Are Told

7. Why is it important that Kottak tells you he is a frequent McDonald's customer?
8. In paragraph 12 Kottak explains where he has done much of his fieldwork. Why does he use that term? What other reinforcement for his basic assertion—McDonald's as a source of ritual—does he give in that paragraph?
9. At the end of paragraph 16, Kottak makes an analogy between McDonald's and religion. Go back to paragraph 12 and find another one. Then look ahead to paragraphs 19 and 20 to find more. What purpose do these analogies serve?
10. In discussing McDonald's advertising campaigns, Kottak cites several instances that reinforce his assertion that the chain is not just an eating

place but part of an American ritual. In paragraphs 24 through 28 find some instances that seem to you to provide such reinforcement.
11. Kottak is an anthropologist, in other words a social scientist trained to study a culture, usually one different from his own. What is the effect of Kottak's use of anthropological methods to discuss a familiar scene?

Some Subjects for Essays

12. Kottak explains the appeal of McDonald's in anthropological terms. Write an essay explaining the appeal of fast-food restaurants in terms of one particular, significant concern, such as price, speed, reliability, convenience. Remember, argue your point on the grounds of only one of these.
13. Describe in detail a fast-food restaurant to someone from another culture who has never seen one. Provide sensory details—sight, smell, touch—and make sure that person will know what to do when he or she gets there.

SEVEN

New Worlds

*T*he selections in Part Seven are concerned with coming to live or living among strangers. Some tell of immigration to a new country or flight from an old one. Others are observations or reflections by men and women who have traveled to, or settled in, a culture very different from their own.

The first three selections tell of the experiences of people coming to America in search of a better, more secure life. The first two delve into the past, the turn of the century when immigration from Europe was at its height. Jacob A. Riis and Irving Howe both describe the same scene: the thousands who passed through Ellis Island into New York City every day. Riis describes it as an eye-witness, Howe as a historian looking at the record. The third selection, more recent, is a woman's personal account of a harrowing escape from Vietnam in 1979.

The next several selections are reflections on living in or visiting a foreign culture. Andrea Lee, a young American who spent a year in the Soviet Union, kept a journal from which the first selection is taken. She describes two scenes of the life of Russian youth: the first day for new students at Moscow University, and a Moscow nightclub frequented by the privileged. Both echo and contrast with her own experience as a young woman in America. In the next selection, Elizabeth Hanson describes a crucial difference between living in Japan and in the United States, the absence of the kind of living space that Americans take for granted.

Laura Bohannan, an American anthropologist, lived with the Tiv, a tribe in Nigeria, West Africa. The Tiv, who have a tradition of storytelling, asked her for a story from her own culture. She chose Hamlet, thinking that its universality would make it comprehensible, but found that the Tiv had decidedly different views from hers (or ours) as to the meaning and morality of the play.

Laura Bohannan is a participant in the story she tells. Jonathan Schell, the author of the next selection, is a witness. He went along on a raid by a squadron of American helicopter troops that landed in a Vietnamese village during the war. The encounter between soldiers and villagers he describes is a telling example of the depersonalizing effect of war.

The final two prose selections are extended reflections on living as strangers in other lands. James Baldwin spent several months in an isolated Swiss mountain village, the only black man most villagers had ever seen. The experience serves as a springboard for serious reflections that far transcend the actual circumstances of his story and his relations with the villagers. George Orwell served in the Imperial Police in Burma in his youth, when that country was still part of the British Empire. The experience he describes—the shooting of an elephant that was threatening the village—gives rise to his reflections on the nature of oppression and colonial rule.

The final selection, a poem by Nikki Giovanni, describes the experience of American Blacks visiting Africa in search of their identity. What they find surprises them.

IN THE GATEWAY OF NATIONS

Jacob A. Riis

Jacob A. Riis (1849–1914) was born in Denmark and came to the
United States as an immigrant at the age of 20. He became a journalist
who crusaded for social reforms at the turn of the century. His autobiography, *The Making of an American* (1901), reflects to some extent
the stereotypes of various nationalities current in his day. Yet Riis also
displays an openness to differences and a lively objection to prejudice,
unusual in that period. In this article, first printed in *Century Magazine* in 1903, he describes a visit to Ellis Island, the New York immigration station through which millions were passing from Europe into
the United States. (Riis had immigrated through Castle Gardens, the
station replaced by Ellis Island in 1892.) In this selection he looks back
as a relatively prosperous, settled citizen of his adopted country, to the
days of his own arrival.

How it all came back to me; that Sunday in early June when I stood, a lonely   1
immigrant lad, at the steamer's rail and looked out upon the New World of
my dreams; upon the life that teemed ashore and afloat, and was all so
strange; upon the miles of streets that led nowhere I knew of; upon the sunlit
harbor, and the gay excursion-boats that went to and fro with their careless
crowds; upon the green hills of Brooklyn; upon the majestic sweep of the
lordly river. I thought that I had never seen anything so beautiful, and I think
so now, after more than thirty years, when I come into New York's harbor
on a steamer. But now I am coming home; then all the memories lay behind.
I squared my shoulder against what was coming. I was ready and eager. But
for a passing moment, there at the rail, I would have given it all for one
familiar face, one voice I knew.

How it all came back as I stood on the deck of the ferry-boat plowing   2
its way from the Battery Park to Ellis Island. They were there, my fellow-
travelers of old: the men with their strange burdens of feather beds, cooking-
pots, and things unknowable, but mighty of bulk in bags of bed-ticking much
the worse for wear. There was the very fellow with the knapsack that had
never left him once on the way over, not even when he slept. Then he used
it as a pillow. It was when he ate that we got fleeting glimpses of its inter-
minable coils of sausage, its uncanny depths of pumpernickel and cheese that
eked out the steamer's fare. I saw him last in Pittsburg, still with his sack.

253

What long-forgotten memories that crowd stirred! The women were there, with their gaudy head-dresses and big gold ear-rings. But their hair was raven black instead of yellow, and on the young girl's cheek there was a richer hue than the pink and white I knew. The men, too, looked like swarthy gnomes compared with the stalwart Swede or German of my day. They were the same, and yet not the same. I glanced out over the bay, and behold! all things were changed. For the wide stretch of squat houses pierced by the single spire of Trinity Church there had come a sky-line of towering battlements, in the shelter of which nestled Castle Garden, once more a popular pleasure resort. My eye rested upon one copper-roofed palace, and I recalled with a smile my first errand ashore to a barber's shop in the old Washington Inn, that stood where it is built. I went to get a bath and to have my hair cut, and they charged me two dollars in gold for it, with gold at a big premium; which charge, when I objected to it, was adjudged fair by a man who said he was a notary—an office I was given to understand was equal in dignity to that of a justice of peace or of the Supreme Court. And when, still unawed, I appealed to the policeman outside, that functionary heard me through, dangling his club from his thumb, and delivered himself of a weary "G'wan, now!" that ended it. There was no more.

"For the loikes o' them!" I turned sharply to the voice at my elbow, and caught the ghost of a grimace on the face of the old apple-woman who sat disdainfully dealing out bananas to the "Dagos" and "sheenies" of her untamed prejudices, sole survival in that crowd of the day that was past. No, not quite the only one. I was another. She recognized it with a look and a nod.   3

A curiously changing procession has passed through Uncle Sam's gateway since I stood at the steamer's rail that June morning in the long ago. Then the tide of Teutonic immigration that peopled the great Northwest was still rising. The last herd of buffaloes had not yet gone over the divide before the white-tented prairie-schooner's advance; the battle of the Little Big Horn was yet unfought. A circle drawn on the map of Europe around the countries smitten with the America-unrest would, even a dozen years later than that, have had Paris for its center. "To-day," said Assistant Commissioner of Immigration McSweeney, speaking before the National Geographic Society last winter, "a circle of the same size, including the sources of the present immigration to the United States, would have its center in Constantinople." And he pointed out that as steamboat transportation developed on the Danube the center would be more firmly fixed in the East, where whole populations, notably in the Balkan States, are catching the infection or having it thrust upon them. Secretary Hay's recent note to the powers in defense of the Rumanian Jews told part of that story. Even the Italian, whose country   4 sent us half a million immigrants in the last four years, may then have to yield first place to the hill men with whom kidnapping is an established industry. I mean no disrespect to their Sicilian brother bandit. With him it is a fine art.

While the statesman ponders the perils of unrestricted immigration, and debates with organized labor whom to shut out and how, the procession moves serenely on. Ellis Island is the nations' gateway to the promised land. There is not another such to be found anywhere. In a single day it has handled seven thousand immigrants. "Handled" is the word; nothing short of it will do.

"How much you got?" shouts the inspector at the head of the long file moving up from the quay between iron rails, and, remembering, in the same breath shrieks out, "Quanto moneta?" with a gesture that brings up from the depths of Pietro's pocket a pitiful handful of paper money. Before he has it half out, the interpreter has him by the wrist, and with a quick movement shakes the bills out upon the desk, as a dice-thrower "chucks" the ivories.

Ten, twenty, forty lire. He shakes his head. Not much, but—he glances at the ship's manifest—is he going to friends?

"Si, si! signor," says Pietro, eagerly; his brother of the vineyard—oh, a fine vineyard! And he holds up a bundle of grapesticks in evidence. He has brought them all the way from the village at home to set them out in his brother's field.

"Ugh," grunts the inspector as he stuffs the money back in the man's pocket, shoves him on, and yells, "Wie viel geld?" at a hapless German next in line. "They won't grow. They never do. Bring 'em just the same." By which time the German has joined Pietro in his bewilderment en route for something or somewhere, shoved on by guards, and the inspector wrestles with a "case" who is trying to sneak in on false pretenses. No go; he is hauled off by an officer and ticketed "S.I.," printed large on a conspicuous card. It means that he is held for the Board of Special Inquiry, which will sift his story. Before they reach the door there is an outcry and a scuffle. The tide has turned against the Italian and the steamship company. He was detected throwing the card, back up, under the heater, hoping to escape in the crowd. He will have to go back. An eagle eye, with a memory that never lets go, has spotted him as once before deported. King Victor Emmanuel has achieved a reluctant subject; Uncle Sam has lost a citizen. Which is the better off?

A stalwart Montenegrin comes next, lugging his gun of many an ancient feud, and proves his title clear. Neither the feud nor the blunderbuss is dangerous under the American sun; they will both seem grotesque before he has been here a month. A Syrian from Mount Lebanon holds up the line while the inspector fires questions at him which it is not given to the uninitiated ear to make out. Goodness knows where they get it all. There seems to be no language or dialect under the sun that does not lie handy to the tongue of these men at the desk. There are twelve of them. One would never dream there were twelve such linguists in the country till he hears them and sees them; for half their talk is done with their hands and shoulders and with the official steel pen that transfixes an object of suspicion like a merciless spear, upon the point of which it writhes in vain. The Syrian wriggles off by good luck, and to-morrow will be peddling "holy earth from Jerusalem," purloined on his way through the Battery, at half a dollar a clod. He represents the purely commercial element of our immigration, and represents it well—or ill, as you take it. He cares neither for land and cattle, nor for freedom to worship or work, but for cash in the way of trade. And he gets it. Hence more come every year.

Looking down upon the crowd in the gateway, jostling, bewildered, and voluble in a thousand tongues—so at least it sounds,—it seems like a hopeless mass of confusion. As a matter of fact, it is all order and perfect system, begun while the steamer was yet far out at sea. By the time the lighters are tied up at the Ellis Island wharf their human cargo is numbered and lettered in groups that correspond with like entries in the manifest, and so are marshaled upon and over the bridge that leads straight into the United States to the man with the pen who asks questions. When the crowd is great and pressing, they camp by squads in little stalls bearing their proprietary stamp, as it were, finding one another and being found when astray by the mystic letter that brings together in the close companionship of a common peril—the pen, one stroke which can shut the gate against them—men and women who in another hour go their way, very likely never to meet or hear of one another again on earth. The sense of the impending trial sits visibly upon the waiting crowd. Here and there a masterful spirit strides boldly on; the mass huddle close, with more or less anxious look. Five minutes after it is over, eating their dinner in the big waiting-room, they present an entirely different appearance. Signs and numbers have disappeared. The groups are recasting themselves on lines of nationality and personal preference. Care is cast to the winds. A look of serene contentment sits upon the face that gropes among the hieroglyphics on the lunch-counter bulletin-board for the things that pertain to him and his: 11

Röget Fisk

Kielbara

Szynka Gotowana

"Ugh!" says my companion, home-bred on fried meat, "I wouldn't eat   12
it." No more would I if it tastes as it reads; but then, there is no telling. That
lunch-counter is not half bad. From the kosher sausage to the big red apples
that stare at one—at the children especially—wherever one goes, it is really
very appetizing. The *röget fisk* I know about; it is good.

The women guard the baggage in their seats while *pater familias* takes   13
a look around. Half of them munch their New World sandwich with an I-
care-not-what-comes-next-the-worst-is-over air; the other half scribble elab-
orately with stubby pencils on postal cards that are all star-spangled and
striped with white and red. It is their announcement to those waiting at
home that they have passed the gate and are within.

Behind carefully guarded doors wait the "outs," the detained immi-   14
grants, for the word that will let down the bars or fix them in place immov-
ably. The guard is for a double purpose: that no one shall leave or enter the
detention—"pen" it used to be called; but the new regime under President
Roosevelt's commission has set its face sternly against the term. The law of
kindness rules on Ellis Island; a note posted conspicuously invites every
employee who cannot fall in with it to get out as speedily as he may. So now
it is the detention—"room" into which no outsider with unfathomed intentions may enter. Here are the old, the stricken, waiting for friends able to
keep them; the pitiful little colony of women without the shield of a man's
name in the hour of their greatest need; the young and pretty and thoughtless, for whom one sends up a silent prayer of thanksgiving at the thought of
the mob at that other gate, yonder in Battery Park, beyond which Uncle
Sam's strong hand reaches not to guide or guard. And the hopelessly bewildered are there, often enough exasperated at the restraint, which they cannot
understand. The law of kindness is put to a severe strain here by ignorance
and stubbornness. In it all they seem, some of them, to be able to make out
only that their personal liberty, their "rights," are interfered with. How
quickly they sprout in the gateway! This German girl who is going to her
uncle flatly refuses to send him word that she is here. She has been taught to
look out for sharpers and to guard her little store well, and detects in the
telegraph toll a scheme to rob her of one of her cherished silver marks. To
all reasoning she turns a deaf and defiant ear: he will find her. The important
thing is that she is here. That her uncle is in Newark makes no impression
on her. Is it not all America?

A name is cried at the door, and there is a rush. Angelo, whose desti-   15
nation, repeated with joyful volubility in every key and accent, puzzled the
officials for a time, is going. His hour of deliverance has come. "Pringvillia-
mas" yielded to patient scrutiny at last. It was "Springfield, Mass.," and
impatient friends are waiting for Angelo up there. His countryman, who is

going to his brother-in-law, but has "forgotten his American name," takes leave of him wistfully. He is penniless, and near enough the "age limit of adaptability" to be an object of doubt and deliberation.

In laying down that limit, as in the case of the other that fixes the amount of money in hand to prove the immigrant's title to enter, the island is a law unto itself. Under the folds of the big flag which drapes the tribunal of the Board of Special Inquiry, claims from every land under the sun are weighed and adjusted. It is ever a matter of individual consideration. A man without a cent, but with a pair of strong hands and with a head that sits firmly on rugged shoulders, might be better material for citizenship in every way than Mr. Moneybags with no other recommendation; and to shut out an aged father and mother for whom the children are able and willing to care would be inhuman. The gist of the thing was put clearly in President Roosevelt's message in the reference to a certain economic standard of fitness for citizenship that must govern, and does govern, the keepers of the gate. Into it enter not only the man's years and his pocket-book, but the whole man, and he himself virtually decides the case. Not many, I fancy, are sent back without good cause. The law of kindness is strained, if anything, in favor of the immigrant to the doubtful advantage of Uncle Sam, on the presumption, I suppose, that he can stand it.

But at the locked door of the rejected, those whom the Board has heard and shut out, the process stops short. At least, it did when I was there. I stopped it. It was when the attendant pointed out an ex-bandit, a black and surly fellow with the strength of a wild boar, who was wanted on the other side for sticking a knife into a man. The knife they had taken from him here was the central exhibit in a shuddering array of such which the doorkeeper kept in his corner. That morning the bandit had "soaked" a countryman of his, waiting to be deported for the debility of old age. I could not help it. "I hope you—" I began, and stopped short, remembering the "notice" on the wall. But the man at the door understood. "I did," he nodded. "I soaked him a couple." And I felt better. I confess it, and I will not go back to the island, if Commissioner Williams will not let me, for breaking his law.

But I think he will, for within the hour I saw him himself "soak" a Flemish peasant twice his size for beating and abusing a child. The man turned and towered above the commissioner with angry looks, but the ordinarily quiet little man presented so suddenly a fierce and warlike aspect that, though neither understood a word of what the other said, the case was made clear to the brute on the instant, and he slunk away. Commissioner Williams's law of kindness is all right. It is based upon the correct observation that not one in a thousand of those who land at Ellis Island needs harsh treatment, but advice and help—which does not prevent the thousandth case from receiving its full due.

Two negroes from Santa Lucia are there to keep the stranded Italian 19
company. Mount Pelée sent them hither, only to be bounced back from an
inhospitable shore. In truth, one wintry blast would doubtless convince them
it were so indeed; their look and lounging attitude betray all too clearly the
careless children of the South. Gipsies from nowhere in particular are here
with gold in heavy belts, but no character to speak of or to speak for them.
They eye the throng making for the ferry with listless unconcern. It makes,
in the end, little difference to them where they are, so long as there is a
chance for a horse trade, or a horse, anyway. There is none here, and they
are impatient only to get away somewhere. Meanwhile they live at the
expense of the steamship company that brought them. They all do. It is the
penalty for differing with the commission and the Board of Special
Inquiry—that and taking them back whence they came without charge.

The railroad ferries come and take their daily host straight from Ellis 20
Island to the train, ticketed now with the name of the route that is to deliver
them at their new homes, West and East. And the Battery boat comes every
hour for its share. Then the many-hued procession—the women are hooded,
one and all, in their gayest shawls for the entry—is led down on a long path-
way divided in the middle by a wire-screen, from behind which come
shrieks of recognition from fathers, brothers, uncles, and aunts that are gathered there in the holiday togs of Mulberry or Division street. The contrast is
sharp—an artist would say all in favor of the newcomers. But they would be
the last to agree with him. In another week the rainbow colors will have been
laid aside, and the landscape will be the poorer for it. On the boat they meet
their friends, and the long journey is over, the new life begun. Those who
have no friends run the gantlet of the boarding house runners, and take their
chances with the new freedom, unless the missionary of "the society" of their
people holds out a helping hand. For at the barge-office gate Uncle Sam lets
go. Through it they must walk alone.

However, in the background waits the universal friend, the padrone. 21
Enactments, prosecutions, have not availed to eliminate him. He will yield
only to the logic of the very situation he created. The process is observable
among the Italians to-day: where many have gone and taken root, others
follow, guided by their friends and no longer dependent upon the padrone.
As these centers of attraction are multiplying all over the country, his grip is
loosened upon the crowds he labored so hard to bring here for his own
advantage. Observant Jews have adopted in recent days the plan of planting
out their people who come here, singly or by families, and the farther apart
the better, with the professed purpose of diverting as much of the inrush as
may be from the city, and thus heading off the congestion of the labor market that perplexes philanthropy in Ludlow street and swells the profits of the
padrone on the other side of the Bowery. Something of the problem will be

solved in that way, though not in a year, or in ten. But what of those who come after? There is still a long way from the Bosporus to China, where the bars are up. Scarce a Greek comes here, man or boy, who is not under contract. A hundred dollars a year is the price, so it is said by those who know, though the padrone's cunning has put the legal proof beyond their reach. And the Armenian and Syrian hucksters are "worked" by some peddling trust that traffics in human labor as do other merchants in food-stuffs and coal and oil. So the thing, as it runs down, everlastingly winds itself up again. It has not yet run down far enough to cause anybody alarm. Three Mediterranean steamers and one from Antwerp, as I write, brought 4700 steerage passengers into port in one day, of whom only 1700 were bound for the West. The rest stayed in New York. The padrone will be able to add yet another tenement, purchased with his profits, to his holdings. In 1891, of 138,608 Italians who landed on Ellis Island, 67,231 registered their final destination as Mulberry street, and Little Italy in Harlem.

Many an emigrant vessel's keel has plowed the sea since the first brought   22
white men greedy for gold. Some have come for conscience sake, some seeking political asylum. Long after the beginning of the last century, ship-loads were sold into virtual slavery to pay their passage money. Treated like cattle, dying by thousands on the voyage, and thrown into the sea with less compunction or ceremony than if they had been so much ballast, still they came. "If crosses and tombstones could be erected on the seas, as in the Western deserts," said Assistant Commissioner McSweeney in the speech before referred to, "the routes of the emigrant vessel from Europe to America would look like crowded cemeteries." They were not made welcome. The sharpers robbed them. Patriots were fearful. The best leaders of American thought mistrusted the outcome of it. The very municipal government of New York expressed apprehension at the handful, less than ten thousand, that came over in 1819–20. Still they came. The Know-nothings had their day, and that passed away. The country prospered and grew great, and the new citizens prospered and grew with it. Evil days came, and they were scorned no longer; for they were found on the side of right, of an undivided Union, of financial honor, stanch and unyielding. To them America had "spelled opportunity." They paid back what they had received, with interest. They saved the country they had made their own. They were of our blood. These are not; they have other traditions, not necessarily poorer. What people has a prouder story to tell than the Italian? Who is more marvelous than the Jew? But their traditions are not ours. Where will they stand when the strain comes?

I was concerned only with the kaleidoscope of the gateway, and I prom-   23
ised myself not to discuss politics, economics, or morals. But this is very cer-

tain: so long as the school-house stands over against the sweat-shop, clean and bright as the flag that flies over it, we need have no fear of the answer. However perplexed the to-day, the to-morrow is ours. We have the making of it. When we no longer count it worth the cost, better shut the gate on Ellis Island. We cannot be too quick about it—for their sake. The opportunity they seek here will have passed then, never to return.

QUESTIONS

Words to Know

Teutonic (paragraph 4), Montenegrin (10), voluble (11), manifest (11), *pater familias*—the father of the family (13), exasperated (14), presumption (16), know-nothings (22), kaleidoscope (23).

Some of the Issues

1. In the first two paragraphs Riis recalls the scenes of 30 years earlier, when he arrived as an immigrant. What similarities between his time of arrival and the time he tells of now does he see? What differences?
2. What is the point of the short anecdote in paragraph 3?
3. In paragraph 4 the kind of information given to the reader changes. What is the difference? How does Riis feel about the changes in the types of immigrants who arrived around the turn of the century as compared with those of 30 years before? In retrospect, can you find any of those feelings reflected in the previous three, more personal paragraphs?
4. How does Riis characterize the possible or actual rejects at Ellis Island? What does he imply about the procedure under which such would-be immigrants are rejected? What in his description would lead you to think it is a fair procedure?
5. At the turn of the century when this selection was written, the problem of letting immigration continue unchecked was already a hot subject. (The controversy resulted in a gradual restriction of immigration in the early 1920s.) Which side does Riis take on this question? How does he argue for his side in the last three paragraphs?
6. Explain the argument he makes in the last paragraph.

The Way We Are Told

7. What does Riis try to tell the reader in the ancedote that concludes the second paragraph? Consider the choice of words and phrases—the way he tells it after 30 years. How do you think he felt at the time? Try to retell the anecdote from the point of view of the twenty-year-old Riis.
8. In paragraph 14 and in paragraphs 16 through 19 Riis discusses "the outs"—the rejected ones. How does Riis feel about them, and how does he try to shape our responses to the idea of sending people back?
9. What does Riis imply are the reasons for restricting immigration; is it a question of the numbers of people who arrive or of the characteristics of recent arrivals?

Some Subjects for Essays

10. Consider the tone of the description of the Italian and the German immigrants, as they are "handled" on Ellis Island (paragraphs 5 through 9). Write a paragraph giving the same account from the point of view of one of the immigrants.
11. Riis explains that there is some sort of balance between humane considerations and the interests of the United States as a whole which shapes immigration policy. In an essay explain what Riis considers this balance of interests to be and comment on its fairness.

ELLIS ISLAND

Irving Howe

Irving Howe, born in New York in 1920, attended City College, has taught at Brandeis and Stanford Universities, and is now professor of English at City University of New York. He is the author or editor of many books in areas of American literature, including biographies of William Faulkner and Sherwood Anderson. He has also written about socialism and communism and edited books of Yiddish stories and poems. The excerpt included here is from *World of Our Fathers* (1976).

Ellis Island in New York Harbor served as the official place of entry for immigrants from Europe from 1892 until 1943. In 1965 it was declared a national historic site and is being renovated as a memorial.

1 "The day of the emigrants' arrival in New York was the nearest earthly likeness to the final Day of Judgment, when we have to prove our fitness to enter Heaven." So remarked one of those admirable journalists who in the early 1900's exposed themselves to the experience of the immigrants and came to share many of their feelings. No previous difficulties roused such overflowing anxiety, sometimes self-destructive panic, as the anticipated test of Ellis Island. Nervous chatter, foolish rumors spread tbrough each cluster of immigrants:

> "There is Ellis Island!" shouted an immigrant who had already been in the United States and knew of its alien laws. The name acted like magic. Faces grew taut, eyes narrowed. There, in those red buildings, fate awaited them. Were they ready to enter? Or were they to be sent back?
>
> "Only God knows," shouted an elderly man, his withered hand gripping the railing.

2 Numbered and lettered before debarking, in groups corresponding to entries on the ship's manifest, the immigrants are herded onto the Customs Wharf. "Quick! Run! Hurry!" shout officials in half a dozen languages.

3 On Ellis Island they pile into the massive hall that occupies the entire width of the building. They break into dozens of lines, divided by metal railings, where they file past the first doctor. Men whose breathing is heavy, women trying to hide a limp or deformity behind a large bundle—these are marked with chalk, for later inspection. Children over the age of two must

walk by themselves, since it turns out that not all can. (A veteran inspector recalls: "Whenever a case aroused suspicion, the alien was set aside in a cage apart from the rest . . . and his coat lapel or shirt marked with colored chalk, the color indicating why he had been isolated.") One out of five or six needs further medical checking—H chalked for heart, K for hernia, Sc for scalp, X for mental defects.

An interpreter asks each immigrant a question or two: can he respond   4
with reasonable alertness? Is he dull-witted? A question also to each child: make sure he's not deaf or dumb. A check for TB, regarded as "the Jewish disease."

Then a sharp turn to the right, where the second doctor waits, a spe-   5
cialist in "contagious and loathsome diseases." Leprosy? Venereal disease? Fauvus, "a contagious disease of the skin, especially of the scalp, due to a parasitic fungus, marked by the formation of yellow flattened scabs and baldness"?

Then to the third doctor, often feared the most. He   6

> stands directly in the path of the immigrant, holding a little stick in his hand. By a quick movement and the force of his own compelling gaze, he catches the eyes of his subject and holds them. You will see the immigrant stop short, lift his head with a quick jerk, and open his eyes very wide. The inspector reaches with a swift movement, catches the eyelash with his thumb and finger, turns it back, and peers under it. If all is well, the immigrant is passed on . . . Most of those detained by the physician are Jews.

The eye examination hurts a little. It terrifies the children. Nurses wait   7
with towels and basins filled with disinfectant. They watch for trachoma, cause of more than half the medical detentions. It is a torment hard to understand, this first taste of America, with its poking of flesh and prying into private parts and mysterious chalking of clothes.

Again into lines, this time according to nationality. They are led to stalls   8
at which multilingual inspectors ask about character, anarchism, polygamy, insanity, crime, money, relatives, work. You have a job waiting? Who paid your passage? Anyone meeting you? Can you read and write? Ever in prison? Where's your money?

For Jewish immigrants, especially during the years before agencies like   9
the Hebrew Immigrant Aid Society (HIAS) could give them advice, these questions pose a dilemma: to be honest or to lie? Is it good to have money or not? Can you bribe these fellows, as back home, or is it a mistake to try? Some are so accustomed to bend and evade and slip a ruble into a waiting

hand that they get themselves into trouble with needless lies. "Our Jews,"
writes a Yiddish paper,

> love to get tangled up with dishonest answers, so that the officials have
> no choice but to send them to the detention area. A Jew who had money
> in his pocket decided to lie and said he didn't have a penny. . . . A woman
> with four children and pregnant with a fifth, said her husband had been
> in America fourteen years. . . . The HIAS man learned that her husband
> had recently arrived, but she thought fourteen years would make a better
> impression. The officials are sympathetic. They know the Jewish immi-
> grants get "confused" and tell them to sit down and "remember." Then
> they let them in.

Especially bewildering is the idea that if you say you have a job waiting for
you in the United States, you are liable to deportation—because an 1885 law
prohibits the importation of contract labor. But doesn't it "look better" to say
a job is waiting for you? No, the HIAS man patiently explains, it doesn't.
Still, how can you be sure *he* knows what he's talking about? Just because he
wears a little cap with those four letters embroidered on it?

Except when the flow of immigrants was simply beyond the staff's 10
capacity to handle it, the average person passed through Ellis Island in about
a day. Ferries ran twenty-four hours a day between the island and both the
Battery and points in New Jersey. As for the unfortunates detained for medical or other reasons, they usually had to stay at Ellis Island for one or two
weeks. Boards of special inquiry, as many as four at a time, would sit in
permanent session, taking up cases where questions had been raised as to the
admissibility of an immigrant, and it was here, in the legal infighting and
appeals to sentiment, that HIAS proved especially valuable.

The number of those detained at the island or sent back to Europe dur- 11
ing a given period of time varied according to the immigration laws then in
effect . . . and, more important, according to the strictness with which they
were enforced. It is a sad irony, though familiar to students of democratic
politics, that under relatively lax administrations at Ellis Island, which sometimes allowed rough handling of immigrants and even closed an eye to corruption, immigrants had a better chance of getting past the inspectors than
when the commissioner was a public-spirited Yankee intent upon literal
adherence to the law.

Two strands of opinion concerning Ellis Island have come down to us, 12
among both historians and the immigrant masses themselves: first, that the
newcomers were needlessly subjected to bad treatment, and second, that
most of the men who worked there were scrupulous and fair, though often
overwhelmed by the magnitude of their task.

The standard defense of Ellis Island is offered by an influential historian   13
of immigration, Henry Pratt Fairchild:

> During the year 1907 five thousand was fixed as the maximum number
> of immigrants who could be examined at Ellis Island in one day; yet
> during the spring of that year more than fifteen thousand immigrants
> arrived at the port of New York in a single day.
>   As to the physical handling of the immigrants, this is [caused] by
> the need for haste. . . . The conditions of the voyage are not calculated to
> land the immigrant in an alert and clear-headed state. The bustle, con-
> fusion, rush and size of Ellis Island complete the work, and leave the
> average alien in a state of stupor. . . . He is in no condition to understand
> a carefully-worded explanation of what he must do, or why he must do
> it, even if the inspector had the time to give it. The one suggestion which
> is immediately comprehensible to him is a pull or a push; if this is not
> administered with actual violence, there is no unkindness in it.

Reasonable as it may seem, this analysis meshed Yankee elitism with a   14
defense of the bureaucratic mind. Immigrants *were* disoriented by the time
they reached Ellis Island, but they remained human beings with all the sen-
sibilities of human beings; the problem of numbers *was* a real one, yet it was
always better when interpreters offered a word of explanation than when
they resorted to "a pull or a push." Against the view expressed by Fairchild,
we must weigh the massive testimony of the immigrants themselves, the
equally large body of material gathered by congressional investigations, and
such admissions, all the more telling because casual in intent, as that of Commissioner Corsi: "Our immigration officials have not always been as humane
as they might have been." The Ellis Island staff was often badly overworked,
and day after day it had to put up with an atmosphere of fearful anxiety
which required a certain deadening of response, if only by way of self-
defense. But it is also true that many of the people who worked there were
rather simple fellows who lacked the imagination to respect cultural styles
radically different from their own.

One intepreter who possessed that imagination richly was a young Italo-   15
American named Fiorello La Guardia, later to become an insurgent mayor
of New York. "I never managed during the years I worked there to become
callous to the mental anguish, the disappointment and the despair I witnessed almost daily. . . . At best the work was an ordeal." For those who cared
to see, and those able to feel, there could finally be no other verdict.

QUESTIONS

Words to Know

anticipated (paragraph 1), taut (1), withered (1), debarking (2), ship's manifest (2), contagious (5), loathsome (5), leprosy (5), trachoma (7), multilingual (8), anarchism (8), polygamy (8), bewildering (9).

Some of the Issues

1. Describe the stages the prospective immigrant goes through in passing through Ellis Island. You may draw a flow chart to accompany your description.
2. In your own words, what are the "two strands of opinion" about Ellis Island (paragraphs 12 and after)?
3. Riis ("In the Gateway of Nations") and Howe describe essentially the same process. Which one is more accepting of it? Explain the reasons for your answer by referring to specific elements in each selection.

The Way We Are Told

4. What impression of the treatment of immigrants does Howe want the reader to have? Is he entirely neutral? Cite words and phrases to support your opinion.

Some Subjects for Essays

5. If you have ever approached an event as if it were some sort of "final Day of Judgment," as described in paragraph 1, give an account of the experiences and of your feelings at the time. Can you, like Riis in the first essay, look back on your experience with a feeling of serenity?
6. Much of what happened at Ellis Island was dictated by bureaucratic processes. Most of us have come in contact with a bureaucracy. Describe your own experience with a bureaucratic process.

FROM VIETNAM, 1979

Vo Thi Tam

Vo Thi Tam was one of the Vietnamese "boat people"—men, women, and children who escaped from South Vietnam after the communist takeover. The harrowing experiences of those who survived filled the television screens and newspapers in 1979; thousands died by drowning, thirst, starvation, and the merciless attack of pirates.

Vo Thi Tam's story is part of *American Mosaic* by Joan Morrison and Charlotte Fox Zabusky (1980), a comprehensive collection of interviews with immigrants to the United States.

My husband was a former officer in the South Vietnamese air force. After the fall of that government in 1975, he and all the other officers were sent to a concentration camp for reeducation. When they let him out of the camp, they forced all of us to go to one of the "new economic zones," that are really just jungle. There was no organization, there was no housing, no utilities, no doctor, nothing. They gave us tools and a little food, and that was it. We just had to dig up the land and cultivate it. And the land was very bad. 1

It was impossible for us to live there, so we got together with some other families and bought a big fishing boat, about thirty-five feet long. 2

Altogether, there were thirty-seven of us that were to leave—seven men, eight women, and the rest children. I was five months pregnant. 3

After we bought the boat we had to hide it, and this is how: We just anchored it in a harbor in the Mekong Delta. It's very crowded there and very many people make their living aboard the boats by going fishing, you know. So we had to make ourselves like them. We took turns living and sleeping on the boat. We would maneuver the boat around the harbor, as if we were fishing or selling stuff, you know, so the Communist authorities could not suspect anything. 4

Besides the big boat, we had to buy a smaller boat in order to carry supplies to it. We had to buy gasoline and other stuff on the black market— everywhere there is a black market—and carry these supplies, little by little, on the little boat to the big boat. To do this we sold jewelry and radios and other things that we had left from the old days. 5

On the day we left we took the big boat out very early in the morning— all the women and children were in that boat and some of the men. My husband and the one other man remained in the small boat, and they were to rendezvous with us outside the harbor. Because if the harbor officials see 6 too many people aboard, they might think there was something suspicious. I think they were suspicious anyway. As we went out, they stopped us and made us pay them ten taels of gold—that's a Vietnamese unit, a little heavier than an ounce. That was nearly all we had.

Anyway, the big boat passed through the harbor and went ahead to the rendezvous point where we were to meet my husband and the other man in the small boat. But there was no one there. We waited for two hours, but we did not see any sign of them. After a while we could see a Vietnamese navy boat approaching, and there was a discussion on board our boat and the end of it was the people on our boat decided to leave without my husband and the other man. [*Long pause.*]

When we reached the high seas, we discovered, unfortunately, that the water container was leaking and only a little bit of the water was left. So we had to ration the water from then on. We had brought some rice and other food that we could cook, but it was so wavy that we could not cook anything at all. So all we had was raw rice and a few lemons and very little water. After seven days we ran out of water, so all we had to drink was the sea water, plus lemon juice.

Everyone was very sick and, at one point, my mother and my little boy, four years old, were in agony, about to die. And the other people on the boat said that if they were agonizing like that, it would be better to throw them overboard so as to save them pain.

During this time we had seen several boats on the sea and had waved to them to help us, but they never stopped. But that morning, while we were discussing throwing my mother and son overboard, we could see another ship coming and we were very happy, thinking maybe it was people coming to save us. When the two boats were close together, the people came on board from there—it happened to be a Thai boat—and they said all of us had to go on the bigger boat. They made us all go there and then they began to search us—cutting off our blouses, our bras, looking everywhere. One woman, she had some rings she hid in her bra, and they undressed her and took out everything. My mother had a statue of Our Lady, a very precious one, you know, that she had had all her life—she begged them just to leave the statue to her. But they didn't want to. They slapped her and grabbed the statue away.

Finally they pried up the planks of our boat, trying to see if there was any gold or jewelry hidden there. And when they had taken everything, they put us back on our boat and pushed us away.

They had taken all our maps and compasses, so we didn't even know which way to go. And because they had pried up the planks of our boat to look for jewelry, the water started getting in. We were very weak by then.

But we had no pump, so we had to use empty cans to bail the water out, over and over again.

That same day we were boarded again by two other boats, and these, too, were pirates. They came aboard with hammers and knives and everything. But we could only beg them for mercy and try to explain by sign language that we'd been robbed before and we had nothing left. So those boats let us go and pointed the way to Malaysia for us.   13

That night at about 9:00 P.M. we arrived on the shore, and we were so happy finally to land somewhere that we knelt down on the beach and prayed, you know, to thank God.   14

While we were kneeling there, some people came out of the woods and began to throw rocks at us. They took a doctor who was with us and they beat him up and broke his glasses, so that from that time on he couldn't see anything at all. And they tied him up, his hands behind him like this [*demonstrates*], and they beat up the rest of the men, too. They searched us for anything precious that they could find, but there was nothing left except our few clothes and our documents. They took these and scattered them all over the beach.   15

Then five of the Malaysian men grabbed the doctor's wife, a young woman with three little children, and they took her back into the woods and raped her—all five of them. Later, they sent her back, completely naked, to the beach.   16

After this, the Malaysians forced us back into the boat and tried to push us out to sea. But the tide was out and the boat was so heavy with all of us on board that it just sank in the sand. So they left us for the night. . . .   17

In the morning, the Malaysian military police came to look over the area, and they dispersed the crowd and protected us from them. They let us pick up our clothes and our papers from the beach and took us in a big truck to some kind of a warehouse in a small town not far away. They gave us water, some bread, and some fish, and then they carried us out to Bidong Island. . . .   18

Perhaps in the beginning it was all right there, maybe for ten thousand people or so, but when we arrived there were already fifteen to seventeen thousand crowded onto thirty acres. There was no housing, no facilities, nothing. It was already full near the beach, so we had to go up the mountain and chop down trees to make room for ourselves and make some sort of a temporary shelter. There was an old well, but the water was very shallow. It was so scarce that all the refugees had to wait in a long line, day and night, to get our turn of the water. We would have a little can, like a small Coke can at the end of a long string, and fill that up. To fill about a gallon, it would take an hour, so we each had to just wait, taking our turn to get our Coke   19 can of water. Sometimes one, two, or three in the morning we would get our water. I was pregnant, and my boys were only four and six, and my old mother with me was not well, but we all had to wait in line to get our water. That was just for cooking and drinking, of course. We had to do our washing in the sea.

The Malaysian authorities did what they could, but they left most of   20
the administration of the camp to the refugees themselves, and most of us were sick. There were, of course, no sanitary installations, and many people had diarrhea. It was very hard to stop sickness under those conditions. My little boys were sick and my mother could hardly walk. And since there was no man in our family, we had no one to chop the wood for our cooking, and it was very hard for us just to survive. When the monsoons came, the floor of our shelter was all mud. We had one blanket and a board to lie on, and that was all. The water would come down the mountain through our shelter, so we all got wet.

After four months in the camp it was time for my baby to be born.   21
Fortunately, we had many doctors among us, because many of them had tried to escape from Vietnam, so we had medical care but no equipment. There was no bed there, no hospital, no nothing, just a wooden plank to lie down on and let the baby be born, that was all. Each mother had to supply a portion of boiling water for the doctor to use and bring it with her to the medical hut when it was time. It was a very difficult delivery. The baby came legs first. But, fortunately, there were no complications. After the delivery I had to get up and go back to my shelter to make room for the next woman.

When we left Vietnam we were hoping to come to the United States,   22
because my sister and her husband were here already. They came in 1975 when the United States evacuated so many people. We had to wait in the camp a month and a half to be interviewed, and then very much longer for the papers to be processed. Altogether we were in the camp seven months.

All this time I didn't know what had happened to my husband, although   23
I hoped that he had been able to escape some other way and was, perhaps, in another camp, and that when I came to the United States I would find him.

We flew out here by way of Tokyo and arrived the first week in July.   24
It was like waking up after a bad nightmare. Like coming out of hell into paradise. If only—. [*Breaks down, rushes from room.*]

Shortly after she arrived in this country, Vo Thi Tam learned that her hus-   25
band had been captured on the day of their escape and was back in a "reeduca-
tion" camp in Vietnam.

QUESTIONS

Some of the Issues

1. What clues are there about the background or class of the refugees?

The Way We Are Told

2. What indications do you have that Vo Thi Tam's is a spoken rather than a written account, the result of an interview?
3. "Third Generation" by Richard Sennett and Jonathan Cobb, like Vo Thi Tam's account, is the result of an interview. Compare and contrast the two accounts.

Some Subjects for Essays

4. Select a friend or relative who you know can tell a story or express a point of view on an interesting issue. Conduct an interview to elicit the material, and write your account.
5. The flow of immigrants to the United States continues, together with controversies about who should be admitted and how new arrivals should be treated. Discuss your views on any current topic concerning recent immigration to the United States, supporting your opinion with evidence.

RUSSIAN JOURNAL

Andrea Lee

Andrea Lee was a 25-year-old graduate student in English at Harvard when she and her husband, a doctoral candidate in Russian history at Harvard, went to Russia in the late 1970s. They spent eight months at Moscow State University, living in a student dormitory, and two more months at Leningrad State University. Since they both spoke Russian and lived among Russian students, they came to know the country and its culture in ways closed to most foreign visitors. Lee records her observations with a good eye for detail. In the following excerpts she describes the opening day of the school year in Moscow and an evening in a nightclub designed for privileged young Muscovites. *Russian Journal* was published in 1981; several of the entries originally appeared in *The New Yorker* in 1980.

September 1   The nights are cold; the apples are ripe on the trees in   1
the university orchard. Today was the first day of school, and though I slept late and missed the cute and much-photographed primary schoolers (marching in starched pinafores, with flowers for the teachers), Tom and I did catch the opening exercises tonight for freshmen here at Moscow State. We had seen the build-up to the ceremony over the past month, as entrance exams took place around us. Outside the immense glass-and-steel humanities building, crowds of parents stood staring anxiously up at the windows of the examination rooms. The children of many of them had spent the past six months in intensive "prepping" courses for three days of tests. This is an expensive procedure, especially for provincial families, whose children must come to live in Moscow during the half year. The expense is often worthwhile, however, since these all-day examinations really do determine a student's future career. Three papers are posted on the bulletin board outside the building: a description of the exams; a list of appeal procedures for students who fail; and an employment ad from an automobile factory, addressed specifically to candidates whose appeals are turned down. (These young people don't always face a future of factory work. Russian friends have told me that a common tactic after rejection from Moscow State is to try institutes whose prestige is less and which have fewer applications. Determined students can find a place in these humbler schools, as students of, for instance, forest management or soil chemistry.)

The hundreds of students in the auditorium tonight were the happy   2
winners, survivors of a tough selection system; they seemed like freshmen anywhere. Before the ceremony they straggled into the room, smoking cig-

273

arettes, laughing, calling to their friends. A few loners stood gazing at the vast embossed ceiling, obviously overwhelmed by the stupendous size of the building and perhaps as well by the prestige of the institution they were entering. One or two couples strolled in with their arms around each other, but for the most part the sexes stayed in packs, eying each other covertly. By Soviet standards, they were dressed modishly: the girls in bright miniskirts and clumsy platform shoes, the boys in wildly patterned polyester shirts. Among them, a small group stood out in especially naïve clothing: crop-headed boys in tight suits, girls whose tremendous coiled braids were topped with frilly ribbons. These, I guessed, were country kids, in Moscow for the first time. A sophisticated Russian friend had described to me the reaction of these rural students to the university cafeteria: "They all came charging in, wearing these incredible suits—narrow lapels and short trousers. They gawked at everything, and then they started to gobble the food—tough meat and watery soup—as if it was the best thing they'd eaten in their lives." Aside from the provincials, the students made a fairly homogeneous group. I was surprised to find so few representatives of the various Soviet ethnic and racial groups. Most students were clearly Great Russian, the ethnic group that dominates Central European Russia and makes up most of the population of Moscow.

The huge auditorium filled, then quieted, and at seven o'clock the head of the university began to speak. At his first few phrases, I felt stealing irresistibly over me the memory of my own freshman year: the universal confusion; the unexpected liberty; awe; the endlessly proffered, absurd advice, which we ritually ignored. The faraway official, with his plump vest full of medals, was urging the students to uphold the standards of Lenin. He reminded them to follow the principles of the Twenty-fifth Party Congress in their scholarship. He told them that university life itself was an educational experience, that one must be fit in mind as well as body. Two grave, pink-cheeked Komsonol leaders carried in the flag of the Order of Lenin, and the speeches continued. I felt my ears closing, and I guessed that the ears of hundreds of students around me had closed as well. For a few minutes they had all stared up at the platform with the polite forbearance of the young for the pompous old, then the natural life of the crowd took over. Boys elbowed each other and stared at girls; girls put on lipstick and passed notes down the rows to their friends. I could feel the classic freshman sense of universal ogling, and also the question burning in the back of every mind: What will happen tonight? Because what was important was not the ceremony but afterward, when the freshman class had been promised a dance with live music.

The series of long speeches ended with a memorial to the Moscow State University students killed in the Second World War. The freshmen grew quiet as a soldier marched slowly forward with a wreath. I was curious about what they were thinking, these children born in the early sixties, to whom the forlorn hope of crudely armed students in the defense of Moscow could mean little more than an excerpt from a cycle of legends. The young faces around me wore only a strict ceremonial gravity. After a few minutes of silence, a stylishly dressed girl beside me glanced down at her watch and gave a little frown of impatience.

Later Tom and I watched the dance. It was held in the main hall of the dormitory, a dreary marble room whose walls give off a penetrating cold even in the summer. On a small platform in the center, four young men in jeans and suspenders played English and American rock music. Their hair was shoulder-length and their expressions were grim; they pronounced the English words with savage precision. A few girls in miniskirts hovered on the floor below, staring up at the musicians and hurrying to adjust microphones and amplifiers. As the lead singer shook his hair and began to sing "Satisfaction," I had an acute sense of time lag. The music, the setting were those of any small college dance a decade ago in the United States. But there was a naïveté about the crowd which would have been unusual for any group of young Americans. The tiny refreshment stand served only fizzy *limonad*, and we didn't see anyone slip off to drink vodka or beer in a corner. A wall of spectators surrounded the dance floor, where a few shy couples were moving in the strange rhythmless combination of Monkey and Jerk which makes up Russian "pop" dancing. The action, however, was not on the dance floor but among the hovering watchers. Packs of girls and boys approached and fell away from each other, giggling at the near-intersections but never actually meeting. I thought of the formality that seems to govern encounters of sexes in the Soviet Union. Many of my young married Russian friends were introduced by relatives.

So the freshman dance at Moscow State failed as a meeting ground for male and female students. Both sexes listened raptly to the music. Boys roughhoused in corners. Someone upset a tray of *zakuski* (snacks), and the floor was slippery with bologna sandwiches. The band played a slow song, and the few dancers moved heavily and chastely, their heads on the shoulders of their partners. At exactly eleven o'clock a uniformed guard appeared and told the band members to pack up. The dance was over, and in a minute the students had filed obediently away. The freshman class needs its rest, I discovered. Early tomorrow morning they leave on a bus to fulfill another first-year tradition: a month of work in a potato-harvest brigade at a collective farm.

October 5   A popular Moscow night spot right now for trendy Russian youth is the Sinyaya Ptitsa, a dinner-and-dancing club on Pushkin Street. If you arrive there after seven on any evening, there is a line of denim-jacketed kids in their late teens and early twenties waiting without much hope outside its door, which is locked. We got there around 5 P.M. the other day, and were welcomed inside by the manager, a gray-haired gentleman in a stylish Western suit. He looked sleek and prosperous, and there was about him a touch of something I hadn't seen since I left the United States: the high-bouncing M.C. who loves "the kids" and the money they bring him. We paid a three-ruble cover charge and were seated by another sleek character in a French suit. A waiter brought us "cocktails" that were weak and oversweetened; that didn't matter, because we were busy staring at an amazing phenomenon—a Moscow night club that looked like a night club. The lighting was dim and the walls dark tile, with a bright mural depicting a blue bird—the namesake of the café. The tables were grouped around a small dance floor, which faced—wonder of wonders—a bar with bar stools. The recorded music was loud and good. It mainly featured the Swedish group Abba and the Caribbean group Boney M., two wildly popular bands that play soft disco-type rock with English lyrics. (When Boney M. performed live in Moscow a few weeks ago, young people stood in line for more than twenty hours to buy tickets. Scalpers' prices reached a hundred rubles.)

A friend of mine at the university had told me that the Sinyaya Ptitsa was the main hangout for Moscow's *Zolotaya Molodyozh*, "Golden Youth"—the popular name for the spoiled offspring of the Communist elite. I looked around and concluded that he was right. The young clientele looked richer and more bored than any Russians I'd ever seen before. At each table a couple or a threesome leaned back in their seats, smoking with the almost ludicrous cigarette-in-the-air gesture that seems to be the mark of the Soviet snob. I could see packs of Marlboros and Gauloises lying on the tables. Every second person was dressed in denim—the girls in fashionable narrow slit skirts, the boys in name-brand American jeans and jackets. (Labels are very important now in denim-conscious Moscow. I have several times been drawn into debates on the merits of Wrangler versus Levis.) It was an expensive gathering. How many thousands of rubles did these yards of blue jeans represent? How many trips abroad? Many of the girls had fluffy Parisian-looking bobs, a real rarity in this land of long braids and coiled chignons. Everyone seemed to know everyone else; no one laughed or appeared to be having a good time. There was a lot of wandering around between tables for cigarette lighting and brief, intense conversations. I went to the ladies' room and found two beautiful, sulky girls improving their faces with French mascara. Part of their conversation went like this:

"Sasha's here tonight."

"I know. He's here with Olya."

"And so?"   11

A pause while one girl closed and opened her lashes in the mirror. Then: 12
"Well, *I* won't say hello."

After a while couples got up to dance. They danced well, doing an exag-   13
gerated version of the Bump, which was the sexiest thing I'd seen in this city
of chaste, energentic dances. (Most dance floors in Moscow are arenas for
crowds of hefty drunken couples, who do an oddly inncoent kind of bop and
lurch.) Girls in tight dresses danced with boys in very tight pants, and over
it all swirled a kind of psychedelic show of colored lights. I thought of my
friend Elena's tales of dances in Moscow fifteen years ago: they used to call
in the police if anyone did anything other than the waltz or the polka. A
shout went up from the tables as a song came on that has been a hit in Moscow for the past few months. It is a song about Rasputin, by Boney M., and
it gives an informal account of the sexual prowess of the mystic from Siberia.
Its chorus goes like this:

> *Rah! Rah! Rasputin,*
> *Russia's greatest love machine!*
> *It was a shame*
> *How he carried on!*

Everyone was up on the dance floor for this one, still bored-looking, still   14
unsmiling, but singing along. Stomping their Italian leather boots, bumping
their blue-jeaned backsides, the spoiled rich kids of Moscow were celebrating
this cosmopolitan in-joke: an irreverent song about Russia sung in English by
a black group that records in West Germany. I saw the sleek gray-haired
manager standing near the dance floor, snapping his fingers and smiling
complacently as he watched the dancers. His hair was pouffed and swept,
and I bet myself that he owned one of the few blow-dryers in Moscow. I had
been seeing big tips change hands, and I could read his thoughts clearly. He
was watching the growing success of the only Western-style club in town
and thinking: These kids! Right on! Crazy, but I love 'em!

QUESTIONS

Words to Know

pinafore (paragraph 1), embossed (2), covertly (2), gawked (2), homogeneous (2), Great Russian (2), proffered (3), Komsomol (3), phenomenon (7), Rasputin (13), cosmopolitan (14).

Some of the Issues

1. Lee describes the selection system of Moscow University. How does it differ from the American system as you know it?
2. Lee recalls (paragraph 3) that the opening ceremony at Moscow State reminded her of her own experience at freshman orientation. In what respects did you find the description reminded you of your own experience? In what ways did it differ?
3. Lee tells about the dance that concluded freshman orientation (paragraph 5). Do you think that the behavior of freshman students at such events is much the same everywhere?

The Way We Are Told

4. Lee describes the Moscow nightclub and its customers in detail. Which details are purely factual descriptions and which convey judgments? Is it always easy to tell? How would you characterize the overall tone of her description?
5. Lee presents her recollections of Moscow in the form of a journal. Compare it to Carolina Maria de Jesus's "Diary" in Part Three. Quite apart from the obvious differences in content, how do the two records differ?

Some Subjects for Essays

6. Keep a journal or diary for one week, making at least one entry every day. Which of the two journals, Lee's or de Jesus's does yours resemble more closely?
7. In paragraph 2 Lee divides the Soviet freshmen into several groups: extroverts and loners, urban and rural, majority and minority—on the basis of

external observation of appearance, clothing, and habits. Write an essay dividing into three or four sub-groups any group with which you are familiar, for example, students in your college or members of a particular profession. Distinguish each sub-group by means of details describing appearance and behavior.

8. In her journal, Lee describes the Russian graduation ceremony: "The huge auditorium filled, then quieted, and at seven o'clock the head of the university began to speak. At his first few phrases, I felt stealing irresistibly over me the memory of my own freshman year: the universal confusion; the unexpected liberty; awe; the endlessly proffered, absurd advice, which we ritually ignored." In an essay, describe your own first experiences at school or college, contrasting expectations with reality, advice offered and ignored.

BLESSINGS OF EMPTINESS

Elizabeth Hanson

"Blessings of Emptiness" was first published in the *National Observer* in November 1975.

I returned to the United States for a visit this summer after living for two years in Kyoto, Japan. While I was home I learned a lesson about affluence that might serve Americans as a "survival tactic." On the way back to Kyoto, my husband and I helped an elderly Japanese couple, the Hiratas, find their way through the big, empty Seattle airport. Mrs. Hirata looked around in awe as she went down the escalator. "You can hardly see a human shadow," she said. "My daughter says she likes living in America better than in Japan, and after three months here, maybe I agree."

When we landed at Haneda airport in Tokyo, we were immersed in a baggage-claim area that was packed with people. I understood then that Mrs. Hirata wasn't attracted to American life because we have cars and big television sets and lots of appliances. The Japanese have those things too. She liked the United States because of the emptiness.

I realize after living in Japan that emptiness is a natural resource like oil or topsoil, yet in America we take our large country for granted.

The United States has its share of congested urban areas, and many Americans live close together without the benefit of some private green area. Yet the crowded conditions of some cities in the United States are standard in Japan. The effects of this poverty of space are everywhere. In Japan a population half the size of the United States' is packed into a land area about the same size as California, and only about 16 percent of that land is habitable. Housing that would be considered middle class in the United States—a prefabricated three-bedroom house with a quarter-acre lot, for example—is out of the reach of all but the richest Japanese families.

My husband and I were lucky enough to rent a house in Kyoto with two small rooms upstairs and two downstairs. The kitchen is large enough for only one cook. Our yard is a narrow concrete area in the front and back, with a hardy Japanese maple growing over the wall. There is no central heating, no running hot water, no washing machine. We thought the place would be big enough for the two of us, though. We smugly told ourselves that it would be good experience to live Japanese-style in this "typical" house.

We learned soon after moving in that our house is not typical. It is large. Japanese friends comment on the size the minute they take their shoes off and step into the entry hall. They are amazed at how quiet and private it is, despite the fact that we can hear the rumblings of the streetcar a block away and the unique sound mixture of one neighbor playing a samisen, another practicing classical piano, and a third playing Beatles' records. Japanese friends have asked several times why we don't rent our upstairs room to a student boarder. Surely, they say, the house is lonely with just two people.

A white-collar worker typically lives in a three-room apartment with 7 his wife and two or three children; a recent advertisement in Kyoto listed the cost of such a 760-square-foot condominium apartment at $60,000. The rooms are converted from sleeping to living rooms and back again. There is no space for a private children's room, much less a den. Children play in a communal patch of packed earth between the buildings, in a parking lot, or on the streets.

Because their homes are small, the Japanese don't spend as much time 8 in them as Americans do. Men don't bring colleagues home for dinner because a quiet, leisurely meal is impossible in a tiny apartment shared with active children. Japanese meet close friends at restaurants or bars instead of having parties at home. Coffee shops in nearly every neighborhood serve as substitute living rooms, not just as places to grab a snack.

A poverty of space also affects the way people spend their free time. 9 Because many people have only one day off each week, a Sunday outing to a park, zoo, or beach is a constant struggle against crowds. Trains and buses to recreation areas are packed to rush-hour capacity. Families sit nearly side by side in parks, eating their picnics and politely ignoring the people around them.

One has to reserve a tennis court a month in advance to play on a week 10 end. Golf courses are luxuries; persons may have to pay fees of $30 to $50 to play 18 holes. Japanese who say they often play golf get on a real course only a few times a year; usually they must be satisfied with practicing on a driving range. Movies are full on weekends and holidays, with people standing in the aisles.

This summer when I visited my home state, Illinois, I was entranced by 11 the rich, flat grain fields. Just outside the center of Japanese cities one can find rice plots wedged between houses and apartment buildings. The Japanese rely desperately on imports of grain other than rice.

Most Japanese are well fed, but families spend 40 to 50 percent of their 12 income on food. A dozen eggs costs $1.25; a quart of milk, 73 cents; ground beef, $3 a pound. It embarrassed me to hear American friends in the United States complain about food prices and having to eat fish, chicken, or hamburger instead of roast or steak. Most Japanese don't consider eating large pieces of meat every day any more than people in Kansas expect to eat freshly caught seafood.

Sometimes the strains of living in such a society are overwhelming.   13
Each year several teen-agers commit suicide because of the pressure of
studying for entrance examinations to crowded colleges. A few years ago, a
man killed his neighbor and her daughter because he could no longer stand
to hear their piano playing.

Yet the Japanese seem to appreciate what they have and to accept, more   14
or less, that some things are impossible to obtain. If there is no room around
the house for a yard, then a garden enthusiast substitutes a row of carefully
tended potted plants.

I realize after living in Japan how precious mere emptiness can be. I   15
didn't know what an advantage it is to live in a big country until I lived in
a small one. If we Americans understand what a blessing space is, perhaps
we can accept problems of inflation with a sense of balance and perspective.

QUESTIONS

Words to Know

immersed (paragraph 2), samisen (6), entranced (11).

Some of the Issues

1. What is Hanson's thesis? Does she state it explicitly?
2. Explain the intent of the title. How does it contribute to Hanson's thesis?
3. Why does Hanson refer to emptiness as a natural resource?
4. Hanson presents evidence for her argument in a variety of ways. List
   several and show how she uses examples in each case to make her point.
5. What consequences of the crowded conditions in Japan does Hanson
   cite?
6. Does Hanson imply any criticism of Japan? Of America?

The Way We Are Told

7. Hanson alternates personal experiences with more general information.
   How does the sequence of personal experiences reinforce her thesis?
8. Hanson also gives the reader general information designed to support

her argument. What makes that information effective? From what point of view is it selected?

9. For what public do you think this essay is intended? Can you think of a different public for whom different evidence would be needed?

Some Subjects for Essays

10. Hanson's essay compares and contrasts certain conditions in two societies. Write an essay in which you compare and contrast two conditions or institutions with which you are familiar. Consider carefully how to make your comparison effective by selecting the right kinds of evidence, whether personal or general.

11. Identify either a specific "blessing" or a "curse" of life in America. Select your supporting evidence and organizational patterns so as to make your argument effective.

SHAKESPEARE IN THE BUSH

Laura Bohannan

Laura Bohannan, born in New York City in 1922, is a professor of anthropology at the University of Illinois in Chicago. She received her doctorate from Oxford University and later did field work with various peoples in Africa, including the Tiv, a tribe in central Nigeria, with whom this story is concerned. Under the pseudonym Elenore Smith Bowen, she has published a novel about anthropological field work, *Return to Laughter.*

Just before I left Oxford for the Tiv in West Africa, conversation turned to the season at Stratford, "You Americans." said a friend, "often have difficulty with Shakespeare. He was, after all, a very English poet, and one can easily misinterpret the universal by misunderstanding the particular."   1

I protested that human nature is pretty much the same the whole world over; at least the general plot and motivation of the greater tragedies would always be clear—everywhere—although some details of custom might have to be explained and difficulties of translation might produce other slight changes. To end an argument we could not conclude, my friend gave me a copy of *Hamlet* to study in the African bush: it would, he hoped, lift my mind above its primitive surroundings, and possibly I might, by prolonged meditation, achieve the grace of correct interpretation.   2

It was my second field trip to that African tribe, and I thought myself ready to live in one of its remote sections—an area difficult to cross even on foot. I eventually settled on the hillock of a very knowledgeable old man, the head of a homestead of some hundred and forty people, all of whom were either his close relatives or their wives and children. Like the other elders of the vicinity, the old man spent most of his time performing ceremonies seldom seen these days in the more accessible parts of the tribe. I was delighted. Soon there would be three months of enforced isolation and leisure, between the harvest that takes place just before the rising of the swamps and the clearing of new farms when the water goes down. Then, I thought, they would have even more time to perform ceremonies and explain them to me.   3

I was quite mistaken. Most of the ceremonies demanded the presence of elders from several homesteads. As the swamps rose, the old men found it   4

284

too difficult to walk from one homestead to the next, and the ceremonies gradually ceased. As the swamps rose even higher, all activities but one came to an end. The women brewed beer from maize and millet. Men, women, and children sat on their hillocks and drank it.

People began to drink at dawn. By midmorning the whole homestead 5 was singing, dancing, and drumming. When it rained, people had to sit inside their huts: there they drank and sang or they drank and told stories. In any case, by noon or before, I either had to join the party or retire to my own hut and my books. "One does not discuss serious matters when there is beer. Come, drink with us." Since I lacked their capacity for the thick native beer, I spent more and more time with *Hamlet*. Before the end of the second month, grace descended on me. I was quite sure that *Hamlet* had only one possible interpretation, and that one universally obvious.

Early every morning, in the hope of having some serious talk before the 6 beer party, I used to call on the old man at his reception hut—a circle of posts supporting a thatched roof above a low mud wall to keep out wind and rain. One day I crawled through the low doorway and found most of the men of the homestead sitting huddled in their ragged cloths on stools, low plank beds, and reclining chairs, warming themselves against the chill of the rain around a smoky fire. In the center were three pots of beer. The party had started.

The old man greeted me cordially. "Sit down and drink." I accepted a 7 large calabash full of beer, poured some into a small drinking gourd, and tossed it down. Then I poured some more into the same gourd for the man second in seniority to my host before I handed my calabash over to a young man for further distribution. Important people shouldn't ladle beer themselves.

"It is better like this," the old man said, looking at me approvingly and 8 plucking at the thatch that had caught in my hair. "You should sit and drink with us more often. Your servants tell me that when you are not with us, you sit inside your hut looking at a paper."

The old man was acquainted with four kinds of "papers": tax receipts, 9 bride price receipts, court fee receipts, and letters. The messenger who brought him letters from the chief used them mainly as a badge of office, for he always knew what was in them and told the old man. Personal letters for the few who had relatives in the government or mission stations were kept until someone went to a large market where there was a letter writer and reader. Since my arrival, letters were brought to me to be read. A few men also brought me bride price receipts, privately, with requests to change the figures to a higher sum. I found moral arguments were of no avail, since in-laws are fair game, and the technical hazards of forgery difficult to explain to an illiterate people. I did not wish them to think me silly enough to look at any such papers for days on end, and I hastily explained that my "paper" was one of the "things of long ago" of my country.

"Ah," said the old man. "Tell us."   10

I protested that I was not a storyteller. Storytelling is a skilled art among   11
them; their standards are high, and the audiences critical—and vocal in their criticism. I protested in vain. This morning they wanted to hear a story while they drank. They threatened to tell me no more stories until I told them one of mine. Finally, the old man promised that no one would criticize my style "for we know you are struggling with our language." "But," put in one of the elders, "you must explain what we do not understand, as we do when we tell you our stories." Realizing that here was my chance to prove *Hamlet* universally intelligible, I agreed.

The old man handed me some more beer to help me on with my sto-   12
rytelling. Men filled their long wooden pipes and knocked coals from the fire to place in the pipe bowls; then, puffing contentedly, they sat back to listen. I began in the proper style,

"Not yesterday, not yesterday, but long ago, a thing occurred. One night three men were keeping watch outside the homestead of the great chief, when suddenly they saw the former chief approach them."

"Why was he no longer their chief?"   13

"He was dead," I explained. "That is why they were troubled and afraid   14
when they saw him."

"Impossible," began one of the elders, handing his pipe on to his neigh-   15
bor, who interrupted, "Of course it wasn't the dead chief. It was an omen sent by a witch. Go on."

Slightly shaken, I continued. "One of these three was a man who knew   16
things"—the closest translation for scholar, but unfortunately it also meant witch. The second elder looked triumphantly at the first. "So he spoke to the dead chief saying, 'Tell us what we must do so you may rest in your grave,' but the dead chief did not answer. He vanished, and they could see him no more. Then the man who knew things—his name was Horatio—said this event was the affair of the dead chief's son, Hamlet."

There was a general shaking of heads round the circle. "Had the dead   17
chief no living brothers? Or was this son the chief?"

"No," I replied. "That is, he had one living brother who became the   18
chief when the elder brother died."

The old men muttered: such omens were matters for chiefs and elders,   19
not for youngsters; no good could come of going behind a chief's back; clearly Horatio was not a man who knew things.

"Yes, he was," I insisted, shooing a chicken away from my beer. "In our   20 country the son is next to the father. The dead chief's younger brother had become the great chief. He had also married his elder brother's widow only about a month after the funeral."

"He did well," the old man beamed and announced to the others, "I told you that if we knew more about Europeans, we would find they really were very like us. In our country also," he added to me, "the younger brother marries the elder brother's widow and becomes the father of his children. Now, if your uncle, who married your widowed mother, is your father's full brother, then he will be a real father to you. Did Hamlet's father and uncle have one mother?"   21

His question barely penetrated my mind; I was too upset and thrown too far off balance by having one of the most important elements of *Hamlet* knocked straight out of the picture. Rather uncertainly I said that I thought they had the same mother, but I wasn't sure—the story didn't say. The old man told me severely that these genealogical details made all the difference and that when I got home I must ask the elders about it. He shouted out the door to one of his younger wives to bring his goatskin bag.   22

Determined to save what I could of the mother motif, I took a deep breath and began again. "The son Hamlet was very sad because his mother had married again so quickly. There was no need for her to do so, and it is our custom for a widow not to go to her next husband until she has mourned for two years."   23

"Two years is too long," objected the wife, who had appeared with the old man's battered goatskin bag. "Who will hoe your farms for you while you have no husband?"   24

"Hamlet," I retorted without thinking, "was old enough to hoe his mother's farms himself. There was no need for her to remarry." No one looked convinced. I gave up. "His mother and the great chief told Hamlet not to be sad, for the great chief himself would be a father to Hamlet. Furthermore, Hamlet would be the next chief: therefore he must stay to learn the things of a chief. Hamlet agreed to remain, and all the rest went off to drink beer."   25

While I paused, perplexed at how to render Hamlet's disgusted soliloquy to an audience convinced that Claudius and Gertrude had behaved in the best possible manner, one of the younger men asked me who had married the other wives of the dead chief.   26

"He had no other wives," I told him.   27

"But a chief must have many wives! How else can he brew beer and prepare food for all his guests?"   28

I said firmly that in our country even chiefs had only one wife, that they had servants to do their work, and that they paid them from tax money.   29

It was better, they returned, for a chief to have many wives and sons   30
who would help him hoe his farms and feed his people; then everyone loved
the chief who gave much and took nothing—taxes were a bad thing.

I agreed with the last comment, but for the rest fell back on their favor-   31
ite way of fobbing off my questions: "That is the way it is done, so that is
how we do it."

I decided to skip the soliloquy. Even if Claudius was here thought quite   32
right to marry his brother's widow, there remained the poison motif, and I
knew they would disapprove of fratricide. More hopefully I resumed, "That
night Hamlet kept watch with the three who had seen his dead father. The
dead chief again appeared, and although the others were afraid, Hamlet
followed his dead father off to one side. When they were alone, Hamlet's
dead father spoke."

"Omens can't talk!" The old man was emphatic.   33

"Hamlet's dead father wasn't an omen. Seeing him might have been an   34
omen, but he was not." My audience looked as confused as I sounded. "It
was Hamlet's dead father. It was a thing we call a 'ghost.'" I had to use the
English word, for unlike many of the neighboring tribes, these people didn't
believe in the survival after death of any individuating part of the
personality.

"What is a 'ghost?' An omen?"   35

"No, a 'ghost' is someone who is dead but who walks around and can   36
talk, and people can hear him and see him but not touch him."

They objected. "One can touch zombis."   37

"No, no! It was not a dead body the witches had animated to sacrifice   38
and eat. No one else made Hamlet's dead father walk. He did it himself."

"Dead men can't walk," protested my audience as one man.   39

I was quite willing to compromise. "A 'ghost' is the dead man's   40
shadow."

But again they objected. "Dead men cast no shadows."   41

"They do in my country," I snapped.   42

The old man quelled the babble of disbelief that arose immediately and   43
told me with that insincere, but courteous, agreement one extends to the
fancies of the young, ignorant, and superstitious, "No doubt in your country
the dead can also walk without being zombis." From the depths of his bag
he produced a withered fragment of kola nut, bit off one end to show it
wasn't poisoned, and handed me the rest as a peace offering.

"Anyhow," I resumed, "Hamlet's dead father said that his own brother,   44
the one who became chief, had poisoned him. He wanted Hamlet to avenge
him. Hamlet believed this in his heart, for he did not like his father's
brother." I took another swallow of beer. "In the country of the great chief,
living in the same homestead, for it was a very large one, was an important

elder who was often with the chief to advise and help him. His name was
Polonius. Hamlet was courting his daughter, but her father and her brother
. . . [I cast hastily about for some tribal analogy] warned her not to let Hamlet
visit her when she was alone on her farm, for he would be a great chief and
so could not marry her."

"Why not?" asked the wife, who had settled down on the edge of the   45
old man's chair. He frowned at her for asking stupid questions and growled,
"They lived in the same homestead."

"That was not the reason," I informed them. "Polonius was a stranger   46
who lived in the homestead because he helped the chief, not because he was
a relative."

"Then why couldn't Hamlet marry her?"   47

"He could have," I explained, "But Polonius didn't think he would.   48
After all, Hamlet was a man of great importance who ought to marry a
chief's daughter, for in his country a man could have only one wife. Polonius
was afraid that if Hamlet made love to his daughter, then no one else would
give a high price for her."

"That might be true," remarked one of the shrewder elders, "but a   49
chief's son would give his mistress's father enough presents and patronage to
more than make up the difference. Polonius sounds like a fool to me."

"Many people think he was," I agreed. "Meanwhile Polonius sent his   50
son Laertes off to Paris to learn the things of that country, for it was the
homestead of a very great chief indeed. Because he was afraid that Laertes
might waste a lot of money on beer and women and gambling, or get into
trouble by fighting, he sent one of his servants to Paris secretly, to spy out
what Laertes was doing. One day Hamlet came upon Polonius's daughter
Ophelia. He behaved so oddly he frightened her. Indeed"—I was fumbling
for words to express the dubious quality of Hamlet's madness—"the chief
and many others had also noticed that when Hamlet talked one could understand the words but not what they meant. Many people thought that he had
become mad." My audience suddenly became much more attentive. "The
great chief wanted to know what was wrong with Hamlet, so he sent for two
of Hamlet's age mates [school friends would have taken long explanation] to
talk to Hamlet and find out what troubled his heart. Hamlet, seeing that they
had been bribed by the chief to betray him, told them nothing. Polonius,
however, insisted that Hamlet was mad because he had been forbidden to
see Ophelia, whom he loved."

"Why," inquired a bewildered voice, "should anyone bewitch Hamlet   51
on that account?"

"Bewitch him?"   52

"Yes, only witchcraft can make anyone mad, unless, of course, one sees   53
the beings that lurk in the forest."

I stopped being a storyteller, took out my notebook and demanded to   54
be told more about these two causes of madness. Even while they spoke and
I jotted notes, I tried to calculate the effect of this new factor on the plot.
Hamlet had not been exposed to the beings that lurk in the forests. Only his
relatives in the male line could bewitch him. Barring relatives not mentioned
by Shakespeare, it had to be Claudius who was attempting to harm him.
And, of course, it was.

For the moment I staved off questions by saying that the great chief   55
also refused to believe that Hamlet was mad for the love of Ophelia and
nothing else. "He was sure that something much more important was trou-
bling Hamlet's heart."

"Now Hamlet's age mates," I continued, "had brought with them a   56
famous storyteller. Hamlet decided to have this man tell the chief and all his
homestead a story about a man who had poisoned his brother because he
desired his brother's wife and wished to be chief himself. Hamlet was sure
the great chief could not hear the story without making a sign if he was
indeed guilty, and then he would discover whether his dead father had told
him the truth."

The old man interrupted, with deep cunning, "Why should a father lie   57
to his son?" he asked.

I hedged: "Hamlet wasn't sure that it really was his dead father." It was   58
impossible to say anything, in that language, about devil-inspired visions.

"You mean," he said, "it actually was an omen, and he knew witches   59
sometimes send false ones. Hamlet was a fool not to go to one skilled in
reading omens and divining the truth in the first place. A man-who-sees-the-
truth could have told him how his father died, if he really had been poisoned,
and if there was witchcraft in it; then Hamlet could have called the elders
to settle the matter."

The shrewd elder ventured to disagree. "Because his father's brother   60
was a great chief, one-who-sees-the-truth might therefore have been afraid
to tell it. I think it was for that reason that a friend of Hamlet's father—a
witch and an elder—sent an omen so his friend's son would know. Was the
omen true?"

"Yes," I said, abandoning ghosts and the devil; a witch-sent omen it   61
would have to be. "It was true, for when the storyteller was telling his tale
before all the homestead, the great chief rose in fear. Afraid that Hamlet
knew his secret he planned to have him killed."

The stage set of the next bit presented some difficulties of translation. I   62
began cautiously. "The great chief told Hamlet's mother to find out from her
son what he knew. But because a woman's children are always first in her
heart, he had the important elder Polonius hide behind a cloth that hung

against the wall of Hamlet's mother's sleeping hut. Hamlet started to scold his mother for what she had done."

There was a shocked murmur from everyone. A man should never scold his mother.   63

"She called out in fear, and Polonius moved behind the cloth. Shouting,   64
'A rat!' Hamlet took his machete and slashed through the cloth." I paused for dramatic effect. "He had killed Polonius!"

The old men looked at each other in supreme disgust. "That Polonius   65
truly was a fool and a man who knew nothing! What child would not know enough to shout, 'It's me!'" With a pang, I remembered that these people are ardent hunters, always armed with bow, arrow, and machete; at the first rustle in the grass an arrow is aimed and ready, and the hunter shouts "Game!" If no human voice answers immediately, the arrow speeds on its way. Like a good hunter Hamlet had shouted, "A rat!"

I rushed in to save Polonius's reputation. "Polonius did speak. Hamlet   66
heard him. But he thought it was the chief and wished to kill him to avenge his father. He had meant to kill him earlier that evening. . . ." I broke down, unable to describe to these pagans, who had no belief in individual afterlife, the difference between dying at one's prayers and dying "unhousell'd, dis-appointed, unaneled."

This time I had shocked my audience seriously. "For a man to raise his   67
hand against his father's brother and the one who had become his father— that is a terrible thing. The elders ought to let such a man be bewitched."

I nibbled at my kola nut in some perplexity, then pointed out that after   68
all the man had killed Hamlet's father.

"No," pronounced the old man, speaking less to me than to the young   69
men sitting behind the elders. "If your father's brother has killed your father, you must appeal to your father's age mates; *they* may avenge him. No man may use violence against his senior relatives." Another thought struck him. "But if his father's brother had indeed been wicked enough to bewitch Ham-let and make him mad that would be a good story indeed, for it would be his fault that Hamlet, being mad, no longer had any sense and thus was ready to kill his father's brother."

There was a murmur of applause. *Hamlet* was again a good story to   70
them, but it no longer seemed quite the same story to me. As I thought over the coming complications of plot and motive, I lost courage and decided to skim over dangerous ground quickly.

"The great chief," I went on, "was not sorry that Hamlet had killed   71
Polonius. It gave him a reason to send Hamlet away, with his two treacherous age mates, with letters to a chief of a far country, saying that Hamlet should

be killed. But Hamlet changed the writing on their papers, so that the chief killed his age mates instead." I encountered a reproachful glare from one of the men whom I had told undetectable forgery was not merely immoral but beyond human skill. I looked the other way.

"Before Hamlet could return, Laertes came back for his father's 72 funeral. The great chief told him Hamlet had killed Polonius. Laertes swore to kill Hamlet because of this, and because his sister Ophelia, hearing her father had been killed by the man she loved, went mad and drowned in the river."

"Have you already forgotten what we told you?" The old man was 73 reproachful. "One cannot take vengeance on a madman; Hamlet killed Polonius in his madness. As for the girl, she not only went mad, she was drowned. Only witches can make people drown. Water itself can't hurt anything. It is merely something one drinks and bathes in."

I began to get cross. "If you don't like the story, I'll stop." 74

The old man made soothing noises and himself poured me some more 75 beer. "You tell the story well, and we are listening. But it is clear that the elders of your country have never told you what the story really means. No, don't interrupt! We believe you when you say your marriage customs are different, or your clothes and weapons. But people are the same everywhere; therefore, there are always witches and it is we, the elders, who know how witches work. We told you it was the great chief who wished to kill Hamlet, and now your own words have proved us right. Who were Ophelia's male relatives?"

"There were only her father and her brother." Hamlet was clearly out 76 of my hands.

"There must have been many more; this also you must ask of your eld- 77 ers when you get back to your country. From what you tell us, since Polonius was dead, it must have been Laertes who killed Ophelia, although I do not see the reason for it."

We had emptied one pot of beer, and the old men argued the point 78 with slightly tipsy interest. Finally one of them demanded of me, "What did the servant of Polonius say on his return?"

With difficulty I recollected Reynaldo and his mission. "I don't think he 79 did return before Polonius was killed."

"Listen," said the elder, "and I will tell you how it was and how your 80 story will go, then you may tell me if I am right. Polonius knew his son would get into trouble, and so he did. He had many fines to pay for fighting, and debts from gambling. But he had only two ways of getting money quickly. One was to marry off his sister at once, but it is difficult to find a man who will marry a woman desired by the son of a chief. For if the chief's heir commits adultery with your wife, what can you do? Only a fool calls a case against a man who will someday be his judge. Therefore Laertes had to take the second way: he killed his sister by witchcraft, drowning her so he could secretly sell her body to the witches."

I raised an objection. "They found her body and buried it. Indeed 81 Laertes jumped into the grave to see his sister once more—so, you see, the body was truly there. Hamlet, who had just come back, jumped in after him."

"What did I tell you?" The elder appealed to the others. "Laertes was 82 up to no good with his sister's body. Hamlet prevented him, because the chief's heir, like a chief, does not wish any other man to grow rich and powerful. Laertes would be angry, because he would have killed his sister without benefit to himself. In our country he would try to kill Hamlet for that reason. Is this not what happened?"

"More or less," I admitted. "When the great chief found Hamlet was 83 still alive, he encouraged Laertes to try to kill Hamlet and arranged a fight with machetes between them. In the fight both the young men were wounded to death. Hamlet's mother drank the poisoned beer that the chief meant for Hamlet in case he won the fight. When he saw his mother die of poison, Hamlet, dying, managed to kill his father's brother with his machete."

"You see, I was right!" exclaimed the elder. 84

"That was a very good story," added the old man, "and you told it with 85 very few mistakes. There was just one more error, at the very end. The poison Hamlet's mother drank was obviously meant for the survivor of the fight, whichever it was. If Laertes had won, the great chief would have poisoned him, for no one would know that he arranged Hamlet's death. Then, too, he need not fear Laertes' witchcraft; it takes a strong heart to kill one's only sister by witchcraft.

"Sometime," concluded the old man, gathering his ragged toga about 86 him, "you must tell us some more stories of your country. We, who are elders, will instruct you in their true meaning, so that when you return to your own land your elders will see that you have not been sitting in the bush, but among those who know things and who have taught you wisdom."

QUESTIONS

Words to Know

meditation (paragraph 2), homesteads (4), calabash (7), gourd (7), bride price (9), no avail (9), intelligible (11), omen (15), genealogical (22), motif (23), retorted (25), soliloquy (26), fobbing off (31), fratricide (32), quelled (43), babble (43), dubious (50), cunning (57), hedged (58), unhousell'd (66), unaneled (66), toga (86).

Some of the Issues

1. What is the significance of the discussion about "papers" in paragraphs 8 and 9? How does it foretell that the Tivs' interpretation of *Hamlet* may differ from Bohannan's (and ours)?
2. In a number of instances, Bohannan shows that she is knowledgeable about the social customs of the Tiv and is trying to conform to them. Give some specific instances.
3. In paragraphs 23 through 31 two differences between the Tiv and the West are made clear: they relate to the period of mourning for the dead and to the number of wives a chief may have. In what way does the Tivs' view on these matters differ from Western views? Does their view have any advantages for their culture?
4. The Tiv elders are shocked—morally upset—at several parts of the story of *Hamlet*. What specific instances can you cite? Do their moral perceptions differ from ours in those instances?
5. Bohannan makes several efforts to make *Hamlet* more intelligible or acceptable to the Tiv. What are some of these? Does she succeed?
6. Both Bohannan (paragraph 2) and the chief (paragraph 75) say that human nature is much the same everywhere. What evidence do you find in the essay to support or contradict these assertions?

The Way We Are Told

7. Bohannan does not begin the story of her trip to Africa until the third paragraph. How are the first two paragraphs used to set the theme?
8. What does the use of dialog contribute to the telling of the story?

Some Subjects for Essays

9. Bohannan does her best to adapt the story of *Hamlet* to the experiences, customs, and feelings of the Tiv. Have you ever had the experience of having to adapt yourself in some way to a situation in which the rules and assumptions differed greatly from your own? Tell the story.
10. Practice writing short, accurate summaries of stories, plays, movies, or television shows you know.

THE VILLAGE OF BEN SUC

Jonathan Schell

Jonathan Schell is the author of *The Fate of the Earth* (1982), an analysis of the dangers and possible effects of atomic warfare. A frequent contributor to *The New Yorker*, he is also the author of *The Military Half* (1967), *The Time of Illusion* (1976), and the *The Village of Ben Suc* (1967), from which the following selection is taken.

The men got up at five-thirty in the morning and were guided in the dark to a mess tent in a different part of the rubber grove, where they had a breakfast of grapefruit juice, hot cereal, scrambled eggs, bacon, toast, and coffee. At about six-thirty, the sky began to grow light, and they were led back to the airstrip. Strings of nine and ten helicopters with tapered bodies could be seen through the treetops, filing across the gray early-morning sky like little schools of minnows. In the distance, the slow beat of their engines sounded soft and almost peaceful, but when they rushed past overhead the noise was fearful and deafening. By seven o'clock, sixty helicopters were perched in formation on the airstrip, with seven men assembled in a silent group beside each one. When I arrived at the helicopter assigned to me— No. 47—three engineers and three infantrymen were already there, five of them standing or kneeling in the dust checking their weapons. One of them, a sergeant, was a small, wiry American Indian, who spoke in short, clipped syllables. The sixth man, a stocky infantryman with blond hair and a red face, who looked to be about twenty and was going into action for the first time, lay back against an earth embankment with his eyes closed, wearing an expression of boredom, as though he wanted to put these wasted minutes of waiting to some good use by catching up on his sleep. Two of the other six men in the team were also going into combat for the first time. The men did not speak to each other.

At seven-fifteen, our group of seven climbed up into its helicopter, a UH-1 (called Huey), and the pilot, a man with a German accent, told us that four of us should sit on the seat and three on the floor in front, to balance the craft. He also warned us that the flight might be rough, since we would be flying in the turbulent wake of the helicopter in front of us. At seven-twenty, the engines of the sixty helicopters started simultaneously, with a thunderous roar and a storm of dust. After idling his engine for three minutes on the airstrip, our pilot raised his right hand in the air, forming a circle with the forefinger and thumb, to show that he hoped everything would proceed perfectly from then on. The helicopter rose slowly from the airstrip right after the helicopter in front of it had risen. The pilot's gesture was the only indication that the seven men were on their way to something more than a nine-o'clock job. Rising, one after another, in two parallel lines of thirty, the fleet of sixty helicopters circled the base twice, gaining altitude and tightening their formation as they did so, until each machine was not more than twenty yards from the one immediately in front of it. Then the fleet, straightening out the two lines, headed south, toward Ben Suc.

In Helicopter No. 47, one of the men shouted a joke, which only one other man could hear, and they both laughed. The soldier who had earlier been trying to catch a nap on the runway wanted to get a picture of the sixty helicopters with a Minolta camera he had hanging from a strap around his neck. He was sitting on the floor, facing backward, so he asked one of the men on the seat to try to get a couple of shots. "There are sixty choppers here," he shouted, "and every one of them costs a quarter of a million bucks!" The Huey flies with its doors open, so the men who sat on the outside seats were perched right next to the drop. They held tightly to ceiling straps as the helicopter rolled and pitched through the sky like a ship plunging through a heavy sea. Wind from the rotors and from the forward motion blasted into the men's faces, making them squint. At five minutes to eight, the two lines of the fleet suddenly dived, bobbing and swaying from the cruising altitude of twenty-five hundred feet down to treetop level, at a point about seven miles from Ben Suc but heading away from it, to confuse enemy observers on the ground. Once at an altitude of fifty or sixty feet, the fleet made a wide U turn and headed directly for Ben Suc at a hundred miles an hour, the helicopters' tails raised slightly in forward flight. Below, the faces of scattered peasants were clearly visible as they looked up from their water buffalo at the sudden, earsplitting incursion of sixty helicopters charging low over their fields.

All at once, Helicopter No. 47 landed, and from both sides of it the men jumped out on the run into a freshly turned vegetable plot in the village of Ben Suc—the first Vietnamese village that several of them had ever set foot in. The helicopter took off immediately, and another settled in its place. Keeping low, the men I was with ran single file out into the center of the little plot, and then, spotting a low wall of bushes on the side of the plot they had just left, ran back there for cover and filed along the edges of the bushes toward several soldiers who had landed a little while before them. For a minute, there was silence. Suddenly a single helicopter came clattering overhead at about a hundred and fifty feet, squawking Vietnamese from two stubby speakers that stuck out, winglike, from the thinnest part of the fuselage, near the tail. The message, which the American soldiers could not understand, went, "Attention, people of Ben Suc! You are surrounded by Republic of South Vietnam and Allied Forces. Do not run away or you will be shot as V.C. Stay in your homes and wait for further instructions." The metallic voice, floating down over the fields, huts, and trees, was as calm as if it were announcing a flight departure at an air terminal. It was gone in ten seconds, and the soldiers again moved on in silence. Within two minutes, the young men from No. 47 reached a little dirt road marking the village perimeter, which they were to hold, but there were no people in sight except American soldiers. The young men lay down on the sides of embankments and in little hollows in the small area it had fallen to them to control. There was no sign of an enemy.

For the next hour and a half, the six men from No. 47 were to be the   5
masters of a small stretch of vegetable fields which was divided down the center by about fifty yards of narrow dirt road—almost a path—and bounded on the front and two sides (as they faced the road and, beyond it, the center of the village) by several small houses behind copses of low palm trees and hedges and in back by a small graveyard giving onto a larger cultivated field. The vegetable fields, most of them not more than fifty feet square and of irregular shape, were separated by neatly constructed grass covered ridges, each with a path running along its top. The houses were small and trim, most of them with one side open to the weather but protected from the rain by the deep eaves of a thatch-grass roof. The houses were usually set apart by hedges and low trees, so that one house was only half visible from another and difficult to see from the road; they were not unlike a wealthy American suburb in the logic of their layout. An orderly small yard, containing low-walled coops for chickens and a shed with stalls for cows, adjoined each house. Here and there, between the fields and in the copses, stood the whitewashed waist-high columns and brick walls of Vietnamese tombs, which look like small models of the ruins of once-splendid palaces. It was a tidy, delicately wrought small-scale landscape with short views—not overcrowded but with every square foot of land carefully attended to.

Four minutes after the landing, the heavy crackle of several automatic   6
weapons firing issued from a point out of sight, perhaps five hundred yards away. The men, who had been sitting or kneeling, went down on their bellies, their eyes trained on the confusion of hedges, trees, and houses ahead. A report that Mike Company had made light contact came over their field radio. At about eight-ten, the shock of tremendous explosions shattered the air and rocked the ground. The men hit the dirt again. Artillery shells crashed somewhere in the woods, and rockets from helicopters thumped into the ground. When a jet came screaming low overhead, one of the men shouted, "They're bringing in air strikes!" Heavy percussions shook the

ground under the men, who were now lying flat, and shock waves beat against their faces. Helicopter patrols began to wheel low over the treetops outside the perimeter defended by the infantry, spraying the landscape with long bursts of machine-gun fire. After about five minutes, the explosions became less frequent, and the men from the helicopters, realizing that this was the planned bombing and shelling of the northern woods, picked themselves up, and two of them, joined by three soldiers from another helicopter, set about exploring their area.

Three or four soldiers began to search the houses behind a nearby copse.   7
Stepping through the doorway of one house with his rifle in firing position at his hip, a solidly built six-foot-two Negro private came upon a young woman standing with a baby in one arm and a little girl of three or four holding her other hand. The woman was barefoot and was dressed in a white shirt and rolled-up black trousers; a bandanna held her long hair in a coil at the back of her head. She and her children intently watched each of the soldier's movements. In English, he asked, "Where's your husband?" Without taking her eyes off the soldier, the woman said something in Vietnamese, in an explanatory tone. The soldier looked around the inside of the one-room house and, pointing to his rifle, asked, "You have same-same?" The woman shrugged and said something else in Vietnamese. The soldier shook his head and poked his hand into a basket of laundry on a table between him and the woman. She immediately took all the laundry out of the basket and shrugged again, with a hint of impatience, as though to say, "It's just laundry!" The soldier nodded and looked around, appearing unsure of what to do next in this situation. Then, on a peg on one wall, he spotted a pair of men's pants and a shirt hanging up to dry. "Where's *he?*" he asked, pointing to the clothes. The woman spoke in Vietnamese. The soldier took the damp clothing down and, for some reason, carried it outside, where he laid it on the ground.

The house was clean, light, and airy, with doors on two sides and the   8
top half of one whole side opening out onto a grassy yard. On the table, a half-eaten bowl of rice stood next to the laundry basket. A tiny hammock, not more than three feet long, hung in one corner. At one side of the house, a small, separate wooden roof stood over a fireplace with cooking utensils hanging around it. On the window ledge was a row of barley sprouting plants, in little clods of earth wrapped in palm leaves. Inside the room, a kilnlike structure, its walls and top made of mud, logs, and large stones, stood over the family's bedding. At the rear of the house, a square opening in the ground led to an underground bomb shelter large enough for several people to stand in. In the yard, a cow stood inside a third bomb shelter, made of tile walls about a foot thick.

After a minute, the private came back in with a bared machete at his   9
side and a field radio on his back. "Where's your husband, huh?" he asked
again. This time, the woman gave a long answer in a complaining tone, in
which she pointed several times at the sky and several times at her children.
The soldier looked at her blankly. "What do I do with her?" he called to
some fellow-soldiers outside. There was no answer. Turning back to the
young woman, who had not moved since his first entrance, he said, "O.K.,
lady, you stay here," and left the house.

Several other houses were searched, but no other Vietnamese were   10
found, and for twenty minutes the men on that particular stretch of road
encountered no one else, although they heard sporadic machine-gun fire
down the road. The sky, which had been overcast, began to show streaks of
blue, and a light wind stirred the trees. The bombing, the machine-gunning
from helicopters, the shelling, and the rocket firing continued steadily. Suddenly a Vietnamese man on a bicycle appeared, pedalling rapidly along the
road from the direction of the village. He was wearing the collarless, paja-
malike black garment that is both the customary dress of the Vietnamese
peasant and the uniform of the National Liberation Front, and although he
was riding away from the center of the village—a move forbidden by the
voices from the helicopters—he had, it appeared, already run a long gantlet
of American soldiers without being stopped. But when he had ridden about
twenty yards past the point where he first came in sight, there was a burst
of machine-gun fire from a copse thirty yards in front of him, joined immediately by a burst from a vegetable field to one side, and he was hurled off
his bicycle into a ditch a yard from the road. The bicycle crashed into a side
embankment. The man with the Minolta camera, who had done the firing
from the vegetable patch, stood up after about a minute and walked over to
the ditch, followed by one of the engineers. The Vietnamese in the ditch
appeared to be about twenty, and he lay on his side without moving, blood
flowing from his face, which, with the eyes open, was half buried in the dirt
at the bottom of the ditch. The engineer leaned down, felt the man's wrist,
and said, "He's dead." The two men—both companions of mine on No. 47—
stood still for a while, with folded arms, and stared down at the dead man's
face, as though they were giving him a chance to say something. Then the
engineer said, with a tone of finality, "That's a V.C. for you. He's a V.C., all
right. That's what they wear. He was leaving town. He had to have some
reason."

The two men walked back to a ridge in the vegetable field and sat down   11
on it, looking off into the distance in a puzzled way and no longer bothering
to keep low. The man who had fired spoke suddenly, as though coming out
of deep thought. "I saw this guy coming down the road on a bicycle," he

said. "And I thought, you know, Is this it? Do I shoot? Then some guy over there in the bushes opened up, so I cut loose."

The engineer raised his eyes in the manner of someone who has made 12 a strange discovery and said, "I'm not worried. You know, that's the first time I've ever seen a dead guy, and I don't feel bad. I just don't, that's all." Then, with a hard edge of defiance in his voice, he added, "Actually, I'm glad. I'm glad we killed the little V.C."

Over near the copse, the man who had fired first, also a young soldier, 13 had turned his back to the road. Clenching a cigar in his teeth, he stared with determination over his gun barrel across the wide field, where several water buffaloes were grazing but no human beings had yet been seen. Upon being asked what had happened, he said, "Yeah, he's dead. Ah shot him. He was a fuckin' V.C."

QUESTIONS

Words to Know

tapered (paragraph 1), turbulent (2), wake (2), choppers (3), perched (3), pitched (3), incursion (3), copses (5), perimeter (6), explanatory tone (7), machete (9), sporadic (10), National Liberation Front (10), gantlet (10).

Some of the Issues

1. We learn very little about the soldiers who fly Huey No. 47. How would the story change if we knew more about them as individuals?
2. Numbers play a considerable role in the first two paragraphs. Why?
3. Paragraph 8 seems to interrupt the episode that is taking place in 7 and 9. What is its contribution to that episode?
4. What is the evidence that leads the soldiers to decide that the bicyclist was a V.C.?
5. Read George Orwell's "Shooting an Elephant". In it the narrator is under the same kind of pressure to take action as the soldier with the Minolta. Do you see any differences in their situations?

The Way We Are Told

6. Consider the details Schell singles out in the first three paragraphs: the anonymity of the soldiers as contrasted to the references to specific numbers, times, or to the Minolta camera. Why does Schell not record the names of any of the soldiers?

7. Why does Schell single out the fact that No. 47 lands in "a freshly turned vegetable plot" (paragraph 4) and describe the six men as "masters of a small stretch of vegetable fields" (paragraph 5)?

8. In paragraph 5 Schell describes the village. Where does he place his emphasis through his selection of details, and what effect does the description achieve? Contrast it particularly with what we are told in paragraph 6.

9. In paragraphs 7 through 9 (the encounter between the soldiers and the woman), what would you say are the dangers in the kind of communication that is taking place? How does this episode prepare for the events in paragraphs 10 through 12?

10. Does the way in which Schell describes the whole raid change in paragraphs 10 through 12? If so, in what way?

11. Is Schell giving an objective, factual rendering of the events he witnessed, or not? Support your conclusion.

Some Subjects for Essays

12. Write an essay in which you examine in detail Schell's view of what war is like. Use the details of the selection as evidence.

13. Write an account of a specific event, using sensory detail of different kinds to make the reader "feel" the event as much as possible. Like Schell in this selection, avoid direct judgment and do not include yourself in the story.

STRANGER IN THE VILLAGE

James Baldwin

James Baldwin (1924–), is one of America's most distinguished writers, is the author of novels, plays, and volumes of essays. These include *Go Tell It on the Mountain* (1953), *Notes of a Native Son* (1955), *Nobody Knows My Name* (1960), *The Fire Next Time* (1963), *Blues for Mister Charlie* (1964), *One Day When I Was Lost* (1973), and *Just Above My Head* (1979). The essay included here is taken from *Notes of a Native Son*.

From all available evidence no black man had ever set foot in this tiny Swiss village before I came. I was told before arriving that I would probably be a "sight" for the village; I took this to mean that people of my complexion were rarely seen in Switzerland, and also that city people are always something of a "sight" outside of the city. It did not occur to me—possibly because I am an American—that there could be people anywhere who had never seen a Negro.

It is a fact that cannot be explained on the basis of the inaccessibility of the village. The village is very high, but it is only four hours from Milan and three hours from Lausanne. It is true that it is virtually unknown. Few people making plans for a holiday would elect to come here. On the other hand, the villagers are able, presumably, to come and go as they please—which they do: to another town at the foot of the mountain, with a population of approximately five thousand, the nearest place to see a movie or go to the bank. In the village there is no movie house, no bank, no library, no theater; very few radios, one jeep, one station wagon; and, at the moment, one typewriter, mine, an invention which the woman next door to me here had never seen. There are about six hundred people living here, all Catholic—I conclude this from the fact that the Catholic church is open all year round, whereas the Protestant chapel, set off on a hill a little removed from the village, is open only in the summertime when the tourists arrive. There are four or five hotels, all closed now, and four or five *bistros*, of which, however, only two do any business during the winter. These two do not do a great deal, for life in the village seems to end around nine or ten o'clock. There are a few stores, butcher, baker, *épicerie*, a hardware store, and a money-changer—who cannot change travelers' checks, but must send them down to the bank, an operation which takes two or three days. There is something called the *Ballet Haus*, closed in the winter and used for God knows what, certainly not ballet, during the summer. There seems to be only one schoolhouse in the village, and this for the quite young children; I suppose this to mean that their older brothers and sisters at some point descend from these mountains in order to complete their education—possibly, again, to the town just below. The landscape is absolutely forbidding, mountains towering on all four sides, ice and snow as far as the eye can reach. In this white wilderness, men and women and children move all day, carrying washing, wood, buckets of milk or water, sometimes skiing on Sunday afternoons. All week long boys and young men are to be seen shoveling snow off the rooftops, or dragging wood down from the forest in sleds.

   The village's only real attraction, which explains the tourist season, is   3
the hot spring water. A disquietingly high proportion of these tourists are cripples, or semicripples, who come year after year—from other parts of Switzerland, usually—to take the waters. This lends the village, at the height of the season, a rather terrifying air of sanctity, as though it were a lesser Lourdes. There is often something beautiful, there is always something awful, in the spectable of a person who has lost one of his faculties, a faculty he never questioned until it was gone, and who struggles to recover it. Yet people remain people, on crutches or indeed on deathbeds; and wherever I passed, the first summer I was here, among the native villagers or among the lame, a wind passed with me—of astonishment, curiosity, amusement, and outrage. That first summer I stayed two weeks and never intended to return. But I did return in the winter, to work; the village offers, obviously, no distractions whatever and has the further advantage of being extremely cheap. Now it is winter again, a year later, and I am here again. Everyone in the village knows my name, though they scarcely ever use it, knows that I come from America—though, this, apparently, they will never really believe: black men come from Africa—and everyone knows that I am the friend of the son of a woman who was born here, and that I am staying in their chalet. But I remain as much a stranger today as I was the first day I arrived, and the children shout *Neger! Neger!* as I walk along the streets.

   It must be admitted that in the beginning I was far too shocked to have   4
any real reaction. In so far as I reacted at all, I reacted by trying to be pleasant—it being a great part of the American Negro's education (long before he goes to school) that he must make people "like" him. This smile-and-the-world-smiles-with-you routine worked about as well in this situation as it had in the situation for which it was designed, which is to say that it did not work at all. No one, after all, can be liked whose human weight and complexity cannot be, or has not been, admitted. My smile was simply another unheard-of phenomenon which allowed them to see my teeth—they did not, really,

see my smile and I began to think that, should I take to snarling, no one would notice any difference. All of the physical characteristics of the Negro which had caused me, in America, a very different and almost forgotten pain were nothing less than miraculous—or infernal—in the eyes of the village people. Some thought my hair was the color of tar, that it had the texture of wire, or the texture of cotton. It was jocularly suggested that I might let it all grow long and make myself a winter coat. If I sat in the sun for more than five minutes some daring creature was certain to come along and gingerly put his fingers on my hair, as though he were afraid of an electric shock, or put his hand on my hand, astonished that the color did not rub off. In all of this, in which it must be conceded there was the charm of genuine wonder and in which there was certainly no element of intentional unkindness, there was yet no suggestion that I was human: I was simple a living wonder.

I knew that they did not mean to be unkind, and I know it now; it is necessary, nevertheless, for me to repeat this to myself each time that I walk out of the chalet. The children who shout *Neger!* have no way of knowing the echoes this sound raises in me. They are brimming with good humor and the more daring swell with pride when I stop to speak with them. Just the same, there are days when I cannot pause and smile, when I have no heart to play with them; when, indeed, I mutter sourly to myself, exactly as I muttered on the streets of a city these children have never seen, when I was no bigger than these children are now: *Your* mother *was a nigger.* Joyce is right about history being a nightmare—but it may be the nightmare from which no one *can* awaken. People are trapped in history and history is trapped in them. 5

There is a custom in the village—I am told it is repeated in many villages—of "buying" African natives for the purpose of converting them to Christianity. There stands in the church all year round a small box with a slot for money, decorated with a black figurine, and into this box the villagers drop their francs. During the *carnaval* which precedes Lent, two village children have their faces blackened—out of which bloodless darkness their blue eyes shine like ice—and fantastic horsehair wigs are placed on their blond heads; thus disguised, they solicit among the villagers for money for the missionaries in Africa. Between the box in the church and the blackened children, the village "bought" last year six or eight African natives. This was reported to me with pride by the wife of one of the *bistro* owners and I was careful to express astonishment and pleasure at the solicitude shown by the village for the souls of black folk. The *bistro* owner's wife beamed with a pleasure far more genuine than my own and seemed to feel that I might now breathe more easily concerning the souls of at least six of my kinsmen. 6

I tried not to think of these so lately baptized kinsmen, of the price paid 7 for them, or the peculiar price they themselves would pay, and said nothing about my father, who having taken his own conversion too literally never, at bottom, forgave the white world (which he described as heathen) for having saddled him with a Christ in whom, to judge at least from their treatment of him, they themselves no longer believed. I thought of white men arriving for the first time in an African village, strangers there, as I am a stranger here, and tried to imagine the astounded populace touching their hair and marveling at the color of their skin. But there is a great difference between being the first white man to be seen by Africans and being the first black man to be seen by whites. The white man takes the astonishment as tribute, for he arrives to conquer and to convert the natives, whose inferiority in relation to himself is not even to be questioned; whereas I, without a thought of conquest, find myself among a people whose culture controls me, has even, in a sense, created me, people who have cost me more in anguish and rage than they will ever know, who yet do not even know of my existence. The astonishment with which I might have greeted them, should they have stumbled into my African village a few hundred years ago, might have rejoiced their hearts. But the astonishment with which they greet me today can only poison mine.

And this is so despite everything I may do to feel differently, despite   8
my friendly conversations with the *bistro* owner's wife, despite their three-year-old son who has at last become my friend, despite the *saluts* and *bonsoirs* which I exchange with people as I walk, despite the fact that I know that no individual can be taken to task for what history is doing, or has done. I say that the culture of these people controls me—but they can scarcely be held responsible for European culture. America comes out of Europe, but these people have never seen America, nor have most of them seen more of Europe than the hamlet at the foot of their mountain. Yet they move with an authority which I shall never have; and they regard me, quite rightly, not only as a stranger in their village but as a suspect latecomer, bearing no credentials, to everything they have—however unconsciously—inherited.

For this village, even were it incomparably more remote and incredibly   9
more primitive, is the West, the West onto which I have been so strangely grafted. These people cannot be, from the point of view of power, strangers anywhere in the world; they have made the modern world, in effect, even if they do not know it. The most illiterate among them is related, in a way that I am not, to Dante, Shakespeare, Michelangelo, Aeschylus, Da Vinci, Rembrandt, and Racine; the cathedral at Chartres says something to them which it cannot say to me, as indeed would New York's Empire State Building, should anyone here ever see it. Out of their hymns and dances come Beethoven and Bach. Go back a few centuries and they are in their full glory—but I am in Africa, watching the conquerors arrive.

The rage of the disesteemed is personally fruitless, but it is also abso- ¹⁰
lutely inevitable; this rage, so generally discounted, so little understood even
among the people whose daily bread it is, is one of the things that makes
history. Rage can only with difficulty, and never entirely, be brought under
the domination of the intelligence and is therefore not susceptible to any
arguments whatever. This is a fact which ordinary representatives of the
Herrenvolk, having never felt this rage and being unable to imagine it, quite
fail to understand. Also, rage cannot be hidden, it can only be dissembled.
This dissembling deludes the thoughtless, and strengthens rage and adds, to
rage, contempt. There are, no doubt, as many ways of coping with the resulting complex of tensions as there are black men in the world, but no black
man can hope ever to be entirely liberated from this internal warfare—rage,
dissembling, and comtempt having inevitably accompanied his first realization of the power of white men. What is crucial here is that, since white men
represent in the black man's world so heavy a weight, white men have for
black men a reality which is far from being reciprocal; and hence all black
men have toward all white men an attitude which is designed, really, either
to rob the white man of the jewel of his naïveté, or else to make it cost him
dear.

The black man insists, by whatever means he finds at his disposal, that ¹¹
the white man cease to regard him as an exotic rarity and recognize him as
a human being. This is a very charged and difficult moment, for there is a
great deal of will power involved in the white man's naïveté. Most people
are not naturally reflective any more than they are naturally malicious, and
the white man prefers to keep the black man at a certain human remove
because it is easier for him thus to preserve his simplicity and avoid being
called to account for crimes committed by his forefathers, or his neighbors.
He is inescapably aware, nevertheless, that he is in a better position in the
world than black men are, nor can he quite put to death the suspicion that
he is hated by black men therefore. He does not wish to be hated, neither
does he wish to change places, and at this point in his uneasiness he can
scarcely avoid having recourse to those legends which white men have created about black men, the most usual effect of which is that the white man
finds himself enmeshed, so to speak, in his own language which describes
hell, as well as the attributes which lead one to hell, as being as black as night.

Every legend, moreover, contains its residuum of truth, and the root ¹²
function of language is to control the universe by describing it. It is of quite
considerable significance that black men remain, in the imagination, and in
overwhelming numbers in fact, beyond the disciplines of salvation; and this
despite the fact that the West has been "buying" African natives for centuries. There is, I should hazard, an instantaneous necessity to be divorced from
this so visibly unsaved stranger, in whose heart, moreover, one cannot guess

what dreams of vengeance are being nourished; and, at the same time, there are few things on earth more attractive than the idea of the unspeakable liberty which is allowed the unredeemed. When, beneath the black mask, a human being begins to make himself felt one cannot escape a certain awful wonder as to what kind of human being it is. What one's imagination makes of other people is dictated, of course, by the laws of one's own personality and it is one of the ironies of black-white relations that, by means of what the white man imagines the black man to be, the black man is enabled to know who the white man is.

I have said, for example, that I am as much a stranger in this village 13 today as I was the first summer I arrived, but this is not quite true. The villagers wonder less about the texture of my hair than they did then, and wonder rather more about me. And the fact that their wonder now exists on another level is reflected in their attitudes and in their eyes. There are the children who make those delightful, hilarious, sometimes astonishingly grave overtures of friendship in the unpredictable fashion of children; other children, having been taught that the devil is a black man, scream in genuine anguish as I approach. Some of the older women never pass without a friendly greeting, never pass, indeed, if it seems that they will be able to engage me in conversation; other women look down or look away or rather contemptuously smirk. Some of the men drink with me and suggest that I learn how to ski—partly, I gather, because they cannot imagine what I would look like on skis—and want to know if I am married, and ask questions about my *métier*. But some of the men have accused *le sale nègre*— behind my back—of stealing wood and there is already in the eyes of some of them that peculiar, intent, paranoiac malevolence which one sometimes surprises in the eyes of American white men when, out walking with their Sunday girl, they see a Negro male approach.

There is a dreadful abyss between the streets of this village and the 14 streets of the city in which I was born, between the children who shout *Neger!* today and those who shouted *Nigger!* yesterday—the abyss is experience, the American experience. The syllable hurled behind me today expresses, above all, wonder: I am a stranger here. But I am not a stranger in America and the same syllable riding on the American air expresses the war my presence has occasioned in the American soul.

For this village brings home to me this fact: that there was a day, and 15 not really a very distant day, when Americans were scarcely Americans at all but discontented Europeans, facing a great unconquered continent and strolling, say, into a marketplace and seeing black men for the first time. The shock this spectacle afforded is suggested, surely, by the promptness with which they decided that these black men were not really men but cattle. It is true that the necessity on the part of the settlers of the New World of reconciling their moral assumptions with the fact—and the necessity—of slavery enhanced immensely the charm of this idea, and it is also true that this idea expresses, with a truly American bluntness, the attitude which to varying extents all masters have had toward all slaves.

But between all former slaves and slave-owners and the drama which 16 begins for Americans over three hundred years ago at Jamestown, there are at least two differences to be observed. The American Negro slave could not suppose, for one thing, as slaves in past epochs had supposed and often done, that he would ever be able to wrest the power from his master's hands. This was a supposition which the modern era, which was to bring about such vast changes in the aims and dimensions of power, put to death; it only begins, in unprecedented fashion, and with dreadful implications, to be resurrected today. But even had this supposition persisted with undiminished force, the American Negro slave could not have used it to lend his condition dignity, for the reason that this supposition rests on another: that the slave in exile yet remains related to his past, has some means—if only in memory—of revering and sustaining the forms of his former life, is able, in short, to maintain his identity.

This was not the case with the American Negro slave. He is unique 17 among the black men of the world in that his past was taken from him, almost literally, at one blow. One wonders what on earth the first slave found to say to the first dark child he bore. I am told that there are Haitians able to trace their ancestry back to African kings, but any American Negro wishing to go back so far will find his journey through time abruptly arrested by the signature on the bill of sale which served as the entrance paper for his ancestor. At the time—to say nothing of the circumstances—of the enslavement of the captive black man who was to become the American Negro, there was not the remotest possibility that he would ever take power from his master's hands. There was no reason to suppose that his situation would ever change, nor was there, shortly, anything to indicate that his situation had ever been different. It was his necessity, in the words of E. Franklin Frazier, to find a "motive for living under American culture or die." The identity of the American Negro comes out of this extreme situation, and the evolution of this identity was a source of the most intolerable anxiety in the minds and the lives of his masters.

For the history of the American Negro is unique also in this: that the 18 question of his humanity, and of his rights therefore as a human being, became a burning one for several generations of Americans, so burning a question that it ultimately became one of those used to divide the nation. It is out of this argument that the venom of the epithet *Nigger!* is derived. It is an argument which Europe has never had, and hence Europe quite sincerely fails to understand how or why the argument arose in the first place, why its effects are so frequently disastrous and always so unpredictable, why it refuses until today to be entirely settled. Europe's black possessions remained—and do remain—in Europe's colonies, at which remove they represented no threat whatever to European identity. If they posed any problem at all for the European conscience, it was a problem which remained comfortingly abstract: in effect, the black man, *as a man*, did not exist for Europe. But in America, even as a slave, he was an inescapable part of the general social fabric and no American could escape having an attitude toward him. Americans attempt until today to make an abstraction of the Negro, but the very nature of these abstractions reveals the tremendous effects the presence of the Negro has had on the American character.

When one considers the history of the Negro in America, it is of the greatest importance to recognize that the moral beliefs of a person, or a people, are never really as tenuous as life—which is not moral—very often causes them to appear; these create for them a frame of reference and a necessary hope, the hope being that when life has done its worst they will be enabled to rise above themselves and to triumph over life. Life would scarcely be bearable if this hope did not exist. Again, even when the worst has been said, to betray a belief is not by any means to have put oneself beyond its power; the betrayal of a belief is not the same thing as ceasing to believe. If this were not so there would be no moral standards in the world at all. Yet one must also recognize that morality is based on ideas and that all ideas are dangerous—dangerous because ideas can only lead to action and where the action leads no man can say. And dangerous in this respect: that confronted with the impossibility of remaining faithful to one's beliefs, and the equal impossibility of becoming free of them, one can be driven to the most inhuman excesses. The ideas on which American beliefs are based are not, though Americans often seem to think so, ideas which originated in America. They came out of Europe. And the establishment of democracy on the American continent was scarcely as radical a break with the past as was the necessity, which Americans faced, of broadening this concept to include black men. [19]

This was, literally, a hard necessity. It was impossible, for one thing, for Americans to abandon their beliefs, not only because these beliefs alone seemed able to justify the sacrifices they had endured and the blood that they had spilled, but also because these beliefs afforded them their only bulwark against a moral chaos as absolute as the physical chaos of the continent it was their destiny to conquer. But in the situation in which Americans found themselves, these beliefs threatened an idea which, whether or not one likes to think so, is the very warp and woof of the heritage of the West, the idea of white supremacy. [20]

Americans have made themselves notorious by the shrillness and the   21
brutality with which they have insisted on this idea, but they did not invent
it; and it has escaped the world's notice that those very excesses of which
Americans have been guilty imply a certain, unprecedented uneasiness over
the idea's life and power, if not, indeed, the idea's validity. The idea of white
supremacy rests simply on the fact that white men are the creators of civilization (the present civilization, which is the only one that matters; all previous civilizations are simply "contributions" to our own) and are therefore
civilization's guardians and defenders. Thus it was impossible for Americans
to accept the black man as one of themselves, for to do so was to jeopardize
their status as white men. But not so to accept him was to deny his human
reality, his human weight and complexity, and the strain of denying the
overwhelmingly undeniable forced Americans into rationalizations so fantastic that they approached the pathological.

At the root of the American Negro problem is the necessity of the Amer-   22
ican white man to find a way of living with the Negro in order to be able to
live with himself. And the history of this problem can be reduced to the
means used by Americans—lynch law and law, segregation and legal acceptance, terrorization and concession—either to come to terms with this necessity, or to find a way around it, or (most usually) to find a way of doing both
these things at once. The resulting spectacle, at once foolish and dreadful,
led someone to make the quite accurate observation that "the Negro-in-
America is a form of insanity which overtakes white men."

In this long battle, a battle by no means finished, the unforeseeable   23
effects of which will be felt by many future generations, the white man's
motive was the protection of his identity; the black man was motivated by
the need to establish an identity. And despite the terrorization which the
Negro in America endured and endures sporadically until today, despite the
cruel and totally inescapable ambivalence of his status in his country, the
battle for his identity has long ago been won. He is not a visitor to the West,
but a citizen there, an American; as American as the Americans who despise
him, the Americans who fear him, the Americans who love him—the Americans who became less than themselves, or rose to be greater than themselves
by virtue of the fact that the challenge he represented was inescapable. He
is perhaps the only black man in the world whose relationship to white men
is more terrible, more subtle, and more meaningful than the relationship of
bitter possessed to uncertain possessor. His survival depended, and his development depends, on his ability to turn his peculiar status in the Western
world to his own advantage and, it may be, to the very great advantage of
that world. It remains for him to fashion out of his experience that which
will give him sustenance, and a voice.

The cathedral at Chartres, I have said, says something to the people of   24
this village which it cannot say to me; but it is important to understand that
this cathedral says something to me which it cannot say to them. Perhaps
they are struck by the power of the spires, the glory of the windows; but they
have known God, after all, longer than I have known him, and in a different
way, and I am terrified by the slippery bottomless well to be found in the
crypt, down which heretics were hurled to death, and by the obscene, inescapable gargoyles jutting out of the stone and seeming to say that God and
the devil can never be divorced. I doubt that the villagers think of the devil
when they face a cathedral because they have never been identified with the
devil. But I must accept the status which myth, if nothing else, gives me in
the West before I can hope to change the myth.

Yet, if the American Negro has arrived at his identity by virtue of the   25
absoluteness of his estrangement from his past, American white men still
nourish the illusion that there is some means of recovering the European
innocence, of returning to a state in which black men do not exist. This is
one of the greatest errors Americans can make. The identity they fought so
hard to protect has, by virtue of that battle, undergone a change: Americans
are as unlike any other white people in the world as it is possible to be. I do
not think, for example, that it is too much to suggest that the American vision
of the world—which allows so little reality, generally speaking, for any of
the darker forces in human life, which tends until today to paint moral issues
in glaring black and white—owes a great deal to the battle waged by Americans to maintain between themselves and black men a human separation
which could not be bridged. It is only now beginning to be borne in on us—
very faintly, it must be admitted, very slowly, and very much against our
will—that this vision of the world is dangerously inaccurate, and perfectly
useless. For it protects our moral high-mindedness at the terrible expense of
weakening our grasp of reality. People who shut their eyes to reality simply
invite their own destruction, and anyone who insists on remaining in a state
of innocence long after that innocence is dead turns himself into a monster.

The time has come to realize that the interracial drama acted out on   26
the American continent has not only created a new black man, it has created
a new white man, too. No road whatever will lead Americans back to the
simplicity of this European village where white men still have the luxury of
looking on me as a stranger. I am not, really, a stranger any longer for any
American alive. One of the things that distinguishes Americans from other
people is that no other people has ever been so deeply involved in the lives
of black men, and vice versa. This fact faced, with all its implications, it can
be seen that the history of the American Negro problem is not merely shameful, it is also something of an achievement. For even when the worst has been
said, it must also be added that the perpetual challenge posed by this prob-

lem was always, somehow, perpetually met. It is precisely this black-white experience which may prove of indispensable value to us in the world we face today. This world is white no longer, and it will never be white again.

QUESTIONS

Words to Know

bistros—bar-restaurants (paragraph 2), *épicerie*—grocery store (2), forbidding (2), Lourdes (3), faculties (3), infernal (4), jocularly (4), gingerly (4), heathen (7), saddled (7), *saluts*—hellos (8), *bonsoirs*—good evenings (8), remote (9), grafted (9), Chartres (9), disesteemed (10), *Herrenvolk*—master race (10), dissembled (10), reciprocal (10), naïveté (10), exotic (11), malicious (11), remove (11), residuum (12), smirk (13), *métier*—profession (13), *le sale nègre*—the dirty nigger (13), paranoiac (13), malevolence (13), abyss (14), supposition (16), venom (18), epithet (18), tenuous (19), crypt (24), gargoyles (24).

Some of the Issues

1. In paragraphs 2 and 3 Baldwin describes the village and its permanent inhabitants. In what ways are they isolated? In what ways are they not?
2. In the second paragraph Baldwin says that all the villagers were Catholic and adds, "I conclude this from the fact that the Catholic church is open all year round. . . ." Would there have been any other way of verifying that assumption? Why does Baldwin reach his conclusion in that way? What light does it throw on his relationship with the villagers?
3. In paragraphs 3 and 4 Baldwin for the first time describes the villagers' reaction to him. What is that reaction? Why does it shock him? What is his response to it? How does the villagers' reaction differ from that of (white) Americans?
4. What does Baldwin mean when he says, "People are trapped in history and history is trapped in them" (paragraph 5)?
5. What is meant by, "The villagers cannot be, from the point of view of power, strangers anywhere in the world. . . . The most illiterate among them is related, in a way I am not, to Dante, Shakespeare, Michelangelo, Aeschylus, Da Vinci, Rembrandt, and Racine. . . ." (paragraph 9)?

6. In paragraph 9 Baldwin claims that the Cathedral at Chartres means more to the villagers than to him. Then, in paragraph 24, he claims that the same cathedral says something to him that it cannot say to the villagers. Explain the apparent contradiction.

7. Examine paragraph 12 in detail. Why is it "of quite considerable significance that black men remain . . . beyond the disciplines of salvation," while "at the same time there are few things . . . more attractive than the idea of the unspeakable liberty which is allowed the unredeemed." Try to explain the two ideas that Baldwin develops in this paragraph.

8. At the end of paragraph 13 Baldwin links the reactions of the villagers to those of some Americans. How does he develop that theme in paragraphs 14 and 15? How does he relate the reactions of the villagers to those of slave owners in the New World?

9. In paragraphs 17 and 18 Baldwin describes what, in his view, makes the history of the American Negro unique. What are the major points in his argument?

The Way We Are Told

10. The first sentence of the essay indicates one simple but important point. What would be the effect if that sentence were to read, "Several years ago I decided to spend some months in the house of a friend in a small Swiss village"?

11. In paragraphs 6 and 7 Baldwin moves from a specific instance (the "buying" of African natives for conversion to Christianity) to reflections that transcend the example by far. Can you find other instances in which Baldwin also follows a specific point with a general idea or reflection?

12. Explain how the title of the essay is drawn into its first and last paragraph and how it provides a framework for the whole.

Some Subjects for Essays

13. In paragraph 4 Baldwin says, "No one, after all, can be liked whose human weight and complexity cannot be, or has not been, admitted." In an essay, first explain what Baldwin means by this sentence and then examine its validity by referring to Baldwin's observations and your own experience.

14. Have you ever been a stranger? Describe the experience and reflect on it.

SHOOTING AN ELEPHANT

George Orwell

George Orwell was born in India of English parents in 1903. He was
sent back to England to attend Eton as a scholarship student and hated
it. Afterwards he returned to India as a member of the Imperial police
which he quit after five years. His attitude toward that whole experience forms the background of the story included here.

After India he turned to writing, but with small success, and lived
in great poverty for some time, as described in his first published book,
Down and Out in Paris and London (1933). He fought on the Repub-
lican side in the Spanish Civil War, was wounded, and wrote of his
experience in *Homage to Catalonia* (1938).

Success finally came late in his life, with *Animal Farm* (1945), and
1984, both of which expressed his disillusionment with Communism.
1984 was published in 1949, one year before his death from
tuberculosis.

In Moulmein, in lower Burma, I was hated by large numbers of people—the
only time in my life that I have been important enough for this to happen
to me. I was sub-divisional police officer of the town, and in an aimless, petty
kind of way anti-European feeling was very bitter. No one had the guts to
raise a riot, but if a European woman went through the bazaars alone somebody would probably spit betel juice over her dress. As a police officer I was
an obvious target and was baited whenever it seemed safe to do so. When a
nimble Burman tripped me up on the football field and the referee (another
Burman) looked the other way, the crowd yelled with hideous laughter. This
happened more than once. In the end the sneering yellow faces of young
men that met me everywhere, the insults hooted after me when I was at a
safe distance, got badly on my nerves. The young Buddhist priests were the
worst of all. There were several thousands of them in the town and none of
them seemed to have anything to do except stand on street corners and jeer
at Europeans.

All this was perplexing and upsetting. For at that time I had already
made up my mind that imperialism was an evil thing and the sooner I
chucked up my job and got out of it the better. Theoretically—and secretly,
of course—I was all for the Burmese and all against their oppressors, the
British. As for the job I was doing, I hated it more bitterly than I can perhaps
make clear. In a job like that you see the dirty work of Empire at close
quarters. The wretched prisoners huddling in the stinking cages of the lock-

ups, the grey, cowed faces of the long-term convicts, the scarred buttocks of the men who had been flogged with bamboos—all these oppressed me with an intolerable sense of guilt. But I could get nothing into perspective. I was young and ill-educated and I had had to think out my problems in the utter silence that is imposed on every Englishman in the East. I did not even know that the British Empire is dying, still less did I know that it is a great deal better than the younger empires that are going to supplant it. All I knew was that I was stuck between my hatred of the empire I served and my rage against the evil-spirited little beasts who tried to make my job impossible. With one part of my mind I thought of the British Raj as an unbreakable tyranny, as something clamped down, in *saecula saeculorum*, upon the will of prostrate peoples; with another part I thought that the greatest joy in the world would be to drive a bayonet into a Buddhist priest's guts. Feelings like these are the normal by-products of imperialism; ask any Anglo-Indian official, if you can catch him off duty.

One day something happened which in a roundabout way was enlightening. It was a tiny incident in itself, but it gave me a better glimpse than I had had before of the real nature of imperialism—the real motives for which despotic governments act. Early one morning the sub-inspector at a police station the other end of the town rang me up on the 'phone and said that an elephant was ravaging the bazaar. Would I please come and do something about it? I did not know what I could do, but I wanted to see what was happening and I got on to a pony and started out. I took my rifle, an old .44 Winchester and much too small to kill an elephant, but I thought the noise might be useful *in terrorem*. Various Burmans stopped me on the way and told me about the elephant's doings. It was not, of course, a wild elephant, but a tame one which had gone "must." It had been chained up, as tame elephants always are when their attack of "must" is due, but on the previous night it had broken its chain and escaped. Its mahout, the only person who could manage it when it was in that state, had set out in pursuit, but had taken the wrong direction and was now twelve hours' journey away, and in the morning the elephant had suddenly reappeared in the town. The Burmese population had no weapons and were quite helpless against it. It had already destroyed somebody's bamboo hut, killed a cow and raided some fruit-stalls and devoured the stock; also it had met the municipal rubbish van and, when the driver jumped out and took to his heels, had turned the van over and inflicted violences upon it. 3

The Burmese sub-inspector and some Indian constables were waiting for me in the quarter where the elephant had been seen. It was a very poor quarter, a labyrinth of squalid bamboo huts, thatched with palm-leaf, winding all over a steep hillside. I remember that it was a cloudy, stuffy morning 4 at the beginning of the rains. We began questioning the people as to where the elephant had gone and, as usual, failed to get any definite information. That is invariably the case in the East; a story always sounds clear enough at a distance, but the nearer you get to the scene of events the vaguer it becomes. Some of the people said that the elephant had gone in one direction, some said that he had gone in another, some professed not even to have heard of any elephant. I had almost made up my mind that the whole story was a pack of lies, when we heard yells a little distance away. There was a loud, scandalized cry of "Go away, child! Go away this instant!" and an old woman with a switch in her hand came round the corner of a hut, violently shooing away a crowd of naked children. Some more women followed, clicking their tongues and exclaiming; evidently there was something that the children ought not to have seen. I rounded the hut and saw a man's dead body sprawling in the mud. He was an Indian, a black Dravidian coolie, almost naked, and he could not have been dead many minutes. The people said that the elephant had come suddenly upon him round the corner of the hut, caught him with its trunk, put its foot on his back and ground him into the earth. This was the rainy season and the ground was soft; and his face had scored a trench a foot deep and a couple of yards long. He was lying on his belly with arms crucified and head sharply twisted to one side. His face was coated with mud, the eyes wide open, the teeth bared and grinning with an expression of unendurable agony. (Never tell me, by the way, that the dead look peaceful. Most of the corpses I have seen looked devilish.) The friction of the great beast's foot had stripped the skin from his back as neatly as one skins a rabbit. As soon as I saw the dead man I sent an orderly to a friend's house nearby to borrow an elephant rifle. I had already sent back the pony, not wanting it to go mad with fright and throw me if it smelt the elephant.

The orderly came back in a few minutes with a rifle and five cartridges,   5
and meanwhile some Burmans had arrived and told us that the elephant was in the paddy fields below, only a few hundred yards away. As I started forward practically the whole population of the quarter flocked out of the houses and followed me. They had seen the rifle and were all shouting excitedly that I was going to shoot the elephant. They had not shown much interest in the elephant when he was merely ravaging their homes, but it was different now that he was going to be shot. It was a bit of fun to them, as it would be to an English crowd; besides they wanted the meat. It made me vaguely uneasy. I had no intention of shooting the elephant—I had merely sent for the rifle to defend myself if necessary—and it is always unnerving to have a crowd following you. I marched down the hill, looking and feeling a fool, with the rifle over my shoulder and an ever-growing army of people

jostling at my heels. At the bottom, when you got away from the huts, there was a metalled road and beyond that a miry waste of paddy fields a thousand yards across, not yet ploughed but soggy from the first rains and dotted with coarse grass. The elephant was standing eight yards from the road, his left side towards us. He took not the slightest notice of the crowd's approach. He was tearing up bunches of grass, beating them against his knees to clean them and stuffing them into his mouth.

I had halted on the road. As soon as I saw the elephant I knew with   6
perfect certainty that I ought not to shoot him. It is a serious matter to shoot a working elephant—it is comparable to destroying a huge and costly piece of machinery—and obviously one ought not to do it if it can possibly be avoided. And at that distance, peacefully eating, the elephant looked no more dangerous than a cow. I thought then and I think now that his attack of "must" was already passing off; in which case he would merely wander harmlessly about until the mahout came back and caught him. Moreover, I did not in the least want to shoot him. I decided that I would watch him for a little while to make sure that he did not turn savage again, and then go home.

But at that moment I glanced round at the crowd that had followed me.   7
It was an immense crowd, two thousand at the least and growing every minute. It blocked the road for a long distance on either side. I looked at the sea of yellow faces above the garish clothes—faces all happy and excited over this bit of fun, all certain that the elephant was going to be shot. They were watching me as they would watch a conjurer about to perform a trick. They did not like me, but with the magical rifle in my hands I was momentarily worth watching. And suddenly I realized that I should have to shoot the elephant after all. The people expected it of me and I had got to do it; I could feel their two thousand wills pressing me forward, irresistibly. And it was at this moment, as I stood there with the rifle in my hands, that I first grasped the hollowness, the futility of the white man's dominion in the East. Here was I, the white man with his gun, standing in front of the unarmed native crowd—seemingly the leading actor of the piece; but in reality I was only an absurd puppet pushed to and fro by the will of those yellow faces behind. I perceived in this moment that when the white man turns tyrant it is his own freedom that he destroys. He becomes a sort of hollow, posing dummy, the conventionalized figure of a sahib. For it is the condition of his rule that he shall spend his life in trying to impress the "natives," and so in every crisis he has got to do what the "natives" expect of him. He wears a mask, and his face grows to fit it. I had got to shoot the elephant. I had committed myself to doing it when I sent for the rifle. A sahib has got to act like a sahib; he has got to appear resolute, to know his own mind and do definite things. To come all that way, rifle in hand, with two thousand people

marching at my heels, and then to trail feebly away, having done nothing—
no, that was impossible. The crowd would laugh at me. And my whole life,
every white man's life in the East, was one long struggle not to be laughed
at.

But I did not want to shoot the elephant. I watched him beating his   8
bunch of grass against his knees, with that preoccupied grandmotherly air
that elephants have. It seemed to me that it would be murder to shoot him.
At that age I was not squeamish about killing animals, but I had never shot
an elephant and never wanted to. (Somehow it always seems worse to kill a
large animal.) Besides, there was the beast's owner to be considered. Alive,
the elephant was worth at least a hundred pounds; dead, he would only be
worth the value of his tusks, five pounds, possibly. But I had got to act
quickly. I turned to some experienced-looking Burmans who had been there
when we arrived, and asked them how the elephant had been behaving.
They all said the same thing: he took no notice of you if you left him alone,
but he might charge if you went too close to him.

It was perfectly clear to me what I ought to do. I ought to walk up to   9
within, say, twenty-five yards of the elephant and test his behavior. If he
charged, I could shoot; if he took no notice of me, it would be safe to leave
him until the mahout came back. But also I knew that I was going to do no
such thing. I was a poor shot with a rifle and the ground was soft mud into
which one would sink at every step. If the elephant charged and I missed
him, I should have about as much chance as a toad under a steam-roller. But
even then I was not thinking particularly of my own skin, only of the watchful yellow faces behind. For at that moment, with the crowd watching me,
I was not afraid in the ordinary sense, as I would have been if I had been
alone. A white man mustn't be frightened in front of "natives"; and so, in
general, he isn't frightened. The sole thought in my mind was that if anything went wrong those two thousand Burmans would see me pursued,
caught, trampled on and reduced to a grinning corpse like that Indian up
the hill. And if that happened it was quite probable that some of them would
laugh. That would never do. There was only one alternative. I shoved the
cartridges into the magazine and lay down on the road to get a better aim.

The crowd grew very still, and a deep, low, happy sigh, as of people   10
who see the theatre curtain go up at last, breathed from innumerable throats.
They were going to have their bit of fun after all. The rifle was a beautiful
German thing with cross-hair sights. I did not then know that in shooting an
elephant one would shoot to cut an imaginary bar running from ear-hole to
ear-hole. I ought, therefore, as the elephant was sideways on, to have aimed
straight at his ear-hole; actually I aimed several inches in front of this, thinking the brain would be further forward.

When I pulled the trigger I did not hear the bang or feel the kick—one   11 never does when a shot goes home—but I heard the devilish roar of glee that went up from the crowd. In that instant, in too short a time, one would have thought, even for the bullet to get there, a mysterious, terrible change had come over the elephant. He neither stirred nor fell, but every line of his body had altered. He looked suddenly stricken, shrunken, immensely old, as though the frightful impact of the bullet had paralysed him without knocking him down. At last, after what seemed a long time—it might have been five seconds, I dare say—he sagged flabbily to his knees. His mouth slobbered. An enormous senility seemed to have settled upon him. One could have imagined him thousands of years old. I fired again into the same spot. At the second shot he did not collapse but climbed with desperate slowness to his feet and stood weakly upright, with legs sagging and head drooping. I fired a third time. That was the shot that did for him. You could see the agony of it jolt his whole body and knock the last remnant of strength from his legs. But in falling he seemed for a moment to rise, for as his hind legs collapsed beneath him he seemed to tower upward like a huge rock toppling, his trunk reaching skywards like a tree. He trumpeted, for the first and only time. And then down he came, his belly towards me, with a crash that seemed to shake the ground even where I lay.

I got up. The Burmans were already racing past me across the mud. It 12 was obvious that the elephant would never rise again, but he was not dead. He was breathing very rhythmically with long rattling gasps, his great mound of a side painfully rising and falling. His mouth was wide open—I could see far down into caverns of pale pink throat. I waited a long time for him to die, but his breathing did not weaken. Finally I fired my two remaining shots into the spot where I thought his heart must be. The thick blood welled out of him like red velvet, but still he did not die. His body did not even jerk when the shots hit him, the tortured breathing continued without a pause. He was dying, very slowly and in great agony, but in some world remote from me where not even a bullet could damage him further. I felt that I had got to put an end to that dreadful noise. It seemed dreadful to see the great beast lying there, powerless to move and yet powerless to die, and not even to be able to finish him. I sent back for my small rifle and poured shot after shot into his heart and down his throat. They seemed to make no impression. The tortured gasps continued as steadily as the ticking of a clock.

In the end I could not stand it any longer and went away. I heard later 13 that it took him half an hour to die. Burmans were bringing dahs and baskets even before I left, and I was told they had stripped his body almost to the bones by the afternoon.

Afterwards, of course, there were endless discussions about the shooting 14 of the elephant. The owner was furious, but he was only an Indian and could do nothing. Besides, legally I had done the right thing, for a mad elephant has to be killed, like a mad dog, if its owner fails to control it. Among the Europeans opinion was divided. The older men said I was right, the younger men said it was a damn shame to shoot an elephant for killing a coolie, because an elephant was worth more than any damn Coringhee coolie. And afterwards I was very glad that the coolie had been killed; it put me legally in the right and it gave me a sufficient pretext for shooting the elephant. I often wondered whether any of the others grasped that I had done it solely to avoid looking a fool.

QUESTIONS

Words to Know

perplexing (paragraph 2), imperialism (2), supplant (2), British Raj (2), *saecula saeculorum*—for all time (2), prostrate (2), ravaging (3), bazaar (3), *in terrorem*—to spread terror (3), mahout (3), rubbish (3), Dravidian (4), jostling (5), conjurer (7), conventionalized (7), sahib (7), flabbily (11), senility (11), dahs (13).

Some of the Issues

1. Before Orwell begins to tell the story of the shooting of the elephant, he uses two paragraphs to talk about feelings: the feelings of the Burmese toward him as a colonial officer, and his own "perplexing and unsettling" feelings toward the Burmese. Why are Orwell's feelings complex and contradictory? How does this discussion of attitudes set the scene for the narrative that follows?
2. The main topic or theme of the essay is stated in the first few sentences of paragraph 3. After reading the whole essay, explain why the incident Orwell describes gave him "a better glimpse of the real nature of imperialism"? What, according to Orwell, are "the real motives for which despotic governments act"?
3. In paragraph 7 Orwell says, "I perceived in this moment that when the white man turns tyrant it is his own freedom he destroys." Explain the meaning of this sentence; how does it apply to the story Orwell tells?

The Way We Are Told

4. When Orwell begins to tell the story of the elephant, in paragraph 3, he continues to reveal his attitude toward the Burmese in various indirect ways. Try to show how he does this.
5. In paragraph 4 Orwell describes the dead coolie in considerable detail. Compare that description to the one of the elephant's death. How do the descriptions differ? What are some of the words and phrases that show the difference?
6. In paragraphs 5 through 9 Orwell discusses his plans and options regarding the elephant. Paragraphs 5 and 6, however, differ greatly from 7, 8, and 9, both in content and treatment. Characterize the difference.

Some Subjects for Essays

7. Have you ever been placed in a situation in which you were forced to do something that you did not entirely agree with? For example, an employee must often carry out the policies of his or her employer even while disagreeing with them. Write an essay describing such an incident and detail your feelings before, during, and after.
8. Both Orwell and Baldwin ("Stranger in the Village") describe themselves as outsiders among the people with whom they live. Try to explain how the two authors' attitudes differ and account for these differences.
9. Orwell is placed in a position of authority, but finds it restricts his scope of action rather than expands it. Write an essay that asserts the truth of this apparent contradiction. Try to find examples of other situations in which the possession of power limits the possessor.

‖ THEY CLAPPED ‖

Nikki Giovanni

Nikki Giovanni is a graduate of Fisk College. She has published a number of volumes of poetry, including *Black Feeling Black Talk/Black Judgment* (1970), *The Women and the Men* (1975), and *My House*

(1972), from which the following poem is taken. She has also written
an autobiography, *Gemini* (1971).

they clapped when we landed
thinking africa was just an extension
of the black world
they smiled as we taxied home to be met
black to black face not understanding africans lack
color prejudice
they rushed to declare
cigarettes, money, allegiance to the mother land
not knowing despite having read fanon and davenport
hearing all of j.h. clarke's lectures, supporting
nkrumah in ghana and nigeria in the war that there was once
a tribe called afro-americans that populated the whole
of africa
they stopped running when they learned the packages
on the women's heads were heavy and that babies didn't
cry and disease is uncomfortable and that villages are fun
only because you knew the feel of good leather on good
pavement
they cried when they saw mercedes benz were as common
in lagos as volkswagens are in berlin
they shook their heads when they understood there was no
difference between the french and the english and the americans
and the afro-americans or the tribe next door or the country
across the border
they were exasperated when they heard sly and the family stone
in francophone africa and they finally smiled when little boys
who spoke no western tongue said "james brown" with reverence
they brought out their cameras and bought out africa's drums
when they finally realized they are strangers all over
and love is only and always about the lover not the beloved
they marveled at the beauty of the people and the richness
of the land knowing they could never possess either

they clapped when they took off
for home despite the dead
dream they saw a free future

EIGHT

Change

*A*merican society is committed to the idea of change: the newer the model or product, the more likely we are to believe that it is improved, more convenient, more efficient. We think of change as increase: more affluence, more speed, more power; better jobs, faster planes, more powerful computers. Only in the last generation have Americans begun to pay attention to the possible adverse effects of change, to the potential dangers that unrestrained technological development poses to the ecology of the earth or to our very survival.

Even for those who think that change is, on the whole, a beneficial, welcome process, the speed of change may be a source of trouble. That is the warning Alvin Toffler voices in the chapter taken from his book Future Shock. *He questions whether we are going to be able to absorb change at the rate at which we are increasingly subjected to it.*

Adam Smith, in "The Japanese Model," also discusses change and accommodation to it. Opened up to Western influence and technology little more than 100 years ago, wrecked in World War II, Japan today is one of the industrial superpowers which threatens American eminence in several fields. Smith sees Japan as a possible model as well as a warning of what may be to come.

The next two selections both deal with the effect of Western-style development on the less developed countries. Henry Knepler ("Beyond American Expressland") warns the American reader that many cultures see industrialization mainly as a threat to their traditional values. Modernization may cause a severe backlash—has caused it in some instances, in fact. American professionals going to work in the Third World need to be prepared not only for the culture shock they will experience but for the culture shock they may spread where they go.

Ivan Illich questions the very idea of modernization for the less developed countries. He makes the case that imitating the ways of the industrial world will not benefit them, even in such fields as education and health care. On the contrary, that imitation may distract these countries from dealing with their real needs.

W. B. Yeats' poem "The Second Coming," finally, is an enigmatic view of what is to come, one that transcends the religious meaning of the title.

FUTURE SHOCK

Alvin Toffler

The title of Alvin Toffler's *Future Shock* (1970) has, like the earlier term *culture shock*, become part of the English language. Before he wrote that book he was an editor of *Fortune* magazine and a Washington correspondent for several newspapers. He has written for many other magazines, including *Life, Horizon*, and *Playboy*. His latest book is *The Third Wave* (1980). The selection included here is the opening chapter of *Future Shock*.

In the three short decades between now and the twenty-first century, millions of ordinary, psychologically normal people will face an abrupt collision with the future. Citizens of the world's richest and most technologically advanced nations, many of them, will find it increasingly painful to keep up with the incessant demand for change that characterizes our time. For them, the future will have arrived too soon. 1

Western society for the past 300 years has been caught up in a fire storm of change. This storm, far from abating, now appears to be gathering force. Change sweeps through the highly industrialized countries with waves of ever accelerating speed and unprecedented impact. It spawns in its wake all sorts of curious social flora—from psychedelic churches and "free universities" to science cities in the Arctic and wife-swap clubs in California. 2

It breeds odd personalities, too: children who at twelve are no longer childlike; adults who at fifty are children of twelve. There are rich men who playact poverty, computer programmers who turn on with LSD. There are anarchists who, beneath their dirty denim shirts, are outrageous conformists, and conformists who, beneath their button-down collars, are outrageous anarchists. There are married priests and atheist ministers and Jewish Zen Buddhists. We have pop . . . and op . . . and *art cinétique* . . . There are Playboy Clubs and homosexual movie theaters . . . amphetamines and tranquilizers. . . anger, affluence, and oblivion. Much oblivion. 3

Is there some way to explain so strange a scene without recourse to the jargon of psychoanalysis or the murky clichés of existentialism? A strange new society is apparently erupting in our midst. Is there a way to understand it, to shape its development? How can we come to terms with it? 4

Much that now strikes us as incomprehensible would be far less so if we took a fresh look at the racing rate of change that makes reality seem, sometimes, like a kaleidoscope run wild. For the acceleration of change does not 5 merely buffet industries or nations. It is a concrete force that reaches deep into our personal lives, compels us to act out new roles, and confronts us with the danger of a new and powerfully upsetting psychological disease. This new disease can be called "future shock," and a knowledge of its sources and symptoms helps explain many things that otherwise defy rational analysis.

The parallel term "culture shock" has already begun to creep into the 6 popular vocabulary. Culture shock is the effect that immersion in a strange culture has on the unprepared visitor. Peace Corps volunteers suffer from it in Borneo or Brazil. Marco Polo probably suffered from it in Cathay. Culture shock is what happens when a traveler suddenly finds himself in a place where yes may mean no, where a "fixed price" is negotiable, where to be kept waiting in an outer office is no cause for insult, where laughter may signify anger. It is what happens when the familiar psychological cues that help an individual to function in society are suddenly withdrawn and replaced by new ones that are strange or incomprehensible.

The culture shock phenomenon accounts for much of the bewilder- 7 ment, frustration, and disorientation that plagues Americans in their dealings with other societies. It causes a breakdown in communication, a misreading of reality, an inability to cope. Yet culture shock is relatively mild in comparison with the much more serious malady, future shock. Future shock is the dizzying disorientation brought on by the premature arrival of the future. It may well be the most important disease of tomorrow.

Future shock will not be found in *Index Medicus* or in any listing of 8 psychological abnormalities. Yet, unless intelligent steps are taken to combat it, millions of human beings will find themselves increasingly disoriented, progressively incompetent to deal rationally with their environments. The malaise, mass neurosis, irrationality, and free-floating violence already apparent in contemporary life are merely a foretaste of what may lie ahead unless we come to understand and treat this disease.

Future shock is a time phenomenon, a product of the greatly acceler- 9 ated rate of change in society. It arises from the superimposition of a new culture on an old one. It is culture shock in one's own society. But its impact is far worse. For most Peace Corps men, in fact most travelers, have the comforting knowledge that the culture they left behind will be there to return to. The victim of future shock does not.

Take an individual out of his own culture and set him down suddenly 10 in an environment sharply different from his own, with a different set of cues to react to—different conceptions of time, space, work, love, religion, sex, and everything else—then cut him off from any hope of retreat to a more familiar social landscape, and the dislocation he suffers is doubly severe. Moreover, if this new culture is itself in constant turmoil, and if—

worse yet—its values are incessantly changing, the sense of disorientation will be still further intensified. Given few clues as to what kind of behavior is rational under the radically new circumstances, the victim may well become a hazard to himself and others.

Now imagine not merely an individual but an entire society, an entire   11
generation—including its weakest, least intelligent, and most irrational members—suddenly transported into this new world. The result is mass disorientation, future shock on a grand scale.

This is the prospect that man now faces. Change is avalanching upon   12
our heads and most people are grotesquely unprepared to cope with it.

Is all this exaggerated? I think not. It has become a cliché to say that   13
what we are now living through is a "second industrial revolution." This phrase is supposed to impress us with the speed and profundity of the change around us. But in addition to being platitudinous, it is misleading. For what is occurring now is, in all likelihood, bigger, deeper, and more important than the industrial revolution. Indeed, a growing body of reputable opinion asserts that the present moment represents nothing less than the second great divide in human history, comparable in magnitude only with that first great break in historic continuity, the shift from barbarism to civilization.

This idea crops up with increasing frequency in the writings of scientists   14
and technologists. Sir George Thomson, the British physicist and Nobel prizewinner, suggests in *The Foreseeable Future* that the nearest historic parallel with today is not the industrial revolution but rather the "invention of agriculture in the neolithic age." John Diebold, the American automation expert, warns that "the effects of the technological revolution we are now living through will be deeper than any social change we have experienced before." Sir Leon Bagrit, the British computer manufacturer, insists that automation by itself represents "the greatest change in the whole history of mankind."

Nor are the men of science and technology alone in these views. Sir   15
Herbert Read, the philosopher of art, tells us that we are living through "a revolution so fundamental that we must search many past centuries for a parallel. Possibly the only comparable change is the one that took place between the Old and the New Stone Age ..." And Kurt W. Marek, who under the name C. W. Ceram is best-known as the author of *Gods, Graves and Scholars*, observes that "we, in the twentieth century, are concluding an era of mankind five thousand years in length ... We are not, as Spengler supposed, in the situation of Rome at the beginning of the Christian West, but in that of the year 3000 B.C. We open our eyes like prehistoric man, we see a world totally new."

One of the most striking statements of this theme has come from Ken-   16 neth Boulding, an eminent economist and imaginative social thinker. In justifying his view that the present moment represents a crucial turning point in human history, Boulding observes that "as far as many statistical series related to activities of mankind are concerned, the date that divides human history into two equal parts is well within living memory." In effect, our century represents The Great Median Strip running down the center of human history. Thus he asserts, "The world of today . . . is as different from the world in which I was born as that world was from Julius Caesar's. I was born in the middle of human history, to date, roughly. Almost as much has happened since I was born as happened before."

This startling statement can be illustrated in a number of ways. It has   17
been observed, for example, that if the last 50,000 years of man's existence were divided into lifetimes of approximately sixty-two years each, there have been about 800 such lifetimes. Of these 800, fully 650 were spent in caves.

Only during the last seventy lifetimes has it been possible to commu-   18
nicate effectively from one lifetime to another—as writing made it possible to do. Only during the last six lifetimes did masses of men ever see a printed word. Only during the last four has it been possible to measure time with any precision. Only in the last two has anyone anywhere used an electric motor. And the overwhelming majority of all the material goods we use in daily life today have been developed within the present, the 800th, lifetime.

This 800th lifetime marks a sharp break with all past human experience   19
because during this lifetime man's relationship to resources has reversed itself. This is most evident in the field of economic development. Within a single lifetime, agriculture, the original basis of civilization, has lost its dominance in nation after nation. Today in a dozen major countries agriculture employs fewer than 15 percent of the economically active population. In the United States, whose farms feed 200,000,000 Americans plus the equivalent of another 160,000,000 people around the world, this figure is already below 6 percent and it is still shrinking rapidly.

Moreover, if agriculture is the first stage of economic development and   20
industrialism the second, we can now see that still another stage—the third— has suddenly been reached. In about 1956 the United States became the first major power in which more than 50 percent of the non-farm labor force ceased to wear the blue collar of factory or manual labor. Blue collar workers were outnumbered by those in the so-called white-collar occupations—in retail trade, administration, communications, research, education, and other service categories. Within the same lifetime a society for the first time in human history not only threw off the yoke of agriculture, but managed within a few brief decades to throw off the yoke of manual labor as well. The world's first service economy had been born.

Since then, one after another of the technologically advanced countries 21
have moved in the same direction. Today, in those nations in which agriculture is down to the 15 percent level or below, white collars already outnumber blue in Sweden, Britain, Belgium, Canada, and the Netherlands. Ten
thousand years for agriculture. A century or two for industrialism. And now,
opening before us—super-industrialism.

Jean Fourastié, the French planner and social philosopher, has declared 22
that "Nothing will be less industrial than the civilization born of the industrial revolution." The significance of this staggering fact has yet to be
digested. Perhaps U Thant, Secretary General of the United Nations, came
closest to summarizing the meaning of the shift to super-industrialism when
he declared that "The central stupendous truth about developed economies
today is that they can have—in anything but the shortest run—the kind and
scale of resources they decide to have. . . . It is no longer resources that limit
decisions. It is the decision that makes the resources. This is the fundamental
revolutionary change—perhaps the most revolutionary man has ever
known." This monumental reversal has taken place in the 800th lifetime.

This lifetime is also different from all others because of the astonishing 23
expansion of the scale and scope of change. Clearly, there have been other
lifetimes in which epochal upheavals occurred. Wars, plagues, earthquakes,
and famine rocked many an earlier social order. But these shocks and
upheavals were contained within the borders of one or a group of adjacent
societies. It took generations, even centuries, for their impact to spread
beyond these borders.

In our lifetime the boundaries have burst. Today the network of social 24
ties is so tightly woven that the consequences of contemporary events radiate
instantaneously around the world. A war in Vietnam alters basic political
alignments in Peking, Moscow, and Washington, touches off protests in
Stockholm, affects financial transactions in Zurich, triggers secret diplomatic
moves in Algiers.

Indeed, not only do *contemporary* events radiate instantaneously—now 25
we can be said to be feeling the impact of all *past* events in a new way. For
the past is doubling back on us. We are caught in what might be called a
"time skip."

An event that affected only a handful of people at the time of its occur- 26
rence in the past can have large-scale consequences today. The Peloponnesian War, for example, was little more than a skirmish by modern standards.
While Athens, Sparta and several nearby city-states battled, the population
of the rest of the globe remained largely unaware of and undisturbed by the
war. The Zapotech Indians living in Mexico at the time were wholly
untouched by it. The ancient Japanese felt none of its impact.

Yet the Peloponnesian War deeply altered the future course of Greek   27
history. By changing the movement of men, the geographical distribution of
genes, values, and ideas, it affected later events in Rome, and, through Rome,
all Europe. Today's Europeans are to some small degree different people
because that conflict occurred.

In turn, in the tightly wired world of today, these Europeans influence   28
Mexicans and Japanese alike. Whatever trace of impact the Peloponnesian
War left on the genetic structure, the ideas, and the values of today's Europeans is now exported by them to all parts of the world. Thus today's Mexicans and Japanese feel the distant, twice-removed impact of that war even
though their ancestors, alive during its occurrence, did not. In this way, the
events of the past, skipping as it were over generations and centuries, rise up
to haunt and change us today.

When we think not merely of the Peloponnesian War but of the build-   29
ing of the Great Wall of China, the Black Plague, the battle of the Bantu
against the Hamites—indeed, of all the events of the past—the cumulative
implications of the time-skip principle take on weight. Whatever happened
to some men in the past affects virtually all men today. This was not always
true. In short, all history is catching up with us, and this very difference,
paradoxically, underscores our break with the past. Thus the scope of change
is fundamentally altered. Across space and through time, change has a power
and reach in this, the 800th lifetime, that it never did before.

But the final, qualitative difference between this and all previous life-   30
times is the one most easily overlooked. For we have not merely extended
the scope and scale of change, we have radically altered its pace. We have
in our time released a totally new social force—a stream of change so accel-
erated that it influences our sense of time, revolutionizes the tempo of daily
life, and affects the very way we "feel" the world around us. We no longer
"feel" life as men did in the past. And this is the ultimate difference, the
distinction that separates the truly contemporary man from all others. For
this acceleration lies behind the impermanence—the transience—that penetrates and tinctures our consciousness, radically affecting the way we relate
to other people, to things, to the entire universe of ideas, art and values.

To understand what is happening to us as we move into the age of   31
super-industrialism, we must analyze the processes of acceleration and con-
front the concept of transience. If acceleration is a new social force, transience is its psychological counterpart, and without an understanding of the
role it plays in contemporary human behavior, all our theories of personality,
all our psychology, must remain pre-modern. Psychology without the concept of transience cannot take account of precisely those phenomena that are
peculiarly contemporary.

By changing our relationship to the resources that surround us, by vio- 32
lently expanding the scope of change, and, most crucially, by accelerating
its pace, we have broken irretrievably with the past. We have cut ourselves
off from the old ways of thinking, of feeling, of adapting. We have set the
stage for a completely new society and we are now racing toward it. This is
the crux of the 800th lifetime. And it is this that calls into question man's
capacity for adaptation—how will he fare in this new society? Can he adapt
to its imperatives? And if not, can he alter these imperatives?

QUESTIONS

Words to Know

incessant (paragraph 1), abating (2), curious social flora (2), psychedelic (2),
anarchists (3), Zen Buddhists (3), pop (3), op (3), jargon (4), psychoanalysis
(4), clichés (4), existentialism (4), kaleidoscope (5), buffet (5), immersion (6),
Marco Polo (6), Cathay (6), incomprehensible (6), phenomenon (7), disorientation (7), *Index Medicus* (8), malaise (8), neurosis (8), superimposition (9),
dislocation (10), turmoil (10), grotesquely (12), profundity (13), platitudinous
(13), eminent (16), blue collar (20), white collar (20), epochal (23), upheavals
(23), radiate (25), instantaneously (25), Peloponnesian War (26), skirmish
(26), cumulative (29), transience (30), irretrievably (32), crux (32), imperatives (32).

Some of the Issues

1. At the end of paragraph 1, Toffler says that for citizens of the world's
   richest and most technologically advanced nations "the future will have
   arrived too soon." Explain what he means and show how this quotation
   states the theme of the essay.
2. In paragraph 2 Toffler alludes to changes that have taken place in the
   past 300 years. Cite some that seem to you to be among the most
   important.
3. In paragraph 6 Toffler defines culture shock and uses it to define future
   shock. How are they alike, and what are the differences between them?
4. In paragraph 17 Toffler introduces the idea of the 800th lifetime. How

does he use this concept to support his thesis about the rapidity of recent change?

5. Beginning with paragraph 20, Toffler talks about three states of economic development. What are they?

6. In paragraphs 30 through 32 Toffler asserts that the psychological changes brought about by technological change are the most disturbing ones. How does he make this point?

The Way We Are Told

7. What is the argument Toffler makes in paragraph 2 and how does it differ from the one made in paragraph 1? Justify his use of two rather brief paragraphs.

8. Paragraph 3 ends with a two word sentence fragment, a form beginning writers are taught to avoid. Justify its use here.

9. In paragraph 5 Toffler describes future shock as a disease. How does he justify calling it that?

10. Toffler uses several ways to convince us of the reality and importance of "future shock." In paragraphs 1 through 3 he enumerates rapid changes in contemporary life. What means does he use in paragraphs 4 and 5?

11. In paragraphs 14 through 16 Toffler argues his case for future shock in still another way. Explain.

Some Subjects for Essays

12. Consider one item in your life that was unknown to your grandparents when they were your age, such as rapid air travel, antibiotics, or the computer chip. Compare life with and without that item.

13. Do you agree with Toffler's assessment of the effect of rapid change, or do you consider his conclusions to be exaggerated? Argue either way, giving specific examples.

14. Toffler asserts that events throughout the world are more interconnected today than in the past. In a short essay, give one explicit example of such an interconnected series of events.

THE JAPANESE MODEL

Adam Smith

Adam Smith is the pseudonym of George J. W. Goodman, who turned from fiction to writing about economics and finance, particularly the impact of economic policies on society. His books include *The Money Game* (1968), *Supermoney* (1972), *Powers of Mind* (1975), and *Paper Money* (1981). He writes a regular feature for *Esquire*, in which the following selection appeared in October 1980.

"Do you remember," said my visitor, "the stories about Usa?" 1

My visitor was an old friend, an American who lives in the Far East, 2
where he drums up business for his American firm. As for Usa, it is a town
on the main southernmost Japanese island, Kyushu.

"The story used to be," said my visitor, "that because Japanese goods 3
were so cheap and shoddy, they were all sent to Usa before they were
exported to be stamped MADE IN USA, so that people would think they had
been made in the United States."

"I remember," I said. "That's like the story about how the Japanese 4
filched the plans for a battleship but got them just wrong enough so that
when the ship was launched it turned upside down."

"Well," said the Far East hand, "you haven't heard stories like that for 5
twenty-five years. Detroit is reeling from Japanese imports, and you see jog-
gers wearing earphones and carrying little Japanese tape decks not much
larger than cigarette packs. I have to go meet some of my Japanese associates
in New York now. They think New York is charming—and so *cheap*, they
keep saying. Such *bargains*."

The Far East hand left with me a book that is a huge best seller in Japan. 6
It was written by a Harvard professor, Ezra Vogel, and its English-language
edition has sold a respectable twenty-five thousand copies. But in Japan it is
a runaway success: four hundred fifty-five thousand copies sold. The title is
Japan as No. 1: Lessons for America. "The very title," said Edwin Reis-
chauer, a former ambassador to Japan, "will blow the minds of many Americans. Japan today has a more smoothly functioning society [than ours] and
an economy that is running rings around ours." One Japanese official has said
that the United States has now taken the place of Japan's prewar colonies.
The United States supplies the raw materials—the coal, the grain and soy-
beans, the timber—to this superior modern industrial machine, and it gets
back the machine's superior industrial products.

Japan's economic performance has been well documented in Vogel's 7

335

book. In 1952, Japan's gross national product was one third that of France. By the late 1970s, it was larger than those of France and Britain combined, and half as large as that of the United States. Japan is the leading automobile manufacturer. Of the world's twenty-two largest and most modern steel plants, fourteen are in Japan and none are in the United States.

Health? Japan has the world's lowest infant mortality rate. In 1967 the life expectancy of the average Japanese passed that of the average American, and in 1977 Japan's life expectancy rate passed Sweden's to become the highest in the world.   8

Education? About 90 percent of all Japanese graduate from high school, and they generally spend sixty more days a year in high school than do their American counterparts.   9

Crime? In Japan the cities are safe, and the Japanese carry large amounts of cash and don't even worry about it. Americans are accustomed to annual increases in the crime rate; in Japan, the crime rate is going *down.*   10

Labor? The Japanese visitors are shocked again. Professor Vogel says that the American factory seems almost like an armed camp to them: "Foremen stand guard to make sure workers do not slack off. Workers grumble at foremen, and foremen are cross with workers. In the Japanese factory, employees seem to work even without the foreman watching."   11

What are the Japanese doing right? And how have they done it on a crowded group of islands, without enough coal and oil, without significant natural resources, without adequate farmland?   12

The rather chilling answer is that they have done it by a social process— by a kind of group behavior modification. An average Japanese who goes to work for a company is there for life. He works throughout the day in an atmosphere in which consensus is always the goal. If, as his career progresses, he needs retraining, the company will retrain him, so he need not get involved in the protection of rights that American unions strive for. The company's goals are his. The people he sees socially are from the company.   13

The government works the same way, striving for consensus within itself and for consensus with business. Elite bureaucrats, their ties reinforced by social contacts in the geisha houses and on the golf course, form an elaborate old-boy network and move in lockstep through the age ranks.   14

And all this starts very early. Children are taught the value of cooperation, says Vogel, "however annoying they may find group pressures." The group pressure helps to explain the low crime rate. The policeman is part of the group: his little kiosk also contains the neighborhood bulletin board. The criminal, in fact, is encouraged to turn himself in. Even Japanese gangs exist in a consensus with the police.   15

The whole design of group activity is a conscious one. After World War   16
II, the Japanese decided what they needed to survive, and they followed
their decision. They even learned golf and baseball with the same sense of
purpose that they applied to business and government. Americans win arguments; the Japanese win agreements. Americans try for victory; the Japanese
try for consensus.

Nobody can deny Japan its success. What is so chilling is the implication   17
of that success: Japan works and America doesn't. The Japanese leaped from
feudalism to a modern corporate society without the intervening four
hundred years of individualism that have characterized Western Europe and
the United States. Our individualism was all very well in its time, but that
was when energy was plentiful and the world was agricultural. But now we
live in a postagrarian world, and individualism doesn't work anymore: "Our
institutional practices promote adversary relations and litigation, divisiveness
threatens our society," warns Vogel.

What we ought to do, he argues, is to borrow some of the models that   18
have worked for the Japanese: more group direction, more "central leadership oriented to a modern economic order," more cooperation between business and government.

You can see why this is at once so provocative and so chilling. Should   19
we all gather behind the banners of IBM and General Motors? When William H. Whyte Jr. wrote *The Organization Man*, the phenomenon he documented was considered alarming. Do we really want five hundred highly
trained bureaucrats, a close-knit group from elite universities, to establish our
goals and run our government? Our experience with the best and the brightest was not totally happy. Should we teach youngsters not to win, just to tie?

Japanophiles point out that America, too, had groups: New England   20
town meetings, farmers' granges, professional guilds. But in our mobile society, group solidarity has become attenuated. We have lost a sense of
community.

This is not the direction we are going in. Americans complain that their   21
government is too big and directs them too much. They are more and more
suspicious of big business. They distrust, the polls show, all of their
institutions.

There isn't any doubt that we are losing ground in the world, and that   22
we have forgotten what safe cities and a sense of community feel like. Is the
group model what it takes to survive? Could we adopt it? More to the point,
is it the way we want to live?

QUESTIONS

Words to Know

shoddy (paragraph 3), filched (4), consensus (13), kiosk (15), postagrarian (17), litigation (17), "the best and the brightest" (19), Japanophiles (20), granges (20), guilds (20), attenuated (20).

Some of the Issues

1. In paragraphs 1 through 5 Smith cites a conversation with a "Far East hand." What specifics does it contribute to the essay? How does it set up the comparison between the United States and Japan?
2. What do the remarks of the former United States Ambassador and the unnamed Japanese official in paragraph 6 contribute to Smith's argument?
3. Enumerate and explain the different kinds of arguments Smith uses to substantiate his (or Ezra Vogel's) assertion that Japan is number one. Exemplify each kind of argument.
4. What is Smith's main argument? That we should imitate the Japanese? That we cannot expect to follow their example? Try to determine Smith's direction, giving evidence from the essay.
5. What, according to Smith, are the underlying causes of Japanese industrial superiority?
6. Explain the meaning of the sentence in paragraph 19: "Our experience with the best and the brightest was not totally happy. Should we teach our youngsters not to win, just to tie?"

The Way We Are Told

7. Smith's essay can be divided into three parts linked by transitional paragraphs 6 and 12. Write an outline of the essay using this division.
8. Notice the presence of many sentences (and fragments) phrased as questions. Why does Smith use this form? Consider the last paragraph in particular.

Some Subjects for Essays

8. Reread paragraph 19 and try to answer any one of the questions asked in
   it. In your response, consider carefully the Japanese examples Smith has
   cited and argue your answer from them as well as from your own
   experience.
9. Write an essay about one or two products you have recently used. Argue
   that they are either improvements on previous products or they are not.
   Try to account for the change in various ways.

BEYOND AMERICAN EXPRESSLAND

Henry Knepler

Henry Knepler, born in Vienna, Austria, has published a number of
books, including *The Gilded Stage* (1968) and *Man About Paris*
(1970). In addition to teaching at the Illinois Institute of Technology,
he has served as visiting professor at the University of Paris and in
several African countries, and as consultant to international agencies.
The article included here was originally published in *Change* magazine in February 1980.

On national TV news shows in recent months we have seen large crowds— 1
usually separated by gender—shouting in unison, fists raised, eyes wild. They
are the followers of Colonel Quaddafi or the Ayatollah Khomeini, and they
are shouting about us. They sack our embassies and hold our countrymen
hostage. And they have oil. After the shocks of Vietnam and Watergate in
the early 1970s they may well be readying us for the shock of the early 1980s:
that large parts of the world reject not only our democratic institutions—we
are used to that—but our fundamental beliefs in development, modernization, and change.

From Mark Twain and Henry James to our day Americans have pre- 2
ferred to view themselves as the rational, disinterested helpers of the world—
and until recently we have lived the part more consistently than many other
nationalities. We have seen ourselves as hands-on people, pragmatic, progressive, lacking the pretensions to cultural superiority we attribute to the
English and French. We have felt our mixed heritage conditioned us to deal
with cultural diversity. We see—or saw—ourselves as straightforward, with
a tinge of innocence, only a little cleaner in mind and body than the natives
upon whom we visit the rational accomplishments of our culture. Apart from
human rights these accomplishments are mainly managerial and technological and their transfer is now most in evidence in the Third World—a realm
that is increasingly capturing our attention as well as our embassy personnel.

The Third World contains 70 percent of the planet's burgeoning pop- 3
ulation and most of its remaining natural resources; rising numbers of the
million or so Americans who live and work abroad are being sent there.
These are the "new nations," just as ours once was, and we feel an affinity

340

for their birth pangs. In providing our managerial and technological expertise, we mean to ease the pangs and lead these countries into the modern world.

But we are finding more and more that our knowledge and hardware, 4 while giving joy to a few, arouse anger in many. We have begun to realize that the Westernized elites our people have mostly dealt with do not represent the new nations, many of which are really very old cultures. Yet we know that we must work with them. Can we? More precisely, what do the professionals going overseas—the experts, the managers, the engineers— know? What should they be aware of? What can be done to prepare them?

Americans travel to the Third World mainly for business or government 5 purposes. They expect to be respectfully welcomed as experts. They need not do as the natives do. And they therefore find it relatively easy to preserve a false ethnocentric security. One contributing factor, especially for the usually monolingual American, is language—which presents a curious problem in this context. An engineer or business manager may excuse, to himself or to others, his lack of meaningful local contacts on the basis of his ignorance of the local tongue. In many places this will be true, though the local tongue he really needs is often no more esoteric than Spanish or French (the latter, for example, in about half of Africa).

Language apart, the Third World traveler is enveloped in a cocoon of 6 accommodation and service that appears seamless (and confirms his implicit view of the ubiquity of Coca-Cola). First, there are, in many capitals, the great hotels. Some have a kind of supernatural splendor because they contrast so glaringly to the rest of the place—or because some consortium sold a tremendous bill of goods to the government of the new nation: the Hotel Aurassi in Algiers, for example, with its kidney-shaped pool, or the Hotel Ivoire in Abidjan with its hamburgers, skating rink, and saunas. There are the Hiltons and Intercontinentals, veritable Taj Majals of hostelry where one can find *Time* Magazine, Dior ties, scotch, and taxicabs in abundance. With passport, six additional documents, and expense account firmly in place, the traveler may never experience the realities beyond.

When he settles in for a longer stay, the cocoon is spun further. The 7 diligent transferee will read the excellent but slightly out-of-date area handbook for his destination issued by the government. Or he will have brought some paperbacks, knowledgeable but not directly concerned with his particular interest in the country. Usually the traveler confines himself to a handout from his employer. If the company is large and its managers thoughtful, he will get a lot of information. One major engineering corporation, for example, issues a book-size pamphlet to its overseas-bound employees that begins:

> Before any overseas assignment your physician will give you vaccinations and inoculations to protect you from a variety of ills. There is one disease for which there is no immunization and for which we want to prepare you. This illness, for lack of a better term, is called "culture shock."

You can't avoid it, fella, so you might as well face it: This is the standard jaunty introduction. Then, sometimes in more than 100 pages, the traveler learns about everything from history to entry documents to the purchase of soft drinks. He is told, in practical terms, how to cope: how to make life as easy—as American—as possible. The advice boils down to the three W's: wine, women, and work. You are to avoid the first two and do the third.

The company brochure is designed to fill the gaps between the threads   8
of the cocoon, which also includes such comforts as living compounds, company stores, imported goods, and local fixers. These are intended to cushion the culture shock of the American manager or engineer and his wife and children. But the culture shock that he may be spreading among the native population is not dealt with at all. Culture shock is a communicable disease and, to mix metaphors, it is only the tip of the iceberg. It is likely to have explosive implications, not only for the patient but for those with whom he comes in contact.

Consider the American professional going abroad for the first time. He   9
works for a large corporation; even if he works for the government, he sees himself as a private individual entitled to express his personal views freely. The people he deals with are native workers or officials, neither likely to be trained as he was. He may find that the government is monolithic; he may never see—as, it seems, thousands of Americans never saw in the Shah's Iran—a pervasive hostility that nobody dares to, or can, express. To the American both the hostility and the monolithic control are alien. He is not likely to be aware, except theoretically, of monitored telephone calls, opened mail, or interrogations (not necessarily of him but of his local contacts). His native counterparts, on the other hand, will be hard to convince that he does not represent his government. To the less sophisticated that means the police; to the worldly it implies the CIA.

Furthermore, the average American has no experience with ideology,   10
his politics being as pragmatic as his work experience. American political life is, after all, singularly unideological. As a result he may see ideology in terms of what he is acquainted with: competition, a transfer from the realm of commerce. While American political life thrives on consensus, commercial life, at least in theory, thrives on competition. Ideology may then become something in which the other side should be bested. Because the commercial and social or political realms differ widely, this may lead to important misjudgments, and what plays in Peoria may flop in Poona or La Paz.

Finally, the American professional sees himself as an applied scientist,   11
if he is an engineer, or as a manager drawing rational conclusions from available data. Of course, here at home we no longer accept the notion that what
is technologically and economically optimal is therefore socially optimal; we
no longer view the world through the eyes of the white-coated expert pushing buttons. We consider technology assessment, professional ethics, social
implications, and ecology. But in the Third World "progress" has a particularly profound effect. There that middle-class, university-trained professional is an accessory to revolution. His dam will not simply relocate people
as in the peripatetic U.S.A.; it may uproot and destory a way of life. His
factory will not merely boost employment; it will be a magnet drawing people to the city as it once drew them to Manchester or Pittsburgh. It will lure
people from pursuits their ancestors have followed for ages.

One may argue that the professional on his first overseas tour of duty,   12
employed by a big concern, hasn't the power to make such decisions. Not
necessarily true. His bosses fly in and out via Paris or London; he is there all
the time. After six months he knows the lay of the land, the local authorities.
(National governments seem like local authorities to some Americans.) Very
soon his employers rely on him. He may have power he never dreamed of—
and never wished on himself, if he is conscientious. Then when the pipeline
goes through the territory of a hostile tribe or the bridge permits access to
the wrong people, the American plutocrat from the CIA and the country
that sent him are blamed. Alternatively, if there is no explosion, the American may walk through his job never seeing the potential for disaster. He
operates methodically and is offended and disturbed when his logic is not
understood. He comes as a friend and is stereotyped as the Ugly American.

It would be fatuous to suggest that training in intercultural communi-   13
cation could turn this person into a diplomatic expert; too many variables
beyond his control are involved. And even if it did, would the foreign people
he deals with be willing to see him in his new garb? Yet many factors compel
us to transcend our traditional Western-oriented frame of reference, and
attempts to help are under way—from a renewed interest in foreign language training to such global plans as the Education and the World View
program of the Council on Learning. The new Institute for Scientific and
Technological Cooperation, which is being developed by the federal government, will, it is hoped, construe its functions broadly enough to transcend
problems such as technology transfer in order to examine the social context
of the decision-making process.

To avoid the idea that solutions are around the corner, it is best to look   14
at what is being done to prepare the industrial managers and engineers. Most
of the larger schools of business, management, and finance, especially those
on the graduate level, have courses or programs or options related to the

international scene. But these tend to be narrow in scope. The Graduate School of Business Administration at New York University is one of a few that at least mention social and cultural dimensions in their course descriptions (under the heading of "Environmental Factors"). Cornell's Graduate School of Business has a small exchange program with two Belgian universities. In the rest of these international business programs, if intercultural matters are taken up at all, it is likely at the discretion of a particular professor. Among the major exceptions are some institutions that specialize in the field of international relations: the Graduate School of International Management in Glendale, Arizona, which has programs specifically designed for managers going overseas; and the Experiment in International Living in Brattleboro, Vermont, which also offers graduate work in international administration. Both provide a genuine integration of professional and intercultural learning.

In engineering schools the picture worsens considerably. The education 15 of engineers still proceeds as if each student's career were to unroll exclusively in the United States; rarely does a course have some international context. Occasionally courses in technology transfer are offered, but they are generally part of special interdisciplinary sequences (such as Science, Technology, and Society programs), which puts them outside the inner circle of "real" engineering departments. The Science, Technology, and Public Policy program at Washington University in St. Louis, for example, includes a course in technology transfer taught by Robert Morgan, who is also the chief editor of *Science and Technology for Development*, prepared for the United Nations conference on that topic held in Vienna in August 1979. Yet even in this large, comprehensive summary of American efforts and plans, the technical, economic, and strategic matters are transcended by just one reference to the need for "dedicated, capable, culturally sensitive U.S. faculty" to participate in overseas development. Where are they to come from?

The literature of international business and appropriate technology has 16 grown in recent years; journals such as *Technos* and *World Development* are examples. Books like E. F. Schumacher's *Small Is Beautiful* have drawn attention to the differences between Western high technology and the rest of the world. But small is not likely to be beautiful in the usual marketing or civil engineering course, and in electronics small is more likely to refer to sophisticated miniaturization than to labor-intensive small-scale industry. (In fairness, that emphasis may be justified. Engineers and managers are not Renaissance men. Most students need to be prepared for the domestic market, and the schools generally are not, or don't believe themselves to be, equipped to explore matters beyond the domestic.)

The literature of intercultural communications, a comparative new-   17
comer, has not only developed rapidly, but the field has acquired something
like its own taxonomy in the 1970s. Since this growth stems largely from the
foreign student boom in this country, much of the work deals with their
presence here rather than ours abroad. But there is still a significant body of
literature for the overseas-bound American. It began in earnest in the 1960s,
primarily through studies done for or by the Peace Corps. The early 1970s
brought a much wider interest, which can be explained by one statistic: In
1970 the State Department issued fewer than 40,000 passports for business
purposes; by 1975 the number had approached a quarter of a million
annually. We now have such works as the three-volume *Overview of Intercultural Education, Training, and Research*, edited by David Hoopes and
others, and Richard W. Brislin and Paul Pedersen's *Cross-Cultural Orientation Programs*.

Intercultural communication suffers from certain difficulties that are   18
typical of American education. Its troubles parallel those of that university
albatross, the freshman composition course. Students and faculty see it as a
service program, hardly a subject in itself like chemistry or literature. To be
involved may put its practitioner at the fringe of the field in which he works;
it is easier to cross the equator than to cross disciplinary lines. Furthermore,
its cognitive aspects take second place to the development of attitudes and
skills, which are of a lower order academically. Finally, while it would be
better taught in conjunction with the student's major field, it rarely is.

When a corporation hires someone to teach intercultural communica-   19
tion, added troubles arise. As Richard W. Brislin says, "Training personnel
must be able to recognize failure" among those being prepared for overseas
work; not only recognize, it would seem, but act upon. Yet the intercultural
instructor who rejects the young, go-getting assistant vice president as too
insensitive for that big overseas promotion may not be long for the corporate
world. It is as if everyone taking English 101 were assured of a passing grade.

Intercultural communication has begun to overcome the difficulties of   20
its beginnings; now it needs to overcome an orientation that imposes an inap-
propriate simplicity on its practices. National cultures are seen as one homogeneous whole. A useful and intelligent book like *Intercultural Communication: A Reader*, edited by Larry A. Samovar and Richard E. Porter, does
not consider it illogical to include a section on black-white relations in this
country while presenting the varied cultures of India as one. The editors
recognize that differences within the United States—even though we speak
one language—are so great than an intercultural consideration is called for;
yet they lead the reader to expect that Madras and Delhi, or Rabat and
Riyadh, need not be similarly differentiated. The nongeographic differences

are also oversimplified—those between Westernized and non-Westernized elites, and some that are especially important to the American professional abroad: the training and attitudes of workers and skilled persons.

I do not deny the value of the intercultural education now available. To 21 have read Edward Hall's *Silent Language* may console the tired businessman cooling his heels in some outer office in Kuwait. His knowledge of customs may keep him from holding out his left hand instead of his right to accept a gift in Chad. He may learn to cope more patiently and effectively with the vagaries of those vast regions beyond American Expressland. But intercultural communication needs to be tackled in the specific context of professional education and work. Industry, government, and academe must all participate.

Industry, first of all, should face the problem at an earlier stage than it 22 does now. Recruiters should look for candidates with some cultural sensitivity. That is not as difficult as it sounds: A likely prospect's background would include such evidence as relevant college courses, especially among humanities and social science electives; work in foreign languages; or participation in intercultural activities on campus. In addition, preparation for the job abroad should begin long before departure, not when the employee is frantically winding up his affairs. This is not always possible, of course; a contract arrived at after months of negotiations may need to be implemented within a few weeks. But larger corporations with a number of contracts in the works at all times can create a pool of interculturally prepared employees to call on. If incentive pay is given for expertise in difficult tasks or location, why not for intercultural skills? In the long run it would pay industry to go this route.

Second, the federal government can benefit its citizens and its interna- 23 tional relations by diversifying its role. It has occasionally sent experts overseas to advise educational institutions and governments in technological and organizational matters. Such programs would be enhanced if, in addition to the senior advisors, junior professionals were sent abroad, particularly to universities and technological institutes. These young men and women—perhaps faculty on the assistant professor level—would be involved in a two-way process rather than the largely one-way advisory tasks their seniors undertake. They could put their fresh educational expertise to work while learning the needs and attitudes of the host country; they could acquire at the same time an awareness of another culture and its ways of handling (resisting) change. In this somewhat humbler role—somewhere between the expert and the Peace Corps member—the young professional could make his own contribution to international relations.

In the final analysis, however, the job of mediating between different 24 cultures and technology is likely to fall to the institutions of higher education. Room must be made for intercultural communication among other general education courses—not only in undergraduate programs but on the graduate level as well. The subject must be integrated; it is not enough to substitute an intercultural veneer for the Western cultural veneer that general education supplies all too often. A heartening analogy is the recent development of courses in ethics for the professions. These are neither amateur efforts from within the professional schools nor services rendered by humanists in danger of extinction. At their best they truly cross disciplines and draw on both sides. The professional schools must reach out for intercultural education and discard their usual passive role.

The practitioners of intercultural communication must reach out with equal fervor. They will fail if they view these new programs simply as expansions of their present domain. They must learn the methods of the professions they will cooperate with. They must bridge additional disciplines and transcend their social science origins and biases, especially in course design and research. A body of material awaits creation that addresses the intercultural needs of students in the professions: engineering, management, agriculture, architecture. To give one example, La Ray M. Barna, in *Intercultural Communication: A Reader*, warns:

> Typically, the method used to improve chances for successful intercultural communication is simply to gather information about the language and behavior and attitude patterns of the other culture from whatever source is available. This information is seldom sufficient and may or may not be helpful. Unless the traveler has an investigative attitude and a high tolerance of ambiguity, knowledge of "what to expect" [may] blind him to all but what is confirmatory to his preconception.

Studies have established beyond reasonable doubt that American engineers have a low tolerance of ambiguity. This is compounded by the fact that they, as applied scientists, believe themselves to have a thoroughly investigative attitude. But does that attitude transcend the technological? Is it likely to be influenced by the low tolerance of ambiguity? And how can this low tolerance be counteracted if the rest of their education abets it?

Not only a reorientation but an expansion of faculty is called for, hardly an inviting prospect in today's academic climate. One answer is to draw upon a resource hardly tapped so far for intercultural communication: the humanities. Language teachers, for example, could contribute greatly. While few teachers of Arabic or Chinese are available, French and Spanish instructors are not in short supply. Besides reorienting themselves, these instructors would also bring a needed humanistic ingredient: History and literature are conspicuously neglected in intercultural communication. A novel like Ousmane Sembène's *Xala* or a play like Wole Soyinka's *Death and the King's Horseman* provides insights that far outshine the wisdom of statistical information.

An additional resource is the large number of Third World students in   27
American universities, particularly those in engineering. (At some schools as many as half the engineering graduate students are from the Third World.) They can be enlisted to help in the development and teaching of intercultural professional programs. Consider the "informants" who have been used in linguistics courses for many years. Why not cultural informants, involved in lively give-and-take discussions in American classrooms? The domestic students would be helped to overcome their lack of knowledge (which at times verges on xenophobia). The foreign students would enjoy being givers, not only takers. They would have the satisfaction, perhaps with some remuneration, of putting their culture to work with ours. Considering the career prospects of these men and women in their native countries, the effect may be doubly significant.

Pedagogy can be fitted to the needs and structures of the professional   28
programs. Case study methods lend themselves to intercultural communication. In engineering, design problems that cross cultures can be used; this has been demonstrated in the Guided Design program developed by Charles Wales at West Virginia University where students solve fairly extensive design problems by drawing on several engineering and nonengineering disciplines.

To effect the conjunction proposed here, all sides need to go to work.   29
The professional schools must no longer be the passive recipients of outside services. They must stop paying lip service to cultural sensitivity while considering marketing and technology the real thing. Similarly, the intercultural specialist must recognize that the usual social-scientific approach will not necessarily serve. If educators cannot reorient themselves to bridge schools and departments, how can they orient students to bridge cultures?

QUESTIONS

Words to Know

gender (paragraph 1), unison (1), disinterested (2), Third World (2), realm (2), burgeoning (3), affinity (3), expertise (3), elites (4), ethnocentric (5), cocoon (6), implicit (6), ubiquity (6), consortium (6), Taj Mahals (6), monolithic (9), pragmatic (10), optimal (11), ecology (11), accessory (11), peripatetic (11), conscientious (12), plutocrat (12), fatuous (13), garb (13), construe (13), discretion (14), interdisciplinary (15), miniaturization (16), labor-intensive (16), taxonomy (17), albatross (18), cognitive (18), homogeneous (20), vagaries (21), academe (21), implemented (22), enhanced (23), veneer (24), passive (24), fervor (25), biases (25), tolerance of ambiguity (25), confirmatory (25), preconception (25), xenophobia (27), remuneration (27), case study method (28), conjunction (29).

Some of the Issues

1. In paragraph 2 the author describes the image he believes Americans have of themselves. What is this image? Do you agree?
2. Several factors are discussed in the first part of the essay that according to Knepler serve to isolate the American abroad from the culture he is living in. Cite them.
3. Paragraph 6 describes the "cocoon" that envelops Americans who work abroad. Explain that term and show how Knepler supports his argument.
4. In paragraph 10 Knepler asserts that American politics are pragmatic, not ideological. Explain what this means. What evidence can you find to support or contradict this view?
5. The American professional, according to Knepler, is likely to have some specific effects on the country to which he has traveled. Cite some of these that seem to you to be the most important.
6. In paragraphs 18 and 19 Knepler describes intercultural communications as analogous to the freshman English course. How does he make that analogy explicit?
7. The essay suggests some solutions, or partial solutions, to some of the problems it discusses. Cite some of these. Who in each case is to implement them?

The Way We Are Told

8. The author begins with a description of a scene from a TV news broadcast. How is this incident used to set the scene?
9. Why is "real" in quotation marks in paragraph 15?
10. What audiences is this essay addressed to? Cite evidence to support your claim.

Some Ideas for Essays

11. What qualities or experiences would, in your opinion, cause a person to be sensitive to cultural differences? Make a list of such qualities, put them in specific, logical order, and write an essay, devoting a paragraph to each of them.
12. To what extent do you believe you are sensitive to and understanding of cultural differences? To what personal qualities or experiences do you attribute your sensitivity?

EFFECTS OF DEVELOPMENT

Ivan Illich

Ivan Illich was born in Vienna, Austria in 1926 and studied theology in Rome. He received a doctorate from the University of Salzburg in 1951 and was ordained a priest in the Catholic Church in the same year. From 1951 to 1956 he served as a parish priest in a Puerto-Rican neighborhood in New York City. He is now a researcher at the Center for Intercultural Documentation in Cuernavaca, Mexico. He has written a number of books noted for their questioning of accepted values and ideas. Among them are *Deschooling Society* (1971), *Energy and Equity* (1974), *Medical Nemesis* (1976), *Disabling Professions* (1977), and *Toward a History of Needs* (1978). The essay reprinted here first appeared in *The New York Review of Books* in November 1969.

It is now common to demand that the rich nations convert their war machine [1] into a program for the development of the Third World. The poorer four fifths of humanity multiply unchecked while their per capita consumption actually declines. This population expansion and decrease of consumption threaten the industrialized nations, who may still, as a result, convert their defense budgets to the economic pacification of poor nations. And this in turn could produce irreversible despair, because the plows of the rich can do as much harm as their swords. U.S. trucks can do more lasting damage than U.S. tanks. It is easier to create mass demand for the former than for the latter. Only a minority needs heavy weapons, while a majority can become dependent on unrealistic levels of supply for such productive machines as modern trucks. Once the Third World has become a mass market for the goods, products, and processes which are designed by the rich for themselves, the discrepancy between demand for these Western artifacts and the supply will increase indefinitely. The family car cannot drive the poor into the jet age, nor can a school system provide the poor with education, nor can the family icebox insure healthy food for them.

It is evident that only one man in a thousand in Latin America can [2] afford a Cadillac, a heart operation, or a Ph.D. This restriction on the goals of development does not make us despair of the fate of the Third World, and the reason is simple. We have not yet come to conceive of a Cadillac as necessary for good transportation, or of a heart operation as normal healthy

351

care, or of a Ph.D. as the prerequisite of an acceptable education. In fact, we recognize at once that the importation of Cadillacs should be heavily taxed in Peru, that an organ transplant clinic is a scandalous plaything to justify the concentration of more doctors in Bogotá, and that a Betatron is beyond the teaching facilities of the University of São Paolo.

Unfortunately, it is not held to be universally evident that the majority   3
of Latin Americans—not only of our generation, but also of the next and the next again—cannot afford any kind of automobile, or any kind of hospitalization, or for that matter an elementary school education. We suppress our consciousness of this obvious reality because we hate to recognize the corner into which our imagination has been pushed. So persuasive is the power of the institutions we have created that they shape not only our preferences, but actually our sense of possibilities. We have forgotten how to speak about modern transportation that does not rely on automobiles and airplanes. Our conceptions of modern health care emphasize our ability to prolong the lives of the desperately ill. We have become unable to think of better education except in terms of more complex schools and of teachers trained for ever longer periods. Huge institutions producing costly services dominate the horizons of our inventiveness.

We have embodied our world view into our institutions and are now   4
their prisoners. Factories, news media, hospitals, governments, and schools produce goods and services packaged to contain our view of the world. We— the rich—conceive of progress as the expansion of these establishments. We conceive of heightened mobility as luxury and safety packaged by General Motors or Boeing. We conceive of improving the general well-being as increasing the supply of doctors and hospitals, which package health along with protracted suffering. We have come to identify our need for further learning with the demand for ever longer confinement to classrooms. In other words, we have packaged education with custodial care, certification for jobs, and the right to vote, and wrapped them all together with indoctrination in the Christian, liberal or communist virtues.

In less than a hundred years industrial society has molded patent solu-   5
tions to basic human needs and converted us to the belief that man's needs were shaped by the Creator as demands for the products we have invented. This is as true for Russia and Japan as for the North Atlantic community. The consumer is trained for obsolescence, which means continuing loyalty toward the same producers who will give him the same basic packages in different quality or new wrappings.

Industrialized societies can provide such packages for personal con-   6
sumption for most of their citizens, but this is no proof that these societies are sane, or economical, or that they promote life. The contrary is true. The

more the citizen is trained in the consumption of packaged goods and services, the less effective he seems to become in shaping his environment. His energies and finances are consumed in procuring ever new models of his staples, and the environment becomes a by-product of his own consumption habits.

The design of the "package deals" of which I speak is the main cause 7 of the high cost of satisfying basic needs. So long as every man "needs" his car, our cities must endure longer traffic jams and absurdly expensive remedies to relieve them. So long as health means maximum length of survival, our sick will get ever more extraordinary surgical interventions and the drugs required to deaden their consequent pain. So long as we want to use school to get children out of their parents' hair or to keep them off the street and out of the labor force, our young will be retained in endless schooling and will need ever-increasing incentives to endure the ordeal.

Rich nations now benevolently impose a straightjacket of traffic jams, 8 hospital confinements, and classrooms on the poor nations, and by international agreement call this "development." The rich and schooled and old of the world try to share their dubious blessings by foisting their pre-packaged solutions on to the Third World. Traffic jams develop in São Paolo, while almost a million northeastern Brazilians flee the drought by walking 500 miles. Latin American doctors get training at the New York Hospital for Special Surgery, which they apply to only a few, while amoebic dysentery remains endemic in slums where 90 percent of the population live. A tiny minority gets advanced education in basic science in North America—not infrequently paid for by their own governments. If they return at all to Bolivia, they become second-rate teachers of pretentious subjects at La Paz or Cochibamba. The rich export outdated versions of their standard models.

Each car which Brazil puts on the road denies fifty people good trans- 9 portation by bus. Each merchandised refrigerator reduces the chance of building a community freezer. Every dollar spent in Latin America on doctors and hospitals costs a hundred lives, to adopt a phrase of Jorge de Ahumada, the brilliant Chilean economist. Had each dollar been spent on providing safe drinking water, a hundred lives could have been saved. Each dollar spent on schooling means more privileges for the few at the cost of the many; at best it increases the number of those who, before dropping out, have been taught that those who stay longer have earned the right to more power, wealth, and prestige. What such schooling does is to teach the schooled the superiority of the better schooled.

All Latin American countries are frantically intent on expanding their 10 school systems. No country now spends less than the equivalent of 18 percent of tax-derived public income on education—which means schooling—and

many countries spend almost double that. But even with these huge invest-
ments, no country yet succeeds in giving five full years of education to more
than one third of its population; supply and demand for schooling grow geometrically apart. And what is true about schooling is equally true about the
products of most institutions in the process of modernization in the Third
World.

Continued technological refinements of products which are already   11
established on the market frequently benefit the producer far more than the
consumer. The more complex production processes tend to enable only the
largest producer to continually replace outmoded models, and to focus the
demand of the consumer on the marginal improvement of what he buys, no
matter what the concomitant side effects: higher prices, diminished life span,
less general usefulness, higher cost of repairs. Think of the multiple uses for
a simple can opener, whereas an electric one, if it works at all, opens only
some kinds of cans, and costs one hundred times as much.

This is equally true for a piece of agricultural machinery and for an   12
academic degree. The midwestern farmer can become convinced of his need
for a four-axle vehicle which can go 70 m.p.h. on the highways, has an electric windshield wiper and upholstered seats, and can be turned in for a new
one within a year or two. Most of the world's farmers don't need such speed,
nor have they ever met with such comfort, nor are they interested in obsolescence. They need low-priced transport, in a world where time is not
money, where manual wipers suffice, and where a piece of heavy equipment
should outlast a generation. Such a mechanical donkey requires entirely different engineering and design than one produced for the U.S. market. This
vehicle is not in production.

Most of South America needs paramedical workers who can function   13
for indefinite periods without the supervision of an MD. Instead of establishing a process to train midwives and visiting healers who know how to use a
very limited arsenal of medicines while working independently, Latin American universities establish every year a new school of specialized nursing or
nursing administration to prepare professionals who can function only in a
hospital, and pharmacists who know how to sell increasingly more dangerous
drugs.

Some years ago I watched workmen putting up a sixty-foot Coca-Cola   14
sign on a desert plain in the Mexquital. A serious drought and famine had
just swept over the Mexican highland. My host, a poor Indian in Ixmiquilpan,
had just offered his visitors a tiny tequila glass of the costly black sugar-water.
When I recall this scene I still feel anger; but I feel much more incensed
when I remember UNESCO meetings at which well-meaning and well-paid

bureaucrats seriously discussed Latin American school cirricula, and when I think of the speeches of enthusiastic liberals advocating the need for more schools.

The fraud perpetrated by the salesmen of schools is less obvious but much more fundamental than the self-satisfied salesmanship of the Coca-Cola or Ford representative, because the schoolman hooks his people on a much more demanding drug. Elementary school attendance is not a harmless luxury, but more like the coca chewing of the Andean Indian, which harnesses the worker to the boss. 15

The higher the dose of schooling an individual has received, the more depressing his experience of withdrawal. The seventh-grade dropout feels his inferiority much more acutely than the dropout from the third grade. The schools of the Third World administer their opium with much more effect than the churches of other epochs. As the mind of a society is progressively schooled, step by step its individuals lose their sense that it might be possible to live without being inferior to others. As the majority shifts from the land into the city, the hereditary inferiority of the peon is replaced by the inferiority of the school dropout who is held personally responsible for his failure. Schools rationalize the divine origin of social stratification with much more rigor than churches have ever done. 16

Until this day no Latin American country has declared youthful underconsumers of Coca-Cola or cars as lawbreakers, while all Latin American countries have passed laws which define the early dropout as a citizen who has not fulfilled his legal obligations. The Brazilian government recently almost doubled the number of years during which schooling is legally compulsory and free. From now on any Brazilian dropout under the age of sixteen will be faced during his lifetime with the reproach that he did not take advantage of a legally obligatory privilege. This law was passed in a country where not even the most optimistic could foresee the day when such levels of schooling would be provided for only 25 percent of the young. The adoption of international standards of schooling forever condemns most Latin Americans to marginality or exclusion from social life—in a word, underdevelopment. 17

QUESTIONS

Words to Know

Third World (paragraph 1), per capita (1), pacification (1), discrepancy (1), artifacts (1), prerequisite (2), embodied (4), mobility (4), protracted (4), indoctrination (4), patent solutions (5), obsolescence (5), staples (6), confinements (8), dubious (8), foisting (8), geometrically (10), marginal (11), concomitant (11), paramedical (13), midwives (13), arsenal (13), drought (14), UNESCO (14), peon (16), rationalize (16), social stratification (16), compulsory (17), obligatory (17), underdevelopment (17).

Some of the Issues

1. What allusion is Illich making in paragraph 1 when he states "the plows of the rich can do as much harm as their swords"?
2. What is the meaning of Illich's statement, "the rich export outdated versions of their standard models" (paragraph 8)?
3. In paragraph 9, after discussing the increase in money spent on public education, Illich says, "What such schooling does is to teach the schooled the superiority of the better schooled." What point is Illich trying to make?
4. In paragraph 10 Illich appears to make a distinction between education and schooling. What might that distinction be?
5. What accounts for Illich's anger at seeing the Coca-Cola sign in the Mexican desert, and for his greater anger toward UNESCO officials and "enthusiastic liberals" (paragraph 14)?
6. Illich deals with several different aspects of development: medical care, transportation, and education in particular. In what respects is his argument the same in discussing all three? In what respects is it different?
7. Illich tells the reader what kind of transportation, education, and health care services he disapproves of. What might be the components of a system he might look on more favorably?
8. What does Illich say about dropouts (paragraphs 16 and 17)? What, in his opinion, causes the dropout "problem"?

The Way We Are Told

9. Illich's method is to state or imply the commonly accepted view and then contradict it. Give several examples of this method of argument.
10. At times Illich uses a specific example or event or product to stand for a

large category of items. How effective is this part-for-the-whole technique of argument? Cite examples.

Some Subjects for Essays

11. Illich talks about the effect of "development" on the Third World, but perhaps his argument might apply to the United States as well. Some critics of United States health care have deplored the availability of very risky major surgery and expensive but seldom used equipment in hospitals, when preventive health care and clinics are underfunded. Support or oppose this view.
12. Examine the advertisements in one or two issues of a popular magazine designed for a general audience. In your opinion which of the advertised objects are really useful to people? What are the appeals made to the consumer? Are these appeals made on the basis of the products' usefulness or on other factors?
13. The views that Illich expresses about education in poor countries are perhaps the most controversial parts of his article. In an essay, summarize his views and then comment on them.
14. Illich claims that the consumer is trained for obsolescence. Agree or disagree, focusing on the marketing of one product, such as automobiles, appliances, or clothing.

THE SECOND COMING

William Butler Yeats

W. B. Yeats (1865–1939) was born in Dublin of Anglo-Irish parents. He was a leader in establishing the Irish National Theater, for which he wrote several plays. His reputation, however, rests mainly on his lyric poetry, published in volumes such as *The Wild Swans at Coole* (1917) and *The Tower* (1927). He was awarded the Nobel Prize for Literature in 1923. "The Second Coming" was published in his *Collected Poems* (1923).

Turning and turning in the widening gyre
The falcon cannot hear the falconer;
Things fall apart; the centre cannot hold;
Mere anarchy is loosed upon the world,
The blood-dimmed tide is loosed, and everywhere
The ceremony of innocence is drowned;
The best lack all conviction, while the worst
Are full of passionate intensity.

Surely some revelation is at hand;
Surely the Second Coming is at hand.
The Second Coming! Hardly are those words out
When a vast image out of *Spiritus Mundi*
Troubles my sight: somewhere in sands of the desert
A shape with lion body and the head of a man,
A gaze blank and pitiless as the sun,
Is moving its slow thighs, while all about it
Reel shadows of the indignant desert birds.
The darkness drops again; but now I know
That twenty centuries of stony sleep
Were vexed to nightmare by a rocking cradle
And what rough beast, its hour come round at last,
Slouches towards Bethlehem to be born?

NINE

Defining Culture

*T*o many people the word culture, when used in everyday language, means museums, classical music, Shakespeare, and climbing about ancient ruins. The very mention of it makes them slightly nervous. Sometimes we also speak, somewhat vaguely, about a "youth culture" or a "rock culture." To an anthropologist, on the other hand, as a student of the ways of mankind, culture means, as Clyde Kluckhohn puts it, "the total life way of a people." What we say and do, love or hate, find natural or unnatural, are largely conditioned by our being part of a particular society—in other words, our culture.

In the first selection, Marston Bates defines the word natural. He uses incidents from his own experience to show that what is natural to one person may seem quite unnatural to another. Human beings have a great, unique ability to adapt themselves to a vast range of different environments. That fact in turn means that individuals may also differ widely in their views of what is "right." As Bates says, "The outstanding peculiarity of man is the great control of custom, of culture, over behavior."

In the second selection, Clyde Kluckhohn first defines culture and then demonstrates the facts of cultural difference through a set of examples. But he also reminds us of "the inevitables of biology." Biologically speaking, mankind is one, and cultural differences, however great, are all subject to "the same biological equipment" that serves us all.

Peter Freuchen's description of the Eskimo house demonstrates what it means to live in harmony with nature, especially under the harsh conditions of an Arctic climate. Ashley Montagu ("American Men Don't Cry") demonstrates how a culture may inhibit a natural process and condition its members to accept that suppression of their nature.

In the last selection Leonore Tiefer takes up what may seem to be a universal, natural expression—the kiss—and shows that it, too, is a result of cultural conditioning.

ON BEING HUMAN

Marston Bates

Marston Bates (1906–1974), after attending the University of Florida, worked for a time for the United Fruit Company in several Central American countries. His interests gravitated early toward the tropics and, in particular, tropical diseases, which he studied in widely different countries on three continents, mostly while working for the Rockefeller Foundation. In 1952 he became professor of zoology at the University of Michigan. He has written many books, among them *The Nature of Natural History* (1950), *Man in Nature* (1960), and *Gluttons and Libertines* (1967), from which the following excerpt is taken.

Every schoolday morning our son Glenn comes to the bedroom at a quarter to seven with cups of coffee. Nancy, obviously, has done a good job of raising our children—the oldest at home has the alarm clock, and they all take a certain amount of responsibility for keeping their parents in line. The coffee routine has now passed on through all four of them; and when Glenn goes away I don't know what we will do. Look after ourselves, I suppose.

I switch on the light and automatically look at my watch to check on Glenn's timing—we are all slaves of that damned clock. School, office, lecture, railway, dentist. They say it all started with the monastery bells of the Middle Ages; but however it got started, Time now permeates every aspect of our civilization. The slavery starts at an early age: the schools, whatever else they do, manage to instill an acute dread of being tardy in most children. A few rebellious people manage to be tardy for most of their lives, despite the pressures; but we hardly regard them as models of conduct.

Anyway, I try to make some bright crack as I check on Glenn's timing, but it usually falls flat because neither of us feels very chipper before dawn. I reach for a cigarette—a deplorable habit, but again I am a slave—and start the slow process of pulling myself together to face the world for another day.

I have been sleeping on a bed. This seems perfectly natural to me. But if we take "natural" to mean doing what most people do, it is rather odd behavior. My guess would be that perhaps a quarter of the people of the world sleep on beds. I suspect that the commonest sleeping arrangement is matting that can be rolled up and stowed during the day—which is certainly practical from the point of view of space utilization. In warm climates the most practical sleeping arrangement is the hammock—an invention of the American Indians. It is easily taken down if the space is needed; it is portable;

it isolates the sleeper from creeping things on the ground; and it provides maximum ventilation. It takes getting used to; but so do most things.

The paraphernalia involved in Western sleeping become more peculiar when looked at in detail: springs, mattresses, sheets, blankets, pillows, pillow-cases. Beds have a long history in the Graeco-Roman and Western worlds, but this total accumulation must be rather modern. Much of it I find puzzling. Our bed, for instance, has springs; but my wife has put a bedboard over them. Why not just have a board to start with? And then there are all of the rules for making up a bed, for covering it, for airing it. You could write a whole book about beds, and I suspect someone has.

Habitually I sleep naked. This seems to be rather aberrant behavior in our culture—or in most others. To be sure, I keep a dressing gown close at hand, just in case the house should catch on fire. But it appears that most men in the United States nowadays sleep either in pajamas (a word and custom of Hindu origin) or in underclothes (a particulary common habit with college students). A sociologist might study this, to see whether there is any relation between night clothing and geographical region, or median income, or level of education. I remember reading in the Kinsey report on the human male that nudity was an upper-class characteristic, which made me feel smug for a while.

Women, in my limited experience, cling to nightgowns, though they can sometimes be persuaded to take them off. Nightshirts for men became rare about a generation ago; I know a few people who still wear them—eccentrics, I suppose. It is curious how fashion penetrates even into the privacy of the bedroom. It may be, of course, that more women now wear pajamas than wear nightgowns—my figures on the subject are not really statistically significant.

I left myself smoking a cigarette and drinking a cup of coffee. I wish I could break that cigarette habit. Do you suppose anyone starts the morning in bed with a cigar or a pipe? It doesn't seem right, somehow. As for coffee—in England it would be tea—and mostly in the United States in a private home many people find it an absolute necessity to start the day with a cup of coffee.

Finally I get courage enough to crawl out from under the blanket into the world—or at least into the bathroom. Civilization does have advantages. I brush my teeth and exercise my gums just as my dentist has told me to—what a lot of trouble those teeth cause us! Then I shave. This is an ancient practice among some of the so-called "white" races which, along with the Australian blackfellows, are the only peoples with enough facial hair to bother with. It is said that the ancient Egyptians shaved off all body hair, but with us nowadays men limit the shaving process to the face. Our women

shave their legs and their armpits, as I am reminded when I find my razor
out of place. I cut myself, and I think that my wife will scold. She can't
understand why, after some forty years of daily shaving, I haven't learned
better. I don't understand either.

Then I get dressed. What a long cultural history lies behind each action 10
here! The males in our society wear "arctic type" fitted garments, an invention of the barbaric tribes of prehistoric northern Europe. Trousers, neatly
preserved by the acid waters, have been dug up from Danish peat bogs.
These trousers are convenient in cold weather, as any woman can tell you.
The tropical draped garment, which carries over into the dress of our
females, is more comfortable in hot weather. But comfort is a minor consideration in our clothing habits.

Each morning I have to face the problem of what to wear. I have lived 11
much of my life in the tropics, and I hate the feeling of a tie around my
neck and of leather shoes encasing my feet. But a professor is supposed to
wear shoes, tie and coat. He is far less subject to convention than, say, a
banker or a physician is; but there are limits if he doesn't want to be considered a crackpot. I want to play my role well enough to be accepted by the
society in which I live, so most often (on days when I am due to lecture) I
put on a tie and try to look respectable even though I feel like a fraud. My
aim, as I phrase it to myself, is to be "a reasonable facsimile of a proper
professor." But I don't know that I succeed very well.

Breakfast. "Glenn, you *must* finish your cereal." Eating soon after you 12
get up is another of those fundamental laws of nature in the United States.
In other parts of the world the fundamental laws of nature differ, but they
are equally inexorable, whatever their form. Cereal, milk—whoever first had
the idea of getting food by squeezing the udder of a cow or goat?—eggs,
toast, fruit juice. In the South, grits come with the eggs automatically; at
some line in Kentucky and Virginia these give way to hash-browned potatoes. To the west, grits disappear somewhere in Texas.

Thus in the matter of breakfast we have cultural diversity, geographical 13
diversity, individual diversity. We conform with the common usage of our
group in when we eat, what we eat, how we eat it. Sometimes, too, we
diverge. I almost wrote "rebel" but such a strong word hardly seems appropriate for breakfast—though a child's reaction may be a real enough
rebellion.

Quite unintentionally I have got into a curious situation in this breakfast 14
matter. I have never been much given to eating, especially the first thing in
the morning, and I solved the breakfast problem some years ago by the simple expedient of breaking two raw eggs into a glass of orange juice and drinking the mixture. The needed nutrients are present, with no time spent over

the stove, no frying pan to clean—only a glass to rinse out. This seems to me eminently sensible. The rest of the household accepts my behavior, though no one has ever made any move to imitate.

For years I didn't have the courage to order this breakfast in a restaurant. Finally a friend who knew of my home habits persuaded me to try it: he pointed out that restaurants were supposed to serve people's needs, and why should I be afraid of what the waitress would think. This first try was in the French Quarter of New Orleans, and no eyebrows were raised. But when I gave the same order in cafés along the highway driving north, I met incredulity and reluctance. It turned out to be all right if I asked to have the eggs beaten in the juice—I suppose because everyone knows about eggnogs. I still haven't had the courage to order anything except an ordinary breakfast in the dining room of a proper hotel.

Such is the force of opinion governing human conduct even in a trivial detail. My conduct, at least. Then I stop and wonder whether I am peculiar. I suppose the average waitress in the average middle-class restaurant would definitely say "yes." On the waterfront they are used to the idea of raw eggs in beer, but they might think the orange juice odd. So whether I am peculiar or not depends on where I am, which opens up some large questions.

Everyone, really, is peculiar. Any biologist, used to studying the behavior of animals, becomes puzzled when he turns to man—and he is forced to the conclusion that the human animal as a species is peculiar. How did we get this way? And what does it mean?

We could say that human actions are never to be understood in purely biological terms. Like other animals, we have to eat—we need proteins, fats, carbohydrates, assorted vitamins and minerals. There is nothing unusual about these food requirements or about the way the human digestive system works. The process of metabolism with man, as with other animals, results in the accumulation of waste products which must be got rid of. The wastes take the form of urine and feces. The inner workings, then, are biological; but the outward actions, the modes of behavior, are something else again.

What does it mean, to be "natural"? Maybe it is natural for man to hide himself when excreting. Then maybe it is natural not only to hide the fact in the bushes, but also to gloss over the action with a deceptive kind of vocabulary. In many parts of the world the idea of decent and indecent actions is entangled with the use of decent and indecent words. One could argue that is natural for man to treat actions and words as equivalent—at least it seems to be easy enough to start a fight by calling someone a bad name. If excretion, though unfortunately necessary, is naturally bad, one can see how the word for it naturally becomes bad too. But this still leaves puzzles.

"Natural" clearly means quite a number of different things, so that, 20 when we start to talk about it, we can easily become lost in semantic problems. I checked the unabridged Oxford English Dictionary and found eighteen main definitions for "natural," each with a number of subheadings. For our present purposes, however, we can reduce these to three general ideas, which can be most readily distinguished in terms of their opposites. We can use "natural" as distinguished from "supernatural," "artificial" and "unnatural."

Natural and supernatural need concern us little. Our scientific civiliza- 21 tion assumes that the world is orderly and not subject to capricious intervention and control by spirits. There are many cultures in which spirits are just as "real" as sharks or leopards—and a great deal more dangerous and more difficult to cope with. But in theory at least we treat the events of everyday life as the consequence of natural, rather than supernatural, forces.

Artificial is an easy word in some ways, more difficult in others. Essen- 22 tially it means man-made. This is clear in the case of artifacts. An artifical rose is made from wax, glass, paper or what have you, in imitation of nature. Yet, if we stop to think about it, the "natural" rose growing in our garden is also man-made—the product of selection, hybridization and cultivation by man, and unlike anything that occurs in nature without human intervention. We recognize this rather vaguely when we talk about artificial hybrids or artificial selection, but we are, in general, reluctant to face the extent to which our environment has been altered by our own actions—the extent to which, in this sense, it is artificial.

If we use artificial to cover anything made or altered by man, the word 23 really loses much of its usefulness. There is nothing natural left in the environments that most of us live in. To escape from an artifical world we have to go to the north woods of Canada, the forests of the upper Amazon, or the southwestern deserts. So much for the environment. But there is nothing natural left in human behavior, either: it is all governed or modified in varying degree by culture, tradition, opinion. We can hardly talk about artifical manners, for instance, because all manners are artificial; there is no natural man.

There may be a gain in the use of artificial in this very broad sense 24 because we begin to see the extent to which human actions are the consequence of the human condition. We begin to see the hazards of trying to determine what is natural for man by studying apes or monkeys or white rats.

But if everything about man is artificial, if nothing is natural, does this 25 mean that all human actions are unnatural? Clearly not, because we have shifted to another meaning of natural. Unnatural carries the idea of abnormal, unusual, strange. This doesn't help much: you can get into as much trouble with normal and abnormal as with natural and unnatural. We are involved with the cultural context in which all people live: what is unusual for some may be commonplace for others. For us it is unnatural to eat worms; for the Chinese, unnatural to drink milk. Sometimes I am driven to think that calling anything unnatural merely means that the speaker does not approve of it.

All of which sheds little light on the human problem of being natural.   26
In the case of supernatural, most of us have no alternative to being natural during life, whatever may happen afterward. The sorcerers and magicians in our midst may think they escape this kind of naturalness, but the rest of us have come to view their claims dubiously. In the case of artificial, there seems to be no escape from artificiality into naturalness. Only in the case of natural versus unnatural do we have an apparent choice—which boils down to the question of whether or not to act in accord with the usual, the normal, of our particular culture, our way of life. We are faced with the problem of conformity, about which we in the West at least have lately become self-conscious.

One could argue that natural behavior is that usual to, or conforming   27
with, human nature—but for that one needs a fairly definite concept of human nature. The anthropologists, with their descriptions of cultural relativism, and the psychologists, with their emphasis on individual learning and experience, have shown us that this is not easy. One comes to sympathize with the existentialist position that there is no such thing as human nature, that each man makes himself.

But if it is difficult to determine human nature, one can at least discuss   28
the human condition, most easily in physical terms. Man is a mammal and a primate, which immediately defines many characteristics. He cannot spend his whole life swimming, like a dolphin; nor browse on grass, like a cow; nor scramble up a tree trunk unaided, like a squirrel or like some of his monkey relatives. He has an upright posture, with appropriately modifed feet, legs and trunk, which makes him unique among the primates. His hands and arms, not needed for walking, are free for other functions, thus allowing him to develop his great ability at manipulating things. There are limits though: I have often wished, in situations such as cocktail parties, that I had a prehensile tail so that I could manage my drink, my canapé and my cigarette at the same time. A spider monkey would have no trouble.

Man has binocular vision, which enables him to judge distance well; and   29
he can discriminate form and color. Many animals, however, have keener vision. Man's hearing is moderately good, but his sense of smell is quite poor. One could go on with such a list and describe the anatomical and physiological traits of the human animal with some accuracy, and in so doing one aspect of the human condition would be described. But how little this helps

us in understanding ourselves! No matter how much care we devote to the study of the anatomy of the brain, we learn nothing about why "shit" is an indecent word for a necessary action; nothing about why men wear trousers and women skirts in our culture; nothing about food habits or sex habits. Anatomy and physiology tell us nothing about shame, pride or modesty.

Our problem turns on the mind rather than the body: but how do we dissect the mind? It doesn't help much to say that body and mind are not separate entities, but simply different aspects of the physical organism. Maybe we should shift terms and talk, not about mind, but about self-consciousness or awareness. But we are still bogged down in words. How our awareness compares with that of a chimpanzee, a monkey or a dog, we do not know. Certainly we can find comparable expressions of emotions in animals and men, as Charles Darwin showed long ago. Perhaps from this we can infer comparable emotions, but it is difficult to find out about this because we cannot carry on discussions with other animals.

Certainly it is difficult to separate human actions, emotions and attitudes from the human habit of talking. It would be interesting to know how all of this got started. Did those ape-men living in South Africa a half a million years ago "talk" in some way comparable with ours? Did they listen to the advice of a wise old chief, and did they try to be faithful to their mates? Had they developed special ideas about food, sex and excretion—in other words, did they have cultural taboos? Which I suppose is asking how human they were. Their brains were only a little larger than those of modern chimpanzees: a cranial capacity of 450–550 cc., compared with 350–450 for the chimp and with 1200–1500 for modern man. But it is hard to know what this means in terms of behavior.

These Australopithecines—as the South African apemen are properly called—were at least human enough to commit murder. Raymond Dart, in his book *Adventures with the Missing Link*, remarks on the jaw of an adolescent "which had been bashed in by a formidable blow from the front and delivered with great accuracy just to the left of the point of the jaw." Nothing of this sort happens in the case of squabbles among apes and monkeys, though they may be mean enough to each other when cooped up together in a zoo.

We have here direct evidence of a kind of behavior on the part of our remote evolutionary ancestors, though with no clue as to the meaning of the behavior; but even this much is rare. For the most part we have only bones and tools made of materials likely to survive—which tell us nothing about sex habits, or even skin color or body hair. We have, in short, considerable evidence to help us in reconstructing the evolution of the human skeleton, but almost none to help us reconstruct the history of human behavior. Yet our striking peculiarities are in behavior, not in skeleton. We can get ideas about the possible background by watching living monkeys and apes; but man is so different that these inferences must be interpreted with great caution. For the most part we can only speculate about the history of human behavior, bolstering our speculations with whatever evidence we can find. This is no road to certainty; but speculation often is the impetus for scientific investigation, and it can be illuminating.

The outstanding peculiarity of man is the great control of custom, of culture, over behavior. This is obvious enough in the case of such things as food, sex and excretion, but it is far more pervasive. We can't even get out of breath "naturally." If we are late for an appointment we may tend to exaggerate our breathlessness to show how hard we were trying. On the other hand, people of my age try to suppress their panting, trying to hide the deterioration of age—or of too much smoking.   34

The effect of culture on behavior is not limited to actions; it influences all physiology in many ways. This shows up in the psychosomatic diseases— ulcers, dermatitis, asthma and a host of little-understood effects of "mind" on "body." This relationship is especially irritating when you know that a particular worry is causing a distressing physical effect like dermatitis—yet you can't escape the worry. Here is where psychotherapy or drugs, benign or otherwise, come in.   35

Then there is the curious human trait of blushing, whereby thoughts influence peripheral blood circulation. Here again we run into the perplexing problem of consciousness: you can't stop yourself from blushing by deciding not to. The possible origin and meaning of blushing fascinated Darwin, but neither he nor anyone else seems to have arrived at a satisfactory explanation of the phenomenon.   36

There is also the opposite and equally little understood process of influence of conscious thought on inner physiology, as in the exercises of Yoga. Apparently there is little a man can't do to his body if he puts his mind to it.   37

The human habit of hiding physiology brings up the corresponding habit of hiding anatomy. . . . It would be interesting to know how the idea of covering parts of the body got started, but we shall probably never have direct evidence. It is quite likely that clothing started, not as protection against weather, nor as a consequence of a dawning sense of modesty, but rather as one aspect of the general human tendency to tamper with appearance. The list of things that different peoples do to their bodies is both curious and impressive: cutting hair; chipping teeth; painting, tattooing and scarring skin; deforming the infant skull or feet; circumcising the penis; cutting or enlarging the clitoris; cutting holes in ears or nose to hang things from; draping objects around the neck or waist or arms or ankles. The motive among Ubangi women for adorning themselves with ridiculous lip plugs is no dif-   38

ferent from the motive of Western women who use make-up and hair curl-
ers—or from that of men who endure haircuts, shaves and button-down-
collar shirts.

Clothing probably derives from the habit of hanging things around the   39
neck or waist, or perhaps from the habit of painting or scarring the skin. The
advantage of an extra and artificial skin in bad weather would then be a later
and accidental discovery. The concealing function of clothing is surely a sec-
ondary development and even in our society it is difficult to decide whether
modesty or display is more important in the design of clothes: witness the
bikinis, and the street-corner boys with their tight jeans.

I have not been able to think of any animal except man that ornaments   40
itself by picking up additions for skin, fur or feathers. There is no argument
about man's being a peculiar creature. But there is also no argument—
among biologists at least—about his being an animal. The animal heritage is
clear enough in anatomy and physiology—in the form of bones and muscles
and guts; in the need for breathing and eating and excreting and copulating.
But what of our heritage in behavior?

QUESTIONS

Words to Know

monastery (paragraph 2), permeates (2), acute (2), paraphernalia (5), aberrant (6), smug (6), eccentrics (7), arctic (10), barbaric (10), prehistoric (10),
peat bogs (10), encasing (11), inexorable (12), expedient (14), nutrients (14),
incredulity (15), gloss over (19), deceptive (19), semantic (20), unabridged
(20), capricious (21), hybridization (22), dubiously (26), cultural relativism
(27), existentialist (27), prehensile (28), binocular vision (29), dissect (30),
entities (30), cultural taboos (31), cranial (31), formidable (32), impetus (33),
pervasive (34), dermatitis (35), benign (35), phenomenon (36), Yoga (37),
tamper with (38).

Some of the Issues

1. In paragraphs 2 and 3 the words *slave* and *slavery* occur several times.
   Why does Bates use them?
2. In paragraphs 4 through 7 Bates discusses several customs including
   some that are "natural" to him. What is the purpose of this discussion?

3. After discussing several habits related to sleeping, Bates turns to dressing in paragraph 10, and refers to "cultural history." How does this reference differ from the way he has discussed culture in earlier paragraphs?

4. In paragraphs 12 through 15 Bates devotes a great amount of space to breakfast. What is his "problem" with breakfast and what causes it?

5. In paragraph 13 Bates uses the term *cultural diversity*. How do "cultural divisity" and "cultural history" (paragraph 10) differ from each other? How are they related?

6. In paragraph 24 Bates mentions "the hazards of trying to determine what is natural for man by studying apes or monkeys, or white rats." What are these hazards? Recapitulate Bates's argument that man is both an animal and at the same time different from all animals.

7. What would you say is Bates's primary purpose in writing "On Being Human"?

The Way We Are Told

8. Bates begins his essay with personal anecdotes and moves on to more general, analytical observations. However, he continues to intersperse personal material. What effect does this have on the reader? On the effectiveness of his argument?

9. Humor is used in what is really a serious essay. Find some instances of it and decide for yourself if they enhance the effectiveness of the piece.

10. Several times Bates uses the word *natural* in quotation marks (paragraphs 4, 19, and 20). On other occasions he uses the word without quotes. Why?

Some Subjects for Essays

11. Bates suggests that comfort is a minor consideration in our clothing habits. Choose a fashion (that you may or may not follow) that persists even though it is not comfortable: high heels, ties, tight jeans. Why in your opinion do people conform?

12. Bates describes his embarrassment in ordering his "peculiar" breakfast in a restaurant. In an essay, describe an incident when circumstances, such as an unconventional habit, embarrassed you or someone else.

13. Bates says "we are all slaves of that damned clock." Describe, with examples, why and how we are in that predicament, or disagree and tell why we are not slaves.

CUSTOMS

Clyde Kluckhohn

Clyde Kluckhohn (1905–1960) was at the time of his death a professor of anthropology at Harvard. As an undergraduate at Princeton, he became ill and was sent to New Mexico to recover. There he spent a great deal of time in Navaho country, learned the Navaho language, and developed a lifelong interest in Indian peoples. As a Rhodes scholar he studied at Oxford and received an M.A. from that university. At Harvard he played a major role in establishing its Russian Research Center. Among Kluckhohn's books are *To the Foot of the Rainbow* (1927), and several studies of the Navaho. The selection included here is an excerpt from *Mirror for Man* (1949).

Why do the Chinese dislike milk and milk products? Why would the Japanese die willingly in a Banzai charge that seemed senseless to Americans? Why do some nations trace descent through the father, others through the mother, still others through both parents? Not because different peoples have different instincts, not because they were destined by God or Fate to different habits, not because the weather is different in China and Japan and the United States. Sometimes shrewd common sense has an answer that is close to that of the anthropologist: "because they were brought up that way." By "culture" anthropology means the total life way of a people, the social legacy the individual acquires from his group. Or culture can be regarded as that part of the environment that is the creation of man.

This technical term has a wider meaning than the "culture" of history and literature. A humble cooking pot is as much a cultural product as is a Beethoven sonata. In ordinary speech a man of culture is a man who can speak languages other than his own, who is familiar with history, literature, philosophy, or the fine arts. In some cliques that definition is still narrower. The cultured person is one who can talk about James Joyce, Scarlatti, and Picasso. To the anthropologist, however, to be human is to be cultured. There is culture in general, and then there are the specific cultures such as Russian, American, British, Hottentot, Inca. The general abstract notion serves to remind us that we cannot explain acts solely in terms of the biological properties of the people concerned, their individual past experience, and the immediate situation. The past experience of other men in the form of culture enters into almost every event. Each specific culture constitutes a kind of blueprint for all of life's activities.

371

One of the interesting things about human beings is that they try to   3
understand themselves and their own behavior. While this has been particularly true of Europeans in recent times, there is no group which has not
developed a scheme or schemes to explain man's actions. To the insistent
human query "why?" the most exciting illumination anthropology has to
offer is that of the concept of culture. Its explanatory importance is comparable to categories such as evolution in biology, gravity in physics, disease in
medicine. A good deal of human behavior can be understood, and indeed
predicted, if we know a people's design for living. Many acts are neither
accidental nor due to personal pecularities nor caused by supernatural forces
nor simply mysterious. Even those of us who pride ourselves on our individualism follow most of the time a pattern not of our own making. We brush
our teeth on arising. We put on pants—not a loincloth or a grass skirt. We
eat three meals a day—not four or five or two. We sleep in a bed—not in a
hammock or on a sheep pelt. I do not have to know the individual and his
life history to be able to predict these and countless other regularities, including many in the thinking process, of all Americans who are not incarcerated
in jails or hospitals for the insane.

To the American woman a system of plural wives seems "instinctively"   4
abhorrent. She cannot understand how any woman can fail to be jealous and
uncomfortable if she must share her husband with other women. She feels it
"unnatural" to accept such a situation. On the other hand, a Koryak woman
of Siberia, for example, would find it hard to understand how a woman could
be so selfish and so undesirous of feminine companionship in the home as to
wish to restrict her husband to one mate.

Some years ago I met in New York City a young man who did not speak   5
a word of English and was obviously bewildered by American ways. By
"blood" he was as American as you or I, for his parents had gone from Indiana to China as missionaries. Orphaned in infancy, he was reared by a
Chinese family in a remote village. All who met him found him more
Chinese than American. The facts of his blue eyes and light hair were less
impressive than a Chinese style of gait, Chinese arm and hand movements,
Chinese facial expression, and Chinese modes of thought. The biological heritage was American, but the cultural training had been Chinese. He returned
to China.

Another example of another kind: I once knew a trader's wife in Ari-   6
zona who took a somewhat devilish interest in producing a cultural reaction.
Guests who came her way were often served delicious sandwiches filled with
a meat that seemed to be neither chicken nor tuna fish yet was reminiscent
of both. To queries she gave no reply until each had eaten his fill. She then
explained that what they had eaten was not chicken, not tuna fish, but the

rich, white flesh of freshly killed rattlesnakes. The response was instantaneous—vomiting, often violent vomiting. A biological process is caught in a cultural web.

A highly intelligent teacher with long and successful experience in the public schools of Chicago was finishing her first year in an Indian school. When asked how her Navaho pupils compared in intelligence with Chicago youngsters, she replied, "Well, I just don't know. Sometimes the Indians seem just as bright. At other times they just act like dumb animals. The other night we had a dance in the high school. I saw a boy who is one of the best students in my English class standing off by himself. So I took him over to a pretty girl and told them to dance. But they just stood there with their heads down. They wouldn't even say anything." I inquired if she knew whether or not they were members of the same clan. "What difference would that make?"

"How would you feel about getting into bed with your brother?" The teacher walked off in a huff, but, actually, the two cases were quite comparable in principle. To the Indian the type of bodily contact involved in our social dancing has a directly sexual connotation. The incest taboos between members of the same clan are as severe as between true brothers and sisters. The shame of the Indians at the suggestion that a clan brother and sister should dance and the indignation of the white teacher at the idea that she should share a bed with an adult brother represent equally nonrational responses, culturally standardized unreason.

All this does not mean that there is no such thing as raw human nature. The very fact that certain of the same institutions are found in all known societies indicates that at bottom all human beings are very much alike. The files of the Cross-Cultural Survey at Yale University are organized according to categories such as "marriage ceremonies," "life crisis rites," "incest taboos." At least seventy-five of these categories are represented in every single one of the hundreds of cultures analyzed. This is hardly surprising. The members of all human groups have about the same biological equipment. All men undergo the same poignant life experiences such as birth, helplessness, illness, old age, and death. The biological potentialities of the species are the blocks with which cultures are built. Some patterns of every culture crystallize around focuses provided by the inevitables of biology: the difference between the sexes, the presence of persons of different ages, the varying physical strength and skill of individuals. The facts of nature also limit culture forms. No culture provides patterns for jumping over trees or for eating iron ore.

QUESTIONS

Words to Know

Banzai charge (paragraph 1), shrewd (1), cliques (2), James Joyce (2), Scarlatti (2), Picasso (2), Hottentot (2), Inca (2), insistent (3), query (3), illumination (3), incarcerated (3), instinctively (4), abhorrent (4), gait (5), reminiscent (6), connotation (8), incest taboos (8), clan (8), life crisis rites (9), poignant (9), potentialities (9), species (9), crystallize (9), inevitable (9).

Some of the Issues

1. In paragraph 2 Kluckhohn gives us two different meanings of the word *culture*. Explain the difference between them.
2. Explain what the author means when he says in paragraph 3 that "why" is a persistent human question. What does he mean when he says anthropology offers "the concept of culture" as an "illumination" of that question?
3. Explain the meaning of the two anecdotes in paragraphs 5 and 6. Are they simply to present examples of cultural differences? Do they indicate more than that?
4. In what way does the anecdote in paragraphs 7 and 8 differ from the preceding two?
5. What is the point Kluckhohn tries to make when, at the end of paragraph 8, he sums up with the term "culturally standardized unreason"? Can you cite additional examples?
6. In paragraph 9, after citing several examples of cultural differences, Kluckhohn asserts that "at bottom all human beings are very much alike." Is he contradicting himself? Sum up Kluckhohn's arguments for both diversity and similarity.

The Way We Are Told

7. Read once more the three anecdotes told in paragraphs 5 through 8 and consider the order in which they are told. Is there a purpose in this order?
8. Read Marston Bates's "On Being Human" which deals with much the same subject as Kluckhohn's essay. Cite the differences in the way the two authors make their argument.

9. Find places in Bates's and Kluckhohn's essays that closely parallel each other in content or form.
10. Can you draw any conclusions from the two essays as to differences in the audiences they are intended for?

Some Subjects for Essays

11. Cultural differences can occur in many ways, often near to home. Describe a time when you encountered cultural differences—in a friend's house, with a fellow student, in some unfamiliar setting—and examine the effect on you as well as, perhaps, yours on the others involved.
12. Select a particular life situation and argue either for or against conformity in that situation. Weddings, examinations, travel, government offices, shopping, parties are some possibilities.

THE ESKIMO HOUSE

Peter Freuchen

Peter Freuchen (1886–1957) was a famous Danish explorer. He founded the town of Thule in Greenland, managing "the northernmost house in the world" there from 1910 to 1919. He was married to an Eskimo woman who died on an expedition in 1921. Not long after that he lost a foot through frostbite, which ended his days as an Arctic explorer. Later he said that the incident had turned him into a writer. He continued to travel widely in Arctic Russia and Greenland, however, and acted in a film based on his novel *Eskimo*. In the 1930s he wrote several novels about far northern life. The following selection is from his nonfiction work *Book of the Eskimo*, which appeared after his death in 1961.

The familiar igloo is used by the Polar Eskimos only as a temporary shelter during travels. Most of the winter they live in permanent winter houses made of stones and peat. Permanent, that is, for the winter, for each spring they are left by the inhabitants and automatically become public property the next fall.

You enter the winter house through an entrance tunnel, usually about fifteen feet long so as to provide both ventilation and protection against the outside cold. Since the house usually faces the sea, it is on a hill which the horizontal tunnel cuts into. The floor of the tunnel is laid with flat stones, the walls are piled up stones, and the ceiling is made of flat stones covered with peat or turf. It is low, so that you have to crawl in on your hands and knees.

In the tunnel, you will find a strange little instrument, a little saber of wood or bone, called a *tilugtut*. When snow is falling or drifting outside, thousands of snow crystals will be lodged in the long hair of your skin clothes. If you enter the warm house like that, they will melt and make your clothes wet and heavy. Moreover, if you soon have to go out again, they will freeze. The tilugtut is used to beat the clothes free of snow while still in the entrance tunnel. During this procedure, it is a good idea to call out a few remarks, like: "Somebody comes visiting, as it happens!" so that the people inside are prepared to see you. It is true that an Eskimo home is open to visitors at almost any time of day or night, but there are strained relationships everywhere in the world, and it is neither wise—nor polite—to show up in the house without a word of warning!

The entrance tunnel ends up just inside the front wall of the house itself, and you find yourself a couple of feet below the level of the floor, which you then step onto. Now you are in a room, rarely more than fifteen feet in diameter and roughly circular, inasmuch as the wide front wall, the converging side walls, and the narrower back wall of the house are curved evenly into each other. It is about nine feet high from floor to ceiling, but the roof slants toward the back wall. Besides, the whole back half of the room is filled from wall to wall by a big platform about three feet high. Since the house is sunk a little into the earth to give it extra protection against the gales, the platform usually represents the level of the ground outside. It is laid with flat stones which are extended along the front edge so as to create an overhang, under which there is storage space. On the sides, they extend into two side platforms that rest on stone supports, but also have storage space under them. What is left of the floor, which is also laid with flat stones, is then only a space about seven feet square in the front center part of the house. It serves well when game or frozen meat has to be brought in for the family meal.

The walls of the house are double, two layers of stones with peat or earth 5
filled in between them. The roof is made of flat stones, deftly built up and overlapping each other, at last reaching so far toward the center that a main stone slab can rest on them, their outer ends being weighed down with boulders for stability. The size of a house largely depends upon how many large flat stone slabs can be found for this purpose. Only when an extra large house is wanted will the Eskimos solve the problem by building pillars up from the platform to support the ceiling.

Lumber in sizes sufficient to support a roof was rare before the white 6
man came to Thule. Sometimes the Eskimos could barter a few little pieces of wood from the whalers, precious objects that they guarded with their lives. Also, they would find a little driftwood on their shores, and some of them believed that it came from forests that covered the bottom of the ocean like those in the white man's country. Actually, the driftwood was supplied by the rivers of Siberia and had drifted across the Polar Basin. After several years in salt water, it had chipped and was hard and difficult to work with. But its presence caused the Eskimos never completely to forget the use of wood.

The platform in the house is the family's sleeping bunk. Here they sleep 7
in a neat row with their feet toward the back wall. Against the back wall are usually piled extra clothes and skins so that it isn't too cold. The bunk is covered with a thick layer of dried grass, upon which skins of musk ox and caribou are spread. The family and its eventual guests sleep under blankets made of fox, hare, caribou, and eider duck skins. The natural colors of these animals' feathers and fur are used to make beautiful patterns.

Only when it is overcrowded are the side bunks used for sleeping, but 8
they are less desirable because they are colder. Otherwise, the blubber lamps

are placed on the side bunks. One of them may be used to place a piece of meat or game on for everybody to nibble on. Then there is a bucket or seal-skin basin for ice to thaw in for drinking water. Whenever possible, the lady of the house gets this ice from one of the icebergs floating in the fjord by the beach. That water tastes fresh and sweet. A dipper is placed in the basin or bucket for everybody to use when drinking, and this dipper is usually passed around after each meal.

On the other side bunk, there would then be knives, trays, and other   9 household gear. The storage space under the bunks is used for skins and other property. On the walls may be pegs of caribou ribs or antler for hanging things on. Under the ceiling is suspended a framework of wood or bones. As it is for drying clothes on, it is directly above one of the blubber lamps. It is very important especially for the kamiks and stockings. Every evening, when the master of the house comes home from the day's hunting, his wife takes his kamiks and stockings and hangs them up to dry overnight. In the morn-ing she chews them carefully till they are pliable and soft enough for his feet, and she puts new dried grass in between the soles.

For this purpose, the women go every fall up to the rocks to cut grass   10 off, dry it in the sun, and carry it home. The best harvest is naturally around the bird cliffs, and they have to get a whole year's supply for their family before winter.

Both men and women are usually undressed around the house. The wife   11 is only in her scant foxskin panties, and she sits placidly on the main bunk most of the time. Her cooking pots are suspended from the ceiling over the blubber lamp; everything is within her easy reach, and no bustling around is necessary. Since she has to cut and sew the skin garments of the entire family, that is what busies her most. Like a Turkish tailor, she sits with her legs stretched out at right angles to the body, her favorite position, with her work between her toes. Her most important tool is the *ulo*, a curved knife with a handle in the middle of the blade. From intuition, she cuts her skins in the proper pieces and sews them together, rarely measuring anything. The furs of the blue and the white fox are woven together in intricate patterns, and her work puts the finest Paris furrier to shame. With small, hardly visible stitches she weaves her narwhal sinew thread in and out until the skin pieces look as if they had grown together.

No wonder the needle is one of the most important Eskimo tools. It can   12 be fatal, during a trip, if a torn garment cannot be repaired to protect against the cold, or new garments cannot be sewn. It is perfectly truthful to say that the lack of needles has caused the death of many travelers in the Arctic. For this reason, the woman's ability to sew well is one of her chief attractions.

The husband also undresses in the house. He may keep his bearskin   13 trousers on, or he may be in the nude. When his clothes have dried, he ties them together in a bundle with a thong and hangs them up under the ceiling by a hook. That is in order to get as few lice in them as possible.

The house has one window, which is in the front wall above the entrance. The windowpane is made out of the intestines of the big bearded seal, which are split and dried and sewn together, then framed with sealskin, and the whole thing is put in the wall opening and fastened to the sides. One cannot see through such a window, but it lets quite a good light through. At one side there is a little peephole to look out of. More important, the ventilation of the house is provided through another and larger opening in the upper corner of the windowpane. Fresh air comes in through the entrance tunnel and is often regulated by a skin covering the entrance hole. This skin, when weighed down with a couple of stones, will also keep the dogs out of the house when the family is asleep. The dogs are rarely allowed in the house, anyway, but in very rough weather they may be resting in the entrance tunnel.   14

The flow of air out through the hole in the windowpane is regulated by a whisk of hay stuck in it. It is easy to see when the air is getting close because the flame in the blubber lamp starts to burn low. And although no draft is ever felt, the house is always well ventilated.   15

Although the blood and blubber from the killed game smeared over the floor and side bunks often give the new observer the impression of an animal cave, he will soon realize that the stone house is ingeniously suited to the arctic conditions. And it is well heated and lighted by the blubber lamps.   16

The Eskimo lamp is cut out of soapstone. It has a deep depression in the middle, at one side of which a whisk of long-burning moss is placed. Lumps of blubber are put in the lamp, and as the moss burns, the blubber melts and is sucked up in the moss to be consumed. By placing the lamp on three stones or on a tripod, and slanting it at the right angle, one can regulate the flow of blubber to the side where the moss-wick is. A stick serves to open or close the wick, making it narrow or wide according to whether a large or a small flame is wanted. This demands great practice, and only Eskimo women know this art to perfection. The lamp is kept burning at all times; only when the house goes to sleep the flame is made very narrow, and the lamp is filled up with fresh blubber. If it is properly regulated it burns easily through the period of sleep.   17

There are two types of lamps. One is oval, with a slanting bottom to help the regular flow of the blubber; the other is kind of shell-shaped, with a row of little knobs along the long curved side. This latter is a prototype of the Thule Culture, and is the one used by the Polar Eskimos.   18

This is rather significant, for there are few household possessions that play as big a part in Eskimo domestic life as the lamp. The wife has to tend the lamp, and it belongs under her jurisdiction. The more lamps she can take   19 care of the cleverer she is, and many lamps are a sign of wealth and prestige. Since there rarely is any permanent place called home, the lamps become the symbol of the home.

QUESTIONS

Words to Know

peat (paragraph 1), converging (4), gales (4), deftly (5), barter (6), blubber (8), fjord (8), kamiks (9), thong (13).

Some of the Issues

1. Freuchen's main purpose is to describe the Eskimo house. Is the description detailed enough to allow you to make drawings from it? If so, draw a bird's-eye view and then a picture of the interior layout.
2. Describe the construction and functions of the entrance tunnel.
3. In describing the house, Freuchen also tells us explicitly and implicitly about Eskimo life and customs. Give examples.
4. What do we learn and what can we infer about the role of men and women in Eskimo culture from Freuchen's essay?
5. What indications are we given that the Eskimo house and way of living are practical, comfortable, and adapted to the needs of the people?
6. Freuchen explains how Eskimos use materials found in nature for various purposes, for which other more technological societies use manufactured materials. Cite specific examples.
7. Some aspects of Eskimo life may seem strange and even repugnant: chewing boots and stockings (paragraph 9) and blood and blubber "smeared on the floor" (paragraph 16). How does Freuchen make such things appear acceptable to the reader?

The Way We Are Told

8. Who is the "you" in the first paragraph and later? Is the "you" familiar with Eskimo life?
9. What is the organizing principle of Freuchen's description?

Some Subjects for Essays

10. Describe a living space or working space you know well. Let your
    description focus on the physical qualities of the space as Freuchen's
    does, but also indicate how the space is suited to its inhabitants and the
    purpose it serves.
11. Lead a visitor through a room or a street. Consider carefully how to
    organize your information to be clear and effective. What details not
    exclusively descriptive might you want to add to make your description
    more effective?
12. The lamp in Freuchen's essay and the sewing machine in Kazin's essay
    ("The Kitchen") are focal points physically and spirtually of the rooms
    described and of the lives of the inhabitants of those rooms. Compare
    the two symbolic objects in their various roles.

AMERICAN MEN DON'T CRY

Ashley Montagu

Ashley Montagu served as professor of anthropology at several universities including Rutgers, Harvard, and Princeton. His many books include *On Being Human* (1950), *The Natural Superiority of Women* (1953), *Culture and the Evolution of Man* (1962), *The Nature of Human Aggression* (1962), *Man and the Computer* (1972), and *The American Way of Life* (1952), from which the following selection is an excerpt.

American men don't cry because it is considered unmasculine to do so. Only sissies cry. Crying is a "weakness" characteristic of the female, and no American male wants to be identified with anything in the least weak or feminine. Crying, in our culture, is identifed with childishness, with weakness and dependence. No one likes a crybaby, and we disapprove of crying even in children, discouraging it in them as early as possible. In a land so devoted to the pursuit of happiness as ours, crying really is rather un-American. Adults must learn not to cry in situations in which it is permissible for a child to cry. Women being the "weaker" and "dependent" sex, it is only natural that they should cry in certain emotional situations. In women, crying is excusable. But in men, crying is a mark of weakness. So goes the American credo with regard to crying.

"A little man," we impress on our male children, "never cries. Only sissies and crybabies do." And so we condition males in America not to cry whenever they feel like doing so. It is not that American males are unable to cry because of some biological time clock within them which causes them to run down in that capacity as they grow older, but that they are trained not to cry. No "little man" wants to be like that "inferior creature," the female. And the worst thing you can call him is a sissy or a crybaby. And so the "little man" represses his desire to cry and goes on doing so until he is unable to cry even when he wants to. Thus do we produce a trained incapacity in the American male to cry. And this is bad. Why is it bad? Because crying is a natural function of the human organism which is designed to restore the emotionally disequilibrated person to a state of equilibrium. The return of the disequilibrated organ systems of the body to steady states or dynamic stability is known as homeostasis. Crying serves a homeostatic function for the organism as a whole. Any interference with homeostatic mechanisms is likely to be damaging to the organism. And there is good reason to believe that the American male's trained incapacity to cry is seriously damaging to him.

It is unnecessary to cry whenever one wants to cry, but one should be   3
able to cry when one ought to cry—when one needs to cry. For to cry under certain emotionally disequilibrating conditions is necessary for the maintenance of health.

To be human is to weep. The human species is the only one in the whole   4
of animated nature that sheds tears. The trained inability of any human being to weep is a lessening of his capacity to be human—a defect which usually goes deeper than the mere inability to cry. And this, among other things, is what American parents—with the best intentions in the world— have achieved for the American male. It is very sad. If we feel like it, let us all have a good cry—and clear our minds of those cobwebs of confusion which have for so long prevented us from understanding the ineluctable necessity of crying.

QUESTIONS

Words to Know

represses (paragraph 2), disequilibrated (2), equilibrium (2), dynamic (2), homeostasis (2), ineluctable (4).

Some of the Issues

1. Montagu makes an assertion in the first line of the essay. With what arguments does he support it?
2. Define the difference between the topics of paragraph 1 and paragraph 2. How do they relate to one another?
3. Montagu attributes American men's reluctance to cry not to nature but to environment and training. Does he give evidence to support his view or does he present it as a given?

The Way We Are Told

4. What is the effect of the second sentence? What would be the effect if Montagu were to continue to write such simple sentences?
5. Montagu uses quotation marks extensively. Define the effect they have.

Some Subjects for Essays

6. In American culture certain assumptions are often made about men's or women's fitness to assume certain roles: A woman's place is in the home. Girls aren't good in math. Men aren't the caring, loving creatures that women are. Only mothers know how to mother, not fathers. Agree or disagree with any one such assumption. Do not be neutral. Come down on one side or the other and provide as much evidence for your opinion as you can.
7. Montagu explains how young boys in America are trained not to cry. Consider how children are raised in America or in another country you know well. How does the typical upbringing of boys and girls differ? Consider such factors as the selection of toys, attention given to appearance and keeping clean, restrictions or encouragement of physical activity, acceptance of anger or fighting. Write an essay commenting on the similarities and differences you find in the raising of boys and girls, and evaluate the results of different kinds of upbringing.
8. Recent years have seen an increase in the number of women in traditionally "male" professions such as engineering and a somewhat lesser growth in the number of men in traditionally "female" jobs such as nursing and elementary school teaching. Write an essay giving your opinion of these trends.

THE KISS

Leonore Tiefer

Leonore Tiefer is a professor of psychiatry at the Downstate Medical
Center in Brooklyn, New York, where she also directs the Center for
Human Sexuality. Her research is concerned with the complex psychological, social, and political causes of human behavior. "The Kiss"
appeared in *Human Nature* magazine in July 1978.

Nothing seems more natural than a kiss. Consider the French kiss, also   1
known as the soul kiss, deep kiss, or tongue kiss (to the French, it was the
Italian kiss, but only during the Renaissance). Western societies regard this
passionate exploration of mouths and tongues as an instinctive way to express
love and to arouse desire. To a European who associates deep kisses with
erotic response, the idea of one without the other feels like summer without
sun.

Yet soul kissing is completely absent in many cultures of the world,   2
where sexual arousal may be evoked by affectionate bites or stinging slaps.
Anthropology and history amply demonstrate that, depending on time and
place, the kiss may or may not be regarded as a sexual act, a sign of friendship, a gesture of respect, a health threat, a ceremonial celebration, or a disgusting behavior that deserves condemnation.

In my pursuit of the story of the kiss, two themes most appealed to me: 3
the remarkable cultural and historical variation in styles and purposes of kissing; and the anatomical, evolutionary underpinning that has made the kiss
such a successful signal. In spite of its cultural variants, the kiss is not an
accident of civilization, an arbitrary gesture. There are reasons we kiss
instead of bumping shoulders or tugging each other's ear lobes.

One of the first modern studies to dispel the belief that sexual behavior   4
is universally the same (and therefore instinctive) was *Patterns of Sexual
Behavior*, written in 1951 by Clellan Ford and Frank Beach. Ford and Beach
compared many of the sexual customs of 190 tribal societies that were
recorded in the Human Relations Area Files at Yale University.

Unfortunately, few of the field studies mentioned kissing customs at all.   5
Of the 21 that did, some sort of kissing accompanied intercourse in 13
tribes—the Chiricahua, Cree, Crow, Gros Ventre, Hopi, Huichol, Kwakiutl,
and Tarahumara of North America; the Alorese, Keraki, Trobrianders, and
Trukese of Oceania; and in Eurasia, among the Lapps. Ford and Beach noted
some variations: The Kwakiutl, Trobrianders, Alorese, and Trukese kiss by

sucking the lips and tongue of their partners; the Lapps like to kiss the mouth and nose at the same time. (I would add Margaret Mead's observation of the Arapesh. They "possess the true kiss," she wrote; they touch lips, but instead of pressing, they mutually draw the breath in.)

But sexual kissing is unknown in many societies, including the Balinese, 6 Chamorro, Manus, and Tinguian of Oceania; the Chewa and Thonga of Africa; the Siriono of South America; and the Lepcha of Eurasia. In such cultures the mouth-to-mouth kiss is considered dangerous, unhealthy, or disgusting, the way most Westerners would regard a custom of sticking one's tongue into a lover's nose. Ford and Beach report that when the Thonga first saw Europeans kissing they laughed, remarking, "Look at them—they eat each other's saliva and dirt."

Deep kissing apparently has nothing to do with the degree of sexual 7 inhibition or repression in a culture. Donald S. Marshall, an anthropologist who studied a small Polynesian island he called Mangaia, found that all Mangaian women are taught to be orgasmic and sexually active; yet kissing, sexual and otherwise, was unknown until Westerners (and their popular films) arrived on the island. In contrast, John C. Messenger found that on a sexually repressed Irish island where sex is considered dirty, sinful, and, for women, a duty to be endured, tongue kissing was unknown as late as 1966.

Many tribes across the African continent and elsewhere believe that the 8 soul enters and leaves through the mouth and that a person's bodily products can be collected and saved by an enemy for harmful purposes. In these societies, Sir James Frazer wrote in *The Golden Bough,* the possible loss of saliva would cause a kiss to be regarded as a dangerous gesture. The "soul kiss" is taken literally. (It was taken figuratively in Western societies; recall Marlowe's "Sweet Helen, make me immortal with a kiss! Her lips suck forth my soul. . . .")

Although the deep kiss is relatively rare around the world as a part of 9 sexual intimacy, other forms of mouth or nose contact are common—particularly the "oceanic kiss," named for its prevalence among cultures in Oceania, but not limited to them. The Tinguians place their lips near the partner's face and suddenly inhale. Balinese lovers bring their faces close enough to catch each other's perfume and to feel the warmth of the skin, making contact as they move their heads slightly. Paul d'Enjoy, a French anthropologist writing in 1897, described a kiss practiced by the Chinese, Yakuts, and Mongolians: The nose is pressed to the cheek, followed by a nasal inhalation and finally a smacking of lips.

The oceanic kiss may be varied by the placement of nose and cheek, 10 vigor of the inhalation, the nature of accompanying sounds, action of the arms, and so on; and it is used for affectionate greeting as well as for sexual play. Some observers think that the so-called Eskimo or Malay kiss of rubbing noses is actually a mislabeled oceanic kiss: The kisser is simply moving his or her nose rapidly from one cheek to the other of the partner, bumping noses en route.

Small tribes and obscure Irish islanders are not the only groups to   11
eschew tongue kissing. The advanced civilizations of China and Japan, which regarded sexual proficiency as high art, apparently cared little about it. In their voluminous production of erotica—graphic displays of every possible sexual position, angle of intercourse, variation of partner and setting— mouth-to-mouth kissing is conspicuous by its absence. Japanese poets have rhapsodized for centuries about the allure of the nape of the neck, but they have been silent on the mouth; indeed, kissing is acceptable only between mother and child. (The Japanese have no word for kissing—though they recently borrowed from English to create "kissu.") Intercourse is "natural"; a kiss, pornographic. When Rodin's famous sculpture, *The Kiss*, came to Tokyo in the 1920s as part of a show of European art, it was concealed from public view behind a bamboo curtain.

Among cultures of the West, the number of nonsexual uses of the kiss   12
is staggering. The simple kiss has served any or all of several purposes: greet- ing and farewell, affection, religious or ceremonial symbolism, deference to a person of higher status. (People also kiss icons, dice, and other objects, of course, in prayer, for luck, or as part of a ritual.) Kisses make the hurt go away, bless sacred vestments, seal a bargain. In story and legend a kiss has started wars and ended them, and awakened Sleeping Beauty and put Brunnhilde to sleep.

QUESTIONS

Words to Know

dispel (paragraph 4), repression (7), Marlowe (8), prevalence (9), eschew (11), nape (11), Rodin (11), icon (12), Brunnhilde (12).

Some of the Issues

1. What is Tiefer's basic assertion about kissing? What kinds of evidence does she present?
2. Tiefer lists several different kinds of kisses "natural" to different societies. What are they?
3. Tiefer opens her essay with the sentence, "Nothing seems more natural than a kiss." Read Bates's essay "On Being Human" and compare his definitions of natural to the way Tiefer uses the word here.

The Way We Are Told

4. Consider the opening sentence of paragraph 1. Why does Tiefer use "seems" rather than "is"?
5. Paragraphs 1 and 2 and contrastive. What words and phrases make that contrast explicit?
6. Define as far as you can the intended audience for this essay.

Some Subjects for Essays

7. Select a group of products, activities, or type of persons of which you have some knowledge: bicycles, sports, teachers, and so on. Establish the main sets and subsets, and write an essay using your classification as an organizing principle.

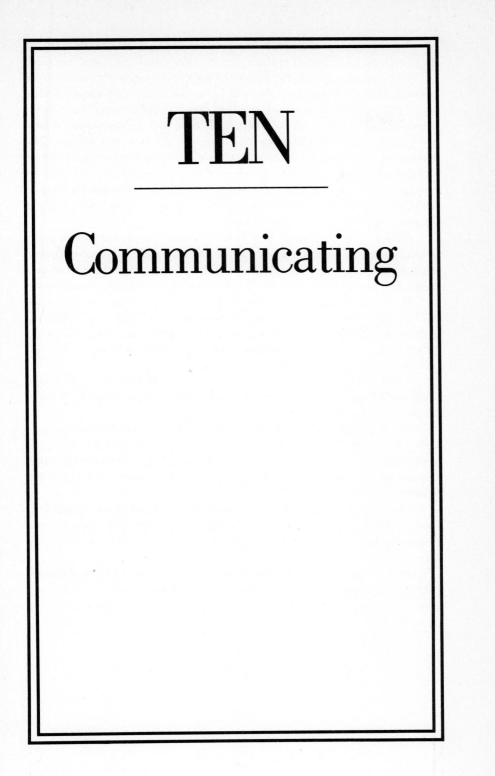

TEN

Communicating

*H*ow do we communicate? The first answer that is likely to come to most peoples' minds is through words: we speak, we listen, we read, we write. But that is only the tip of the iceberg. We also communicate in nonverbal ways, through gestures and body movements. We speak a "body language" that is often more revealing and less fully under our control than what we put into words. Most people have had the experience of having someone say flattering words that they knew were not sincere. The realization may have come through the inflection of the person's voice or through body language that was somehow out of tune with the words. In contacts with other cultures, the understanding or misunderstanding of body language can be very important. There are cultures in which shaking the head means yes and nodding means no.

Peter Farb's "How to Talk About the World" points out that in order to understand all the multitude of sensory impressions that constantly flow our way, we need to categorize them. Different people, different cultures create different categories on the basis of their own needs and experiences.

In "The Logic of Nonstandard English" William Labov compares the relative effectiveness of nonstandard and standard English as means of communication. He finds evidence that the former may actually be more effective and that standard English may trap its user into vague generalizations and meaningless clichés.

Robin Lakoff ("You Are What You Say") describes both the language used by and about women, demonstrating that both provide ample room for put-downs of the "weaker sex."

Myrna Knepler, in "Sold at Fine Stores Everywhere, Naturellement", talks about a particular gambit in the language of advertising: the snob appeal that the use of French has for Americans, as well as the opposite: the use of English to enhance the sales appeal of some products to the French.

The final two essays discuss nonverbal communication. Edward T. Hall's "Private Space" describes the differences between German and American feelings about privacy and the misunderstandings they may cause.

In "The Hand Purse" Desmond Morris analyzes a widely used gesture that has different meanings in different parts of Europe.

HOW TO TALK ABOUT
THE WORLD

Peter Farb

Peter Farb (1929–1980) was trained as a linguist and developed wide-ranging interests in the role language plays in human behavior. He also took a particular interest in American Indians. His books include *Man's Rise to Civilization as Shown by the Indians of North America.* He is co-author of *Consuming Passions: The Anthropology of Eating* (1980). The selection included here comes from *Word Play: What Happens When People Talk* (1974).

If human beings paid attention to all the sights, sounds, and smells that besiege them, their ability to codify and recall information would be swamped. Instead, they simplify the information by grouping it into broad verbal categories. For example, human eyes have the extraordinary power to discriminate some ten million colors, but the English language reduces these to no more than four thousand color words, of which only eleven basic terms are commonly used. That is why a driver stops at all traffic lights whose color he categorizes as *red*, even though the lights vary slightly from one to another in their hues of redness. Categorization allows people to respond to their environment in a way that has great survival value. If they hear a high-pitched sound, they do not enumerate the long list of possible causes of such sounds: a human cry of fear, a scream for help, a policeman's whistle, and so on. Instead they become alert because they have categorized high-pitched sounds as indicators of possible danger.

Words, therefore, are more than simply labels for specific objects; they are also parts of sets of related principles. To a very young child, the word *chair* may at first refer only to his highchair. Soon afterward, he learns that the four-legged object on which his parents sit at mealtimes is also called a *chair*. So is the thing with only three legs, referred to by his parents as a *broken chair*, and so is the upholstered piece of furniture in the living room. These objects form a category, *chair*, which is set apart from all other categories by a unique combination of features. A *chair* must possess a seat, legs, and back; it may also, but not necessarily, have arms; it must accommodate only one person. An object that possesses these features with but a single exception—it accommodates three people—does not belong to the category *chair* but rather to the category *couch*, and that category in turn is described by a set of unique features.

391

Furthermore, Americans think of *chairs* and *couches* as being related   3
to each other because they both belong to a category known in English as
household furniture. But such a relationship between the category *chair* and
the category *couch* is entirely arbitrary on the part of English and some other
speech communities. Nothing in the external world decrees that a language
must place these two categories together. In some African speech communities, for example, the category *chair* would most likely be thought of in
relation to the category *spear*, since both are emblems of a ruler's authority.

The analysis of words by their categories for the purpose of determining   4
what they mean to speakers of a particular language—that is, what the
native speaker, and not some visiting linguist, feels are the distinguishing
features or components of that word—is known as "componential analysis"
or "formal semantic analysis." The aim, in brief, is to determine the components or features that native speakers use to distinguish similar terms from
one another so that more exact meanings can be achieved.

Anyone who visits an exotic culture quickly learns that the people are   5
linguistically deaf to categories he considers obvious, yet they are extraordinarily perceptive in talking about things he has no easy way to describe. An
English-speaking anthropologist studying the Koyas of India, for example,
soon discovers that their language does not distinguish between dew, fog, and
snow. When questioned about these natural phenomena, the Koyas can find
a way to describe them, but normally their language attaches no significance
to making such distinctions and provides no highly codable words for the
purpose. On the other hand, a Koya has the linguistic resources to speak
easily about seven different kinds of bamboo—resources that the visiting
anthropologist utterly lacks in his own language. More important than the
significance, or the lack of it, that a language places on objects and ideas is
the way that language categorizes the information it does find significant. A
pig, for example, can be categorized in several ways: a mammal with cloven
hoofs and bristly hairs and adapted for digging with its snout; a mold in
which metal is cast; a British sixpence coin. The Koyas categorize the pig in
none of these ways; they simply place it in the category of animals that are
edible. Their neighbors, Muslims, think of it in a different way by placing it
in the category of defiled animals.

Everyone, whether he realizes it or not, classifies the items he finds in   6
his environment. Most speakers of English recognize a category that they call
livestock, which is made up of other categories known as *cattle, horses,
sheep,* and *swine* of different ages and sexes. An English speaker who is
knowledgeable about farm life categorizes a barnyardful of these animals in
a way that establishes relationships based on distinguishing features. For
example, he feels that a *cow* and a *mare*, even though they belong to differ-

ent species, are somehow in a relationship to each other. And of course they are, because they both belong to the category of Female Animal under the general category of Livestock. The speaker of English unconsciously groups certain animals into various sub-categories that exclude other animals:

	LIVESTOCK			
	Cattle	*Horses*	*Sheep*	*Swine*
Female	cow	mare	ewe	sow
Intact Male	bull	stallion	ram	boar
Castrated Male	steer	gelding	wether	barrow
Immature	heifer	colt/filly	lamb	shoat/gilt
Newborn	calf	foal	yearling	piglet

A table such as this shows that speakers of English are intuitively aware of certain contrasts. They regard a *bull* and a *steer* as different—which they are, because one belongs to a category of Intact Males and the other to a category of Castrated Males. In addition to discriminations made on the basis of livestock's sex, speakers of English also contrast mature and immature animals. A *foal* is a newborn horse and a *stallion* is a mature male horse.

The conceptual labels by which English-speaking peoples talk about barnyard animals can now be understood. The animal is defined by the point at which two distinctive features intersect: sex (male, female, or castrated) and maturity (mature, immature, or newborn). A *stallion* belongs to a category of horse that is both intact male and mature; a *filly* belongs to a category of horse that is both female and immature. Nothing in external reality dictates that barnyard animals should be talked about in this way; it is strictly a convention of English and some other languages.

In contrast, imagine that an Amazonian Indian is brought to the United States so that linguists can intensively study his language. When the Indian returns to his native forests, his friends and relatives listen in disbelief as he tells about all the fantastic things he saw. He summarizes his impressions of America in terms of the familiar categories his language has accustomed him to. He relates that at first he was bewildered by the strange animals he saw on an American farm because each animal not only looked different but also seemed to represent a unique concept to the natives of the North American tribe. But after considerable observation of the curious folkways of these peculiar people, at last he understood American barnyard animals. He figured out that some animals are good for work and that some are good for food. Using these two components—rather than the Americans' features of sex and maturity—his classification of livestock is considerably different. He categorized *stallion, mare,* and *gelding* as belonging to both the Inedible and Work (Riding) categories. The *bull* also belonged to the Inedible category but it was used for a different kind of Work as a draught animal. He further placed a large number of animals—*cow, ewe, lamb, sow,* and so on—in the category of Edible but Useless for Work. Since his method of categorizing the barnyard failed to take into account the breeding process, which depends upon the categories of sex and maturity, he no doubt found it inexplicable that some animals—*ram, colt, boar,* and so on—were raised even though they could not be eaten or used for work.

To an American, the Amazonian Indian's classification of barnyard animals appears quite foolish, yet it is no more foolish than the American's system of classification by the features of sex and maturity. Speakers of each language have the right to recognize whatever features they care to. And they have a similar right to then organize these features according to the rules of their own speech communities. No one system is better than another in making sense out of the world in terms that can be talked about; the systems are simply different. A speaker of English who defines a *stallion* as a mature, male horse is no wiser than the Amazonian who claims it is inedible and used for riding. Both the speaker of English and the speaker of the Amazonian language have brought order out of the multitudes of things in the environment—and, in the process, both have shown something about how their languages and their minds work.

QUESTIONS

Words to Know

codify (paragraph 1), categorization (1), semantic (4), linguistically (5), perceptive (5), codable (5), defiled (5), convention (7).

Some of the Issues

1. Why, according to Farb, do we categorize information?
2. What is Farb's overall purpose in writing this essay?
3. Read Lakoff's "You Are What You Say." Like Farb, she talks about words

referring to color near the start of her essay. Why do both use the same
example? How do their purposes differ?
4. What does Farb mean (paragraph 5) when he says that a visitor may find
   the natives of a given culture are "linguistically deaf" to categories he
   considers obvious? How does he support that assertion?
5. Try to think of a classification for livestock that differs both from the one
   Farb gives in paragraph 6 and the one his imaginary Amazonian Indian
   develops in paragraph 8. Under what circumstances would your category
   be used?

The Way We Are Told

6. Farb's first example concerns colors, his second chairs, and his most
   extended one, livestock. Can you justify both the choices and the order in
   which they are given?
7. In paragraph 3, Farb briefly refers to a possible re-categorization of chairs
   in an African culture. Why does he do so at that point?

Some Subjects for Essays

8. Develop a classification for some group of things with which you are
   familiar: college courses, video games, shoes. Describe your method,
   explaining the criteria on which it is based and its possible uses.
9. Politicians in America are generally classified as Democrats or Republi-
   cans, omitting the smaller parties. In what other ways could you classify
   politicians, and what purposes would each of the different classifications
   serve? Develop your ideas in an essay.

THE LOGIC OF
NONSTANDARD ENGLISH

William Labov

William Labov, a professor of linguistics and psychology at the University of Pennsylvania, is the author of *The Social Stratification of English in New York City* (1966), *The Study of Nonstandard English* (1970), and *Sociolinguistic Patterns* (1972). The selection included here is an excerpt from *Language in the Inner City* (1972). BEV, referred to in the selection, stands for Black English Vernacular.

There are undoubtedly many verbal skills which children from ghetto areas must learn in order to do well in the school situation, and some of these are indeed characteristic of middle-class verbal behavior. Precision in spelling, practice in handling abstract symbols, the ability to state explicitly the meaning of words, and a richer knowledge of the Latinate vocabulary, may all be useful acquisitions. But is it true that all of the middle-class verbal habits are functional and desirable in the school situation? Before we impose middle-class verbal style upon children from other cultural groups, we should find out how much of this is useful for the main work of analyzing and generalizing, and how much is merely stylistic—or even dysfunctional. In high school and college, middle-class children spontaneously complicate their syntax to the point that instructors despair of getting them to make their language simpler and clearer. In every learned journal one can find examples of jargon and empty elaboration, as well as complaints about it.

Our work in the speech community makes it painfully obvious that in many ways working-class speakers are more effective narrators, reasoners, and debaters than many middle-class speakers who temporize, qualify, and lose their argument in a mass of irrelevant detail. Many academic writers try to rid themselves of that part of middle-class style that is empty pretension and keep that part that is needed for precision. But the average middle-class speaker that we encounter makes no such effort; he is enmeshed in verbiage, the victim of sociolinguistic factors beyond his control.

I will not attempt to support this argument here with systematic quantitative evidence, although it is possible to develop measures which show how far middle-class speakers can wander from the point. I would like to contrast two speakers dealing with roughly the same topic—matters of belief. The first is Larry H., a fifteen-year-old core member of the Jets, being interviewed by John Lewis. Larry is one of the loudest and roughest members of the Jets, one who gives the least recognition to the conventional rules of politeness. For most readers of this book, first contact with Larry would produce some fairly negative reactions on both sides. It is probable that you would not like him any more than his teachers do. Larry causes trouble in and out of school. He was put back from the eleventh grade to the ninth, and has been threatened with further action by the school authorities.

> JL: What happens to you after you die? Do you know?   4
>
> LARRY: Yeah, I know. (What?) After they put you in the ground, your   5
> body turns into—ah—bones, an' shit.
>
> JL: What happens to your spirit?   6
>
> LARRY: Your spirit—soon as you die, your spirit leaves you. (And   7
> where does the spirit go?) Well, it all depends . . . (On what?) You
> know, like some people say if you're good an' shit, your spirit goin'
> t'heaven. . . 'ni'n if you bad, your spirit goin' to hell. Well, bullshit!
> Your spirit goin' to hell anyway, good or bad.
>
> JL: Why?   8
>
> LARRY: Why? I'll tell you why. 'Cause, you see, doesn' nobody really   9
> know that it's a God, y'know, 'cause I mean I have seen black gods,
> pink gods, white gods, all color gods, and don't nobody know it's
> really a God. An' when they be sayin' if you good, you goin'
> t'heaven, tha's bullshit, 'cause you ain't goin' to no heaven, 'cause
> it ain't no heaven for you to go to.

Larry is a paradigmatic speaker of black English vernacular as opposed   10 to standard English. His grammar shows a high concentration of such characteristic BEV forms as negative inversion ("don't nobody know"), negative concord ("you ain't goin' to no heaven"), invariant *be* ("when they be sayin'"), dummy *it* for standard *there* ("it ain't no heaven"), optional copula deletion ("if you're good . . . if you bad") and full forms of auxiliaries ("I have seen"). The only standard English influence in this passage is the one case of "doesn't" instead of the invariant "don't" of BEV. Larry also provides a paradigmatic example of the rhetorical style of BEV: he can sum up a complex argument in a few words, and the full force of his opinions comes through without qualification or reservation. He is eminently quotable, and his interviews give us many concise statements of the BEV point of view. One can almost say that Larry speaks the BEV culture. . . .

It is the logical form of this passage which is of particular interest here.   11 Larry presents a complex set of interdependent propositions which can be explicated by setting out the standard English equivalents in linear order.

The basic argument is to deny the twin propositions:

> (A) If you are good, (B) then your spirit will go to heaven. (~A) If you are bad, (C) then your spirit will go to hell.

Larry denies B and asserts that if A or ~ A, then C. His argument may   12
be outlined as follows:

1. Everyone has a different idea of what God is like.
2. Therefore nobody really knows that God exists.
3. If there is a heaven, it was made by God.
4. If God doesn't exist, he couldn't have made heaven.
5. Therefore heaven does not exist.
6. You can't go somewhere that doesn't exist.
   (~B) Therefore you can't go to heaven.
   (C) Therefore you are going to hell.

The argument is presented in the order: C, because 2 because 1, therefore 2,   13
therefore ~B because 5 and 6. Part of the argument is implicit: the connection 2 therefore ~B leaves unstated the connecting links 3 and 4, and in this interval Larry strengthens the propositions from the form 2 "Nobody knows if there is . . ." to 5 "There is no. . . ." Otherwise, the case is presented explicitly as well as economically. The complex argument is summed up in Larry's last sentence, which shows formally the dependence of ~B on 5 and 6:

> An' when they be sayin' if you good, you goin' t'heaven, (The proposition if A, then B)
> tha's bullshit, (is absurd)
> 'cause you ain't goin' to no heaven (because B)
> 'cause it·ain't no heaven for you to go to (because 5 and 6).

This hypothetical argument is not carried on at a high level of seriousness. It   14
is a game played with ideas as counters, in which opponents use a wide variety of verbal devices to win. There is no personal commitment to any of these propositions, and no reluctance to strengthen one's argument by bending the rules of logic as in the 2–5 sequence. But if the opponent invokes the rules of logic, they hold. In John Lewis's interviews, he often makes this move, and the force of his argument is always acknowledged and countered within the rules of logic. In this case, he pointed out the fallacy that the argument 2-3--4-5-6 leads to ~C as well as ~B, so it cannot be used to support Larry's assertion C:

JL: Well, if there's no heaven, how could there be a hell?   15

LARRY: I mean—ye-eah. Well, let me me tell you, it ain't no hell,   16
'cause this is hell right here, y'know! (This is hell?) Yeah, this is hell
right here!

Larry's answer is quick, ingenious, and decisive. The application of the   17
3-4-5 argument to hell is denied, since hell is here, and therefore conclusion
C stands. These are not ready-made or preconceived opinions, but new propositions devised to win the logical argument in the game being played. The
reader will note the speed and precision of Larry's mental operations. He
does not wander, or insert meaningless' verbiage. The only repetition is 2,
placed before and after 1 in his original statement. It is often said that the
nonstandard vernacular is not suited for dealing with abstract or hypothetical
questions, but in fact speakers from the BEV community take great delight
in exercising their wit and logic on the most improbable and problematical
matters. Despite the fact that Larry does not believe in God and has just
denied all knowledge of him, John Lewis advances the following hypothetical question:

JL: ... but, just say that there is a God, what color is he? White or   18
black?

LARRY: Well, if it is a God ... I wouldn' know what color, I couldn'   19
say,—couldn' nobody say what color he is or really *would* be.

JL: But now, jus' suppose there was a God—   20

LARRY: Unless'n they say ...   21

JL: No, I was jus' saying jus' suppose there is a God, would he be white   22
or black?

LARRY: ... He'd be white, man.   23

JL: Why?   24

LARRY: Why? I'll tell you why. 'Cause the average whitey out here got   25
everything, you dig? And the nigger ain't got shit, y'know? Y'un-
nerstan'? So—um—for—in order for *that* to happen, you know it
ain't no black God that's doin' that bullshit.

No one can hear Larry's answer to this question without being con-   26
vinced that they are in the presence of a skilled speaker with great "verbal
presence of mind," who can use the English language expertly for many
purposes. Larry's answer to John Lewis is again a complex argument. The
formulation is not standard English, but it is clear and effective even for
those not familiar with the vernacular. The nearest standard English equiv-

alent might be: "So you know that God isn't black, because if he were, he wouldn't have arranged things like that."

The reader will have noted that this analysis is being carried out in stan- 27 dard English, and the inevitable challenge is: why not write in BEV, then, or in your own nonstandard dialect? The fundamental reason is, of course, one of firmly fixed social conventions. All communities agree that standard English is the proper medium for formal writing and public communication. Furthermore, it seems likely that standard English has an advantage over BEV in explicit analysis of surface forms, which is what we are doing here. We will return to this opposition between explicitness and logical statement in subsequent sections on grammaticality and logic. First, however, it will be helpful to examine standard English in its primary natural setting, as the medium for informal spoken communication of middle-class speakers.

Let us now turn to the second speaker, an upper-middle-class, college- 28 educated black adult (Charles M.) being interviewed by Clarence Robins in our survey of adults in central Harlem.

CR: Do you know of anything that someone can do, to have someone 29 who has passed on visit him in a dream?

CHARLES: Well, I even heard my parents say that there is such a thing 30 as something in dreams, some things like that, and sometimes dreams do come true. I have personally never had a dream come true. I've never dreamt that somebody was dying and they actually died, (Mhm) or that I was going to have ten dollars the next day and somehow I got ten ten dollars in my pocket. (Mhm). I don't particularly believe in that, I don't think it's true. I do feel, though, that there is such a thing as—ah—witchcraft. I do feel that in certain cultures there is such a thing as witchcraft, or some sort of *science* of witchcraft; I don't think that it's just a matter of believing hard enough that there is such a thing as witchcraft. I do believe that there is such a thing that a person can put himself in a state of *mind* (Mhm), or that—er—something could be given them to intoxicate them in a certain—to a certain frame of mind— that—that could actually be considered witchcraft.

Charles M. is obviously a good speaker who strikes the listener as well- 31 educated, intelligent, and sincere. He is a likeable and attractive person, the kind of person that middle-class listeners rate very high on a scale of job suitability and equally high as a potential friend. His language is more moderate and tempered than Larry's; he makes every effort to qualify his opinions and seems anxious to avoid any misstatements or overstatements. From these qualities emerge the primary characteristic of this passage—its verbosity. Words multiply, some modifying and qualifying, others repeating or padding the main argument. The first half of this extract is a response to the initial question on dreams, basically:

1. Some people say that dreams sometimes come true.
2. I have never had a dream come true.
3. Therefore I don't believe 1.

Some characteristic filler phrases appear here: *such a thing as, some things like that,* and *particularly.* Two examples of dreams given after 2 are afterthoughts that might have been given after 1. Proposition 3 is stated twice for no obvious reason. Nevertheless, this much of Charles M.'s response is well-directed to the point of the question. He then volunteers a statement of his beliefs about witchcraft which shows the difficulty of middle-class speakers who (a) want to express a belief in something but (b) want to show themselves as judicious, rational, and free from superstitions. The basic proposition can be stated simply in five words: *But I believe in witchcraft.* However, the idea is enlarged to exactly 100 words and it is difficult to see what else is being said. In the following quotations, padding which can be removed without change in meaning is shown in parentheses.

1. "I (do) feel, though, that there is (such a thing as) witchcraft." *Feel* seems to be a euphemism for *'believe'.*
2. "(I do feel that) in certain cultures (there is such a thing as witchcraft)." This repetition seems designed only to introduce the word *culture,* which lets us know that the speaker knows about anthropology. Does *certain cultures* mean 'not in ours' or 'not in all'?
3. "(or some sort of *science* of witchcraft.)" This addition seems to have no clear meaning at all. What is a "science" of witchcraft as opposed to just plain witchcraft? The main function is to introduce the word *science,* though it seems to have no connection to what follows.
4. "I don't think that it's just (a matter of) believing hard enough that (there is such a thing as) witchcraft." The speaker argues that witchcraft is not merely a belief; there is more to it.
5. "I (do) believe that (there is such a thing that) a person can put himself in a state of mind . . . that (could actually be considered) witchcraft." Is witchcraft as a state of mind different from the state of belief, denied in 4?
6. "or that something could be given them to intoxicate them (to a certain frame of mind) . . ." The third learned word, *intoxicate,* is introduced by this addition. The vacuity of this passage becomes

more evident if we remove repetitions, fashionable words and stylistic decorations:

> But I believe in witchcraft.
> I don't think witchcraft is just a belief.
>
> A person can put himself or be put in a state of mind that
> is witchcraft.

Without the extra verbiage and the "OK" words like *science, culture,* [33] and *intoxicate,* Charles M. appears as something less than a first-rate thinker. The initial impression of him as a good speaker is simply our long-conditioned reaction to middle-class verbosity. We know that people who use these stylistic devices are educated people, and we are inclined to credit them with saying something intelligent. Our reactions are accurate in one sense. Charles M. is more educated than Larry. But is he more rational, more logical, more intelligent? Is he any better at thinking out a problem to its solution? Does he deal more easily with abstractions? There is no reason to think so. Charles M. succeeds in letting us know that he is educated, but in the end we do not know what he is trying to say, and neither does he.

QUESTIONS

Words to Know

explicitly (paragraph 1), Latinate (1), dysfunctional (1), spontaneously (1), syntax (1), jargon (1), temporize (2), enmeshed (2), verbiage (2), sociolinguistic (2), quantitative (3), paradigmatic (10), inversion (10), concord (10), copula (10), deletion (10), auxiliaries (10), invariant (10), rhetorical style (10), interdependent (11), propositions (11), explicated (11), hypothetical (14), fallacy (14), assertion (14), ingenious (17), formulation (26), subsequent (27), verbosity (31), filler phrases (32), judicious (32), padding (32), euphemism (32), intoxicate (32), vacuity (32).

Some of the Issues

1. In paragraph 1 Labov begins by listing characteristics of middle-class verbal behavior. What are these? What advantages does he cite for middle-class style? What are the implications of his calling it a "style"?

2. What is the point made by Labov in paragraph 1 about "jargon and empty elaboration"?
3. What is Labov's basic attitude toward Black English Vernacular?
4. Thoughout this selection Labov makes a distinction between the use of language as a tool of thought and of language style. How does this distinction help support his argument? In your opinion, are the two as easily separable as Labov indicates?
5. Sum up the evidence Labov gives for considering Larry to be a more effective communicator than Charles.
6. What does Labov mean to suggest in saying (paragraph 5) that Larry's argument is hypothetical, not carried on at a high level of seriousness, and is like a game. Do these characteristics make it more or less like "intellectual" arguments?
7. Examine the logic of the second part of Larry's argument: if there was a God he would be white.

The Way We Are Told

8. At the beginning of paragraph 3 Labov states that he will not attempt to support his argument with systematic, quantitative evidence, although he claims that it would be possible to do so. What is the effect of this disclaimer? What evidence does he give to support his argument? Is it convincing?
9. In paragraph 3 Labov says, "For most readers of this book, first contact with Larry would produce some fairly negative reactions . . ." Who are the likely readers of the book from which this selection is taken?
10. At other times Labov refers also to readers' reactions, or, as in paragraph 10 "our" reactions to Charles. What does he assume our reactions to be? In what direction does he wish to push our reactions?
11. In paragraph 7 Labov anticipates a possible objection to his thesis about BEV. What is the objection and how does he deal with it?

Some Subjects for Essays

12. Look at several pieces of your own writing. If possible, examine some essays you wrote in high school and some more recent ones. Look carefully for any examples of verbosity, jargon, euphemisms, temporizing, and so on. In an essay, classify, exemplify, and explain what you have found.

13. Look at several pieces of published nonfictional writing (some of your textbooks may be a place to start). Examine them in the same way as suggested in question 12 and construct your essay as a report that classifies and exemplifies the results.

14. In two places (paragraphs 1 and 7) Labov discusses the advantages of standard English. Write your own carefully reasoned defense of it or argue that its importance has been overrated.

YOU ARE WHAT YOU SAY

Robin Lakoff

Robin Lakoff is a professor of linguistics at the University of California, Berkeley. She was educated at Radcliffe, the University of Indiana, and Harvard, and is the author of *Language and Women's Place*. The essay included here comes from the July 1974 issue of *Ms* magazine.

"Women's language" is that pleasant (dainty?), euphemistic, never-aggressive way of talking we learned as little girls. Cultural bias was built into the language we were allowed to speak, the subjects we were allowed to speak about, and the ways we were spoken of. Having learned our linguistic lesson well, we go out in the world, only to discover that we are communicative cripples—damned if we do, and damned if we don't.

If we refuse to talk "like a lady," we are ridiculed and criticized for being unfeminine. ("She thinks like a man" is, at best, a left-handed compliment.) If we do learn all the fuzzy-headed, unassertive language of our sex, we are ridiculed for being unable to think clearly, unable to take part in a serious discussion, and therefore unfit to hold a position of power.

It doesn't take much of this for a woman to begin feeling she deserves such treatment because of inadequacies in her own intelligence and education.

"Women's language" shows up in all levels of English. For example, women are encouraged and allowed to make far more precise discriminations in naming colors than men do. Words like *mauve, beige, ecru, aquamarine, lavender*, and so on, are unremarkable in a woman's active vocabulary, but largely absent from that of most men. I know of no evidence suggesting that women actually *see* a wider range of colors than men do. It is simply that fine discriminations of this sort are relevant to women's vocabularies, but not to men's; to men, who control most of the interesting affairs of the world, such distinctions are trivial—irrelevant.

In the area of syntax, we find similar gender-related peculiarites of speech. There is one construction, in particular, that women use conversationally far more than men: the tag-question. A tag is midway between an outright statement and a yes-no question; it is less assertive than the former, but more confident than the latter.

A *flat statement* indicates confidence in the speaker's knowledge and is fairly certain to be believed; a *question* indicates a lack of knowledge on some point and implies that the gap in the speaker's knowledge can and will

405

be remedied by an answer. For example, if, at a Little League game, I have had my glasses off, I can legitimately ask someone else: "Was the player out at third?" A *tag question*, being intermediate between statement and question, is used when the speaker is stating a claim, but lacks full confidence in the truth of that claim. So if I say, "Is Joan here?" I will probably not be surprised if my respondent answers "no"; but if I say, "Joan is here, isn't she?" instead, chances are I am already biased in favor of a positive answer, wanting only confirmation. I still want a response, but I have enough knowledge (or think I have) to predict that response. A tag question, then, might be thought of as a statement that doesn't demand to be believed by anyone but the speaker, a way of giving leeway, of not forcing the addressee to go along with the views of the speaker.

Another common use of the tag-question is in small talk when the   7
speaker is trying to elicit conversation: "Sure is hot here, isn't it?"

But in discussing personal feelings or opinions, only the speaker nor-   8
mally has any way of knowing the correct answer. Sentences such as "I have a headache, don't I?" are clearly ridiculous. But there are other examples where it is the speaker's opinions, rather than perceptions, for which corroboration is sought, as in "The situation in Southeast Asia is terrible, isn't it?"

While there are, of course, other possible interpretations of a sentence   9
like this, one possibility is that the speaker has a particular answer in mind—"yes" or "no"—but is reluctant to state it baldly. This sort of tag question is much more apt to be used by women than by men in conversation. Why is this the case?

The tag question allows a speaker to avoid commitment, and thereby   10
avoid conflict with the addressee. The problem is that, by so doing, speakers may also give the impression of not really being sure of themselves, or looking to the addressee for confirmation of their views. This uncertainty is reinforced in more subliminal ways, too. There is a peculiar sentence intonation-pattern, used almost exclusively by women, as far as I know, which changes a declarative answer into a question. The effect of using the rising inflection typical of a yes-no question is to imply that the speaker is seeking confirmation, even though the speaker is clearly the only one who has the requisite information, which is why the question was put to her in the first place:

(Q) When will dinner be ready?

(A) Oh . . . around six o'clock . . .?

It is as though the second speaker were saying, "Six o'clock—if that's okay with you, if you agree." The person being addressed is put in the position of having to provide confirmation. One likely consequence of this sort of speech-pattern in a woman is that, often unbeknownst to herself, the speaker builds a reputation of tentativeness, and others will refrain from taking her seriously or trusting her with any real responsibilities, since she "can't make up her mind," and "isn't sure of herself."

Such idiosyncrasies may explain why women's language sounds much more "polite" than men's. It is polite to leave a decision open, not impose your mind, or views, or claims, on anyone else. So a tag-question is a kind of polite statement, in that it does not force agreement or belief on the addressee. In the same way a request is a polite command, in that it does not force obedience on the addressee, but rather suggests something be done as a favor to the speaker. A clearly stated order implies a threat of certain consequences if it is not followed, and—even more impolite—implies that the speaker is in a superior position and able to enforce the order. By couching wishes in the form of a request, on the other hand, a speaker implies that if the request is not carried out, only the speaker will suffer; noncompliance cannot harm the addressee. So the decision is really left up to addressee. The distinction becomes clear in these examples:

Close the door.
Please close the door.
Will you close the door?
Will you please close the door?
Won't you close the door?

In the same ways as words and speech patterns used *by* women undermine her image, those used *to describe* women make matters even worse. Often a word may be used of both men and women (and perhaps of things as well); but when it is applied to women, it assumes a special meaning that, by implication rather than outright assertion, is derogatory to women as a group.

The use of euphemisms has this effect. A euphemism is a substitute for a word that has acquired a bad connotation by association with something unpleasant or embarrassing. But almost as soon as the new word comes into common usage, it takes on the same old bad connotations, since feelings about the things or people referred to are not altered by a change of name; thus new euphemisms must be constantly found.

There is one euphemism for *woman* still very much alive. The word, of course, is *lady. Lady* has a masculine counterpart, namely *gentleman,* occasionally shortened to *gent.* But for some reason *lady* is very much commoner than *gent (leman).*

The decision to use *lady* rather than *woman,* or vice versa, may considerably alter the sense of a sentence, as the following examples show:

(a)   A woman (lady) I know is a dean at Berkeley.
(b)   A woman (lady) I know makes amazing things out of shoelaces and
      old boxes.

The use of *lady* in (a) imparts a frivolous, or nonserious, tone to the   16
sentence: the matter under discussion is not one of great moment. Similarly,
in (b), using *lady* here would suggest that the speaker considered the "amazing things" not to be serious art, but merely a hobby or an aberration. If
woman is used, she might be a serious sculptor. To say *lady doctor* is very
condescending, since no one ever says *gentleman doctor* or even *man doctor*. For example, mention in the San Francisco *Chronicle* of January 31,
1972, of Madalyn Murray O'Hair as the *lady atheist* reduces her position to
that of scatterbrained eccentric. Even *woman atheist* is scarcely defensible:
sex is irrelevant to her philosophical position.

Many women argue that, on the other hand, *lady* carries with it over-   17
tones recalling the age of chivalry: conferring exalted stature on the person
so referred to. This makes the term seem polite at first, but we must also
remember that these implications are perilous: they suggest that a "lady" is
helpless, and cannot do things by herself.

Lady can also be used to infer frivolousness, as in titles of organizations.   18
Those that have a serious purpose (not merely that of enabling "the ladies"
to spend time with one another) cannot use the word *lady* in their titles, but
less serious ones may. Compare the *Ladies' Auxiliary* of a men's group, or
the *Thursday Evening Ladies' Browning and Garden Society* with *Ladies'
Liberation* or *Ladies' Strike for Peace*.

What is curious about this split is that *lady* is in origin a euphemism—   19
a substitute that puts a better face on something people find uncomfortable—for *woman*. What kind of euphemism is it that subtly denigrates the
people to whom it refers? Perhaps *lady* functions as a euphemism for *woman*
because it does not contain the sexual implications present in *woman*: it is
not "embarrassing" in that way. If this is so, we may expect that, in the
future, *lady* will replace woman as the primary word for the human female,
since *woman* will have become too blatantly sexual. That this distinction is
already made in some contexts at least is shown in the following examples,
where you can try replacing *woman* with *lady*:

(a)   She's only twelve, but she's already a woman.
(b)   After ten years in jail, Harry wanted to find a woman.
(c)   She's my woman, see, so don't mess around with her.

Another common substitute for *woman* is *girl*. One seldom hears a man   20
past the age of adolescence referred to as a boy, save in expressions like

"going out with the boys," which are meant to suggest an air of adolescent frivolity and irresponsibility. But women of all ages are "girls": one can have a man—not a boy—Friday, but only a girl—never a woman or even a lady—Friday; women have girlfriends, but men do not—in a nonsexual sense—have boyfriends. It may be that this use of *girl* is euphemistic in the same way the use of *lady* is: in stressing the idea of immaturity, it removes the sexual connotations lurking in *woman*. *Girl* brings to mind irresponsibility: you don't send a girl to do a woman's errand (or even, for that matter, a boy's errand). She is a person who is both too immature and too far from real life to be entrusted with responsibilities or with decisions of any serious or important nature.

Now let's take a pair of words which, in terms of the possible relationships in an earlier society, were simple male-female equivalents, analogous to *bull: cow*. Suppose we find that, for independent reasons, society has changed in such a way that the original meanings now are irrelevant. Yet the words have not been discarded, but have acquired new meanings, metaphorically related to their original senses. But suppose these new metaphorical uses are no longer parallel to each other. By seeing where the parallelism breaks down, we discover something about the different roles played by men and women in this culture. One good example of such a divergence through time is found in the pair, *master: mistress*. Once used with reference to one's power over servants, these words have become unusable today in their original master-servant sense as the relationship has become less prevalent in our society. But the words are still common. 21

Unless used with reference to animals, *master* now generally refers to a man who has acquired consummate ability in some field, normally nonsexual. But its feminine counterpart cannot be used this way. It is practically restricted to its sexual sense of "paramour." We start out with two terms, both roughly paraphrasable as "one who has power over another." But the masculine form, once one person is no longer able to have absolute power over another, becomes usable metaphorically in the sense of "having power over *something*." *Master* requires as its object only the name of some activity, something inanimate and abstract. But *mistress* requires a masculine noun in the possessive to precede it. One cannot say: "Rhonda is a mistress." One must be *someone's* mistress. A man is defined by what he does, a woman by her sexuality, that is, in terms of one particular aspect of her relationship to men. It is one thing to be an *old master* like Hans Holbein, and another to be an *old mistress*. 22

The same is true of the words *spinster* and *bachelor*—gender words for "one who is not married." The resemblance ends with the definition. While *bachelor* is a neuter term, often used as a compliment, *spinster* normally is used pejoratively, with connotations of prissiness, fussiness, and so on. To be 23 a bachelor implies that one has the choice of marrying or not, and this is what makes the idea of a bachelor existence attractive, in the popular literature. He has been pursued and has successfully eluded his pursuers. But a spinster is one who has not been pursued, or at least not seriously. She is old, unwanted goods. The metaphorical connotations of *bachelor* generally suggest sexual freedom; of *spinster*, puritanism or celibacy.

These examples could be multiplied. It is generally considered a *faux* pas, in society, to congratulate a woman on her engagement, while it is correct to congratulate her fiancé. Why is this? The reason seems to be that it is impolite to remind people of things that may be uncomfortable to them. To congratulate a woman on her engagement is really to say, "Thank goodness! You had a close call!" For the man, on the other hand, there was no such danger. His choosing to marry is viewed as a good thing, but not something essential. 24

The linguistic double standard holds throughout the life of the relationship. After marriage, bachelor and spinster become man and wife, not man and woman. The woman whose husband dies remains "John's widow"; John, however, is never "Mary's widower." 25

Finally, why is it that salesclerks and others are so quick to call women customers "dear," "honey," and other terms of endearment they really have no business using? A male customer would never put up with it. But women, like children, are supposed to enjoy these endearments, rather than being offended by them. 26

In more ways than one, it's time to speak up. 27

QUESTIONS

Words to Know

euphemistic (paragraph 1), bias (1), linguistic (1), left-handed compliment (2), unassertive (2), syntax (5), gender-related (5), confirmation (6), leeway (6), small talk (7), elicit (7), corroboration (8), baldly (9), subliminal (10), intonation pattern (10), declarative (10), inflection (10), requisite (10), idiosyncrasies (11), couching (11), noncompliance (11), implication (12), derogatory (12), frivolous (16), moment (16), aberration (16), condescending (16), atheist (16), overtones (17), chivalry (17), exalted (17), perilous (17), denigrates (19), blatantly (19), connotations (20), lurking (20), analogous (21), metaphorically (21), consummate (22), paramour (22), paraphrasable (22), neuter (23), pejoratively (23), eluded (23), puritanism (23), celibacy (23), *faux pas*—misstep (24), double standard (25).

Some of the Issues

1. In paragraph 1 Lakoff says, "we are damned if we do, and damned if we don't." What does she mean by that?
2. In paragraph 2 Lakoff refers to a "left-handed compliment." Why "left-handed"? What is implied in this phrase?
3. Paragraphs 5 through 10 are devoted to tag questions. Why, according to Lakoff, are such questions characteristic of women's speech?
4. What does Lakoff mean in paragraph 11 when she says that women's language is more "polite" than men's language? Is politeness considered a virtue here?
5. In paragraphs 21 to 23 Lakoff discusses pairs of male-female terms. Can you add further examples to that list?
6. Cite examples of the ways, in recent times, we have tried to avoid male-female stereotyping, for example, by replacing "mailman" with "letter carrier."
7. Paragraphs 1 to 11 deal with the way women talk and paragraphs 12 to 15 with the way women are talked about. Sum up the major parts of the argument in each of these sections.

The Way We Are Told

8. Examine the first two paragraphs and show how Lakoff uses words with strong connotations (emotional impact) to reinforce her argument.
9. Who is Lakoff's audience? Is it one that needs convincing or one that looks for reinforcement? Cite reasons for your answer.
10. Who is the "we" in the first two paragraphs?

Some Subjects For Essays

11. Search for examples of language used by groups other than women: minorities, certain occupations. Select one such group and write an essay describing what you have found.
12. Keep a notebook for two weeks in which you record examples of women's language and men's language. At the end of that period look over your notes, try to classify them, and write an analytical paper about the results.

SOLD AT FINE STORES EVERYWHERE, NATURELLEMENT

Myrna Knepler

Myrna Knepler is an assistant professor of linguistics at Northeastern Illinois University in Chicago. The following selection is reprinted from the February 1978 issue of *Verbatim*, a magazine about language.

Why is is that a high priced condominium is advertised in American newspapers as a *de luxe* apartment while French magazines try to sell their more affluent readers *appartements de grand standing?* Madison Avenue, when constructing ads for high priced non-necessary items, may use French phrases to suggest to readers that they are identified as super-sophisticated, subtly sexy, and privy to the secrets of old world charm and tradition. In recent years French magazines aimed at an increasingly affluent public have made equally canny use of borrowed English words to sell their wares.

The advertising pages of the *New Yorker* and the more elegant fashion and home decorating magazines often depend on blatant flattery of the reader's sense of exclusiveness. Time and time again the reader is told "only *you* are elegant, sophisticated, discriminating and rich enough to use this product." Of course the "you" must encompass a large enough group to insure adequate sales. Foreign words, particularly prestigious French words, may be used to reinforce this selling message.

French magazines often use English words in their advertising to suggest to potential consumers a slightly different but equally flattering self-image. The reader is pictured as someone in touch with new ideas from home and abroad who has not forgotten the traditional French arts of living, but is modern enough to approach them in a completely up-to-date and casual manner.

Of course, each language has borrowed words from the other which have, over the course of time, been completely assimilated. It is not these that the advertiser exploits but rather words that are foreign enough to evoke appealing images of an exotic culture. When the French reader is urged to try "Schweppes, le 'drink' des gens raffinés" or an American consumer is told that a certain manufacturer has "the *savoir faire* to design *la crème de la crème* of luxurious silky knits," the foreign words do not say anything that could not be as easily said by native ones. What they do convey is something else. They invite the reader to share in the prestige of the foreign language and the power of the images associated with that language's country of origin.

In each country a knowledge of the other's language is an important   5
sign of cultivation. Today, English is the language studied by an overwhelming majority of French students, and the ability to speak it well is increasingly valued as a symbol of prestige as well as a marketable skill. Despite the decrease in foreign language study in the United States, French has maintained its reputation as a language people ought to know. Adding a few obvious foreign words from the prestige language not only increases the prestige of the product itself but also flatters the reader by reminding him that he has enough linguistic talent to understand what is being said. As in the "only-*you*-are-elegant,-sophisticated,-discriminating-and-rich enough" appeal, the advertiser must be careful not to exclude too many potential customers, and the foreign expressions are usually transparent cognates or easily understood words. A French reader may be urged to buy cigarettes by being told that "partout dans le monde c'est YES á Benson and Hedges" while the *New Yorker* reader can consider a vacation on "an island [off the coast of South Carolina] where change hasn't meant commercialism, and tranquility still comes *au naturelle*."

Even monolinguals are not excluded from this flattery. The word can   6
be given in the foreign language and then translated; the reader is still in on the secret: "'goût' is the French word for taste and Christolfe is the universal word for taste in vases."

The prestige of a foreign term and its possible ambiguity for the reader   7
may serve to disguise a negative fact about the product. A necklace of Perle de Mer advertised in an American magazine is not composed of real pearls made by nature in the seas but of simulated pearls produced by a large American manufacturer. By the same token, when a French advertisement for a packaged tour offers "aller et retour en classe coach" the prestige of the English word *coach* disguises the fact that it is the less luxurious form of airline transportation that is being offered.

But the most important function of borrowed words in advertising is to   8
project an image of their country of origin in order to create for the reader the illusion that the product, and by implication its user, will share in the good things suggested by that image. French names like *Grand Prix, Coupe De Ville*, and *Monte Carlo* attached to American car models help the advertiser to get across the message that the car is luxurious, sophisticated, and elegantly appointed and that driving such an automobile reflects positively on the taste of its potential owner. In almost all cases French names are

reserved for the more expensive models while American words are favored for small meat-and-potatoes cars like *Charger, Maverick, Pinto* and *Bronco.* Similarly, the French reader is likely to encounter a large number of American technical terms in ads for appliances, radio and television equipment, cameras, and "gadgets de luxe," since the manufacturer benefits by associating American mechanical skill with his products. An advertisement for French-made hi-fi equipment appearing in a French magazine spoke of the product's "push-pull ultra linéaire, 6 haut-parleurs, 2 elliptiques et 4 tweeters . . . montés sur baffle."

Images, which are used again and again, are often based on myths of   9
the other country's culture. Words like *tomahawk* and *trading posts* are used in French advertisements to evoke images of a western-movie America of naturalness, freedom, and adventure in order to sell products like "Chemise de 'cow girl,'" "bottes Far West," and vests in the style of "Arizona Bill," irrespective of the real West that is or was. The name *Monte Carlo* attached to an American-made car trades on the American consumer's image of a once-exclusive vacation spot, now available as part of low-cost travel packages. Thus the name *Monte Carlo* can convey to an automobile a prestige that the real trip to Monte Carlo has long since lost.

Those images that are not completely mythic are usually gross stereo-   10
types of the other country's culture. Few Americans would recognize the image of American life presented in French advertising—a new world filled with eternally youthful, glamourously casual, up-to-date men and women devoted to consuming the products of their advanced technology. Similarly, few French men and women would recognize the nation of elegant and knowing consumers of food, wine, and sophisticated sex pictured in American ads.

The image of France as a nation of lovers, bold yet unusually subtle in   11
their relations with the opposite sex, is often called upon to sell perfume and cosmetics, sometimes of French origin but packaged and advertised specifically for the American market. An ad which appeared several years ago in the *New Yorker* showed a bottle of perfume labeled "voulez-vous" implanted next to a closeup of a sexy and elegant woman, her face shadowed by a male hand lighting her cigarette. The text: "The spark that starts the fire. Voulez-vous a new perfume." *Audace, Robe d'un Soir,* and *Je Reviens* are other perfumes advertised in American magazines with pictures and copy that reinforce the sexual suggestiveness of the prominently featured French name on the label.

It may be surprising for Americans to learn that English names are   12
given to perfumes sold in France to enhance their romantic image. *My Love, Partner,* and *Shocking* are some examples. Advertisements for French-made

men's cosmetics in French magazines may refer to products such as *l'after-shave* and *le pre-shave*. Givenchy's *Gentleman* is advertised to Frenchmen as an eau de toilette for the man who dares to appear at business lunches in a turtleneck sweater and has the courage to treat love in a casual manner.

The recent swelling of the list of Americanisms used in French adver-   13
tising and in French speech has pained many Frenchmen and has even caused the government to take action. For a number of years the leader in this "war against anglicisms" has been René Etiemble, a professor at the Sorbonne. Etiemble, through magazine articles, radio and television appearances and his widely read book, *Parlez-vous franglais?*, struggles vehemently against what he most often refers to as an "invasion" of American terms. He does little to disguise his strong anti-American sentiments. American words are rejected as agents of a vulgar American culture and both are seen as threats to the French way of life. According to Etiemble "[the] heritage of words [is the] heritage of ideas: with *le twist* and *la ségrégation, la civilisation cocolcoolique*, the American manner of not living will disturb and contaminate all that remains of your cuisine, wines, love and free thought." It would be difficult to find a stronger believer in the power of words than Etiemble.

In response to the concerns of Etiemble and others, a series of commit-   14
tees composed of highly placed French scientists and language experts were charged with the task of finding Gallic equivalents for such popular terms as *le meeting, le marketing, le management,* and *le know-how*. The recommended replacements are: *la réunion, la commercialisation, la direction,* and, of course, *le savoir faire*. The replacements do not seem to have taken root.

At the end of 1975 a more radical step was taken. The French National   15
Assembly passed a law banning the use of all foreign words in advertising in those cases in which a native alternative has been officially suggested, and instituting a fine against violators.

Both Etiemble and the government purists rely strongly on the "logical"   16
argument that most loan words are not needed because there already exists a native equivalent with exactly the same meaning. Yet a look at the advertising pages of French and American magazines will show that borrowed words are used again and again when there are obvious native equivalents. Certainly the English words in "c'est YES á Benson and Hedges" and "Le'drink' des gens raffinés" could be translated without loss of literal meaning—but they are not.

It is precisely because of the connotations associated with the culture of   17
its country of origin, not its denotations, that advertisers find the borrowed word attractive.

QUESTIONS

Words to Know

affluent (paragraph 1), Madison Avenue (1), privy (1), blatant (2). potential (3), assimilated (4), exploits (4), *raffinés*—refined (4), *savoir faire*—sophistication, literally know-how (4), *crème de la crème*—the very best (4), discriminating (5), cognates (5), *partout dans le monde*—throughout the whole world (5), monolinguals (6), ambiguity (7), *Perle de Mer*—"Pearls of the Sea" (7), *aller et retour*—round trip (7), elegantly appointed (8), *haut-parleurs*—loud speakers (8), *montés sur*—mounted on (8), *chemise*—shirt (9), *bottes*—boots (9), mythic (10), *Voulez-vous*—Are you willing? (11), *Audace*—Boldness (11), *Robe d'un Soir*—Evening wrap (11), *Je Reviens*— I will return (11), anglicisms (13), *Parlez-vous franglais?*—Do you speak franglais? (13), vehemently (13), Gallic (14), connotations (17), denotations (17).

Some of the Issues

1. According to Knepler, what classes of people are addressed through the use of French words in American advertising, and vice versa? How do her examples substantiate her argument?
2. Advertisers use foreign words to provide a sense of exclusivity for the reader; at the same time, they want to make sure their message comes across. How is this done? Cite some examples.
3. What kinds of products are likely to be sold in America with the use of French words? What kinds of products will use English to enhance sales appeal in France?
4. Paragraph 7 presents cases in which the foreign language disguises negative information. Explain the examples.
5. What kind of stereotype of America does French advertising play upon?

The Way We Are Told

6. Consider the first three paragraphs. Why does paragraph 1 begin with a question? Is it answered? How do paragraphs 2 and 3 relate to the first paragaraph?
7. In paragraphs 9 through 11 Knepler discusses the myths the Americans

and the French believe about each other's culture. What means does Knepler use to make the reader believe in the unreality of these respective views?

Some Subjects for Essays

8. Examine several magazine advertisements for a particular kind of product, for example, automobles, clothes, liquor. What flattering images of the potential consumer are used to sell the product? Explain the effect in detail.
9. Write an essay comparing and contrasting the reality of a specific place, type of person, or institution you know with the myth or stereotype about it.

PRIVATE SPACE

Edward T. Hall

Edward T. Hall, a professor of anthropology at Northwestern University, has taught at several other institutions and been in government service in Washington. His research has been concerned with cross-cultural issues related to body language (kinesics). In particular, he did pioneering work in proxemics: the investigation of the relative distances by which people of different cultures spearate themselves from each other, as, for example, in conversation. Among his books are *The Silent Language* (1954), *The Hidden Dimension* (1966), and *Beyond Culture* (1976). The selection included here comes from *The Hidden Dimension*.

I shall never forget my first experience with German proxemic patterns, which occurred when I was an undergraduate. My manners, my status, and my ego were attacked and crushed by a German in an instance where thirty years' residence in this country and an excellent command of English had not attentuated German definitions of what constitutes an intrusion. In order to understand the various issues that were at stake, it is necessary to refer back to two basic American patterns that are taken for granted in this country and which Americans therefore tend to treat as universal.

First, in the United States there is a commonly accepted, invisible boundary around any two or three people in conversation which separates them from others. Distance alone serves to isolate any such group and to endow it with a protective wall of privacy. Normally, voices are kept low to avoid intruding on others and if voices are heard, people will act as though they had not heard. In this way, privacy is granted whether it is actually present or not. The second pattern is somewhat more subtle and has to do with the exact point at which a person is experienced as actually having crossed a boundary and entered a room. Talking through a screen door while standing outside a house is not considered by most Americans as being inside the house or room in any sense of the word. If one is standing on the threshold holding the door open and talking to someone inside, it is still defined informally and experienced as being *outside*. If one is in an office building and just "pokes his head in the door" of an office he's still outside the office. Just holding on to the doorjamb when one's body is inside the room still means a person has one foot "on base" as it were so that he is not quite inside the other fellow's territory. None of these American spatial definitions is

418

valid in northern Germany. In every instance where the American would consider himself *outside* he has already entered the German's territory and by definition would become involved with him. The following experience brought the conflict between these two patterns into focus.

It was a warm spring day of the type one finds only in the high, clean, clear air of Colorado, the kind of day that makes you glad you are alive. I was standing on the doorstep of a converted carriage house talking to a young woman who lived in an apartment upstairs. The first floor had been made into an artist's studio. The arrangement, however, was peculiar because the same entrance served both tenants. The occupants of the apartment used a small entryway and walked along one wall of the studio to reach the stairs to the apartment. You might say that they had an "easement" through the artist's territory. As I stood talking on the doorstep, I glanced to the left and noticed that some fifty to sixty feet away, inside the studio, the Prussian artist and two of his friends were also in conversation. He was facing so that if he glanced to one side he could just see me. I had noted his presence, but not wanting to appear presumptuous or to interrupt his conversation, I unconsciously applied the American rule and assumed that the two activities—my quiet conversation and his conversation—were not involved with each other. As I was soon to learn, this was a mistake, because in less time than it takes to tell, the artist had detached himself from his friends, crossed the intervening space, pushed my friend aside, and with eyes flashing, started shouting at me. By what right had I entered his studio without greeting him? Who had given me permission?

I felt bullied and humiliated, and even after almost thirty years, I can still feel my anger. Later study has given me greater understanding of the German pattern and I have learned that in the German's eyes I really had been intolerably rude. I was already "inside" the building and I intruded when I could *see* inside. For the German, there is no such thing as being inside the room without being inside the zone of intrusion, particularly if one looks at the other party, no matter how far away.

Recently, I obtained an independent check on how Germans feel about visual intrusion while investigating what people look at when they are in intimate, personal, social, and public situations. In the course of my research, I instructed subjects to photograph separately both a man and a woman in each of the above contexts. One of my assistants, who also happened to be German, photographed his subjects out of focus at public distance because, as he said, "You are not really supposed to look at other people at public distances *because it's intruding.*" This may explain the informal custom behind the German laws against photographing strangers in public without their permission.

Germans sense their own space as an extension of the ego. One sees a   6
clue to this feeling in the term "Lebensraum," which is impossible to translate because it summarizes so much. Hitler used it as an effective psychological lever to move the Germans to conquest.

In contrast to the Arab, the German's ego is extraordinarily exposed, and   7
he will go to almost any length to preserve his "private sphere." This was
observed during World War II when American soldiers were offered oppor-
tunities to observe German prisoners under a variety of circumstances. In
one instance in the Midwest, German P.W.s were housed four to a small hut.
As soon as materials were available, each prisoner built a partition so that he
could have *his own space*. In a less favorable setting in Germany when the
Wehrmacht was collapsing, it was necessary to use open stockades because
German prisoners were arriving faster than they could be accommodated.
In this situation each soldier who could find the materials built his own tiny
dwelling unit, sometimes no larger than a foxhole. It puzzled the Americans
that the Germans did not pool their efforts and their scarce materials to create a larger, more efficient space, particularly in view of the very cold spring
nights. Since that time I have observed frequent instances of the use of architectural extensions of this need to screen the ego. German houses with balconies are arranged so that there is visual privacy. Yards tend to be well
fenced; but fenced or not, they are sacred.

The American view that space should be shared is particularly trouble-   8
some to the German. I cannot document the account of the early days of
World War II occupation when Berlin was in ruins but the following situation was reported by an observer and it has the nightmarish quality that is
often associated with inadvertent cross-cultural blunders. In Berlin at that
time the housing shortage was indescribably acute. To provide relief, occupation authorities in the American zone ordered those Berliners who still had
kitchens and baths intact to share them with their neighbors. The order
finally had to be rescinded when the already overstressed Germans started
killing each other over the shared facilities.

Public and private buildings in Germany often have double doors for   9
soundproofing, as do many hotel rooms. In addition, the door is taken very
seriously by Germans. Those Germans who come to America feel that our
doors are flimsy and light. The meanings of the open door and the closed
door are quite different in the two countries. In offices, Americans keep doors
open; Germans keep doors closed. In Germany, the closed door does not
mean that the man behind it wants to be alone or undisturbed, or that he is
doing something he doesn't want someone else to see. It's simply that Germans think that open doors are sloppy and disorderly. To close the door preserves the integrity of the room and provides a protective boundary between
people. Otherwise, they get too involved with each other. One of my Ger-

man subjects commented, "If our family hadn't had doors, we would have
had to change our way of life. Without doors we would have had many,
many more fights . . . When you can't talk, you retreat behind a door. . . . If
there hadn't been doors, I would always have been within reach of my
mother."

Whenever a German warms up to the subject of American enclosed   10
space, he can be counted on to comment on the noise that is transmitted
through walls and doors. To many Germans, our doors epitomize American
life. They are thin and cheap; they seldom fit; and they lack the substantial
quality of German doors. When they close they don't sound and feel solid.
The click of the lock is indistinct, it rattles and indeed it may even be absent.

The open-door policy of American business and the closed-door patterns   11
of German business culture cause clashes in the branches and subsidiaries of
American firms in Germany. The point seems to be quite simple, yet failure
to grasp it has caused considerable friction and misunderstanding between
American and German managers overseas. I was once called in to advise a
firm that has operations all over the world. One of the first questions asked
was, "How do you get the Germans to keep their doors open?" In this company the open doors were making the Germans feel exposed and gave the
whole operation an unusually relaxed and unbusinesslike air. Closed doors,
on the other hand, gave the Americans the feeling that there was a conspiratorial air about the place and that they were being left out. The point is
that whether the door is open or shut, it is not going to mean the same thing
in the two countries.

The orderliness and hierarchical quality of German culture are com-   12
municated in their handling of space. Germans want to know where they
stand and object strenuously to people crashing queues or people who "get
out of line" or who do not obey signs such as "Keep out," "Authorized personnel only," and the like. Some of the German attitudes toward ourselves
are traceable to our informal attitudes toward boundaries and to authority
in general.

However, German anxiety due to American violations of order is noth-   13
ing compared to that engendered in Germans by the Poles, who see no harm
in a little disorder. To them lines and queues stand for regimentation and
blind authority. I once saw a Pole crash a cafeteria line just "to stir up those
sheep."

Germans get very technical about intrusion distance, as I mentioned   14
earlier. When I once asked my students to describe the distance at which a
third party would intrude on two people who were talking, there were no
answers from the Americans. Each student knew that he could tell when he
was being intruded on but he couldn't define intrusion or tell how he knew
when it had occurred. However, a German and an Italian who had worked

in Germany were both members of my class and they answered without any hesitation. Both stated that a third party would intrude on two people if he came within seven feet!

Many Americans feel that Germans are overly rigid in their behavior, unbending and formal. Some of this impression is created by differences in the handling of chairs while seated. The American doesn't seem to mind if people hitch their chairs up to adjust the distance to the situation—those that do mind would not think of saying anything, for to comment on the manners of others would be impolite. In Germany, however, it is a violation of the mores to change the position of your chair. An added deterrent for those who don't know better is the weight of most German furniture. Even the great architect Mies van der Rohe, who often rebelled against German tradition in his buildings, made his handsome chairs so heavy that anyone but a strong man would have difficulty in adjusting his seating position. To a German, light furniture is anathema, not only because it seems flimsy but because people move it and thereby destroy the order of things, including intrusions on the "private sphere." In one instance reported to me, a German newspaper editor who had moved to the United States had his visitor's chair bolted to the floor "at the proper distance" because he couldn't tolerate the American habit of adjusting the chair to the situation.

QUESTIONS

Words to Know

proxemic (see headnote) (paragraph 1), attenuated (1), spatial (2), presumptuous (3), *Wehrmacht*—the German Army (7), inadvertent (8), rescinded (8), integrity (9), epitomize (10), conspiratorial (11), hierarchical (12), queues (12), regimentation (13), deterrent (15), anathema (15).

Some of the Issues

1. What are the "two basic American patterns" Hall refers to in paragraph 1?
2. Describe the basic differences between the German and the American views of private space.

3. In what way do Germans protect and reinforce their concept of private space?
4. State Hall's purpose in presenting the differences between German and American concepts of privacy. Is it simply to present the facts, or does he have a more general purpose?
5. State Hall's thesis regarding German "private space." Do his examples support it sufficiently to be credible?

The Way We Are Told

6. Hall begins with a reference to a personal experience (paragraph 1), but does not return to it until paragraph 3. What is the function of paragraph 2? Is this way of telling his experience effective, or should he have omitted the personal reference in paragraph 1, cut off as it is from the rest of the story?
7. Why does Hall refer (paragraph 3) to the weather, to Colorado, to the young woman as he tells the story? What does this information contribute?
8. In paragraph 5 and then again in paragraphs 6 through 8 Hall moves on to other examples. Do you see any order in this progression?

Some Subjects for Essays

9. Hall explains that concepts of space can differ widely from culture to culture. They may also differ among individuals. Have you ever offended someone, or been offended, because you intruded in some way on the other person's space? If so, describe the event.
10. Another concept that can differ from culture to culture is time: punctuality, being late or early. In America, for example, being more than five minutes late for an appointment may be offensive. On the other hand, arriving at a party at eight o'clock on the nose is likely to make you early, even if you were invited for eight. Write an essay about what it means to be "on time" in different circumstances in your culture.

THE HAND PURSE

Desmond Morris

Desmond Morris, the senior author of the study which is excerpted here, was born in Wiltshire, England in 1928. Trained as a zoologist, he developed an interest in human behavior and turned eventually to writing full-time. He is also an artist, which in part explains his interest in human gestures, combining the visual element with his interest in human actions. His books include *The Naked Ape* (1961), which was made into a film; *Intimate Behavior* (1972); and *Manwatching: A Field Guide to Human Behavior* (1977).

    Gestures (1979), from which this selection is taken, is the result of extensive research done by serveral investigators who collected data from about 1,200 people in 40 locations in Europe. They investigated the meaning of 20 "key" gestures pictured on page 425. "The Hand Purse" is gesture 4.

The hand purse is a multi-message gesture. Many gestures have more than one meaning, as you travel from place to place, but it is unusual to find one with such a variety of meanings, even over a wide range of territory. The explanation lies in the primary source of the hand purse, as a 'baton signal'. [1]

Baton actions occur when the hands 'beat time' to the spoken words. When a speaker emphasizes his words in this way, he uses a variety of hand postures, depending on the mood of his statements. If in a forceful or hostile mood, he tends to employ a clenched fist, his fingers unconsciously adopting a 'power grip' posture. If, by contrast, he is making a fine point, or requesting greater precision or clarity, he is more likely to display the typical 'precision grip' so characteristic of the human species, namely the bringing together of the tips of the digits as if holding some very small object. The digits involved vary, but there are two basic arrangements, the thumb-and-forefinger-tips touch, and the five-fingertips touch. [2]

Speakers perform these precision grips without, of course, actually gripping anything. The small object is imagined, not held, and the hands make the gripping action *in vacuo*. Because this is done unconsciously, as part of the general flow of gesticulation during animated conversations, the movements, like most baton signals, are not identified or named as specific gestures. In the case of the five-fingertips touch, we have therefore had to invent a name—the hand purse. We have used this term because the action is similar to 'pursing the lips', that is, bringing them tightly together, as if pulled close by the draw-string of a purse. [3]

Pursing the hand, as a basic form of baton signal, is common and wide-   4
spread. Indeed, such is the repeated need for precision during verbal inter-
actions, that is probably worldwide, like the clenched fist, the begging hand,
the repelling hand, and many of the other fundamental baton postures. But
in the case of the hand purse, special developments have occurred. In certain
regions, it has gone beyond the simple act of beating time for emphasis, and
has grown into a specific symbolic gesture. In this role it is no longer dependent on verbal exchanges, but can also be performed *instead* of speech.

It is this growth, from a simple baton signal into a fully fledged, sym-   5
bolic gesture, that has enabled the hand purse to have different meanings in
different parts of the world today. The original precision message is capable
of a variety of special extensions, evolving separately as distinct local traditions. In one region, the primary signal of 'precise emphasis' has changed
into 'please be more precise', or 'what are you trying to say?', or 'you idiot,
what *are* you trying to say?'. In this way, it can become a gestural equivalent
of a question mark. It can either accompany a spoken query, or act as a
substitute for it. When performed silently, the gesturer simply purses his
hand at his companion, who infers from the context why he is being questioned and answers accordingly.

The use of the hand purse as a symbolic query was commented on as   6
long ago as 1832 by the Neapolitan Andrea de Jorio, who wrote: 'bringing
the fingers together in a point means bringing your ideas together: "make
one word out of all the other words and tell me what you mean; what are
you talking about?"' In other words, make one, small, precise statement that
will clarify the situation. This implies a certain degree of impatience on the
part of the gesturer and, although irritation is not always implicit, it is frequently present when the gesture is used in this way.

A totally different meaning has arisen elsewhere. From the basic sta-   7
statement of precise emphasis, the message has become transformed into 'this
thing has precision'. From there it has changed to 'this has class', to 'high
quality', to 'excellent', to 'good'. So, although the hand purse may be a query,
often an irritable one, in one region, it can also be a satisfied or excited signal
of excellence in another.

To confuse matters further, in a third region the gesture has an addi-   8
tional meaning, namely strong criticism or sarcasm. To transmit this signal,
the pursed hand is pulled downwards through the air, while the face makes
a glum grimace. The verbal equivalent would be 'that's marvellous', spoken
with heavy sarcasm and meaning the exact opposite. At a sporting event, the
gesture would by saying '*what* a good team you have', meaning 'what a *bad*
team you have'. In this special case, as a sarcasm gesture, it appears to be a
corrupted version of the hand purse meaning 'excellent' or 'good', because

in areas where the gesture is used as a straightforward signal of excellence there is also a frequent tendency to use the down-pull movement of the hand. It seems likely that, in the 'sarcasm region', the gesture has simply 'gone sour' in its usage. The same fate can befall a word. For example, to say that someone is 'precious' today would be taken by most people to be an insult, rather than that he was 'of great value', even though that is the original meaning of the word. Once such a process has begun, it is difficult to put into reverse, and it can quickly spread throughout a whole culture, the original complimentary meaning of the word or gesture becoming too risky to use because it can so easily be misread.

In yet another region, the hand purse message 'be precise' has become 'be careful'. From there it has changed to 'take it slowly' and to the simple message 'slowly'. 9

So, from the simple baton gesture there have evolved four apparently completely separate symbolic messages in different parts of the world: *query*, *good*, *sarcastic criticism*, and *slowly*. But in addition to these modified baton signals, there are also several other distinct hand purse symbolisms. In certain areas, the gesture means 'lots'. It might be 'lots of people', or 'a crowd', or it might simply mean 'many', 'plenty', or 'much'. The symbolic root here is the bringing together of all the fingers in a clump or cluster—the combining of individual units into a tight group. 10

Another, more complex piece of symbolism concerns the use of the gesture as a signal of fear. Here the symbolic starting-point appears to be the squeezing together of the fingertips 'like a tight sphincter' of a frightened person. Some gesturers take this symbolism further by slightly opening and closing the pursed hand, as if the panic has become so great that the anal sphincter is no longer able to control itself. In some regions there is even a special word associated with the use of the gesture, which, roughly translated, means 'to dirty yourself'. Others who use this same fear gesture ascribe it to a different symbolism, with the opening and closing of the fingers representing either the fast heartbeat of panic, or the trembling of terror, but these are probably no more than polite, modern alternatives. The image of the pursed hand as an orifice is certainly an old one, as this passage from the sixteenth-century writings of Rabelais will testify: ' . . . the Englishman lift up on a high into the aire his two hands severally, clunching in all the tops of his fingers together, after the manner, which, *à la Chinonnese*, they call the hen's arse . . .' Strangely, this particular image seems to have survived in a few places, because to some people today the hand purse means 'you've laid an egg', and is employed as a gross insult, true to the original Rabelaisian usage. 11

All together this totals six major symbolic meanings which can be trans- 12 mitted by this simple hand gesture in different regions today. This multi-message potential of the hand purse can obviously create a problem for the traveller or tourist, who can easily make mistakes when using the gesture, or when interpreting its use by others. In almost every area of Europe it has a special local meaning, and as the visitor passes from one to the other, his own way of understanding the gesture must be repeatedly revised if he is to avoid embarrassing misunderstandings.

QUESTIONS

Words to Know

in vacuo—in the empty air (paragraph 3), gesticulation (3), symbolic (4), extensions (5), query (5), infers (5), implicit (6), grimace (8), sphincter (11), ascribe (11), orifice (11), Rabelais (11).

Some of the Issues

1. What does Morris mean when he says that the hand purse is a multi-message gesture. Can you give examples of other multi-message gestures?
2. Look at the illustration. How many of the gestures have meaning to you?
3. What distinction does Morris make between "baton signals" and "symbolic gestures"?
4. What are the different meanings of the hand purse as described by Morris? How does Morris explain the variations in meaning?

The Way We Are Told

5. To write *Gestures*, the book from which this selection is taken, Morris and his associates conducted research in 40 locations in Europe, using 1,200 informants in all. What other sources of information does Morris use?

Some Subjects for Essays

6. Select one of the illustrated symbolic gestures—one with which you are familiar—and show how it is used. Give examples of words or phrases it replaces. Does it have more than one meaning?

7. Have you ever been involved in an embarrassing or funny situation caused by a misunderstanding of a gesture or of words? Describe it in an essay.

8. Examine your own use of gestures. What gestures do you use to accompany and punctuate your speech? Describe them in an essay.

9. Observe the gestures of another person for some time. Write an essay about that person in which a description of gestures plays an important part.